CONSTRUCTING THE AMERICAN PAST

CONSTRUCTING THE AMERICAN PAST

A SOURCE BOOK OF A PEOPLE'S HISTORY

VOLUME 2

Fourth Edition

ELLIOTT J. GORN
Purdue University

RANDY ROBERTS
Purdue University

TERRY D. BILHARTZ
Sam Houston State University

New York   San Francisco   Boston
London   Toronto   Sydney   Tokyo   Singapore   Madrid
Mexico City   Munich   Paris   Cape Town   Hong Kong   Montreal

Vice President and Publisher: Priscilla McGeehon
Executive Marketing Manager: Sue Westmoreland
Supplements Editor: Kelly Villella
Media Supplements Editor: Pat McCarthy
Production Manager: Joseph Vella
Project Coordination, Text Design, and Electronic Page Makeup: Shepherd, Inc.
Photo Research: Photosearch, Inc.
Cover Designer/Manager: Wendy Ann Fredericks
Cover Illustration: *Subway, 1934*, Lily Furedi. © Smithsonian American Art Museum,
    Washington, D.C./Art Resource, NY
Senior Manufacturing Buyer: Dennis J. Para
Printer and Binder: The Maple-Vail Book Manufacturing Group
Cover Printer: John P. Pow

For permission to use copyrighted material, grateful acknowledgment is made to the copy-right holders on pp. 323–326, which are hereby made part of this copyright page.

Library of Congress Cataloging-in-Publication Data

Constructing the American past: a source book of a people's history/[edited by] Elliott
J. Gorn, Randy Roberts, Terry D. Bilhartz.—4th ed.
    p. cm.
  Includes bibliographical references and index.
  ISBN 0-321-09342-9 (v. 1)—ISBN 0-321-09340-2 (v. 2)
  1. United States—History—Sources. I. Gorn, Elliott J., 1951- II. Roberts, Randy, 1951-
III. Bilhartz, Terry D.

E173.C69 2001
973—dc21   2001038425

Please visit our website at http://www.ablongman.com

ISBN 0-321-09340-2

3 4 5 6 7 8 9 10—MA—04 03

For our children
Jade Rachel Yee-Gorn
Alison MacKenzie Roberts
Kelly Rankin Roberts
Teri Noel Bilhartz
Rocky Bilhartz and Lindsey Lee Barton

Contents

Preface

Every historian knows the feeling. You're working in an archive, sleepy and bored, when something jumps out at you. Maybe a letter written by someone who has been dead a hundred years boldly states an idea that was just a glimmer in your mind; or a diary that turns up unexpectedly takes you into the inner life of someone who seemed so unknowable before; or an eyewitness account of clashing armies makes you see and hear and smell the battlefield. Doing history can be as exciting as any act of discovery and exploration.

We developed this anthology to communicate some of that excitement to students. All three of us take pride in our work as teachers and writers of history. Sometimes, however, those two sides of the historian's job seem terribly distant from each other. Bridging that gap is our task here. We have tried to put some of our best teaching between these covers. We hope students will learn the challenges, the rigors, and the joys of hands-on history. Our goal is to present students with exciting documents on a series of topics that will help them learn to think critically.

Each chapter centers on a particular problem in American history. The introductions, documents, and study questions direct students to participate in the past. What was it like, for example, to be at a religious revival at the beginning of the nineteenth century? Who attended them and why? Our chapter on camp meetings offers eyewitness accounts. To give another example, what really happened at Wounded Knee, South Dakota, in 1890? Students read descriptions of the clash between the Sioux and the U.S. cavalry from a variety of vantage points: the voices of the Sioux, the letters of military officers, and the statements of government officials.

The fourth edition of *Constructing the American Past* contains major changes, including cuts and revisions in most chapters, as well as new chapters on the Constitution of 1787, the Cold War, and the Vietnam War, and an epilogue on the Election of 2000. The changes in this edition were specifically designed to sharpen the work, to improve its classroom usefulness, and to incorporate a still wider range of American experiences across ethnic, class, and gender lines. Almost every chapter in this fourth edition includes both male and female voices, as well as voices from diverse social and ethnic populations.

As we compiled these volumes, we also compiled numerous debts. We want to thank the library staffs at Purdue, Miami, Stanford, and Sam Houston State Universities; at the Museum of the City of New York; the Western College Archives; the archives of the Southern Regional Council, Atlanta; the Library of Congress; the New York Public Library; the Newberry Library; the American Antiquarian Society; the Huntington Library; and the Wisconsin Center for Film and Theater Research.

Many colleagues and graduate students have made suggestions and corrected us when we went astray. We especially acknowledge the assistance of Arthur Casciato, Allan Winkler, Jack Kirby, Mary Frederickson, James Hamill, Lynn Depew, Linnea Dietrich, Joshua Brown, Margo Horn, Timothy Gilfoyle, Paul Hutton, Howard Shorr, Gary Bell, Greg Cantrell, James Olson, Roseanne Barker, Ken Hendrickson, Caroline Crimm, Ty Cashion, Joseph Rowe, and Robert Shadle.

Terry Bilhartz still remembers with appreciation the following teachers and colleagues in a 1987 National Endowment for the Humanities Summer Institute on Classic Texts in Early American History who gave inspiration for the first edition of this work: Richard D. Brown, Karen O. Kupperman, Harry S. Stout, John P. Demos, Robert A. Gross, Stephen Nissenbaum, R. Kent Newmyer, Phillip Boucher, Alan V. Briceland, Jerald Combs, Donald R. Hickey, Richard L. Hillard, Graham Hodges, John Ifovic, Thomas W. Jodziewicz, Lawrence Kazura, Patricia O'Malley, Jacqueline Peterson, Bruce Stuart, William Swagerty, Alan S. Thompson, Louis P. Towles, Kerry A. Trask, James A. Trask, and Daniel E. Williams.

Several outside readers have strengthened our work. We acknowledge with gratitude the comments we received from James R. Sweeney, Old Dominion University; Brian Dirck, Anderson University; Margaret A. Lowe, Bridgewater State College; Michael Krenn, University of Miami; Lisa Tolbert, The University at North Carolina at Greensboro; Vernon Burton, University of Illinois at Urbana-Champaign; and Juliana Barr, Rutgers University.

Many of the events and documents in this collection were first used in our own classrooms. We thank all of our students over the years who have helped teach us about teaching. We dedicate this work to our children, our representatives in the next generation, who will construct their own pasts in order to understand themselves and their future. To this illustrious list, which includes Jade Rachel Yee-Gorn, Alison MacKenzie Roberts, Kelly Rankin Roberts, Rocky Bilhartz and Teri Noel Bilhartz, we add for this fourth edition the name of Rocky's adorable fiancée, Lindsey Lee Barton.

Introduction
Constructing the Past

History is *constructed;* human beings make their lives. The generation that decided to end slavery in America, for example, chose that path, just as generations before had opted to continue enslaving African Americans. The discipline of history assumes that the unfolding of the past is not ordained by God or nature, but by humankind.

But there is another meaning to the phrase *"constructing* the American past." There is no single correct narrative for any given historical episode. Historians have interpreted the Civil War for over a hundred years, and they continue to argue over what were the causes of the war, why the North won and the South lost, whether or not the war might have been averted, and countless other questions. It is not true that one interpretation of history is as valid as another; some historians argue with better logic, larger context, more evidence than others. But no written history is perfect because the past is so complex, because documentation is always incomplete and contradictory, and because historians are never totally free of socially shaped assumptions and their own personal biases.

Constructing the American Past, volume II, challenges you to become an historian. Each chapter provides background information and documentary evidence for a particular historical episode. Your goal is to reconstruct what happened, to put events in context, and to explore their meanings. Was being an immigrant at the turn of the century a positive or negative experience? What was at stake in the Scopes "Monkey" trial in the 1920s? What was it like to live through the Great Depression? There are no easy answers, but the sources allow you to construct an historical story and offer your own ideas.

Each chapter begins with a brief essay that sets the historical context for the episode. Following the essay is a selection of primary documents, with each document or group of documents preceded by an introductory headnote. Three sets of study questions follow the documents. The "Defining Terms" section invites readers to review the chapter's key figures, events, and ideas; "Probing the Sources" questions raise specific points about the sources; "Interpreting the Sources" questions seek more speculative responses about the meaning and importance of the chapter's subject. "Additional Reading" provides suggestions for other sources and readings on the subject. The best way to introduce you to this book is to give you a sample of what we are trying to do.

INSIDE THE JUNGLE

Historical Context

A cow grazes in Texas. A month later, part of it is being eaten by a family in New Jersey. This would not have happened before the Civil War, yet it was commonplace by 1900. What happened? Technology was important—the railroad connected the Great Plains with the East, so that shipping goods over hundreds, even thousands of miles now took but a few days. Also refrigeration allowed freshly butchered beef to be preserved. But equally important was the mental leap of thinking of meat as just one more product in the marketplace.

The key was keeping goods cheap through mass production. If thousands of cattle—which required a lot of space to raise—could be brought together and slaughtered systematically, and every part of each animal made into a commodity with a market value, then costs would come down, manufacturers might ship dressed meat to distant places for less money than local butchers could produce it, and beef would be consumed by more and more new customers. Butchers—skilled tradesmen whose labor was expensive—could be replaced by countless unskilled workers who performed but one task over and over, such as cutting off a particular part of the cow as it came down the "disassembly line." These ideas did not occur all at once, but slowly a handful of Chicago entrepreneurs in competition with each other turned what had been a locally based business into a national industry. The result was the famous Packingtown on Chicago's South Side, roughly a mile-and-a-half square bordered by Thirty-Ninth and Fifty-First Streets, and by Halsted and Western, filled with meatpacking plants and slaughterhouses.

Packingtown stank. It was ugly, dangerous, and unhealthy. Entering Packingtown from the north, a visitor was greeted—or perhaps insulted—by two prominent landmarks. The main entrance to the Union Stockyards was an imposing stone and iron gate that dwarfed humans and served as a grim portent of the serious and difficult work inside. Snaking its way to the west of the stockyards was Bubbly Creek, a branch of the Chicago River named for the carbolic acid gas that rose to the surface from the decaying wastes. The gasses of Bubbly Creek mixed with the odors of dying animals and decaying meat, and a series of uncovered dumps gave Packingtown its unforgettable smell.

Forty thousand people lived and worked in Packingtown. Most resided in poorly constructed frame houses that were often firetraps. Unlike better South Side neighborhoods, Packingtown's roads were largely unpaved and its sewage facilities were inadequate. The uncollected garbage, open sewers, and accumulated filth lowered health standards as well as human morale. Tuberculosis was the major scourge, but bronchitis, diphtheria, and other contagious diseases also claimed their victims. Children were especially vulnerable; one out of every three infants did not live to a second birthday.

The residents of Packingtown, mostly immigrants from central Europe and Scandinavia at the turn of the century, tolerated these dreadful conditions for a chance to work in the packinghouses. For them, the words *job* and *work* were magical. Mary McDowell, an early observer of the immigrants, remarked that *job* was the first English word the new arrivals learned: "The children lisp it; the aged cling to it to the end. A steady job or 'Please give me a job' is ever at the front of their minds or on the tips of their tongues." The jobs they acquired were difficult and dangerous—very dangerous. And for risking lives and limbs, unskilled workers were paid between fifteen and eighteen cents per hour, barely enough to starve by inches. Seasoned or cynical immigrants might take refuge in the old Yiddish proverb: "If the rich could pay people to die for them, the poor would make a wonderful living."

Many of the jobs the immigrants filled bordered on torture. Historian James R. Barrett, in his study of Chicago's packinghouse workers, has written, "Each job had its own dangers: the dampness and cold of the packing rooms and hide cellar; the sharp blade of the beef boner's knife; the noxious dust of the wool department and fertilizer plant; the wild charge of a half-crazed steer on the killing floor." And the frantic pace forced on the workers increased the chances of serious injury. Often the results read more like battlefield casualty reports than worker accidents. During the first six months of 1910, Swift and Company reported 3,500 injuries serious enough to require a physician's care. And in 1917 Armour workers became ill or injured over 22,000 times.

A man named Upton Sinclair came to Packingtown in 1904. He did not come as a worker looking for a job but as a writer in pursuit of a subject. Workers had just lost a major strike, and Sinclair went to the stockyards to observe their lives. Thirty-five years old, he had been a novelist for many years. The literary marketplace rewarded sensational writing, and the ambitious young Sinclair had been successful with tales of love and blood and revenge. But he was also ambitious to produce "art." Writing dime novels, even though it supported his family and paid for his education, failed to satisfy his soul. Sinclair's early efforts at serious fiction were commercial and artistic failures. His character's, like the author himself, were consumed with the idea of individual genius, with the rather romantic notion of the suffering and misunderstood artist dedicated to the singularity of his private vision. But then Upton Sinclair had what amounted to a religious conversion—he discovered socialism.

The turn of the century became known as the "progressive era." Government at the local, state, and federal levels intervened more than ever before in the workings of the economy to protect citizens' welfare. The Roosevelt, Taft, and Wilson administrations all attempted to restore competition to a few of those industries where corporate oligopolies had emerged; states instituted electoral reforms that were designed to assure widened citizen participation; local governments across the country attempted to regulate public utilities in the name of fairness. But even as such reforms tried to adjust society, many Americans called for much more sweeping change.

In 1889, Edward Bellamy wrote a utopian novel, *Looking Backward*, that became an instant best-seller. Bellamy envisioned an America where factories and stores were owned collectively and citizens ran the economy democratically. For the next twenty-five years, collectivist ideas became widely expressed. Various organizations for bringing the enormous new corporations under public control were advanced, but after 1900, the Socialist Party was the most noteworthy. Socialists wanted to nationalize the means of production—factories, mills, and mines must be owned by the state; no more private profits for capitalists and low wages for workers. Capitalism might have been around from the beginning, socialists argued, but corporations were new, and they so concentrated private wealth and power that they threatened American democracy. Through the political process the socialists would attempt to remake America. They saw their cause as a patriotic calling. The Socialist Party never threatened to displace the Democrats or Republicans, but before World War I, dozens of socialists became legislators, mayors, and councilmen, while the Socialist Party candidate for President, Eugene V. Debs, garnered nearly one million votes (six percent of the electorate) in 1912.

Sinclair remained an ambitious writer, but by 1904, his faith in the socialist cause led his work away from depicting suffering artists toward analyzing the plight of American workers. New magazines like *McClure's* had published so-called "muckraking" journalists such as Ida Tarbell and Lincoln Stephens, but Sinclair was much more radical than them. He went to Packingtown, studied the factories, the workers, and the "Back-of-the-Yards" neighborhoods. He wrote rapidly and intensely. His novel, *The Jungle,* was first published in serial form in 1905, not in the mainstream press but in the *Appeal to Reason,* a popular socialist newspaper based in Girard, Kansas.

The Jungle came out in book form in 1906 and was an instant success. Sinclair told the story of the Rudkus family, Lithuanian immigrants who came to America only to be used and discarded by the companies that owned Packingtown. The human and sanitary abuses Sinclair catalogued shocked Americans in 1906, and they continue to shock us today. Although *The Jungle* followed the style of literary realism, the conventions of the early twentieth century forced Sinclair to use euphemisms to discuss certain problems in the workplace. For example, he often remarks that there were no places in the packinghouses for the workers to wash their hands. The early twentieth century reader would understand that Sinclair meant that no toilet facilities were provided and that human urine and feces accumulated on the floors of the packinghouses. Despite his attempts to preserve literary delicacy, some reviewers were scandalized by Sinclair's violations of good taste and aesthetics. A reviewer for *The Outlook* declared, "to disgust the reader by dragging him through every conceivable horror, physical and moral, and to depict with lurid excitement and with offensive minuteness the life in jail and brothel—all is to overstep the object."

THE DOCUMENTS

Introduction to Document 1

The publication of *The Jungle* and the wide readership it attracted gave ammunition to the politicians who were seeking reforms in the meatpacking industry. President Roosevelt entered the fight to demand change. The result of the ferment was the Meat Inspection Act of 1906. Far from a perfect piece of legislation, it represented a compromise between the meatpacking companies and the reformers. It helped to restore confidence in the American packing industry. However, it did little for the residents of Packingtown. As Sinclair later remarked, "I aimed at the public's heart, and by accident I hit it in the stomach."

DOCUMENT 1 *From* **The Jungle**

Upton Sinclair

Jurgis heard of these things little by little, in the gossip of those who were obliged to per-petrate them. It seemed as if every time you met a person from a new department, you heard of new swindles and new crimes. There was, for instance, a Lithuanian who was a cattle-butcher for the plant where Marija had worked, which killed meat for canning only; and to hear this man describe the animals which came to his place would have been worth while for a Dante or a Zola. It seemed that they must have agencies all over the country, to hunt out old and crippled and diseased cattle to be canned. There were cat-tle which had been fed on "whiskey-malt," the refuse of the breweries, and had become what the men called "steerly"—which means covered with boils. It was a nasty job killing these, for when you plunged your knife into them they would burst and splash foul-smelling stuff into your face; and when a man's sleeves were smeared with blood, and his hands steeped in it, how was he ever to wipe his face, or to clear his eyes so that he could see? It was stuff such as this that made the "embalmed beef" that had killed several times as many United States soldiers as all the bullets of the Spaniards; only the army beef, besides, was not fresh canned, it was old stuff that had been lying for years in the cellars.

Then one Sunday evening, Jurgis sat puffing his pipe by the kitchen stove, and talk-ing with an old fellow whom Jonas had introduced, and who worked in the canning-rooms at Durham's; and so Jurgis learned a few things about the great and only Durham canned goods, which had become a national institution. They were regular alchemists at Durham's; they advertised a mushroom-catsup, and the men who made it did not know what a mushroom looked like. They advertised "potted chicken,"—and it was like the boarding-house soup of the comic papers, through which a chicken had walked with rub-bers on. Perhaps they had a secret process for making chickens chemically—who knows? said Jurgis's friend; the things that went into the mixture were tripe, and the fat of pork, and beef suet, and hearts of beef, and finally the waste ends of veal, when they had any. They put these up in several grades, and sold them at several prices; but the contents of the cans all came out of the same hopper. And then there was "potted game" and "pot-ted grouse," "potted ham," and "devilled ham"—de-vyled, as the men called it. "De-vyled" ham was made out of the waste ends of smoked beef that were too small to be sliced by the machines; and also tripe, dyed with chemicals so that it would not show white; and trimmings of hams and corned beef; and potatoes, skins and all; and finally the hard cartilaginous gullets of beef, after the tongues had been cut out. All this ingenious mixture was ground up and flavored with spices to make it taste like something. Anybody who could invent a new imitation had been sure of a fortune from old Durham, said Jurgis's informant; but it was hard to think of anything new in a place where so many sharp wits had been at work for so long; where men welcomed tuberculosis in the cattle they were feeding, because it made them fatten more quickly; and where they bought up all the old rancid butter left over in the grocery-stores of a continent, and "oxidized" it by a forced-air process, to take away the odor, rechurned it with skim-milk, and sold it in bricks in the cities! Up to a year or two ago it had been the custom to kill horses in the yards—ostensibly for fertilizer; but after long agitation the newspapers had been able to make the public realize that the horses were being canned. Now it was against the law to kill horses in Packingtown, and the law was really complied with—for the present, at any rate. Any day, however, one might see sharp-horned and shaggy-haired creatures running with the sheep—and yet what a job you would have to get the public to believe that a good part of what it buys for lamb and mutton is really goat's flesh!

There was another interesting set of statistics that a person might have gathered in Packingtown—those of the various afflictions of the workers. . . . There were the men in the pickle-rooms, for instance, where old Antanas had gotten his death; scarce a one of these that had not some spot of horror on his person. Let a man so much as scrape his finger pushing a truck in the pickle-rooms, and he might have a sore that would put him out of the world; all the joints in his fingers might be eaten by the acid, one by one. Of the butchers and floorsmen, the beef-boners and trimmers, and all those who used knives, you could scarcely find a person who had the use of his thumb; time and time again the base of it had been slashed, till it was a mere lump of flesh against which the man pressed the knife to hold it. The hands of these men would be criss-crossed with cuts, until you could no longer pretend to count them or to trace them. They would have no nails,—they had worn them off pulling hides; their knuckles were swollen so that their fingers spread out like a fan. There were men who worked in the cooking-rooms, in the midst of steam and sickening odors, by artificial light; in these rooms the germs of tuberculosis might live for two years, but the supply was renewed every hour. There were the beef-luggers, who carried two-hundred-pound quarters into the refrigerator-cars; a fearful kind of work, that began at four o'clock in the morning, and that wore out the most powerful men in a few years. There were those who worked in the chilling-rooms, and whose special disease was rheumatism; the time-limit that a man could work in the chilling-rooms was said to be five years. There were the wool-pluckers, whose hands went to pieces even sooner than the hands of the pickle-men; for the pelts of the sheep had to be painted with acid to loosen the wool, and then the pluckers had to pull out this wool with their bare hands, till the acid had eaten their fingers off. There were those who made the tins for the canned-meat; and their hands, too, were a maze of cuts, and each cut represented a chance for blood-poisoning. Some worked at the stamping-machines, and it was very seldom that one could work long there at the pace that was set, and not give out and forget himself, and have a part of his hand chopped off. . . . As for the other men, who worked in tank-rooms full of steam, and in some of which there were open vats near the level of the floor, their peculiar trouble was that they fell into the vats; and when they were fished out, there was never enough of them left to be worth exhibiting,—sometimes they would be overlooked for days, till all but the bones of them had gone out to the world as Durham's Pure Leaf Lard! . . .

During this time that Jurgis was looking for work occurred the death of little Kristoforas, one of the children of Teta Elzbieta. . . . Perhaps it was the smoked sausage he had eaten that morning—which may have been made out of some of the tubercular pork that was condemned as unfit for export. At any rate, an hour after eating it, the child had begun to cry with pain, and in another hour he was rolling about on the floor in convulsions. Little Kotrina, who was all alone with him, ran out screaming for help, and after a while a doctor came, but not until Kristoforas had howled his last howl. No one was really sorry about this except poor Elzbieta, who was inconsolable. Jurgis announced that so far as he was concerned the child would have to be buried by the city, since they had no money for a funeral; and at this the poor woman almost went out of her senses, wringing her hands and screaming with grief and despair. Her child to be buried in a pauper's grave! And her stepdaughter to stand by and hear it said without protesting! It was enough to make Ona's [Jurgis's wife] father rise up out of his grave and rebuke her! If it had come to this, they might as well give up at once, and be buried all of them together! . . . In the end Marija said that she would help with ten dollars; and Jurgis being still obdurate, Elzbieta went in tears and begged the money from the neighbors, and so little Kristoforas had a mass and a hearse with white plumes on it, and a tiny plot in a graveyard with a wooden cross to mark the place. The poor mother was not the same for months after that; the mere sight of the floor where little Kristoforas had crawled about would make her weep. He had never had a fair chance, poor little fellow, she would say. He had been handicapped from his birth. If only she had heard about it in time, so that she might have had the great doctor to cure him of his lameness! . . . Some time ago, Elzbieta was told, a Chicago billionnaire had paid a fortune to bring a great European surgeon over to cure his little daughter of the same disease from which Kristoforas had suffered. And because this surgeon had to have bodies to demonstrate upon, he announced that he would treat the children of the poor, a piece of magnanimity over which the papers became quite eloquent. Elzbieta, alas, did not read the papers, and no one had told her; but perhaps it was as well, for just then they would not have had the car-fare to spare to go every day to wait upon the surgeon, nor for that matter anybody with the time to take the child.

All this while that he was seeking for work, there was a dark shadow hanging over Jurgis; as if a savage beast were lurking somewhere in the pathway of his life, and he knew it, and yet could not help approaching the place. There were all stages of being out of work in Packingtown, and he faced in dread the prospect of reaching the lowest. There is a place that waits for the lowest man—the fertilizer-plant!

The men would talk about it in awe-stricken whispers. Not more than one in ten had ever really tried it; the other nine had contented themselves with hearsay evidence and a peep through the door. There were some things worse than even starving to death. They would ask Jurgis if he had worked there yet, and if he meant to; and Jurgis would debate the matter with himself. As poor as they were, and making all the sacrifices that they were, would he dare to refuse any sort of work that was offered to him, be it as horrible as ever it could? Would he dare to go home and eat bread that had been earned by Ona, weak and complaining as she was, knowing that he had been given a chance, and had not had the nerve to take it?—And yet he might argue that way with himself all day, and one glimpse into the fertilizer-works would send him away again shuddering. He was a man, and he would do his duty; he went and made application—but surely he was not also required to hope for success!

The fertilizer-works of Durham's lay away from the rest of the plant. Few visitors ever saw them, and the few who did would come out looking like Dante, of whom the peasants declared that he had been into hell. To this part of the yards came all the "tankage," and waste products of all sorts; here they dried out the bones—and in suffocating cellars where the daylight never came you might see men and women and children bending over whirling machines and sawing bits of bone into all sorts of shapes, breathing their lungs full of the fine dust, and doomed to die, every one of them, within a certain definite time. Here they made the blood into albumen, and made other foul-smelling things into things still more foul-smelling. In the corridors and caverns where it was done you might lose yourself as in the great caves of Kentucky. In the dust and the steam the electric lights would shine like far-off twinkling stars—red and blue, green and purple stars, according to the color of the mist and the brew from which it came. For the odors in these ghastly charnel-houses there may be words in Lithuanian, but there are none in English. The person entering would have to summon his courage as for a cold-water plunge. He would go on like a man swimming under water; he would put his handkerchief over his face, and begin to cough and choke; and then, if he were still obstinate, he would find his head beginning to ring, and the veins in his forehead to throb, until finally he would be assailed by an overpowering blast of ammonia fumes, and would turn and run for his life, and come out half-dazed. . . .

The boss of the grinding room had come to know Jurgis by this time, and had marked him for a likely man; and so when he came to the door about two o'clock this breathless hot day, he felt a sudden spasm of pain shoot through him—the boss beckoned to him! In ten minutes more Jurgis had pulled off his coat and overshirt, and set his teeth together and gone to work. Here was one more difficulty for him to meet and conquer!

His labor took him about one minute to learn. Before him was one of the vents of the mill in which the fertilizer was being ground-rushing forth in a great brown river, with a spray of the finest dust flung forth in clouds. Jurgis was given a shovel, and along with half a dozen others it was his task to shovel this fertilizer into carts. That others were at work he knew by the sound, and by the fact that he sometimes collided with them; otherwise they might as well not have been there, for in the blinding dust-storm a man could not see six feet in front of his face. When he had filled one cart he had to grope around him until another came, and if there was none on hand he continued to grope till one arrived. In five minutes he was, of course, a mass of fertilizer from head to feet; they gave him a sponge to tie over his mouth, so that he could breathe, but the sponge did not prevent his lips and eyelids from caking up with it and his ears from filling solid. He looked like a brown ghost at twilight—from hair to shoes he became the color of the building and of everything in it, and for that matter a hundred yards outside it. The building had to be left open, and when the wind blew Durham and Company lost a great deal of fertilizer.

Working in his shirt-sleeves, and with the thermometer at over a hundred, the phosphates soaked in through every pore of Jurgis's skin, and in five minutes he had a headache, and in fifteen was almost dazed. The blood was pounding his brain like an engine's throbbing; there was a frightful pain in the top of his skull, and he could hardly control his hands. Still, with the memory of his four months' siege behind him, he fought on, in a frenzy of determination; and half an hour later he began to vomit—he vomited until it seemed as if his inwards must be torn to shreds. A man could get used to the fertilizer-mill, the boss had said, if he would only make up his mind to it; but Jurgis now began to see that it was a question of making up his stomach.

At the end of that day of horror, he could scarcely stand. He had to catch himself now and then, and lean against a building and get his bearings. Most of the men, when they came out, made straight for a saloon—they seemed to place fertilizer and rattlesnake poison in one class. But Jurgis was too ill to think of drinking—he could only make his way to the street and stagger on to a car. He had a sense of humor, and later on, when he became an old hand, he used to think it fun to board a street-car and see what happened. Now, however, he was too ill to notice it—how the people in the car began to gasp and sputter, to put their handkerchiefs to their noses, and transfix him with furious glances. Jurgis only knew that a man in front of him immediately got up and gave him a seat; and that half a minute later the two people on each side of him got up; and that in a full minute the crowded car was nearly empty—those passengers who could not get room on the platform having gotten out to walk.

Of course Jurgis had made his home a miniature fertilizer-mill a minute after entering. The stuff was half an inch deep in his skin—his whole system was full of it, and it would have taken a week not merely of scrubbing, but of vigorous exercise, to get it out of him. As it was, he could be compared with nothing known to men, save that newest discovery of the savants, a substance which emits energy for an unlimited time, without being itself in the least diminished in power. He smelt so that he made all the food at the table taste, and set the whole family to vomiting; for himself it was three days before he could keep anything upon his stomach—he might wash his hands, and use a knife and fork, but were not his mouth and throat filled with the poison? . . .

With one member trimming beef in a cannery, and another working in a sausage factory, the family had a first-hand knowledge of the great majority of Packingtown swindles. For it was the custom, as they found, whenever meat was so spoiled that it could not be used for anything else, either to can it or else to chop it up into sausage. With what had been told them by Jonas, who had worked in the pickle-rooms, they could now study the whole of the spoiled-meat industry on the inside, and read a new and grim meaning into that old Packingtown jest—that they use everything of the pig except the squeal.

Jonas had told them how the meat that was taken out of pickle would often be found sour, and how they would rub it up with soda to take away the smell, and sell it to be eaten on free-lunch counters; also of all the miracles of chemistry which they performed, giving to any sort of meat, fresh or salted, whole or chopped, any color and any flavor and any odor they chose. In the pickling of hams they had an ingenious apparatus, by which they saved time and increased the capacity of the plant—a machine consisting of a hollow needle attached to a pump; by plunging this needle into the meat and working with his foot, a man could fill a ham with pickle in a few seconds. And yet, in spite of this, there would be hams found spoiled, some of them with an odor so bad that a man could hardly bear to be in the room with them. To pump into these the packers had a second and much stronger pickle which destroyed the odor—a process known to the workers as "giving them thirty per cent." Also, after the hams had been smoked, there would be found some that had gone to the bad. Formerly these had been sold as "Number Three Grade," but later on some ingenious person had hit upon a new device, and now they would extract the bone, about which the bad part generally lay, and insert in the hole a white-hot iron. After this invention there was no longer Number One, Two, and Three Grade—there was only Number One Grade. The packers were always originating such schemes—they had what they called "boneless hams," which were all the odds and ends of pork stuffed into casings; and "California hams," which were the shoulders, with big knuckle-joints, and nearly all the meat cut out; and fancy "skinned hams," which were made of the oldest hogs, whose skins were so heavy and coarse that no one would buy them—that is, until they had been cooked and chopped fine and labelled "head cheese"!

It was only when the whole ham was spoiled that it came into the department of Elzbieta. Cut up by the two-thousand-revolutions-a-minute flyers, and mixed with half a ton of other meat, no odor that ever was in a ham could make any difference. There was never the least attention paid to what was cut up for sausage; there would come all the way back from Europe old sausage that had been rejected, and that was mouldy and white—it would be dosed with borax and glycerine, and dumped into the hoppers, and made over again for home consumption. There would be meat that had tumbled out on the floor, in the dirt and sawdust, where the workers had tramped and spit uncounted billions of consumption germs. There would be meat stored in great piles in rooms; and the water from leaky roofs would drip over it, and thousands of rats would race about on it. It was too dark in these storage places to see well, but a man could run his hand over these piles of meat and sweep off handfuls of the dried dung of rats. These rats were nuisances, and the packers would put poisoned bread out for them; they would die, and then rats, bread and meat would go into the hoppers together. This is no fairy story and no joke; the meat would be shovelled into carts, and the man who did the shovelling would not trouble to lift out a rat even when he saw one—there were things that went into the sausage in comparison with which a poisoned rat was a tidbit. There was no place for the men to wash their hands before they ate their dinner, and so they made a practice of washing them in the water that was to be ladled into the sausage. There were the butt-ends of smoked meat, and the scraps of corned beef, and all the odds and ends of the waste of the plants, that would be dumped into old barrels in the cellar and left there. Under the system of rigid economy which the packers enforced, there were some jobs that it only paid to do once in a long time, and among these was the cleaning out of the waste-barrels. Every spring they did it; and in the barrels would be dirt and rust and old nails and stale water—and cart load after cart load of it would be taken up and dumped into the hoppers with fresh meat, and sent out to the public's breakfast. Some of it they would make into "smoked" sausage—but as the smoking took time, and was therefore expensive, they would call upon their chemistry department, and preserve it with borax and color it with gelatine to make it brown. All of their sausage came out of the same bowl, but when they came to wrap it they would stamp some of it "special," and for this they would charge two cents more a pound.

Such were the new surroundings in which Elzbieta was placed, and such was the work she was compelled to do. It was stupefying, brutalizing work; it left her no time to think, no strength for anything. She was part of the machine she tended, and every faculty that was not needed for the machine was doomed to be crushed out of existence. There was only one mercy about the cruel grind—that it gave her the gift of insensibility. Little by little she sank into a torpor—she fell silent. She would meet Jurgis and Ona in the evening, and the three would walk home together, often without saying a word. Ona, too, was falling into a habit of silence—Ona, who had once gone about singing like a bird. She was sick and miserable, and often she would barely have strength enough to drag herself home. And there they would eat what they had to eat, and afterwards, because there was only their misery to talk of, they would crawl into bed and fall into a stupor and never stir until it was time to get up again, and dress by candle-light, and go back to the machines. They were so numbed that they did not even suffer much from hunger, now; only the children continued to fret when the food ran short.

Yet the soul of Ona was not dead—the souls of none of them were dead, but only sleeping; and now and then they would waken, and these were cruel times. The gates of memory would roll open—old joys would stretch out their arms to them, old hopes and dreams would call to them, and they would stir beneath the burden that lay upon them, and feel its forever immeasurable weight. They could not even cry out beneath it; but anguish would seize them, more dreadful than the agony of death. It was a thing scarcely to be spoken—a thing never spoken by all the world, that will not know its own defeat. . . .

Introduction to Document 2

The response to *The Jungle* came quickly. But was the book an accurate depiction of life in Packingtown? Historians have differed on this point. Certainly Sinclair exaggerated the plight that any one family might endure. Moreover, some have questioned how well he knew the packing industry; he spent only a few weeks in Packingtown, did not go into the factories very much, and gathered most of his information through interviews. Ralph Chaplin, also a writer and a political radical, declared in his autobiography *Wobbly,* "I thought it a very inaccurate picture of the stockyards district which I knew so well, but I waited for each installment eagerly and read it with great interest." Above all, Sinclair minimized the resources of workers to improve their own lives even when they were feeling the brunt of an economic system that sought to buy their labor as cheaply as possible. For example, like many other middle-class Protestants of his day, Sinclair was appalled by drinking, so he interpreted workers' saloons as places of evil rather than community institutions. Read the following autobiography of Antanas Kaztauskis, a Lithuanian immigrant who lived and worked in Packingtown. Kaztauskis's story was published in the magazine *The Independent* three months before Sinclair began his research for *The Jungle.* As you read, think about how this autobiography confirms or contradicts Sinclair's depiction of the lives of immigrant workers. Ask yourself about the role of unions, political organizations, churches, schools, and ethnic communities in daily life. How did working-class people adjust to their lives in America, what values and institutions did they cling to, how did they reinterpret the American dream for themselves?

DOCUMENT 2 *Antanas Kaztauskis's Story*

. . . We were tired out when we reached the stockyards, so we stopped on the bridge and looked into the river out there. It was so full of grease and dirt and sticks and boxes that it looked like a big, wide, dirty street, except in some places, where it boiled up. It made me sick to look at it. When I looked away I could see on one side some big fields full of holes, and these were the city dumps. On the other side were the stockyards, with twenty tall slaughter house chimneys. The wind blew a big smell from them to us. Then we walked on between the yards and the dumps and all the houses looked bad and poor. In our house my room was in the basement. I lay down on the floor with three other men and the air was rotten. I did not go to sleep for a long time. I knew then that money was everything I needed. My money was almost gone and I thought that I would soon die unless I got a job, for this was not like home. Here money was everything and a man without money must die.

The next morning my friends woke me up at five o'clock and said, "Now, if you want life, liberty and happiness," they laughed, "you must push for yourself. You must get a job. Come with us." And we went to the yards. Men and women were walking in by thousands as far as we could see. We went to the doors of one big slaughter house. There was a crowd of about 200 men waiting there for a job. They looked hungry and kept watching the door. At last a special policeman came out and began pointing to men, one by one. Each one jumped forward. Twenty-three were taken. Then they all went inside, and all the others turned their faces away and looked tired. I remember one boy sat down and cried, just next to me, on a pile of boards. Some policemen waved their clubs and we all walked on. I found some Lithuanians to talk with, who told me they had come every morning for three weeks. Soon we met other crowds coming away from other slaughter houses, and we all walked around and felt bad and tired and hungry.

That night I told my friends that I would not do this many days, but would go some place else. "Where?" they asked me, and I began to see then that I was in bad trouble, because I spoke no English. Then one man told me to give him $5 to give the special policeman. I did this and the next morning the policeman pointed me out, so I had a job. I have heard some big talk since then about my American freedom of contract, but I do not think I had much freedom in bargaining for this job with the Meat Trust. My job was in the cattle killing room. I pushed the blood along the gutter. Some people think these jobs make men bad. I do not think so. The men who do the killing are not as bad as the ladies with fine clothes who come every day to look at it, because they have to do it. The cattle do not suffer. They are knocked senseless with a big hammer and are dead before they wake up. This is done not to spare them pain, but because if they got hot and sweating with fear and pain the meat would not be so good. I soon saw that every job in the room was done like this—so as to save everything and make money. One Lithuanian, who worked with me, said, "They get all the blood out of those cattle and all the work out of us men." This was true, for we worked that first day from six in the morning till seven at night. The next day we worked from six in the morning till eight at night. The next day we had no work. So we had no good, regular hours. It was hot in the room that summer, and the hot blood made it worse.

I held this job six weeks and then I was turned off. I think some other man had paid for my job, or perhaps I was too slow. The foreman in that room wanted quick men to make the work rush, because he was paid more if the work was done cheaper and quicker. I saw now that every man was helping himself, always trying to get all the money he could. At that time I believed that all men in Chicago were grafters when they had to be. They only wanted to push themselves. Now, when I was idle I began to look about, and everywhere I saw sharp men beating out slow men like me. Even if we worked hard it did us no good. I had saved $13-$5 a week for six weeks makes $30, and take off $15 for six weeks' board and lodging and $2 for other things. I showed this to a Lithuanian, who had been here two years, and he laughed. "It will be taken from you," he said. He had saved a hundred dollars once and had begun to buy a house on the instalment plan, but something had happened that he did not know about and his landlord put him out and kept the hundred dollars. I found that many Lithuanians had been beaten this way. At home we never made a man sign contract papers. We only had him make the sign of a cross and promise he would do what he said. But this was no good in Chicago. So these sharp men were beating us.

I saw this, too, in the newspaper. I was beginning to learn English, and at night in the boarding house the men who did not play cards used to read the paper to us. The biggest word was "Graft" in red letters on the front page. Another word was "Trust." This paper kept putting these two words together. Then I began to see how every American man was trying to get money for himself. . . . I felt very bad and sorrowful in that month. I kept walking around with many other Lithuanians who had no job. Our money was going and we could find nothing to do. At night we got homesick for our fine green mountains. We read all the news about home in our Lithuanian Chicago newspaper, *The Katalikas*. It is a good paper and gives all the news. In the same office we bought this song, which was written in Brooklyn by P. Brandukas. He, too, was homesick. It is sung all over Chicago now and you can hear it in the summer evenings through the open windows. In English it is something like this:

> Oh, Lithuania, so dear to me,
> Good-by to you, my Fatherland.
> Sorrowful in my heart I leave you,
> I know not who will stay to guard you.
>
> Is it enough for me to live and enjoy between my neighbors,
> In the woods with the flowers and birds?
> Is it enough for me to live peaceful between my friends?
> No, I must go away from my old father and mother.
>
> > The sun shines bright,
> > The flowers smell sweet,
> > The birds are singing,
> > They make the country glad;
> But I cannot sing because I must leave you.

Those were bad days and nights. At last I had a chance to help myself. Summer was over and Election Day was coming. The Republican boss in our district, Jonidas, was a saloonkeeper. A friend took me there. Jonidas shook hands and treated me fine. He taught me to sign my name, and the next week I went with him to an office and signed some paper, and then I could vote. I voted as I was told, and then they got me back into the yards to work, because one big politician owns stock in one of those houses. Then I felt that I was getting in beside the game. I was in a combine like other sharp men. Even when work was slack I was all right, because they got me a job in the street cleaning department. I felt proud, and I went to the back room in Jonidas's saloon and got him to write a letter to Alexandria to tell her she must come soon and be my wife.

But this was just the trouble. All of us were telling our friends to come soon. Soon they came—even thousands. The employers in the yard liked this, because those sharp foremen are inventing new machines and the work is easier to learn, and so these slow Lithuanians and even green girls can learn to do it, and then the Americans and Germans and Irish are put out and the employer saves money, because the Lithuanians work cheaper. This was why the American labor unions began to organize us all just the same as they had organized the Bohemians and Poles before us.

Well, we were glad to be organized. We had learned that in Chicago every man must push himself always, and Jonidas had taught us how much better we could push ourselves by getting into a combine. Now, we saw that this union was the best combine for us, because it was the only combine that could say, "It is our business to raise your wages." . . . I joined the Cattle Butchers' Union. This union is honest and it has done me a great deal of good. It has raised my wages. The man who worked at my job before the union came was getting through the year an average of $9 a week. I am getting $11. In my first job I got $5 a week. The man who works there now gets $5.75.

It has given me more time to learn to read and speak and enjoy life like an American. I never work now from 6 A.M. to 9 P.M. and then be idle the next day. I work now from 7 A.M. to 5.30 P.M., and there are not so many idle days. The work is evened up.

With more time and more money I live much better and I am very happy. So is Alexandria. She came a year ago and has learned to speak English already. Some of the women go to the big store the day they get here, when they have not enough sense to pick out the clothes that look right, but Alexandria waited three weeks till she knew, and so now she looks the finest of any woman in the district. We have four nice rooms, which she keeps very clean, and she has flowers growing in boxes in the two front windows. We do not go much to church, because the church seems to be too slow. But we belong to a Lithuanian society that gives two picnics in summer and two big balls in winter, where we have a fine time. I go one night a week to the Lithuanian Concertina Club. On Sundays we go on the trolley out into the country.

But we like to stay at home more now because we have a baby. When he grows up I will not send him to the Lithuanian Catholic school. They have only two bad rooms and two priests, who teach only in Lithuanian from prayer books. I will send him to the American school, which is very big and good. The teachers there are Americans and they belong to the Teachers' Labor Union, which has three thousand teachers and belongs to our Chicago Federation of Labor. I am sure that such teachers will give him a good chance. . . .

The union is doing another good thing. It is combining all the nationalities. The night I joined the Cattle Butchers' Union I was led into the room by a negro member. With me were Bohemians, Germans and Poles, and Mike Donnelly, the President, is an Irishman. He spoke to us in English and then three interpreters told us what he said. We swore to be loyal to our union above everything else except the country, the city and the State—to be faithful to each other—to protect the women workers—to do our best to understand the history of the labor movement, and to do all we could to help it on. Since then I have gone there every two weeks and I help the movement by being an interpreter for the other Lithuanians who come in. That is why I have learned to speak and write good English. The others do not need me long. They soon learn English, too, and when they have done that they are quickly becoming Americans.

But the best thing the union does is to make me feel more independent. I do not have to pay to get a job and I cannot be discharged unless I am no good. For almost the whole 30,000 men and women are organized now in some one of our unions and they all are directed by our central council. No man knows what it means to be sure of his job unless he has been fired like I was once without any reason being given.

So this is why I joined the labor union. There are many better stories than mine, for my story is very common. There are thousands of immigrants like me. Over 300,000 immigrants have been organized in the last three years by the American Federation of Labor. The immigrants are glad to be organized if the leaders are as honest as Mike Donnelly is. You must get money to live well, and to get money you must combine. I cannot bargain alone with the Meat Trust. I tried it and it does not work. . . .

Introduction to Document 3

The Jungle stirred up a storm of criticism. President Theodore Roosevelt obtained an advance copy of the book and appointed a committee to investigate the Chicago stockyards. The committee's report was detailed but mixed—there were breaches of cleanliness, but also many plants that were quite hygienic. The passage reprinted here describes a plant that seemed to confirm many of *The Jungle's* accusations. Remember, however, that Sinclair wrote an indictment of capitalism—his point was that the power of the packinghouses and their desire for profit necessarily caused them to cut corners, to cheat workers and sell adulterated meat. The following report went to Congress and became evidence that helped pass Senator Albert Beveridge's bill to regulate the packing industry. Even in this most critical part of the investigators' report, note that they slight Sinclair's main concern, the working conditions of the employees in Packingtown.

 DOCUMENT 3 *House Congressional Record, June 4, 1906*

The SPEAKER laid before the House a message from the President of the United States; which, with the accompanying documents, was referred to the Committee on Agriculture, and ordered to be printed.

The message is as follows:

The Senate and House of Representatives:

I transmit herewith the report of Mr. James Bronson Reynolds and Commissioner Charles P. Neill, the special committee whom I appointed to investigate into the conditions in the stock yards of Chicago and report thereon to me. This report is of a preliminary nature. I submit it to you now because it shows the urgent need of immediate action by the Congress in the direction of providing a drastic and thoroughgoing inspection by the Federal Government of all stock yards and packing houses and of their products, so far as the latter enter into interstate or foreign commerce. The conditions shown by even this short inspection to exist in the Chicago stock yards are revolting. It is imperatively necessary in the interest of health and of decency that they should be radically changed. Under the existing law it is wholly impossible to secure satisfactory results. . . .

I urge the immediate enactment into law of provisions which will enable the Department of Agriculture adequately to inspect the meat and meat food products entering into interstate commerce and to supervise the methods of preparing the same, and to prescribe the sanitary conditions under which the work shall be performed. . . .

Theodore Roosevelt
The White House, June 4, 1906

Condition of the Yards

Before entering the buildings we noted the condition of the yards themselves as shown in the pavement, pens, viaducts, and platforms. The pavement is mostly of brick, the bricks laid with deep grooves between them, which inevitably fill with manure and refuse. Such pavement can not be properly cleaned and is slimy and malodorous when wet, yielding clouds of ill-smelling dust when dry. The pens are generally uncovered except those for sheep; these latter are paved and covered. The viaducts and platforms are of wood. Calves, sheep, and hogs that have died en route are thrown out upon the platforms where cars are unloaded. On a single platform on one occasion we counted fifteen dead hogs, on the next ten dead hogs. The only excuse given for delay in removal was that so often heard—the expense.

Buildings

Lighting—The buildings have been constructed with little regard to either light or ventilation. The workrooms, as a rule, are very poorly lighted. A few rooms at the top of the buildings are well lighted because they can not escape the light, but most of the rooms are so dark as to make artificial light necessary at all times. Many inside rooms where food is prepared are without windows, deprived of sunlight, and without direct communication with the outside air. They may be best described as vaults in which the air rarely changes. . . .

Ventilation—Systematic ventilation of the workrooms is not found in any of the establishments we visited. In a few instances electric fans mitigate the stifling air, but usually the workers toil without relief in a humid atmosphere heavy with the odors of rotten wood, decayed meats, stinking offal, and entrails.

Equipment—The work tables upon which the meat is handled, the floor carts on which it is carried about, and the tubs and other receptacles into which it is thrown are generally of wood. In all the places visited but a single porcelain-lined receptacle was seen. Tables covered with sheet iron, iron carts, and iron tubs are being introduced into the better establishments, but no establishment visited has as yet abandoned the extensive use of wooden tables and wooden receptacles. These wooden receptacles are frequently found water soaked, only half cleansed, and with meat scraps and grease accumulations adhering to their sides, and collecting dirt. This is largely true of meat racks and meat conveyors of every sort, which were in nearly all cases inadequately cleansed, and grease and meat scraps were found adhering to them, even after they had been washed and returned to service.

Sanitary conveniences—Nothing shows more strikingly the general indifference to matters of cleanliness and sanitation than do the privies for both men and women. The prevailing type is made by cutting off a section of the workroom by a thin wooden partition rising to within a few feet of the ceiling, These privies usually ventilate into the workroom, though a few are found with a window opening into the outer air. Many are located in the inside corners of the workrooms, and thus have no outside opening whatever. They are furnished with a row of seats, generally without even side partitions. These rooms are sometimes used as cloakrooms by the employees. Lunch rooms constructed in the same manner, by boarding off a section of the workroom, often adjoin the privies, the odors of which add to the generally insanitary state of the atmosphere.

Abominable as the above-named conditions are, the one that affects most directly and seriously the cleanliness of the food products is the frequent absence of any lavatory provisions in the privies. Washing sinks are either not furnished at all or are small and dirty. Neither are towels, soap, or toilet paper provided. Men and women return directly from these places to plunge their unwashed hands into the meat to be converted into such food products as sausages, dried beef, and other compounds. Some of the privies are situated at a long distance from the workrooms, and men relieve themselves on the killing floors or in a corner of the workrooms. Hence, in some cases the fumes of the urine swell the sum of nauseating odors arising from the dirty, blood-soaked, rotting, wooden floors—fruitful culture beds for the disease germs of men and animals. . . .

Treatment of Meats and Prepared Food Products

A particularly glaring instance of uncleanliness was found in a room where the best grade of sausage was being prepared for export. It was made from carefully selected meats, and was being prepared to be eaten uncooked. In this case the employee carted the chopped-up meat across a room in a barrow, the handles of which were filthy with grease. The meat was then thrown out upon tables, and the employee climbed upon the table, handled the meat with his unwashed hands, knelt with his dirty apron and trousers in contact with the meat he was spreading out, and, after he had finished his operation, again took hold of the dirty handles of the wheelbarrow, went back for another load, and repeated this process indefinitely. Inquiry developed the fact that there was no water in this room at all, and the only method the man adopted for cleaning his hands was to rub them against his dirty apron or on his still filthier trousers.

As an extreme example of the entire disregard on the part of employees of any notion of cleanliness in handling dressed meat, we saw a hog that had just been killed, cleaned, washed, and started on its way to the cooling room fall from the sliding rail to a dirty wooden floor and slide part way into a filthy men's privy. It was picked up by two employees, placed upon a truck, carried into the cooling room and hung up with other carcasses, no effort being made to clean it. . . .

All of [the] canned products bear labels, of which the following is a sample:

The contents of this package have been inspected according to the act of Congress of March 3, 1891.

QUALITY GUARANTEED

The phraseology of these labels is wholly unwarranted. The Government inspectors pass only upon the healthfulness of the animal at the time of killing. They know nothing of the process through which the meat has passed since this inspection. They do not know what else may have been placed in the cans in addition to "inspected meat." As a matter of fact, they know nothing about the "contents" of the can upon which the packers place these labels—do not even know that it contains what it purports to contain. The legend "Quality guaranteed" immediately following the statement as to Government inspection is wholly unjustifiable. It deceives and is plainly designed to deceive the average purchaser, who naturally infers from the label that the Government guarantees the contents of the can to be what it purports to be. . . .

Treatment of Employees

The lack of consideration for the health and comfort of the laborers in the Chicago stock yards seem to be a direct consequence of the system of administration that prevails. The various departments are under the direct control of superintendents who claim to use full authority in dealing with the employees and who seem to ignore all considerations except those of the account book. Under this system proper care of the products and of the health and comfort of the employees is impossible, and the consumer suffers in consequence. The insanitary conditions in which the laborers work and the feverish pace which they are forced to maintain inevitably affect their health. Physicians state that tuberculosis is disproportionately prevalent in the stock yards, and the victims of this disease expectorate on the spongy wooden floors of the dark workrooms, from which falling scraps of meat are later shoveled up to be converted into food products.

Even the ordinary decencies of life are completely ignored. In practically all cases the doors of the toilet rooms open directly into the working rooms, the privies of men and women frequently adjoin, and the entrances are sometimes no more than a foot or two apart. In other cases there are no privies for women in the rooms in which they work, and to reach the nearest it is necessary to go up or down a couple of flights of stairs. In one noticeable instance the privy for the women working in several adjoining rooms was in a room in which men chiefly were employed, and every girl going to use this had to pass by the working places of dozens of male operatives and enter the privy, the door of which was not 6 feet from the working place of one of the men operatives. As previously noted, in the privies for men and women alike there are no partitions, but simply a long row of open seats. Rest rooms, where tired women workers might go for a short rest, were found as rare exceptions, and in some establishments women are even placed in charge of privies chiefly for the purpose, it was stated, to see that the girls did not absent themselves too long from their work under the excuse of visiting them. In some instances what was called a rest room was simply one end of the privy partitioned off by a 6-foot partition from the remaining inclosure. A few girls were found using this, not only as a rest room, but as the only available place in which to sit to eat their luncheon.

Much of the work in connection with the handling of meat has to be carried on in rooms of a low temperature, but even here a callous disregard was everywhere seen for the comfort of those who work in these rooms. Girls and women were found in rooms registering a temperature of 38° F. without any ventilation whatever, depending entirely upon artificial light. The floors were wet and soggy, and in some cases covered with water, so that the girls had to stand in boxes of sawdust as a protection for their feet. In a few cases even drippings from the refrigerator rooms above trickled through the ceiling upon the heads of the workers and upon the food products being prepared. . . .

The neglect on the part of their employers to recognize or provide for the requirements of cleanliness and decency of the employees must have an influence that can not be exaggerated in lowering the morals and discouraging cleanliness on the part of the workers employed in the packing houses. The whole situation as we saw it in these huge establishments tends necessarily and inevitably to the moral degradation of thousands of workers, who are forced to spend their working hours under conditions that are entirely unnecessary and unpardonable, and which are a constant menace not only to their own health, but to the health of those who use the food products prepared by them. . . .

Introduction to Document 4

The meatpacking industry had been very resistant to federal regulation, but the public had been so stirred up by *The Jungle* and subsequent publicity that some sort of federal regulation was all but inevitable. Packinghouses quickly turned to damage control—the industry must win back public confidence by seeming to be out front on reform. Even advertising shifted toward issues of cleanliness. "The Massachusetts State Board of Health Endorses William Underwood Company's Products," an advertisement in a 1906 issue of *Outlook* magazine declared; "The report shows their ABSOLUTE PURITY and freedom from improper adulterants and preservatives. . . . [and] recommends the Wm. Underwood Co.'s CANNING PLANTS as MODELS to be copied by others in the same business." Louis F. Swift, President of one of the largest packing houses in Chicago, published the following open letter, also in *The Outlook* on June 23, 1906.

DOCUMENT 4 *Letter from Louis F. Swift*

Swift & Company,
Union Stock Yards.
Office of the President.

Chicago, June 14, 1906.

Government Supervision of the Meat Industry

No. 1. All cattle, sheep, and hogs purchased by Swift & Company are U.S. Government inspected, both before and after dressing. Those condemned in the ante-mortem inspection are refused and disposed of under local health authorities' supervision.

No. 2. The animals condemned by the Federal inspectors after dressing are destroyed under the inspector's supervision. Ante-mortem and post-mortem inspection is now furnished by the Government only when requested and not compulsory under present law. Swift & Company have always been strong advocates of thorough Government inspection both before and after slaughter, and we desire an extension of these regulations to cover all packing and slaughtering establishments, in order that uniform regulations may govern the entire industry; and to be compulsory.

No. 3. All processes in the preparation of meats to be under Federal inspection, which should require (*a*) that the meats are from healthy animals proper for food; (*b*) that the conditions under which the work is conducted are sanitary.

No. 4. The Government should pay the cost of inspection, thus affording the packer the same protection given the consumer. The packer does not produce any animals, and under Government inspection will not accept any showing traces of disease in the live examination. The packer now stands the loss of any animals condemned in the post-mortem examination, and to add an inspection fee is unfair.

Swift & Company want to be fully understood when they say that the same *open-door policy* which has prevailed in their plants will continue, the public being welcome to inspect the conditions under which the work is conducted, Further, we desire the continuance of Government inspection for all of our own plants and its strict compulsory enforcement in all other plants, regulating both the inspection of dressed meats and all food products, and the conditions under which the work is performed.

I desire to fix firmly in the minds of the readers of The Outlook the aim for integrity governing our purpose to supply the world with wholesome meats, and to decry the promiscuous attacks upon the industry in general.

We are obliged to The Outlook for the courtesy of its columns to dissipate any suspicion which may exist (through the wholesale, condemnation of the industry), and to maintain the confidence that has been enjoyed in the past, and made possible the progress accomplished in twenty years in the preparation of the world's supply of meat.

Louis F. Swift, President.

POSTSCRIPT

Louis Swift endorsed in almost every detail Senator Beveridge's bill, which became the Meat Inspection Act of 1906. One reason that the large meat packers supported the bill can be found in a single sentence in Swift's letter: "we desire the continuance of Government inspection for all of our own plants and its strict compulsory enforcement in all other plants, regulating both the inspection of dressed meats and all food products, and the conditions under which the work is performed." Many small independent butchers objected to the Meat Inspection Act because they simply would not be able to afford the equipment and labor to comply with its provisions. The large packers saw this as an opportunity to drive out some small competitors and increase their markets. Moreover, with the federal government acting as an impartial guarantor of cleanliness, the public at home and abroad would be reassured and would return to buying meat from the packing companies. In exchange for a bit of federal interference, the large packers would operate in a much more stable marketplace.

After presenting documents, each chapter in this book offers study questions and a bibliography. Questions called "Probing the Sources" tend to ask for detail about the documents, while those under the heading "Interpreting the Sources" are more concerned with analysis. Each chapter ends with a short list of recommended readings.

QUESTIONS

Defining Terms

Identify in the context of the chapter each of the following:

Upton Sinclair   Packingtown
socialists   muckraking
Meat Inspection Act   Jurgis Rudkus
Antanas Kaztauskis   Reynolds-Neill Report
damage control   Louis Swift

Probing the Sources

1. What did Upton Sinclair mean when he said that he aimed at the public's heart but hit it in the stomach?
2. Do you think Sinclair exaggerated conditions in Packingtown? How or why?
3. Compare the specific points in Sinclair's account with those of the Reynolds-Neill Report.
4. What dangers did conditions in the meatpacking industry hold for consumers? What role did the federal government play in protecting consumers?

Interpreting the Sources

1. What was Sinclair's attitude toward immigrants? Did he see them as active or passive?
2. How does Kaztauskis's account of the role of friends and family differ from Sinclair's?
3. Why do you think meatpackers like Swift were in favor of regulating their industry?

ADDITIONAL READING

Conditions in the stockyards and the environment of Packingtown are discussed in James R. Barrett, *Work and Community in the Jungle: Chicago's Packinghouse Workers* (1988); and Louise Carroll Wade, *Chicago's Pride: The Stockyards; Packingtown, and the Environs in the Nineteenth Century* (1988). On the life of Upton Sinclair, see Floyd Dell, *Upton Sinclair: A*

Study in Social Protest (1927); Jon Yoder, *Upton Sinclair* (1975); Leon Harris, *Upton Sinclair, American Rebel* (1975); and Sinclair's own *The Autobiography of Upton Sinclair* (1962). On literary radicalism see Daniel Aaron, *Writers on the Left* (1969); and James Burkhart Gilbert, *Writers and Partisans: A History of Literary Radicalism in America,* (1968). For a classic revisionist interpretation of American progressive reform, see Gabriel Kolko, *The Triumph of Conservatism* (New York, 1963). Finally, see James Harvey Young, *Securing the Federal Food and Drug act of 1906* (1989).

Reconstruction and the Rise of the Ku Klux Klan

HISTORICAL CONTEXT

In a letter to the House of Representatives dated April 19, 1872, President Ulysses S. Grant described a "grand system of criminal associations pervading most of the Southern States." Investigations by the attorney general, by the Joint Committee of Congress upon Southern Outrages, and by local officials all revealed that a terroristic organization known as the Ku Klux Klan, or KKK, exercised enormous influence in the South and worked in defiance of federal Reconstruction. Grant alleged that members swore oaths of obedience and secrecy that they considered more binding than their allegiance to the United States. "They are organized and armed," the president declared. "They effect their objects by personal violence, often extending to murder. They terrify witnesses, they control juries in the State courts, and sometimes in the courts of the United States." Klansmen spied on, murdered, and intimidated their enemies and thereby destroyed the rule of law. Their goals, according to Grant, were

> by force and terror, to prevent all political action not in accord with the views of the members, to deprive colored citizens of the right to bear arms, and of the right of a free ballot, and to suppress the schools in which colored children were taught, and to reduce the colored people to a condition closely allied to that of slavery.

The Ku Klux Klan, in other words, threatened to seize by terror what the South had lost on the battlefield. Voting, bearing arms, education, free thought—all were integral to democracy, and all were menaced by the Klan.

The KKK originated in informal organizations that Confederate men joined immediately after the Civil War. The agenda of these organizations became increasingly political as Andrew Johnson's Reconstruction policies were replaced by the more stringent ones of the so-called radical Republicans in Congress. The South was now occupied by enemy troops, its cities burned, farms barren, elected officials disgraced, and population decimated. Those who had been slaves, black men and women stigmatized as ineradicably inferior, were now to be treated as equal citizens of a democracy. There was even talk of confiscating southern agricultural land and redistributing it so that blacks and poor whites could become independent farmers, a plan, as it turned out, too radical for most radical Republicans, whose devotion to private property—even that of former rebels—brooked no exceptions.

For African-Americans, the era of Reconstruction was a time of relative freedom. Many took the opportunity to leave the land they had been bound to and sought opportunity in southern cities and in the North. Certainly some whites feared the possible loss of their labor force. Equally threatening, the former slaves were more free to worship, work, learn, and acquire power and money than ever before. Many whites alleged that blacks were incapable of handling freedom, that black politicians were corrupt; black workers, slothful; and black masses, ignorant. But the unspoken and perhaps deeper fear was that African-Americans were indeed capable of good citizenship and would compete with their former masters. In other words, the comforting idea that any white, no matter how degraded, was "better than a nigger" no longer held. If radical Reconstruction failed to secure real economic opportunity for the former slaves, it did insist that African-Americans be treated as equal citizens under the law, an idea antithetical to the old southern economic and social structure, indeed to white southern identity.

But it was not just the new position of blacks that threatened white southerners. Republican rule included policies for changing the region to conform more with the tone of northern society. The "carpetbaggers" and "scalawags" generally were not corrupt individuals but people who genuinely believed that the South's salvation would come through railroads, new industries, and public schools—in short, institutions associated with economic progress in the free-labor North. Radical Reconstruction not only proposed to change racial mores but aimed to make a premodern social and economic system modern. Such drastic changes, imposed, as it appeared to many white southerners, by upstart blacks and alien Yankees, were terrifying.

The Ku Klux Klan was a response to the social, cultural, and economic changes that many white southerners found so disturbing. It might best be seen as the extreme wing of the "redeemers," those whites who sought political redemption from Reconstruction. African-Americans and southern Unionists, with the aid of the federal government and the Republican party, were able to govern several states for a few years after the Civil War, but eventually the political experience, popularity, and just plain brutality of the redeemers won the day. The Klan specialized in the latter.

Klansmen typically dressed in white robes and hoods, and they tried to convince their black victims that they were the ghosts of the Confederate dead. Blacks were intimidated, not so much by the transparent ghostly ruse, but by the violence the Klansmen dealt out. By the 1860s, their pattern was clear: several Klansmen would surround a victim's house at night, shoot into the windows, set fire to the structure, poison livestock, or simply drag the inhabitants out and shoot, whip, or hang them. Usually the victims were individuals who had stood up for their rights, blacks who voted, ran for office, or refused to take whites' insults. Occasionally there was open warfare between Klansmen and black militias. White citizens, too, who dared support blacks or who expressed Unionist sympathies were terrorized by the night riders.

It is impossible to know how many southern men ever joined the Klan—it was, after all, a secret organization—but through the late 1860s and into the early 1870s, the Klan was very successful in intimidating both blacks and whites. When the federal government outlawed the organization and began prosecuting its members, the

Klan lost some of its effectiveness, but by then violence, along with social ostracism and economic coercion, had become part of the arsenal of redeemer politics. Redemption came to state and local government but succeeded only because the federal government lost its resolve to make sure that all citizens were treated, as promised in the Constitution, with equality. Slowly, African-Americans' rights to vote, to speak out freely, and to participate equally in social life were stripped away.

Perhaps even more important than the political disenfranchisement of African-Americans that followed Reconstruction was their reduction to economic peonage. Slavery died at Appomattox, but new forms of economic and political servitude soon took its place, and they lasted for a century. In the years following the Civil War, most blacks became tenant farmers with no land of their own, and most of these sharecropped, work that offered little more freedom or material comfort than slavery. As a sharecropper, a former slave might farm a white man's land; buy tools, supplies, and food from him; and rent a shack for the family from him. Owner and renter would split the proceeds of the harvest, but the black farmer's debt for the goods that the white man had furnished would almost certainly exceed any profit. Indebted to the white planter, former slaves would be unable to leave; year after year they would have to stay on the land, trying to pay off a debt that grew ever larger.

THE DOCUMENTS

The following documents reveal the Ku Klux Klan from various points of view. The initiation oath of the Knights of the White Camelia (a part of the Klan) reveals the style, tone, and purposes of this organization. Despite the Klan's high rhetoric of defending southern honor, the passages from the narratives of former slaves and from congressional hearings give testimony to how the Klan used violence to accomplish its goals. Note here the reasons for which the victims felt they were being attacked. Congressman Stevenson's speech summarizes the federal findings on the scope of Klan activities and reveals the conflict over values and ideology between southern redeemers and northern Reconstructionists. Finally, *Experience of a Northern Man Among the Ku-Klux* gives a good sense of how northerners viewed the South and how some of them even visualized colonizing it and remaking its society to conform to northern norms. As you read these selections, ask yourself how and why the problem of race relations spilled over into issues related to ideology, economics, and labor.

Introduction to Document 1

The initiation oath of the Knights of the White Camelia reveals the attraction of such organizations. The Knights originated during the early days of the Klan in the late 1860s. Note the claims to religious faith and patriotism and the chivalric mandate: to protect the weak and defenseless against the outrages of "lawless" blacks. Aside from the reassertion of crude white supremacy, the KKK must have been very popular for its sense of mystery, pageantry, and special rituals; individuals were made to feel that they belonged to something splendid and grand. To whom would such appeals be most compelling?

DOCUMENT 1 *Initiation Oath of the Knights of the White Camelia*

I do solemnly swear, in the presence of these witnesses, never to reveal, without authority, the existence of this Order, its objects, its acts, and signs of recognition; never to reveal or publish, in any manner whatsoever, what I shall see or hear in this Council; never to divulge the names of the members of the Order, or their acts done in connection therewith; I swear to maintain and defend the social and political superiority of the White Race on this Continent; always and in all places to observe a marked distinction between the White and African races; to vote for none but white men for any office of honor, profit or trust; to devote my intelligence, energy and influence to instil these principles in the minds and hearts of others; and to protect and defend persons of the White Race, in their lives, rights and property, against the encroachments and aggressions of an inferior race.

I swear, moreover, to unite myself in heart, soul and body with those who compose this Order; to aid, protect and defend them in all places; to obey the orders of those, who, by our statutes, will have the right of giving those orders. . . .

The oath having been taken by the candidate, the C[ommander] shall now say:

Brother, by virtue of the authority to me delegated, I now pronounce you a Knight of the [White Camelia]. . . .

Brothers: You have been initiated into one of the most important Orders, which have ever been established on this continent: an Order, which, if its principles are faithfully observed and its objects diligently carried out, is destined to regenerate our unfortunate country and to relieve the White Race from the humiliating condition to which it has lately been reduced in this Republic. It is necessary, therefore, that before taking part in the labors of this Association, you should understand fully its principles and objects and the duties which devolve upon you as one of its members.

As you may have already gathered from the questions which were propounded to you, and which you have answered so satisfactorily, and from the clauses of the Oath which you have taken, our main and fundamental object is the *maintenance of the supremacy of the white race* in this Republic. History and physiology teach us that we belong to a race which nature has endowed with an evident superiority over all other races, and that the Maker, in thus elevating us above the common standard of human creation, has intended to give us over inferior races, a dominion from which no human laws can permanently derogate. The experience of ages demonstrate that, from the origin of the world, this dominion has always remained in the hands of the Caucasian Race; whilst all the other races have constantly occupied a subordinate and secondary position; a fact which triumphantly confirms this great law of nature. Powerful nations have succeeded each other in the face of the world, and have marked their passage by glorious and memorable deeds; and among those who have thus left on this globe indelible traces of their splendor and greatness, we find none but descended from the Caucasian stock. We see, on the contrary, that most of the countries inhabited by the other races have remained in a state of complete barbarity; whilst the small number of those who have advanced beyond this savage existence, have, for centuries, stagnated in a semi-barbarous condition, of which there can be no progress or improvement. And it is a remarkable fact that as a race of men is more remote from the Caucasian and approaches nearer to the black African, the more fatally that stamp of inferiority is affixed to its sons, and irrevocably dooms them to eternal imperfectibility and degradation.

Convinced that we are of these elements of natural ethics, we know, besides, that the government of our Republic was established by white men, for white men alone, and that it never was in the contemplation of its founders that it should fall into the hands of an inferior and degraded race. We hold, therefore, that any attempt to wrest from the white race the management of its affairs in order to transfer it to control of the black population, is an invasion of the sacred prerogatives vouchsafed to us by the Constitution, and a violation of the laws established by God himself; that such encroachments are subversive of the established institutions of our Republic, and that no individual of the white race can submit to them without humiliation and shame.

It, then, becomes our solemn duty, as white men, to resist strenuously and persistently those attempts against our natural and constitutional rights, and to do everything in our power in order to maintain, in this Republic, the supremacy of the Caucasian race, and restrain the black or African race to that condition of social and political inferiority for which God has destined it. This is the object for which our Order was instituted; and, in carrying it out, we intend to infringe no laws, to violate no rights, and to resort to no forcible means, except for purposes of legitimate and necessary defense.

As an essential condition of success, this Order proscribes absolutely all social equality between the races. If we were to admit persons of African race on the same level with ourselves, a state of personal relations would follow which would unavoidably lead to political equality; for it would be a virtual recognition of *status*, after which we could not consistently deny them an equal share in the administration of our public affairs. The man who is good enough to be our familiar companion, is good enough also to participate in our political government; and if we were to grant the one, there could be no good reason for us not to concede the other of these two privileges.

There is another reason, Brothers, for which we condemn this social equality. Its toleration would soon be a fruitful source of intermarriages between individuals of the two races; and the result of this *misceganation [sic]* would be gradual amalgamation and the production of a degenerate and bastard offspring, which would soon populate these States with a degraded and ignoble population, incapable of moral and intellectual development and unfitted to support a great and powerful country. We must maintain the purity of the white blood, if we would preserve for it that natural superiority with which God has ennobled it.

To avoid these evils, therefore, we take the obligation *to observe a marked distinction between the two races*, not only in the relations of public affairs, but also in the more intimate dealings and intercourse of private life which, by the frequency of their occurrence, are more apt to have an influence on the attainment of the purposes of the Order.

Now that I have laid before you the objects of this Association, let me charge you specially in relation to one of your most important studies as one of its members. Our statutes make us bound to respect sedulously the rights of the colored inhabitants of this Republic, and in every instance, to give to them whatever lawfully belongs to them. It is an act of simple justice not to deny them any of the privileges to which they are legitimately entitled; and we cannot better show the inherent superiority of our race than by dealing with them in that spirit of firmness, liberality and impartiality which characterizes all superior organizations. Besides, it would be ungenerous for us to undertake to restrict them to the narrowest limits as to the exercise of certain rights, without conceding to them, at the same time, the fullest measure of those which we recognize as theirs; and a fair construction of a white man's duty towards them would be, not only to respect and observe their acknowledged rights, but also to see that these are respected and observed by others.

Introduction to Documents 2 and 3

Despite the Klan's lofty rhetoric, the following testimonies by its victims reveal the terrorism for which the organization was renowned. Ask yourself who became Klan victims and why. The three statements in Document 2 were made by former slaves looking back on their experiences from a distance of several decades; the statements are taken from oral histories collected during the 1930s by the Federal

Writers Project. The two statements in Document 3 come from testimony before a congressional committee investigating Klan activities in the early 1870s.

 DOCUMENT 2 *Testimony of Victims of the Ku Klux Klan*

Pierce Harper

After de colored people was considered free an' turned loose de Klu Klux broke out. Some of de colored people commenced to farming like I tol' you an' all de ol' stock dey could pick up after de Yankees left dey took an' took care of. If you got so you made good money an' had a good farm de Klu Klux'd come an' murder you. De gov'ment built de colored people school houses an' de Klu Klux went to work an' burn 'em down. Dey'd go to de jails an' take de colored men out an' knock dere brains out an' break dere necks an' throw 'em in de river.

Dere was a man dat dey taken, his name was Jim Freeman. Dey taken him an' destroyed his stuff an' him 'cause he was making some money. Hung him on a tree in his front yard, right in front of his cabin. Dere was some young men who went to de schools de gov'ment opened for de colored folks. Some white widder woman said someone had stole something she own', so dey put these young fellers in jail 'cause dey suspicioned 'em. De Klu Kluxes went to de jail an' took 'em out an' kill 'em. Dat happen de second year after de War.

After de Klu Kluxes got so strong de colored men got together an' made a complaint before de law. De Gov'nor told de law to give 'em de ol' guns in de commissary what de Southern soldiers had use, so dey issued de colored men old muskets an' told 'em to protect theirselves.

De colored men got together an' organized the 'Malicy [Militia]. Dey had leaders like regular soldiers, men dat led 'em right on. Dey didn't meet 'cept when dey heard de Klu Kluxes was coming to get some of de colored folks. Den de one who knowed dat tol' de leader an' he went 'round an' told de others when an' where dey's meet. Den dey was ready for 'em. Dey'd hide in de cabins an' when de Klu Kluxes come dere dey was. Den's when dey found out who a lot of de Klu Kluxes was, 'cause a lot of 'em was killed. Dey wore dem long sheets an' you couldn't tell who dey was. Dey even covered dere horses up so you couldn't tell who dey belong to. Men you thought was your friend was Klu Kluxes. You deal wit' 'em in de stores in de day time an' at night dey come out to your house an' kill you.

Sue Craft

My teacher's name Dunlap—a white teacher teachin de cullud. De Ku Klux whupped him fo' teachin' us. I saw de Ku Klux ridin' a heap dem days. Dey had hoods pulled ovah dere faces. One time dey come to our house twict. Fus' time dey come quiet. It was right 'fore de 'lection o' Grant jus' after slavery. It was fus' time cullud people 'lowed t' vote. Dey ast my father was he goin' to vote for Grant. He tell 'em he don' know he goin' vote. After 'lection dey come back, whoopin' an' hollerin. Dey shoot out de winder lights. It was 'cause my father voted for Grant. Dey broke de do' open. My father was a settin' on de bed. I 'member he had a shot gun in his han'. Well, dey broke de do' down, an' then father he shoot, an' dey scattered all ovah de fence.

Morgan Ray

. . . I heard a lot about the Klu Klux, but it warn't till long afterwards dat I evan see 'em. It was one night after de work of de day was done and I was takin' a walk near where I worked. Suddenly I hear the hoof beats of horses and I natcherly wuz curious and waited

Ku Klux Klan "mode of torture." (Library of Congress)

beside de road to see what was comin'. I saw a company of men hooded and wearin' what looked like sheets. Dey had a young cullud man as dere prisoner. I wuz too skairt to say anything or ask any questions. I just went on my sweet way. Later I found out dey acclaimed de prisoner had assaulted a white woman. Dey strung him up when he wouldn't confess, and shot him full of holes and threw his body in de pond.

 DOCUMENT 3 *Congressional Inquiry into Klan Activities*

Atlanta, Georgia, October 25, 1871.

Joseph Addison (White) Sworn and Examined
BY THE CHAIRMAN:

Question: What is your age, where were you born, where do you live, and what is your present occupation?

Answer: I am about twenty-four years old; I was born in Muscogee County, and now live in Haralson County; I have been living there ever since I was a little bit of a boy; I am a farmer.

Question: During the war which side were you on?

Answer: I never fought a day in the rebel army; I was not in it at all.

Question: Which side were your feelings on?

Answer: My feelings were on the side of what you call the radical party now.

Question: What did they call it then?

Answer: I was what you call a Union man then.

Question: Were your opinions well known?

Answer: Yes, sir; I reckon I am well known.

Question: Have you seen any people, or do you know of any, in your county, called Ku-Klux?

Answer: Yes, sir.

Question: Tell us what you know about them.

Answer: Do you want me to state just about all how they did?

Question: Yes.

Answer: I will tell you how they did me. . . . My wife looked out and said, "Lord have mercy! Joe, it is the Ku-Klux." I jumped out of the door and ran. One of them was right in the back yard, and he jabbed the end of his six-shooter almost against my head, and said, "Halt! God damn you." I said, "I will give up." I asked them what they were doing that for; they said that I had been stealing. I said, "You men here know I have not." They said, "We gave you time once to get away, and, God damn you, you have not gone; now, God damn you, you shall not go, for we allow to kill you." I said, "If you do not abuse me or whip me, I will go the next morning." They said they would not abuse me or whip me, but they would kill me. I said, "Let me go and see my wife and children." They said, "No, God damn you." I turned away from the man; he jammed his pistol in my face, and said, "God damn you, go on, or I will kill you." They took me about eighty or ninety yards from there into a little thicket. The man on my right was a high, tall man; the one on my left was a low, chunky fellow. The man on my right stepped back, and said to the little fellow on my left, "Old man, we have got him here now; do as you please with him." There were some little hickories near him; he looked at them, but did not take them. They were all standing right around me with their guns pointing at me. Just as he turned around, I wheeled and run; but before I had run ten yards I heard a half a dozen caps bursted at me. Just as I made a turn to go behind some buildings and little bushes, I heard two guns fired. I must have gone seventy or eighty yards, and then I heard what I thought was a pistol fired. I heard a bullet hit a tree. I run on eight or ten steps further, and then I heard a bullet hit a tree just before me. Every one of them took after me, and run me for a hundred and fifty yards. I ran down a little bluff and ran across a branch. When I got across there, I could not run any further, for my shoes were all muddy. I cut the strings of my old shoes, and left them there. I stopped to listen, but I never saw anything more of them. I then went around and climbed up on the fence, and sat there and watched until dark. I then went to the house and got some dry clothes, and then went back where I had fixed a place in the woods to sleep in, and went to bed. That was the last I heard of them that night. They came back Sunday night before court commenced on Monday, in Haralson County. My wife would not stay there by herself, but went to her sister-in-law's, Milton Powell's wife. They came in on them on Sunday night, or about two hours and a half before day Monday morning. They abused her and cursed her powerfully, and tried to make her tell where I was. They said that if she did not tell them they would shoot her God-damned brains out. I was laying out close by there, and I stood there and heard them. They shot five or six shots in the yard; some of them said they shot into the house. They scared my wife and sister-in-law so bad that they took the children and went into the woods and staid there all night. That was the last time they were there. . . .

Question: Have they ever molested you since then?

Answer: No, sir; they have never been on me any more since then.

Question: Do you still stay there?

Answer: No, sir; I have done moved now. I moved off, and left my hogs and my crop and everything there, what little I made. I did not make much crop this year, for I was afraid to work, and now I am afraid to go back there to save anything.

Atlanta, Georgia, October 26, 1871.

Thomas M. Allen (Colored) Sworn and Examined

By the Chairman:

Question: What is your age, where were you born, and where do you now live?

Answer: I am now thirty-eight years old. I was born in Charleston, South Carolina, and I am living here at present; that is, my family is here; I am pastor of the Baptist church at Marietta, Jasper County.

Question: How long have you been living in this State?

Answer: I came to this State the year that James K. Polk died, about 1849.

Question: How do you connect your coming here with his death?

Answer: I landed in Savannah at the time they were firing cannon there, and asked what was the matter.

Question: Were you a slave?

Answer: Partly so. My father was a white man and he set us free at his death. They stole us from Charleston and run me and my brother and mother into this State. He left us ten thousand dollars each to educate us, and give us trades, and for that money they stole us away.

Question: Were you kept in slavery until the time of emancipation?

Answer: Yes, sir; I was held as a slave; I hired my time.

Question: You never were able to assert your freedom before emancipation?

Answer: No, sir, I could not do it. . . .

Question: Have you been connected with political affairs in this State since the war?

Answer: Yes, sir. When the constitutional convention was called, I took an active part, and did all I could, of course. Afterwards I ran for the legislature and was elected.

Question: In what year?

Answer: I was elected in 1868; the colored members were expelled that year.

Question: From what county were you elected?

Answer: From Jasper County.

Question: Were you reinstated in your seat in the legislature?

Answer: Yes, sir.

Question: Have you witnessed any violence towards any of your race, yourself or any others?

Answer: Yes, sir. After we were expelled from the legislature, I went home to Jasper County; I was carrying on a farm there. On the 16th of October, a party of men came to my house; I cannot say how many, for I did not see them. . . . About 2 o'clock my wife woke me up, and said that there were persons all around the house; that they had been there for half an hour, and were calling for me. I heard them call again, and I asked them what they wanted, and who they were. . . .

They asked me to come out. At this time my brother-in-law waked up and said, "Who are they, Thomas?" I said, "I do not know." . . .

He put on his shoes and vest and hat; this was all he was found with after he was killed. He opened the door and hollered, "Where are you?"

He hollered twice, and then two guns were fired. He seemed to fall, and I and my wife hollered, and his wife hollered. I jumped up, and ran back to the fire-place, where I started to get a light, and then started to go over the partition to him. I threw a clock down, and then I thought of the closet there, and went through it to him, and my wife closed the door. I hollered for Joe, a third man on the place, to come up and bring his gun, for Emanuel was killed. He did not come for some time, and then I was so excited that I could not recognize his voice. After a time I let him in. We made up a light, and then I saw my brother-in-law laying on his back as he fell. I examined him; there were four or five number one buck-shot in his breast. . . .

Question: What do you know about this organization of men they call Ku-Klux?
Answer: I have never seen one in my life; I have seen a great many people who have seen them. I have a Ku-Klux letter here that I got on the day of the election for the constitution.
Question: Will you read it?
Answer: Yes, sir; this is it.

To Thomas Allen:
Tom, you are in great danger; you are going heedless with the radicals, against the interest of the conservative white population, and I tell you if you do not change your course before the election for the ratification of the infernal constitution, your days are numbered, and they will be but few. Just vote or use your influence for the radicals or for the constitution, and you go up certain. My advice to you, Tom, is to stay at home if you value your life, and not vote at all, and advise all of your race to do the same thing. You are marked and closely watched by K.K.K. (or in plain words Ku-Klux.)

Take heed; a word to the wise is sufficient.
By order of Grand Cyclops.

Question: Where did you get this?
Answer: It was dropped in the shop the morning of the election, when I was running for the legislature. I showed it to a great many men in town; I showed it to Colonel Preston, a friend of mine. He asked where I got it, and I told him. He said, "Tear it up." I said, "No, it may be of service to my children if not to me." He said, "You need not talk so slack about it; there may be heaps of Ku-Klux in the State, and they might get hold of your talk. . . ."
Question: What is the feeling of your people in regard to their personal safety?
Answer: They do not consider that they have any safety at all, only in the cities; that is the truth. In a great many places the colored people call the white people master and mistress, just as they ever did; if they do not do it they are whipped. They have no safety at all except in a large place like this. If I could have stayed at home I would not have been here. I left all my crops and never got anything for them. My wife had no education, and when I came away everything went wrong. There are thousands in my condition.
Question: Is that the reason so many of your people come to the large cities?
Answer: Yes, sir, that is the reason. Mr. Abram Turner, a member of the legislature, from Putnam County, the county adjoining mine, was shot down in the street in open day. He was a colored man. They have elected another in his place, a democrat.
Question: When was he elected?
Answer: Last fall.
Question: He has been killed since?
Answer: Yes, sir, shot down in broad open day. . . .

Question: Was he a republican?

Answer: Yes sir, I knew him very well; he was a good man, a harmless man; I married him to his wife.

Question: Do the people of your race feel that they have the protection of the laws?

Answer: By no means.

Question: What is their hope and expectation for the future?

Answer: They expect to get protection from the Federal Government at Washington; that is all. You ask any one of my people out there, even the most ignorant of them, and they will tell you so. . . . I believe that many of the jurymen, and lawyers too, are members of the Ku-Klux; I believe it positively; I would say so on my deathbed.

Question: How much have you been over the State?

Answer: I have traveled all over the State.

Question: Have you communicated pretty freely with the people of your own race?

Answer: Yes, sir.

Question: Have you received information from them about the Ku-Klux?

Answer: Yes, sir, occasionally.

Question: In how large a portion of the State do you find reports of Ku-Klux operations?

Answer: I find it in the counties of what is known among us as the Black Belt. Wherever the negroes are in the majority, there the Ku-Klux range more than in any other places. Up in Cobb County they are very peaceable. The democrats are always elected there to the general assembly. The whites have about seven hundred majority. The colored people get along splendidly there. In those counties where the whites are largely in the majority, the colored people get along very well; but go into the counties where the negroes are in the majority, and there is always trouble; for instance, in Monroe County, or Warren County, or anywhere in the Black Belt, there is always trouble between the whites and the colored people.

Question: Are the colored people riotous in disposition? Are they inclined to make trouble?

Answer: I suppose the colored people are as peaceable as any people in the world. The colored people of Madison, when the white people went to the jail and murdered a man there, could have burned up the town and killed all the white people there.

Introduction to Document 4

Congressman Job E. Stevenson from Ohio delivered the following address in the House of Representatives on May 30, 1872. He argued that the Klan was not merely a brutal organization devoted to terror, but part of a political conspiracy to overthrow Reconstruction and reenslave African Americans. As you read the excerpts from this speech, note Stevenson's characterization of the newly conquered South. Why did he believe that the North must stop the Klan? What were his political motivations for opposing the Klan?

 DOCUMENT 4 *Speech to the House of Representatives*

Hon. Job E. Stevenson of Ohio

Mr. Speaker: The gravest question before Congress is the Kuklux Conspiracy, its origin and extent, character and actions, plans and purposes, condition and prospects.

Origin

It originated in hostility to the Government, in enmity against the Union. It is the successor of the southern confederacy, rebellion in disguise, war at midnight. It rose like an exhalation from the unsodden grave of the "lost cause." . . .

A Political Conspiracy

Such being the origin . . . of this great conspiracy, we may well inquire against whom its terrors are aimed. It strikes exclusively at the Unionists of the South, principally at the freedmen. No man can deny that it is political. The oath swears the member to oppose Radicalism, to oppose the Radical party, to oppose the political equality of the races.

General Forrest said: "It is a protective political military organization. Its objects originally were protection against Loyal Leagues and the Grand Army of the Republic; but after it became general, it was found that political matters and interests could best be promoted within it, and it was then made a political organization, giving its support, of course, to the Democratic party." . . .

It appears that in the States of Georgia, Louisiana, Tennessee, and South Carolina from the spring election in 1868 to the election for President in 1868, the Republican vote was reduced eighty-five thousand by intimidation and violence. . . .

Commanders

The forces of the conspiracy are controlled by such men as Generals Gordon, Hampton, and Forrest, and under them by inferior officers, running down from grade to grade, to captains of companies, or chiefs of klans or cyclops of dens. The organization begins at the den and extends to the precinct, the county, the congressional district, the State, the South. It is compact, connected, consistent, moving as a perfect body from the head to the humblest member, as an army in the field, with sterner discipline than that of an army. . . .

Authority

These commands bind the members by an oath enforced by fear; administered with strange ceremonies, emphasized by penalty of death. At midnight the member is led blindfold to the den, and there, on his knees, hears the ritual and takes the oath. And as the bandage drops from his eyes he sees circles of men in frightful disguises armed with revolvers leveled on his head, and the Grand Cyclops says: "And this you do under penalty of a traitor's doom, which is death! death! death!" In some dens there are symbols of horror. In one in North Carolina, two skulls, one of a white man, a Union soldier, whose grave was rifled and his skull taken for the den; and the other the skull of a freedman, who had been murdered; and a vial of blood of the colored victim; the member is sworn "by these skulls and this blood."

Thus members are sworn to obey their superior officers on penalty of death, and under that oath they are compelled to take the field at the command and to do any deed he may order, even to murder. Scores of members have confessed and testified that they have committed outrages and murders at the command of their officers.

Outrages

The outrages vary from threats and intimidations to scourging, wounding, maiming, and killing by shooting, drowning, hanging, and burning. If we could know the whole truth it would appear that since the war this conspiracy has outraged more than thirty thousand men, women, and children—peaceful, innocent, defenseless citizens of the Republic. . . .

Excuses

Among the excuses made by those who control and defend this organization is that they feared the negroes; yet all Southern men of intelligence testify that the negroes of the South have behaved better than any other people ever did under similar circumstances. . . . They pretend that the Government of the United States has oppressed them, yet that Government, to which they had forfeited property, liberty, and life, spared their lives, allowed them their liberty, and returned them their property. No confiscated estates are withheld from their owners; although some abandoned property was taken, the only rebel estate remaining in the hands of the Government is Arlington [Robert E. Lee's estate], and gentlemen in both Houses of Congress propose to remove the remains of our soldiers and give that cemetery back to its rebel owners. No life has been taken for treason. Jefferson Davis is as free as the air, a citizen of the Republic. Few political privileges are denied, few leaders are unamnestied. The only issue that can be made on amnesty is whether the remnant should be forthwith relieved. The difference between parties on this question is whether the Republican party has been derelict in not restoring to political power even Jefferson Davis. . . .

Financial Results of Reconstruction

What has been the financial result of reconstruction? The Government and the peoples of the North forgave to the people of the South and caused them to repudiate debts amounting to more than twenty-five hundred million dollars. We relieved them by constitutional amendments, and by the generosity of our people, of debts nearly double the property their own crimes had left. If the Government and the people of the North had merely withheld their hands from the South, and left the conquered rebels to their own financial devices, the South would have sunk in bankruptcy and ruin as a man thrown into the sea with a millstone at his neck. The Government and people of the North rescued them, fed them, advanced money and property, restored peace and order, and gave them the opportunity to revive their fortunes.

The white people of the South continually upbraid the colored people, saying, "The negro will not work." Yet wherever you go you see scores of white men lounging on the piazzas of the hotels, shifting their chairs to keep out of the sun, moving only to get "refreshments," while freedmen are laboring in the fields earning money to enable the whites to lounge. The laborers of the South have produced in cotton and other agricultural products since the war nearly $4,000,000,000, more than double the value of property in 1865. And the people have saved so much of these gains, that they had in 1870 $2,700,000,000 against $1,600,000,000 at the end of the war, having increased their property since the war over $1,000,000,000. And they had in 1870, $6,000,000 more than their State assessments in 1860, excluding slaves. That is the financial result of reconstruction. . . .

Financial Effects of Kuklux

They have not yet ceased reckless destruction of their own property. The Kuklux conspiracy is fatal to values. It disturbs business, disorganizes labor, paralyzes industry and commerce. The documents show the fall of property in those States where the conspiracy has been acting by the millions. . . . The Kuklux conspiracy has cost the South more than all the carpet-baggers of all the States (including the Louisiana leader of the new movement), have been able to misappropriate.

Depopulation

The conspiracy is driving away the people. Here is a copy of the *Freedmen's Repository*, giving an account of the emigration from this country to Liberia, showing that last fall a ship took out of the country from Virginia one passenger; from Florida, five; from North Carolina, five; from Georgia, sixty-six; and from Clay Hill, York county, South Carolina, one hundred and sixty-six. And at the head of this South Carolina party was Rev. Elias Hill, a description of whom is given here, a Baptist preacher, a cripple, whom the Kuklux scourged because he preached the gospel, taught school, and belonged to the Republican party. He was driven with a colony of one hundred and sixty-six souls out of South Carolina, out of the United States of America, even to Liberia.

Here were two hundred and thirty-eight industrious people driven at once from the United States to Africa.

Before the war these colored people—men, women, and children—were valued by their owners at $500 each. Now they are driven out of the country by outrage, scourging, and murder; and we are told that the United States Government must not interfere to protect them. Imagine Elias Hill in the wilds of Africa, telling the bushmen how the great American Republic protects its citizens.

Present Condition of the Conspiracy

But, Mr. Speaker, what is the present condition of this organization? . . .

Those who imagine that because the conspirators are now still, they will remain so, do not understand them. In South Carolina the members of this organization raided in 1868, outraged and murdered Union people, and changed votes by scores of thousands. From that time until 1870 they were quiet, and then they raided again until more than three thousand outrages were committed in less than six months. The conspiracy is so organized that it may remain quiescent for a year or for two years, ready to be called into the field by the blast of the bugle, or by the click of the telegraph. Within one week this "military political" organization could throw into action a quarter of a million men, armed with the revolver, the bowie-knife, . . . with bayonets captured from State militia, and revolving rifles furnished from New York city.

Its Power

Shall we trust them? Are we blind—blind to the red rivers of blood they have shed; deaf to the cries of their thousands of victims? Are we mad to forget our own interests and safety? These conspirators have power, if they dare—and they are men who have dared death at the cannon's mouth—to sweep the whole South at the next presidential election; and if the result depends on the South, they can seat their candidate in the presidential chair. . . . *Whoever shall be the Democratic candidate will be the candidate of the Kuklux conspiracy. If the Democrats elect the next President it will be by Kuklux votes and violence; and the man thus elected will be the Kuklux President.*

Introduction to Document 5

Benjamin Bryant's *Experience of a Northern Man Among the Ku-Klux* argues that, while the South had been defeated, the region's way of life remained stubbornly unchanged. Bryant began with the problem of education, stating that the southern aristocracy kept both African Americans and poor whites in ignorance. The Klan had arisen to maintain this situation. Keeping the masses poor and ignorant, according to Bryant, was the Klan's main goal. Document 5 contains excerpts from Bryant's preface and book.

DOCUMENT 5   *From* **Experience of a Northern Man Among the Ku-Klux**

Benjamin Bryant

In order to better inform my readers of my intention for writing a book, I will say before entering into the main body of the work, that I have just returned from a long visit in the South, and have witnessed things which have occurred in the States late in Rebellion, and have kept a record of all, for the interest of the Northern people, and also, to give in detail the present situation of the people who are living there. . . .

As education is the great aim of every true American citizen, I will first inform you of its progress. The South has not had the advantages to aid in the development of education like the people of the North; but it has always been discouraged by the aristocracy of the South; and in so doing they have deprived the poor white people of education and other intelligences, as well as the black man. . . .

A great many freedmen are working on shares with their former masters, and are generally doing well, but are working for one-half, one-third, or one-fourth of their former pay, and are working under their master's hand, calling their former masters, "master," and denouncing the Proclamation of Emancipation. They hate that "old Northern woman" who is teaching the "nigger school," and resist all aid to free schools, and say, "I can live without education; I don't want it and will not have it."

"You are a good negro, and you may live on my land all your life-time."

That black man will work there for some time, and make one or two bales of cotton and give it to his master, as he calls him, to sell; and he will sell it and bring Tom, the good and smart negro, what he has a mind to.

Well, some day Tom will walk by the school-house and have a word or two with the teacher. Tom will tell him about his cotton. The teacher will say, "How much cotton did you have?"

"So much."

"How much money did you get?"

Tom says, "I got fifty dollars."

The school teacher will say, "Is that all? You should have more than that."

"How much more?"

"You should have twenty-five dollars more."

Tom says, "I am going to see him." . . .

[Tom's former master asked who told him he deserved more money.]

"The school teacher told me so."

"Who, that damn'd Yankee?"

"Yes sir."

"He told you that you could get more pay if you should go North, did he?"

"Yes sir. He told John, that black boy that lives with Mr. Brown, that he was free and should go to school. Yes, master, he told all the colored people to send their children and let them learn something." . . .

"Where is he from?"

"Massachusetts."

"We will fix him," says Tom's master. "Hitch up my horse; I am going away."

He will then go to the fork of the roads and tell everybody about what the damn'd Yankee school teacher told his niggers. If he stays here long he will have every nigger in the place think that he is as good as a white man. Well, we must run him away. Send him word to leave by Monday. If not, we will fix him.

Monday has come—Tuesday has come. The nigger-school teacher has not gone yet. We must get together. (This is not talked in the presence of Tom, but Tom is in the next room and hears it all.)

"Tom, you go and tell Mr. Brown and Mr. Bond to come here, and on your way back go round by the Pugh Place and tell Mr. Pollock to come, too, and bring every one that he can."

They will all meet and talk the matter over, and agree to meet on Wednesday night at 10 o'clock, all dressed in uniform, ready to commence their secret midnight demonstration. They went to his house and took him out, and tied a large rope round his neck, and he was seen down on his knees praying. But the party who saw him was a colored man (in the woods), and he says that he could go to the spot where he was hung with his feet up, tied to the branch of an oak tree, and a log of wood round his neck, and his tongue from five to seven inches out of his mouth. This punishment will be applied to that class of Northern people who will go South and settle, and have not received full information how to act. You know it is an old saying, and a good one too, when you are in Rome, act as a Roman, and when you are in the South, you must act as a Southern man. What are these actions? First, I will say, you must act with the majority, let their actions be good or bad. You must denounce all free schools for white or black children. You must not come South and pay more for labor than the established price, which is all the way from five to ten dollars per month, but an extra good hand, who has always been farming, may in some cases get from fifteen to sixteen dollars per month. Never give a black man, or a poor white man who cannot read, any advice to post themselves upon matters pertaining to their own welfare. Never speak a good word for New England, because her States demand human rights before the law, for all men. Never say anything about Bunker Hill, because that is in Massachusetts. Never express your political opinion, let it be Republican or Democratic, for we know that both parties wanted to maintain the Union. And, above all, you must hate niggers. There has been many a good enterprising Northern man driven from the newly established homestead because he did not know the existing circumstances. This organization, known as the "Invisible Empire," or Ku-Klux, does exist in the Southern States. There is a number of Northern people in both of the political parties that have manifested a strong unbelief in regard to the Ku-Klux Klans, but I will say a word on a verified fact, and truth, which is today being witnessed by every peace-loving and upright citizen.

Introduction to Document 6

In *The Grand Army of the Republic Versus the Ku Klux Klan,* W. H. Gannon proposed that 100,000 former soldiers be allowed to colonize the South. These men would be given land and money, and, presumably, their example would show southerners the value of Northern industriousness and the free-labor system. Such a plan would also help alleviate the unemployment caused by swings of the business cycle. The following excerpts are taken from the chapter "How to Extirpate Ku-Kluxism from the South" in Gannon's book.

 DOCUMENT 6   *"How to Extirpate Ku-Kluxism From the South"*

W. H. Gannon

. . . In view of the fact, that the present phase of the difficulty between the North and the South has already continued for eight long and dreary years, whereas half that time sufficed in which to annihilate the whole of rebel armies, the conclusion is inevitable that the Northern People are making some very serious mistake in conducting their case in its present form; and consequently, that they must make some radical change in their Southern policy, before they can hope to gain their cause at the South. . . :

(1.) That the fatal mistake of the Northern People in their Southern policy since the dispersion of the rebel armies, has been their reliance upon United States Marshals and United States soldiers, almost exclusively, to represent them at the South; (2.) that their true course to pursue towards the South is to colonize it with at least One Hundred Thousand (100,000) intelligent, respectable, and industrious Northern Working Men; (3.) that, inasmuch as the Federal Government found no very great difficulty, any time during the late war, in inducing a million of Northern men to exchange the security, peace, and enjoyment of their homes for the dangers and privations of prolonged active warfare in the face of a determined and powerful enemy at the South and to remain there year after year, until the overthrow of their antagonists left them free to return to their homes,— there are 100,000 of those same men who would gladly return South now with the implements of peace in their hands, to make their homes there, provided they had the means to enable them to do so; (4.) that One Thousand (1000) Dollars per man would be all sufficient to establish them comfortably there; (5.) that the required funds would readily enough be forthcoming, were the proper parties to ask the public for them; and (6.) that the proper parties to collect the required funds, and to select the proposed colonists, and superintend the suggested undertaking, generally, are the GRAND ARMY OF THE REPUBLIC, and the various WORKING MEN'S SOCIETIES throughout the North. . . .

All purely patriotic considerations aside, the success of this plan would, in a mere speculative and economic point of view, prove highly beneficial to the industrial and business interests of the North. Its operations, if extended to anything like National proportions, would necessarily open a vast field for utilizing the immense mass of well disposed and intelligent, but adventurous young energy now wandering aimless about the North; they would provide acceptable and remunerative employment, at the South, for multitudes of Northern working people who find it impossible to secure the means of a decent support for themselves and their families in their present abodes. For, while individual Northern enterprise in that direction is not just now advisable, yet throughout the whole civilized world, there is not another so favorable an opening for co-operative Northern enterprise, if it be united, systematic, and of a legitimate character, as the South, in its present condition, offers to it. Every associated enterprise, such as this plan suggests, if judiciously located and properly managed for developing the natural resources of the South, instead of (as some have done) plunging into mad attempts at competition with great Northern industries, would handsomely compensate the laborer for his work, besides, after the first year, paying cent-per-cent, per annum on every dollar of capital invested in it. Once settled at the South, the colonist, amidst congenial social surroundings that this plan would secure to him, could not, with a tithe of the industry, fail to secure an ample competency for themselves and their dependents, without that incessant toil which, for even a scanty and precarious support, the North exacts from every person who depends solely upon manual labor, for their livelihood within its great centers of population. Thus they would materially benefit themselves in all the relations of life, and, at the same time, leave a freer field to, and open a new market for, the industry of those of their fraternity who are established at the North. It would, also, give a new and lasting impetus to legitimate business of all kinds throughout the whole country. Therefore, leaving Southern interests and political considerations out of the question altogether, this plan deserves the serious attention of the Working men and the Business men of the North.

QUESTIONS

Defining Terms

Identify in the context of the chapter each of the following:

racism   Reconstruction

redeemers   carpetbaggers and scalawags

sharecroppers   Knights of the White Camelia
Job Stevenson   Benjamin Bryant
miscegenation   Liberia

Probing the Sources

1. Who were the victims of Klan violence? Why were whites sometimes attacked by the Klan in addition to African Americans?

2. Under what political circumstances did the Klan arise?

3. What were its stated goals? What were its goals as you can infer them by its members' actions?

4. How did northerners characterize southerners? How did southerners characterize northerners?

Intrepreting the Sources

1. Who opposed the Klan and why? Was the Ku Klux Klan a political organization? A terrorist organization?

2. Did the Klan's racist ideology fulfill goals beyond the simple expression of irrational hatred?

3. Did opponents of the Klan want to stop racism, or did they have an additional agenda?

4. Was the Klan successful? Why or why not?

ADDITIONAL READING

On the Ku Klux Klan, see Allen Trelease, *White Terror: The Ku Klux Klan Conspiracy and Southern Reconstruction* (1971), and David Mark Chalmers, *Hooded Americanism: The History of the Ku Klux Klan* (1981). For various interpretations of Reconstruction, see John Hope Franklin, *Reconstruction After the Civil War* (1961); Kenneth M. Stampp, *The Era of Reconstruction, 1865–1877* (1965); and Eric Foner, *Reconstruction: America's Unfinished Revolution, 1863–1877* (1988). On African Americans during Emancipation, see W. E. B. DuBois, *Black Reconstruction* (1935); and Leon F. Litwack, *Been in the Storm So Long: The Aftermath of Slavery* (1979). For the era's legacy, see Jay R. Mandle, *Not Slave, Not Free: The African American Economic Experience Since the Civil War* (1992). On the reborn Klan of the 1920s, see Leonard Moore, *Citizen Klansmen* (1992) and Nancy MacLain, *Behind the Mask of Chivalry: The Making of the Second Ku Klux Klan* (1994).

2

The Great Strike of 1877

HISTORICAL CONTEXT

The year 1876 was one of celebration. The centennial of the Declaration of Independence was heralded with speeches, fireworks, and prayers. In Philadelphia, a great exhibition made palpable the nation's progress in technology and the arts. Self-congratulations seemed in order, for the Union had been preserved, the railroad now linked both coasts, and new inventions like the telephone and the Corliss engine promised a bright and prosperous future.

Yet these were not altogether happy times. Reconstruction in the South seemed more and more torturous as the Ku Klux Klan continued its rampage of violence and whites found ways to limit blacks' newly won freedom. In the summer of 1876, word came from out west that General George Armstrong Custer and over two hundred cavalrymen had been wiped out at the battle of the Little Bighorn, and during the following year, Chief Joseph and his Nez Percés tribe gave the army all it could handle. Moreover, corruption tainted business and government at the highest levels, as a series of scandals rocked the Grant administration, Wall Street, and especially the nation's largest business: the railroads.

Worst of all, a severe economic depression continued into its fourth year. Millions were unemployed, and many who had jobs experienced severe wage cuts. In New York City, roughly one-quarter of the labor force was out of work, and police brutally dispersed angry crowds of the unemployed. Some workers questioned the logic of celebrating a hundred years of freedom when families went hungry in the streets, and a handful of laborers even began calling for a second American Revolution. In the best of times, the concentration of wealth in the hands of relatively few entrepreneurs raised questions in many workers' minds. These were not the best of times.

Labor organizing and militancy had a long history in America. Before the Civil War, as the old artisan system broke down, as the division of labor grew more specialized, and as manufacturing wealth began to concentrate—in other words, as the dividing line between employers and employees grew ever sharper—labor unions formed in several crafts and industries. Their record was spotty; sometimes they succeeded in gaining worker control over wages, hours, and hiring practices; sometimes they failed. Some workers and labor leaders criticized the system of production and distribution itself, asking why a relative handful of individuals should own so much wealth while most families barely scratched out a living.

But nothing on the scale of the Great Strike of 1877 had ever happened before. In the middle of that year, most of the nation's vast new transcontinental railroad system—the very symbol of American progress, wealth, and modernity—was shut down by angry employees. Tracks, engines, and switching yards were destroyed, related businesses were forced to close, and workers in other industries organized themselves for strikes. Rather suddenly, America looked less like a special land of opportunity for all and more like the London of Charles Dickens, where poverty ground down the working class, or like Paris, where the masses organized themselves for bloody revolution.

The strike began on July 16, in the town of Martinsburg, West Virginia. The Baltimore & Ohio Railroad on that day announced a 10 percent wage cut for all employees, the second such cut in eight months and part of the policy for all railroads across the country. Workers grumbled that companies continued to pay generous dividends to stockholders during the depression, but that those who labored were forced to take starvation wages. Men gathered and talked through the day. When the crew of one train abandoned their posts, other men refused to replace them, and soon everyone threw down their tools. Workers then rode all of the engines into the roundhouse and announced to B&O officials that no trains would move through Martinsburg until their pay was restored.

Local sheriffs and militia were powerless to get the engines running, for the strikers grew too numerous. As they left Wheeling, state troops sent by the governor of West Virginia were met by angry workers, and when they got to Martinsburg, they found themselves overwhelmed by an orderly but determined crowd. Equally important, the soldiers themselves came mostly from laboring families and were sympathetic to the strikers. Finally, at the urging of the governor of West Virginia and the president of the B&O line, President Hayes dispatched three hundred federal troops, who guarded strikebreakers sent from Baltimore. But by now thousands had gathered, including miners and canal workers, all angered by the conditions of labor in their industries. The federal soldiers managed to get trains moving out of Martinsburg, but soon strikers were ambushing these, side-railing and detaining them. Worse, the strike was spreading. Workers, one Baltimore leader declared,

> know what it is to bring up a family on ninety cents a day, to live on beans and cornmeal week in and week out, to run in debt at the stores until you cannot get trusted any longer, to see the wife breaking down under privation and distress, and the children growing up sharp and fierce like wolves day after day because they don't get enough to eat.

The incidents begun in Martinsburg were repeated across the country. The strike was not well organized; during the depression, the small gains made by unions in previous years had been nearly wiped out, and the workers' organizations that did exist tended to be very conservative. The faith of many workers in equal opportunity meant that unions generally were not terribly strong, and as the need for labor solidarity in the face of ever larger companies grew apparent, owners used lockouts, blacklists, scabs, espionage, firings, and prosecutions to keep unions out of their shops. The lack of organization and preparation for a major strike gave the upheaval considerable spontaneity, as workers in various communities responded to local situations and did their best to control events. But sometimes things got out of hand.

The strike reached its climax in Pittsburgh. The Pennsylvania Railroad was America's largest private enterprise, controlling 6,000 miles of track and creating over 20,000 jobs. Three days after the Martinsburg incident began, Pennsylvania Railroad managers ordered that all trains running east from Pittsburgh be "doubleheaders," meaning that two engines pull twice the usual number of cars. Doubleheaders meant harder work, increased danger of accidents, and more layoffs. Once again, brakemen, conductors, flagmen, and others walked off the job, and they were joined by angry workers from other industries. Once again, the state militia was called in, but as an officer explained, "The sympathy of the people, the sympathy of the troops, my own sympathy, was with the strikers proper. We all felt that those men were not receiving enough wages." Soon the soldiers laid down their weapons and fraternized with the strikers. But then 600 fresh troops from Philadelphia were called in; since they were not from the local area, they had less sympathy for the workers. A crowd of 6,000, including women and children there to support their husbands and fathers, began jeering and throwing rocks; the militia opened fire and, in five minutes, killed 20 people. When the soldiers retreated to the roundhouse, strikers armed themselves and attacked them, burned the roundhouse, tore up tracks, and destroyed over 2,000 cars and 100 engines.

And so the upheaval rolled across the country; in St. Louis, Chicago, Cincinnati, Buffalo, and countless other towns, workers from various industries refused to accept low wages, authoritarian owners, or armed coercion. For a few days, workers stopped the wheels of business and rejected the sovereignty of management. The general strike that had begun with the railroads gripped all parts of industry.

But the strike ended as quickly as it had begun. Lacking organization, the workers failed to make their demands clear, and the ability of laborers to counter management quickly eroded. The federal government mobilized thousands of troops, and cities reorganized their police forces. Soldiers rolled into a town, drove off strikers, secured management's property, allowed strikebreakers to restart businesses, then moved on to the next town. Occasionally workers won concessions from management; more often, not. In all, over a hundred laborers were killed.

The strikes threw disturbing new features of American life into bold relief. At the time of the uprising, about fifty corporations controlled eighty thousand miles of line, and employed hundreds of thousands of workers. As companies competed and sometimes drove each other out of business, the railroads were concentrated in fewer and fewer hands. A handful of men enjoyed private fortunes and paid themselves dividends even during depressions, but most of their employees would be wage laborers for life and would never rise to become independent entrepreneurs, that status so exalted by journalists and orators. And the railroads, it was clear, had merely led the way, for America now was no longer the land of small shopkeepers and apprentices, but of capitalists and workers.

The notion that America had escaped the curse of class conflict-Europe's curse of a rich upper class and an oppressed working class—seemed no longer plausible, if it had ever been true. The events of 1877 made it abundantly clear that a deep chasm divided and would continue to divide the rich and the poor in America. The Great Strike also gave a glimpse of how government would respond to this state of affairs. In the past, civic officials had often taken the part of the workers, for they represented local control rather than the distant power of faceless corporations. But

Strike of 1877: People standing amongst debris. (Carnegie Library of Pittsburgh)

in 1877, as in future conflicts (and there would be many intense labor struggles in the coming decades), state and federal power were the creatures of the rich and powerful. When the government intervened, it was to protect private property against the claims of workers.

THE DOCUMENTS

Introduction to Documents 1 and 2

The documents in this section are as much about how individuals responded to the strike as about the strike itself. Document 1 appeared in a leading journal of the day, the *North American Review*, in September 1877. It is a letter written by an anonymous striker justifying the actions of those who had taken part in the uprising.

   Document 2 is an article that the *North American Review* solicited from Colonel Thomas Scott, the president of the Pennsylvania Railroad. Note how he identified his own interests with those of the nation, as did the writer of Document 1. Compare the striker's assumption (in Document 1) that all value is created by labor with the railroad president's belief that the best interests of his company and of the nation were one. How did each writer define patriotism? How did they differ on what constitutes fairness?

DOCUMENT 1   *"Fair Wages"*

by a Striker

The newspapers have fallen into line to defend the railway companies, who thus have brought all the great guns of public opinion to bear on one side of the fight, so the strikers have got the worst of it before the community. We have been so handled that if a workingman stands out to speak his mind, the public have theirs so full of pictures of him and his doings in the illustrated papers, that he is listened to as if he was a convicted rough pleading in mitigation of penalty, instead of an honest and sincere man asking for a fair show. I would not have any one mistake what my principles are and have been. I don't envy any man his wealth, whether it is ill-gotten or not. I am a workingman, therefore an honest one, and would refuse a dollar I did not earn, for I am neither a beggar to accept charity nor a thief to take what belongs to another, however he came by it. If it be his according to law, I, for one, am ready to protect him in his legal rights, and in return I want to be protected in what I believe to be mine.

Forty years ago my father came over to this country from Sweden. He had a small business and a large family. In Europe business does not grow as fast as children come, and poverty over there is an inheritance. He heard that North America was peopled and governed by workingmen, and the care of the States was mainly engaged in the welfare and prosperity of labor. That moved him, and so I came to be born here. He, and millions like him, made this country their home, and their homes have mainly made this country what it is. Until lately the States kept their faith and promise to the people, and we, the people, showed ours when trouble came; an assessment of blood was made on our shares of liberty, and we paid it. That is our record. We did not fight for this party or that party, but for the country and against all that were against the United States. . . .

So it was before the war, but since then, it seems to me, the power has got fixed so long in one set of hands that things are settling down into a condition like what my father left behind him in Europe forty years ago, and what stands there still. I mean the slavery of labor. The landed aristocracy over there made the feudal system, just as the moneyed men of this continent are now making a ruling class. As the aristocracy used to make war on each other, so in our time the millionnaires live on each other's ruin. As the feudal lords hired mercenary soldiers to garrison their strongholds and to prey on the common people, so the railway lords and stock-exchange barons hire a mercenary press to defend their power, the object of both being the same: the spoils of labor. It looks very like as though this country was settling down into the form and system we fled from in Europe.

The rights and value of labor were acknowledged here forty years ago because the country wanted hands. Now we have made it rich, it turns our own earnings against us, and its prosperity becomes our disaster. We are told to look at Europe and perceive that this condition of affairs is the inevitable result of growth, of population, of wealth; but we look over there, and find that discontent, rebellion, and war are also the inevitable results, and it was to avoid such results these States declared themselves free, that Americans should have a government that was not a conspiracy.

That government has been regarded by the laboring classes of Europe and by our people as the stronghold of the workingman, and in this our present difficulty we are referred to its Constitution which should afford us a remedy for our grievances, the ballot-box is the panacea for all and every complaint. It is not so; and those who point to the remedy know it to be a sham,—they know they can buy idlers and vagabonds enough to swell the ranks of wealth and run up a majority whenever a show of hands is required. They recruit the very men that wrecked Pittsburgh, and would pillage New York if they dared to face us, the workingmen, that fill the ranks of the militia.

We are sick of this game, we are soul-weary of looking around for some sympathy or spirit of justice, and, finding none, we turn to each other and form brotherhoods and unions, depots of the army of labor, officered by the skilled mechanic.

This organized force is now in process of formation, and prepared to meet the great questions of the age: Has labor any rights? If so, what are they? Our claim is simple. We demand *fair wages*.

We say that the man able and willing to work, and for whom there is work to do, is entitled to wages sufficient to provide him with enough food, shelter, and clothing to sustain and preserve his health and strength. We contend that the employer has no right to speculate on starvation when he reduces wages below a living figure, saying, if we refuse that remuneration, there are plenty of starving men out of work that will gladly accept half a loaf instead of no bread.

We contend that to regard the laboring class in this manner is to consider them as the captain of a slave-ship regards his cargo, who throws overboard those unable to stand their sufferings. Let those who knew the South before the war go now amongst the mining districts of Pennsylvania, and compare the home of the white laborer with the quarters of the slave; let them compare the fruits of freedom with the produce of slavery!

But we know the question is a difficult one to settle,—we do not want to force it on with threats. The late strike was not intended to break out as it did; things broke loose and took a direction we regretted. We find ourselves answerable for results we had no share in or control over. Nevertheless we accept the event as a symptom of the disorder that is consuming our body and pray the country to look to it,—it is not a passing complaint. Let me put this matter in a plain way, as we understand it, and use round numbers instead of fractions, as we have to deal with hundreds of millions,-dividing the subject into sections.

1. In the United States the amount of capital invested in railway property last year was $4,470,000,000, made up of $2,250,000,000 capital stock and $2,220,000,000 bonded debt. The gross earnings were $500,000,000, or about eight and a half per cent on the capital. The running expenses (of which the bulk was for labor) were $310,000,000, leaving $185,000,000 as [profit] interest to the capitalist, or barely four per cent on his investment.

Labor is admitted into this enterprise as a preferential creditor, to be paid out of gross earnings before the most preferred mortgagee or bond holder receives a dollar. For as capital could not build the roads nor equip them without labor, so the enterprise, when complete, cannot be run without labor.

Capital, therefore, takes a back seat when it comes to the push, and acknowledges not only that labor has the largest interest in the concern, but takes the first fruits.

I take the railroad as a sample out of all enterprises, and if we could get at figures, there is no doubt it is a fair sample of the crowd. If, then, labor is the more important and essential factor in the result, when it comes to the question which of the two shall suffer in moments of general distress, the capitalist in his pocket or the laborer in his belly, we think the answer has been already settled by the rights assumed by one and acknowledged by the other.

2. It is manifestly unjust that the workingman should be subject to under wages in bad times, if he has not the equivalent of over wages in good times. If railroad companies in concert with the laboring class had established a tariff of labor, and paid a bonus on wages at every distribution of dividends, that bonus being in proportion to the profits of the road, so that each man becomes a shareholder in his very small way, then he would have submitted to bear his share of distress when all were called on to share trouble, but to share it equally and alike.

3. When folks say that labor and capital must find, by the laws of demand and supply, their natural relations to each other in all commercial enterprises, and neither one has any rights it can enforce on the other, they take for granted that the labor "market" is, like the produce market, liable to natural fluctuations. If that were so, we should not complain. But it is not. The labor market has got to be like the stock and share market; a few large capitalists control it and make what prices they please. This sort of game may ruin the gamblers in stocks, and injure those who invest, but the trouble is confined mostly to those who deserve to lose or those who can afford it.

But not so when the same practice operates in the labor market. The capitalist must not gamble with the bread of the workingman, or if he does, let him regard where that speculation led France one hundred years ago, when the financiers made a corner in flour, and the people broke the ring with the axe of the guillotine.

4. When the railway companies obtained privileges and rights over private property, and became by force of law the great landowners of the state, holding its movable property as well, and controlling every avenue and department of business, public and private, they became powerful monopolies. The state endowed them with powers to frame laws of their own and deprived citizens of their property, means, facilities of transport, to vest it all in these corporations. Thus endowed, they cannot pretend they are no more than ordinary commercial enterprises. They are responsible to the state for the result of their operations, if they disturb fatally the order of our concerns. They are not independent. The state has claims upon them it has not on private concerns. They may not accept liabilities and then decline responsibility. It behooves the state to decide what the people are entitled to in return for all they have conceded to these companies, and to enforce such claims.

5. The English Parliament legislated on the question of the number of hours a workingman should labor. It limits them to so many. It legislates for his health and supply of light and water. In all these matters the capitalist has an interest. (He does as much for his horse.) But when it comes to the question of a proper amount of food and clothing, of warmth and shelter, the government declines to interfere. It leaves the question of fair wages to be adjusted between employer and employed.

And so I leave it, fearing I have put the matter in rough language, but not intentionally rude, having a deep and loyal faith in the humanity and justice that abide in the hearts of all this community, and wishing that God had given me the power to touch them.

A "Striker"

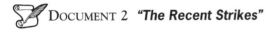 DOCUMENT 2 *"The Recent Strikes"*

by the President of the Pennsylvania Railroad

Philadelphia, August 13, 1877

Allen Thorndike Rice, Esq.,
Editor of the *North American Review*

My *Dear Sir,*

On the 16th of July it became known that the firemen and freight brakemen of the Baltimore and Ohio Railroad were on a strike at Martinsburg, West Virginia, and that no freight trains were allowed to pass that point in either direction. This proved to be the beginning of a movement which spread with great rapidity from New York to Kansas, and from Michigan to Texas, which placed an embargo on the entire freight traffic of more than twenty thousand miles of railway, put passenger travel and the movement of the United States mails at the mercy of a mob, subjected great commercial centres like Chicago and St. Louis to the violent disturbance of all their business relations, and made the great manufacturing city of Pittsburgh for twenty-four hours such a scene of riot, arson, and bloodshed as can never be erased from the memory of its people. . . .

I do not wish, and happily it is not necessary, to fill your pages with the mere recital of the distressing cases of violence and outrage which marked the course of these riots unexampled in American history. Suffice it to say that the conduct of the rioters is entirely inconsistent with the idea that this movement could have been directed by serious, right-minded men bent on improving the condition of the laboring classes. How wages could be improved by destroying property, the existence of which alone made the payment of any wages at all possible, it is difficult to understand. Nothing but the insanity of passion, played upon by designing and mischievous leaders, can explain the destruction of vast quantities of railroad equipment absolutely necessary to the transaction of its business, by men whose complaint was that the business done by the full equipment in possession of the railways did not pay them sufficient compensation for their labor. . . .

It must not for a moment, however, be understood that the greatest portion, or, indeed, any considerable portion, of the outrages upon life and property which have disgraced our recent history were actually committed by railway employés. It is not true that the majority, or even any large portion, of these men have been disloyal to the trust reposed in them. Probably ninety per cent of the men on all the important lines of the country where strikes occurred were faithful to their duties, and either remained at work, or stood ready to resume it as soon as they were relieved from the actual intimidation to which they were subjected by the rioters and their leaders. It was the dissatisfied element—which exists in that branch of industry as in all others—which perpetrated or allowed the perpetration of most of the overt acts of violence, such as stopping trains, forcing men therefrom, uncoupling cars, disconnecting engines, and other lawless doings of the kind, and which made itself amenable also to the charge of directly attacking the interests of the government and society at large as well as of the railway companies.

As General Hurlbut of Illinois so forcibly expresses it, in a paper recently published, "they permitted themselves to be the nucleus around which the idle, vicious, and criminal element could gather. Reinforced by these dark and disreputable allies, they destroyed property, stopped commerce, deranged the mails, burned great public buildings, broke up tracks, and thus paralyzed the natural circulation of the Commonwealth." It is in the menace to the general interests of society involved in these disturbances that the real gravity of the situation with which this country is now called to deal exists. "The railroad system is today a supreme necessity to maintain life, furnish ready markets, and to bring about the enormous interchange of products which makes the country one. Stop it, and in ten days many parts of the country would near the starvation-point, and within a month there would be no hamlet in the vast territory drained by these channels but would feel to the core of its business the effects of the stoppage of this regular and unusual circulation."

The enormous mechanical changes and progress of the past century have brought about a complete revolution, so gradual that perhaps it has not been generally apprehended, in the very condition of things in the United States. The water lines, which, at the date of the framing of the Constitution, were our important channels of internal commerce, have been almost superseded by the new iron highways. Upon these is borne a traffic so essentially national, so closely interwoven with the interests not only of our own but other countries, that it demands the most efficient and speedy protection against all unlawful interference. . . .

It is well known that the government uses the railway lines of the country, both as postal and military highways, in such form as its interests may require. The Constitution of the United States imposes upon the government the duty of thoroughly protecting inter-State commerce. When it is considered that the stock and bond holders of the various railway companies, whenever the interests of the government required it, paid taxes upon their coupons, their dividends, and their gross receipts, that they promptly met every call made by the Federal authorities, and that the entire equipment of the various lines was often placed at the disposal of the government for the prompt movement of the national forces and their supplies, to the exclusion often of other and more profitable traffic, it would seem but a matter of equity that the government should insure such protection to these railways as would preserve their usefulness and keep them always in condition to render similar services when they may be required. But over and beyond such considerations as these, the absolute dependence of the whole community upon this great system of railways for almost its very existence as a civilized body would seem to impose upon the Federal government in the last resort the supreme duty of preventing any lawless and violent interference with the regular and certain operation of every railway in the United States.

This insurrection, which extended through fourteen States, and in many cases successfully defied the local authorities, presents a state of facts almost as serious as that which prevailed at the outbreak of the Civil War. Unless our own experience is to differ entirely from other countries,—and it is not easy to see why it should, with the increasing population of our large cities and business centres, and the inevitable assemblage at such points of the vicious and evil-disposed,—the late troubles may be but the prelude to other manifestations of mob violence, with this added peril, that now, for the first time in American history, has an organized mob learned its power to terrorize the law-abiding citizens of great communities. With our recent experience before us, it is believed that no thoughtful man can argue in favor of delay by the proper authorities in dealing with lawless and riotous assemblages. Delay simply leads to destruction of property, and may lead in the end to the destruction of life. . . .

With the approach of winter, and the loss of outdoor employment which severe weather even in the most prosperous times entails, the country will have to deal not only with the deserving among the unemployed, who can be reached and helped through local organizations, but with vast numbers of idle, dangerous, and in many cases desperate men, who have been allowed unfortunately to catch a glimpse of their possible power for mischief. Such men, unless confronted by a thorough organization in the cities, States, and other communities, backed by the power of the Federal government and an unmistakable public opinion, will need but little urging to renew the scenes which have already brought such disgrace upon the American name. . . .

The magnitude of the evil to be met and dealt with can hardly be overstated. The remedy to be provided should be equally prompt and effective. It must be discussed and adopted in the interest of the whole country, and not of any particular class; for the interests of all classes of our citizens are the same in the maintenance of domestic peace and civil order. . . .

My own railway experience, extending over a period of thirty years, leads me to believe that the managers of American railways in general may fearlessly appeal to their past relations with the faithful among their employés, to prove that they at least have always endeavored to treat the interests of employers and employed as identical, and have never failed to take into prompt and respectful consideration every grievance which has been fairly and properly presented to them. I am sure that it has been the purpose of the company with which I am connected to at all times pay its employés the best compensation that the business of the country would warrant; and I have no doubt that this will be the policy of the company for all future time, as it is founded on sound business principles no less than upon the instincts of humanity.

Very truly yours,
Thomas A. Scott

Introduction to Documents 3 and 4

The next two documents come from Allan Pinkerton and Samuel Gompers. Pinkerton became famous as a private detective. During the Civil War, his company provided the federal government with (often incorrect) intelligence reports of Confederate troop strength and movements. After the war, Pinkerton's agency sold its services to private businesses, providing industrial espionage, guards, strikebreakers, and agents provocateurs. Pinkerton assumed that the Great Strike of 1877 was part of a much larger conspiratorial plot, imported to the United States from Europe and designed to destroy the country. The excerpt reprinted here is from a book entitled *Strikers, Communists, Tramps and Detectives* (1878).

Samuel Gompers, on the other hand, worked as a cigar maker in New York City during the strike. He eventually rose from worker, then local union leader, to president of the American Federation of Labor, a coalition of craft unions founded in 1886. In his later life, Gompers always insisted that organized labor must stay out of politics, must eschew socialism, and must not question owners' rights to hold property and manage it; unions existed to improve wages and working conditions, not to make workers co-owners or managers. Gompers's passage was written fifty years after the Great Strike and published in his memoirs.

DOCUMENT 3 *From* **Strikers, Communists, Tramps and Detectives**

Allan Pinkerton

It was everywhere; it was nowhere. A condition of sedition which can be located, fixed, or given boundaries, may, by any ordinary community or government, be subdued. This uprising, in its far-reaching extent, was so alarmingly sudden that it seemed like the hideous growth of a night. It was as if the surrounding seas had swept in upon the land from every quarter, or some sudden central volcano had upraised its hideous head and belched forth burning rivers that coursed out upon the country in every direction. No general action for safety could be taken. Look where we might, some fresh danger was presented. No one had prophesied it; no one could prevent it; no one was found brave enough or wise enough to stop its pestilential spread. Its birth was spontaneous; its progress like a hurricane; its demise a complete farce.

But, looking over the destruction wrought, the consideration of the now clearly established fact, that our country has arrived at such an age and condition that it contains the dormant elements which require only a certain measure of turbulent handling to at any moment again bring to the surface even a stronger and more concentrated power of violence and outlawry, becomes not only a most wise policy, but an urgent necessity. . . .

The great strike has left everybody poorer. Who has been bettered? Who can point to a single instance where a body of workingmen has been benefited by their participation?

Who shall pay for the enforced idleness of millions; the ruin to vast business interests; the misery brought upon innocent working men and women; and for the hundreds of lives sacrificed upon this altar of human ignorance, blindness, and frenzy?

Looking at the matter from any point of consideration, no good thing can be seen in it, unless it may be judged a good thing to know that we have among us a pernicious communistic spirit which is demoralizing workingmen, continually creating a deeper and more intense antagonism between labor and capital, and so embittering naturally restless elements against the better elements of society, that it must be crushed out completely, or we shall be compelled to submit to greater excesses and more overwhelming disasters in the near future.

The "strike" is essentially an institution of continental Europe, and, like all other good and bad emanations from that part of the world, gradually but surely found its way into England, Scotland, and Ireland, and from thence was transplanted to this country. Riot, which has always existed, has become the constant companion of the strike everywhere. Through my Scotch and English experiences I have become well acquainted with the characteristics of strikes in those countries. One marked difference in them there is in the fact that women, in almost every instance after the strike is inaugurated, seem the most savage in preventing the breaking of the strike by the employment of "nobs," as the "scabs" are called there, and in both inciting and participating in riots. . . .

A good deal has been written and said regarding the causes of our great strike of '77. To my mind they seem clear and distinct. For years, and without any particular attention on the part of the press or the public, animated by the vicious dictation of the International Society, all manner of labor unions and leagues have been forming. No manufacturing town, nor any city, has escaped this baleful influence. Though many of these organizations have professed opposition to communistic principles, their pernicious influence has unconsciously become powerful among them. Other organizations have openly avowed them. They have become an element in politics. The intelligent workingmen, not being altogether ready for the acceptance of these extreme doctrines, have given them no political support, and their violent propagators have been obliged to fall back upon agitation of subjects which would antagonize labor and capital. For years we have been recovering from the extravagances of the war period. Labor has gradually, but surely, been becoming cheaper, and its demand less. Workingmen have not economized in the proportion that economy became necessary. Want and penury followed. Workingmen consequently have become discontented and embittered. They have been taught steadily, as their needs increased, that they were being enslaved and robbed, and that all that was necessary for bettering their condition was a general uprising against capital. So that when, under the leadership of designing men, that great class of railroad employees—than whom no body of workingmen in America were ever better compensated—began their strike, nearly every other class caught the infection, and by these dangerous communistic leaders were made to believe that the proper time for action had come.

DOCUMENT 4 ". . . A Declaration of Protest in the Name of American Manhood . . ."

Samuel Gompers

During the summer of 1876 the unemployment situation grew steadily worse. A feeling of desperation was growing as week after week slipped by and still the unemployed had no dependable means of earning a livelihood. The city authorities selected that time to suspend improvements on public works. The workingmen protested against this course as a harmful, cruel policy. Our next effort was in the form of demonstrations. First, we called a mass meeting in Tompkins Square early in August. Crowds met quietly on the appointed day. We had police protection instead of police aggression. . . .

Mass meetings for organization and as unemployment demonstrations continued. We tried to organize discontent for constructive purposes. Mayor Ely paid no more attention to our needs than other Mayors had done, but wageearners did heed our gospel of organization and solidarity. I am recounting in some detail a picture of cumulative misery in order to bring out why revolt brought a whisper of hope. The crash that broke the months of strain came in the revolt of the railroad workers in July, 1877. That was in the pioneer period of railroading. The Union Pacific had been completed but a short time before, uniting the eastern and western coasts in a new effort to conquer distance. The railway unions were but fledglings. In fierce competitive fights, railroad managements cut passenger and freight rates far below the maintenance level. They were preparing to shift the resulting losses upon their employes by wage cuts. In 1873, wages of railroad workers had been reduced ten per cent; a similar wage reduction was announced for June 1, 1877. Railroad officials had organized and united upon a uniform policy. They did not even consider consultation with their employes. They handed down an order that meant another ten-per-cent reduction in the standards of living of their employes. Although both employment and pay on the railroads were irregular, unemployment was general in all other lines of work, and railroad workers were obliged either to accept conditions, bad as they were, or join the already large ranks of tramps. In addition to cutting wages, the railroads announced employes were to be required to use company hotels which still further reduced real wages.

Made desperate by this accumulation of miseries, without organizations strong enough to conduct a successful strike, the railway workers rebelled. Their rebellion was a declaration of protest in the name of American manhood against conditions that nullified the rights of American citizens. The railroad strike of 1877 was the tocsin that sounded a ringing message of hope to us all.

The railroad rebellion was spontaneous. In those days before the establishment of collective bargaining as an orderly system for presenting grievances to employers as the preliminary to securing an adjustment based on mutuality, the only way the workers could secure the attention of employers was through some demonstration of protest in the form of a strike. The strike grew steadily until it surpassed in numbers and importance all previous industrial movements. Strikers and sympathetic workmen crowded into the streets. The New York papers said at the time that so far as the arguments were concerned, the workers had the best of the situation, but that they could not win because of the weakness of the unions. The authorities grew apprehensive and asked for military protection. Then the fight was on. Long pent-up resentment found vent in destruction. The primitive weapons, fire and violence, were labor's response to arbitrary force. . . .

When the co-operative factory was abandoned with the close of the strike, I could have continued to work there, but, of course, I had neither the desire nor the willingness to act as superintendent or foreman for the factory although requested by them to do so, so I applied to Hirsch for my old job. That had been filled and there was really no opportunity for work with him. The Cigar Manufacturers' Association had declared that under no circumstances would any leaders of the strike be employed for at least six months. As a consequence, for nearly four months I was out of employment. I had parted with everything of any value in the house, and my wife and I were every day expecting a newcomer in addition to the five children we already had.

My family helped in every way possible. Part of the time they were hungry and without the necessaries of life. Never once did my wife falter. Blacklisted, I desperately sought employment, going home at night where my brave wife prepared soup out of water, salt, pepper, and flour. One night when there was no food in the house and our little girl was very ill I returned home to find a fellow-worker, Jack Polak, had called and offered my wife $30 a week for three months if she would persuade me to give up the union and return to work. I turned to my wife and said, "Well, what did you tell him?" My wife, indignant at the question answered: "What do you suppose I said to him with one child dying and another coming? Of course I took the money." Stunned by the blow I fell in a chair. My wife, all tenderness and sympathy, seeing I didn't understand exclaimed: "Good God, Sam, how could you ask such a question? Don't you know I resented the insult?"

Occasionally, my wife suggested the commissary—but I refused that help, for I wanted to fight my own way. My mother worried over our need. She used to tell brother

Al and the younger children to go over and find out whether we had food. Sophia always kept covered pots on the stove—but sometimes they contained only water. The children would accidently brush aside the covers to fulfill their mission of kindness. Many times my mother sent us food from her none too bountiful supply.

Once I was ready to commit murder. All the children were ill, probably because of winter cold and under-nourishment; they were subject to illness and fever. I walked around looking for work and could not find it, and as I left my wife in the morning again to look for work there were indications that the newcomer was about due, but by previous experience I thought that that condition would last a couple of days. But when I came home, my sister-in-law, who was living with us and sharing whatever little we had, told me that the child was born. There had been nobody to help the mother or the child. I stood by, dazed, and then rushed to the man who had acted as our physician. He was the physician paid by the Hand-in-Hand Society. But he was not in and like a madman I rushed back, but the situation was the same as it was before.

It dawned on me that there was a physician on the next block and I went to him and told him of the condition and that I wanted him to come down and attend to my wife. He asked me if I had money. When I told him I did not, he replied that he was not our regular physician. I said I knew that but my wife was in such a serious condition and the child there and I wanted him to come to attend her right away. He said, "Well, I do not feel like it and I won't do it."

I walked up to him, looked him square in the eye and said, "Yes you will, you will come and see my wife now." He said, "Well, I will not." I put my hand on his coat collar and said, "You will come now with me or you will never make another move." He said he wanted me to pay him and I said: "I have got no money. I have been out of work, but I will promise to pay you everything I can gather tonight, but you will come with me without another minute's hesitation or I will not be responsible for what I will do to you. Come along." He put on his hat and coat and he went with me. While he was attending the mother and child, I went around among the members of my family and gathered up two dollars and gave it to him. He prescribed some medicine and I did not have the money to get the prescription filled and finally prevailed upon the druggist with whom I was acquainted through living in the neighborhood to trust me for it and we pulled her through. The baby was my Al. He was our strike baby, born in the forenoon of February 28, 1878.

Introduction to Documents 5 and 6

Like Samuel Gompers, Mary Harris "Mother" Jones was a labor organizer, and, in the following excerpt from her autobiography, she remembers the strike from a distance of fifty years. Unlike Gompers, Jones was not a political moderate but a socialist known for her militant oratory. She was over forty years old when the strike broke out, and it was her first direct involvement in a labor action. She would be at the eye of the storm as an organizer for another fifty years. Like Gompers, she accused company agents of fomenting the violence and destruction. Note also her point that local businessmen as well as laborers resented big national corporations like the Pennsylvania Railroad.

Document 6 comes from a *New York Times* report on the sermons of Reverend Henry Ward Beecher during the strike. Beecher's congregation, Plymouth Church in Brooklyn, was very wealthy, and Beecher was one of the most famous clergymen in America. Beecher's harsh judgment of the strikers grew out of his attachment to social Darwinist assumptions—that the law of living is survival of the fittest—which just happened to flatter his very successful congregants.

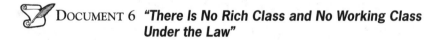

DOCUMENT 5 *The Great Uprising*

Mary Harris "Mother" Jones

One of the first strikes that I remember occurred in the Seventies. The Baltimore and Ohio Railroad employees went on strike and they sent for me to come help them. I went. The mayor of Pittsburgh swore in as deputy sheriffs a lawless, reckless bunch of fellows who had drifted into that city during the panic of 1873. They pillaged and burned and rioted and looted. Their acts were charged up to the striking workingmen. The governor sent the militia.

The Railroads had succeeded in getting a law passed that in case of a strike, the train-crew should bring in the locomotive to the roundhouse before striking. This law the strikers faithfully obeyed. Scores of locomotive were housed in Pittsburgh.

One night a riot occurred. Hundreds of box cars standing on the tracks were soaked with oil and set on fire and sent down the tracks to the roundhouse. The roundhouse caught fire. Over one hundred locomotives, belonging to the Pennsylvania Railroad Company, were destroyed. It was a wild night. The flames lighted the sky and turned to fiery flames the steel bayonettes of the soldiers.

The strikers were charged with the crimes of arson and rioting, although it was common knowledge that it was not they who instigated the fire; that it was started by hoodlums backed by the business men of Pittsburgh who for a long time had felt that the Railroad Company discriminated against their city in the matter of rates.

I knew the strikers personally. I knew that it was they who had tried to enforce orderly law. I knew they disciplined their members when they did violence. I knew, as everybody knew, who really perpetrated the crime of burning the railroad's property. Then and there I learned in the early part of my career that labor must bear the cross for others' sins, must be the vicarious sufferer for the wrongs that others do.

These early years saw the beginning of America's industrial life. Hand and hand with the growth of factories and the expansion of railroads, with the accumulation of capital and the rise of banks, came anti-labor legislation. Came strikes. Came violence. Came the belief in the hearts and minds of the workers that legislatures but carry out the will of the industrialists.

DOCUMENT 6 *"There Is No Rich Class and No Working Class Under the Law"*

Henry Ward Beecher

The Pulpit on the Situation

REV. HENRY WARD BEECHER CONDEMNS THE STRIKE AND DECLARES THAT A FAMILY CAN LIVE ON A DOLLAR A DAY

What right had the working men, the members of those great organizations, to say to any one, 'You shall not work for wages which we refuse.' They had a perfect right to say to the employers, 'We shall not work for you,' but they had no right to tyrannize over their fellow-men. They had put themselves in an attitude of tyrannical opposition to all law and order and they could not be defended. The necessities of the great railroad companies demanded that there should be a reduction of wages. There must be continual shrinkage until things come back to the gold standard, and wages, as well as greenbacks, provisions, and property, must share in it. It was true that $1 a day was not enough to support a man and five children, if a man would insist on smoking and drinking beer. Was not a dollar a day enough to buy bread! Water costs nothing. [Laughter.] Man cannot live by bread, it is true; but the man who cannot live on bread and water is not fit to live. [Laughter.] When a man is educated away from the power of self-denial, he is falsely educated. A family may live on good bread and water in the morning, water and bread at midday, and good water and bread at night. [Continued laughter.] Such may be called the bread of affliction, but it was fit that man should eat of the bread of affliction. Thousands would be glad of a dollar a day, and it added to the sin of the men on strike for them to turn round and say to those men, 'You can do so, but you shall not.' There might be special cases of hardship, but the great laws of political economy could not be set at defiance.

Communism Denounced

HENRY WARD BEECHER'S OPINIONS ON THE LABOR QUESTION

So much discussion has been had, and so much ill will disseminated against Rev. Henry Ward Beecher at communistic meetings during the last week, on account of a misconstruction of the words of his sermon on the 22d inst., that it was shrewdly guessed that Mr. Beecher would take an early opportunity of more clearly defining his position on the question of the rights of laboring men. . . .

We look upon the importation of the communistic and like European notions as abominations. Their notions and theories that the Government should be paternal and take care of the welfare of its subjects and provide them with labor, is un-American. It is the form in which oppression has had its most disastrous scope in the world. The American doctrine is that it is the duty of the Government merely to protect the people while they are taking care of themselves—nothing more than that. "Hands off," we say to the Government; "see to it that we are protected in our rights and our individuality. No more than that." The theories of Europe in regard to the community of property we reject because they are against natural law and will never be practicable. God has intended the great to be great, and the little to be little. No equalization process can ever take place until men are made equal as productive forces. It is a wild vision, not a practicable theory. The European theories of combinations between workmen and trades-unions and communes destroy the individuality of the person, and there is no possible way of preserving the liberty of the people except by the maintenance of individual liberty, intact from Government and intact from individual meddling. Persons have the right to work when or where they please, as long as they please, and for what they please, and any attempt to infringe on this right, and to put good workmen on a level with poor workmen—any such attempt to regiment labor is preposterous. . . .

Our theory is that the Government protects men in their rights, and not Government, but God, gave them those rights. The Government gave me no right of liberty, but God did. The Government protects me in that right. All that the Government has the right to say is, you shall use your rights so as not to injure another's; to secure to every man the liberty that God gave him. Clear the arena! Let each man go into it for what he is! Let him reap what he can sow! Let the Government see that there is fair play between man and man and citizen and citizen! When I hear men say that the Government shall take charge of the railroads, of the telegraphs, and of other forms of industry, and that the proceeds shall be distributed equally among the working men, I say that if all citizens were angels this would be folly. But as men are, only a theorist insane by nature and thrown by meditation into delirium tremens could have invented such a theory. No human being on earth has any rights resulting from the fact that he belongs to a class. In the eye of the law we have rights, but simply of men. The law rubs out all the European distinctions of class and says all men are born equal. We hear of the rich class being arrayed against the working class. There is no rich class and no working class before the law. The way in which these terms are coming now to be used is undemocratic, unphilosophical, and false in fact. It is an American doctrine that every man is to have the full ownership of himself, and the right to develop himself if he can do it.

QUESTIONS

Defining Terms

Identify in the context of the chapter each of the following:

centennial   Martinsburg
Thomas Scott   labor unions
"fair wages"   Allan Pinkerton
Samuel Gompers   *Strikers, Communists, Tramps and Detectives*
Mother Jones   "a family can live on a dollar a day"

Probing the Sources

1. Who were the strikers? What were their goals?
2. What, according to the writers of the documents in this chapter, were the causes of the Great Strike?
3. How did the law and government react to the crisis? Were they consistent? Evenhanded?
4. What did Gompers mean by "American manhood"? Why did he use that phrase?

Interpreting the Sources

1. If they could argue with Gompers, Jones, and the anonymous striker, what do you think Scott, Pinkerton, and Beecher would say? How would Gompers, Jones, and the striker respond?
2. Take the position of either workers or management, and argue over the merits of the strike.
3. Which tactics do you think are justified and which unjustified in civil disputes like labor conflicts?
4. Do you think that the strikers were successful or unsuccessful?
5. What patriotic appeals did each side make? How did they differ?

ADDITIONAL READING

On the 1877 strike, see Philip Foner, *The Great Labor Uprising of 1877* (1977); David O. Stowell, *Street Railroads and the Great Strike of 1877* (1999). and Robert V. Bruce, *1877: Year of Violence* (1959). For discussions of particular aspects of labor in this era, see Melvyn Dubofsky, *Industrialism and the American Worker, 1865–1920* (1985); Herbert Gutman, *Work, Culture and Society in Industrializing America* (1976); Gutman, *Power and Culture: Essays on the American Working Class* (1987); and David Montgomery, *The Fall of the House of Labor: The Workplace, the State, and American Labor Activism, 1865–1925* (1987). An international perspective is provided by Eric Hobsbawm. *The Age of Capital, 1848–1875* (1975). On the poor, see Jacqueline Jones, *The Dispossessed: America's Underclass from the Civil War to the Present* (1992).

When Cultures Collide
Wounded Knee

HISTORICAL CONTEXT

"The 'Great American Desert,' " Charles Nordhoff wrote in 1873, "has disappeared at the snort of the iron horse. . . . The very desert becomes fruitful, and in the midst of the sagebrush and alkali country, you will see corn, wheat, potatoes, and fruits of different kinds growing luxuriantly." For Nordhoff, as for his fellow Americans, settling the West was a poetic ideal, a hymn of progress:

> One can not help but speculate upon what kind of men we Americans shall be when all these now desolate plains are filled; when cities shall be found where now only the lonely depot or the infrequent cabin stands; when the iron and coal of these regions shall have become, as they soon must, the foundation of great manufacturing populations; and when, perhaps, the whole continent will be covered by our Stars and Stripes.

Americans' prose soared as they contemplated their prosperous and powerful republic stretching from sea to shining sea.

In the most concrete sense, the expansion of white settlers westward was part of the same set of processes transforming the rest of society. Imagine, for example, a Nebraska farmer purchasing a Currier and Ives lithograph for his home in 1875, perhaps a scene of pioneers making their way across the continent. He buys the lithograph from a store in Omaha, where the pictures just came off the train from New York. He sells his wheat in the same city, and some of it may find its way onto the tables of railroad workers, who at that moment are worried about rumors of an impending wage cut. Or perhaps our farmer looks at the lithograph and chooses not to buy it, because the low price he will get for his wheat means another lean year in these troubled economic times. He wonders for a moment how he will ever pay off the bank for the new threshing machine that allowed him to grow more wheat. Farmers mechanize, he muses, and grow bigger crops, and, as a result, prices go down. The point, of course, is that industrialization, urbanization, and commercial exchange were all part of a related set of processes. The railroad was one of the ties that bound western farmers to eastern laborers. And underlying the entire transformation—manufacturing, shipping, growing, processing, and financing— was the market economy.

As the quotation from Nordhoff reveals—and as Currier and Ives lithographs of westward expansion made palpable—prosperity, progress, productivity, and individual betterment were highly charged ideals. The marketplace was not just a system of exchange; it generated its own ideology. But shining visions of progress usually did not include those whose land was taken; rather, the myth of progress justified the taking.

When white colonists first came to British North America, there were already millions of native people living in this "uninhabited" land, this "desert," as some colonists called it. European diseases, to which the indigenous peoples had no immunity, quickly wiped out many of them. As whites colonized the new lands, then, they faced greatly weakened tribes that, when not outnumbered, were outgunned. Some groups, after resisting the whites, were simply destroyed, such as the Pequots of New England. The large southeastern tribes—the Creeks, Cherokees, Choctaws, and Chickasaws—were finally conquered during the presidency of Andrew Jackson and forced to relocate west to lands that would be theirs "forever."

By the late nineteenth century, the Sioux of the northern plains were one of the largest and most powerful tribal cultures remaining. During the colonial era, they had occupied lands between Lake Superior and the headwaters of the Mississippi River, but the Ojibwas, armed by the French, drove them west to the plains. The Sioux adapted well to the new environment, cultivating their skills as horsemen and hunters and following the enormous herds of buffalo that roamed the western prairies. Until the Civil War, they ranged from Minnesota to the Rockies and from the Yellowstone River to the Platte, and, with millions of buffalo and thousands of horses, they were masters of these lands.

In 1868, with settlement of the plains by whites accelerating, the federal government sought direct control over the native inhabitants. The Sioux agreed to a treaty granting them the western half of the present state of South Dakota and portions of Nebraska and Wyoming, "for their absolute and undisturbed use and occupation," along with rights to hunt for buffalo beyond reservation boundaries. The treaty seemed to provide not only an endless supply of food, but also peace. "From this day forth," the treaty stated, "all wars between the parties of this agreement shall cease forever." In a few years, however, marksmen and trappers had hunted the buffalo to near extinction, while masses of white settlers had poured in on the new railroads. When gold—"the yellow metal that they worship and that makes them crazy," as one Sioux called it—was discovered on the tribal reservation in the Black Hills, a massive new influx of whites into the region commenced.

Bands of Sioux resisted the occupation of their lands, but as sporadic violence broke out on both sides, the government sent in the army to round up the "hostiles." George Armstrong Custer led the Seventh Cavalry into the Sioux country as part of a larger expedition under the command of General Alfred Terry. In the spring of 1876, Custer divided his forces into three groups to assault the enemy near the Little Bighorn. The entire regiment—over 250 men—was killed by a force of at least 2,500 Indians. The government promptly sent in more troops, who arrested several chiefs and chased the main leader of the uprising, Sitting Bull, and his people into Canada.

Government officials from the military and from the Bureau of Indian Affairs (under the Department of the Interior) now drew up a new treaty, and an accommodating chief, Red Cloud, signed for the tribe. The Sioux lost one-third of their reservation, including the sacred Black Hills. A people who had been hunter-gatherers, with no experience, habits, or capital for agriculture, were left on poor land, without the buffalo herds that had provided food, shelter, clothes, and goods for barter. After another decade of land speculators greedy for profits, railroads coveting rights of way, and squatters clamoring for land, the federal government in 1889 seized half of the remaining Sioux territory and, in the process, divided the one large reservation into five separate units.

In exchange for all of these concessions, the government promised to supply food (which often never came), clothing (which always arrived after the arctic cold), schools for Indian children (where tribal ways were demeaned), and reservation administrators (who were often incompetent political hacks). The old way of life was undermined: agents of the federal government forbade warrior societies and honors, usurped the powers of the chiefs, and banned tribal religious customs, holidays, and ceremonies. The Sioux and other tribes were forced to trade the freedom of the plains for broken promises and confinement to the reservation.

In the midst of this crisis, a new religion swept through the tribes of the western United States, a religion containing both Christian and Native American elements, as seen in the two names given to the movement: the Messiah Craze, as whites called it, and the Ghost Dance. By 1890, word had spread to the plains of a Paiute chief in Nevada named Wavoka who claimed to be "the Christ," returned to earth as an Indian. Throughout the western territories, Native Americans of various tribes listened to Wavoka's message and followed his advice. He promised to renew the earth to what it had been before the coming of the whites. In the spring of 1891, when the grass grew knee-high, the earth would be covered with fresh soil, running water, trees, and buffalo. And all of the old Indians who had died would return as young men and women. Those who did the Ghost Dance would be lifted into the sky, and the new soil would roll over the old and bury the whites; the dancers would then descend to earth and dwell there with their ancestors.

Native Americans across the West donned ghost shirts, painted with symbols that allegedly made them impervious to white men's bullets, and they danced the Ghost Dance. For the Sioux—starved and humiliated, their numbers depleted—the promise of living in peace and plenty was irresistible. Widows would be reunited with their husbands, hunting bands would once again be able to provide food, and an *Indian* messiah would take revenge on the white oppressors. With promises like these, the reservations resounded with the songs and steps of the sacred dance.

Reports of the "Messiah Craze" greatly alarmed whites. There is no doubt that the new religion gave Native Americans the confidence to assert themselves in ways that reservation agents found alarming and citizens saw as threatening. Certainly the idea of a Native American messiah offered tribal members a sense of pride and a new militancy. Many whites, on the other hand, jumped to the conclusion that the Ghost Dance merely proved how wild and barbaric the Native Americans were or that the new religion was a cover for a treacherous attack. Soon army troops were again streaming west, and Native American bands, feeling threatened, began leaving the reservations. The scene was set for tragedy.

THE DOCUMENTS

Introduction to Document 1

Anthropologists call phenomena like the Ghost Dance *revitalization movements*. In times of social stress, people often go back to important elements of their culture and reshape them in powerful ways. The rejuvenated customs or beliefs become a focus of group solidarity and cultural revival.

Z. A. Parker, a teacher on the Pine Ridge reservation in South Dakota, described the Ghost Dance she witnessed at White Clay Creek, June 20, 1890.

DOCUMENT 1 *"The Ghost Dance Observed"*

Z. A. Parker

We drove to this spot about 10.30 oclock on a delightful October day. We came upon tents scattered here and there in low, sheltered places long before reaching the dance ground. Presently we saw over three hundred tents placed in a circle, with a large pine tree in the center, which was covered with strips of cloth of various colors, eagle feathers, stuffed birds, claws, and horns—all offerings to the Great Spirit. The ceremonies had just begun. In the center, around the tree, were gathered their medicine-men; also those who had been so fortunate as to have had visions and in them had seen and talked with friends who had died. A company of fifteen had started a chant and were marching abreast, others coming in behind as they marched. After marching around the circle of tents they turned to the center, where many had gathered and were seated on the ground.

I think they wore the ghost shirt or ghost dress for the first time that day. I noticed that these were all new and were worn by about seventy men and forty women. The wife of a man called Return-from-scout had seen in a vision that her friends all wore a similar robe, and on reviving from her trance she called the women together and they made a great number of the sacred garments. They were of white cotton cloth. The women's dress was cut like their ordinary dress, a loose robe with wide, flowing sleeves, painted blue in the neck, in the shape of a three-cornered handkerchief, with moon, stars, birds, etc., interspersed with real feathers, painted on the waist and sleeves. While dancing they wound their shawls about their waists, letting them fall to within 3 inches of the ground, the fringe at the bottom. In the hair, near the crown, a feather was tied. I noticed an absence of any manner of head ornaments, and, as I knew their vanity and fondness for them, wondered why it was. Upon making inquiries I found they discarded everything they could which was made by white men.

The ghost shirt for the men was made of the same material—shirts and leggings painted in red. Some of the leggings were painted in stripes running up and down, others running around. The shirt was painted blue around the neck, and the whole garment was fantastically sprinkled with figures of birds, bows and arrows, sun, moon, and stars, and everything they saw in nature. Down the outside of the sleeve were rows of feathers tied by the quill ends and left to fly in the breeze, and also a row around the neck and up and down the outside of the leggings. I noticed that a number had stuffed birds, squirrel beads, etc., tied in their long hair. The faces of all were painted red with a black half-moon on the forehead or on one cheek.

As the crowd gathered about the tree the high priest, or master of ceremonies, began his address, giving them directions as to the chant and other matters. After he had spoken for about fifteen minutes they arose and formed in a circle. As nearly as I could count, there were between three and four hundred persons. One stood directly behind another, each with his hands on his neighbor's shoulders. After walking about a few times, chanting, "Father, I come," they stopped marching, but remained in the circle, and set up the most fearful, heart-piercing wails I ever heard—crying, moaning, groaning, and shrieking out their grief, and naming over their departed friends and relatives, at the same time taking up handfuls of dust at their feet, washing their hands in it, and throwing it over their heads. Finally, they raised their eyes to heaven, their hands clasped high above their heads, and stood straight and perfectly still, invoking the power of the Great Spirit to allow them to see and talk with their people who had died. This ceremony lasted about fifteen minutes, when they all sat down where they were and listened to another address, which I did not understand, but which I afterwards learned were words of encouragement and assurance of the coming messiah.

When they rose again, they enlarged the circle by facing toward the center, taking hold of hands, and moving around in the manner of school children in their play of "needle's eye." And now the most intense excitement began. They would go as fast as they could, their heads moving from side to side, their bodies swaying, their arms, with hands gripped tightly in their neighbors', swinging back and forth with all their might. If one, more weak and frail, came near falling, he would be jerked up and into position until tired nature gave way. The ground had been worked and worn by many feet, until the fine, flour-like dust lay light and loose to the depth of two or three inches. The wind, which had increased, would sometimes take it up, enveloping the dancers and hiding them from view. In the ring were men, women, and children; the strong and the robust, the weak consumptive, and those near to death's door. They believed those who were sick would be cured by joining in the dance and losing consciousness. From the beginning they chanted, to a monotonous tune, the words—

Father, I come;
Mother, I come;
Brother, I come;
Father, give us back our arrows.

All of which they would repeat over and over again until first one and then another would break from the ring and stagger away and fall down. One woman fell a few feet from me. She came toward us, her hair flying over her face, which was purple, looking as if the blood would burst through; her hands and arms moving wildly; every breath a pant and a groan; and she fell on her back, and went down like a log. I stepped up to her as she lay there motionless, but with every muscle twitching and quivering. She seemed to be perfectly unconscious. Some of the men and a few of the women would run, stepping high and pawing the air in a frightful manner. Some told me afterwards that they had a sensation as if the ground were rising toward them and would strike them in the face. Others would drop where they stood. One woman fell directly into the ring, and her husband stepped out and stood over her to prevent them from trampling upon her. No one ever disturbed those who fell or took any notice of them except to keep the crowd away.

They kept up dancing until fully 100 persons were lying unconscious. Then they stopped and seated themselves in a circle, and as each one recovered from his trance he was brought to the center of the ring to relate his experience. Each told his story to the medicine-man and he shouted it to the crowd. Not one in ten claimed that he saw anything. I asked one Indian—a tall, strong fellow, straight as an arrow—what his experience was. He said he saw an eagle coming toward him. It flew round and round, drawing nearer and nearer until he put out his hand to take it, when it was gone. I asked him what he thought of it. "Big lie," he replied. I found by talking to them that not one in twenty believed it. After resting for a time they would go through the same performance, perhaps three times a day. They practiced fasting, and every morning those who joined in the dance were obliged to immerse themselves in the creek.

Introduction to Document 2

The Ghost Dance spread, and by autumn, government officials in the West had made their fears known in Washington. The following letters were sent by agents on the reservations to their superiors in the Office of Indian Affairs. The letters give a sense of the anxiety that the Ghost Dance was engendering among whites. It was on the basis of such information that military forces were dispatched to prevent a Sioux outbreak.

 DOCUMENT 2   *Letters from Reservations by United States Agents*

Commissioner of Indian Affairs, Washington, D.C.
United States Indian Service, Office of Indian Agent
Pine Ridge Agency, S. Dak., October 12, 1890

Sir:

In assuming charge of this agency I did so under embarrassing circumstances. I feel that my administration will be badly handicapped owing to the sad mess into which affairs have gotten here. These ghost dances have assumed such proportions that they become very serious. . . . The mistake was made by not nipping it in the bud four months ago when it was in its infancy. They have been permitted to continue in these foolish and harmful practices until they are entirely beyond the control of the police. As yet I have taken no definite action in the matter, my object being to thoroughly acquaint myself with the situation, so that I could act intelligently and wisely when I did make a move. . . .

I intend to act very cautiously until I am convinced that it can not be suppressed without the military, and then I trust I will have the hearty cooperation of the Department.

It is useless for me to undertake to describe the foolish manner in which they conduct themselves during these dances. I can only say it injures them physically, mentally, and morally, and undoes all the Department has done for them in the past. What makes the situation so serious is that every Indian on the reservation is armed with a Winchester rifle, and when they are requested to stop these dances they strip themselves and are ready to fight. Why any Indian on the reservation is permitted to have a gun I am not informed. They certainly have no use for them except to endanger the lives of those who try to suppress them in some wrongdoing. If it were not for this fact alone, we would not have any trouble in controlling them with the police. . . .

Very respectfully,
D. F. Royer
United States Indian Agent

Hon. T. F. Morgan
Commissioner of Indian Affairs, Washington, D.C.

United States Indian Service
Rosebud Agency, S. Dak., November 2, 1890

Sir:

I deem it my duty to call the attention of the Department to the extremely disaffected and troublesome state of a portion of the Indians on this and other Sioux agencies.

The coming new order of things as preached to this people during the past seven months is the return to earth of their forefathers, the buffalo, elk, and all other game, the

Oglala Sioux Ghost Dance, drawing by Frederic Remington. (Amon Carter Museum, Fort Worth)

complete restoration of their ancient habits, customs, and power, and the annihilation of the white man. This movement, which some three weeks ago it was supposed had been completely abandoned, while not so openly indulged in, is continually gaining new adherents, and they are daily becoming more threatening and defiant of the authorities.

This latter phase of the case may in a measure be attributed to the scant supply of rations, to which my attention has been almost daily called by the Indians, and especially to the reduction in the quantity of beef as compared to the issue of former years. They kill cows and oxen issued to them for breeding and working purposes, make no secret of doing so, and openly defy arrest. They say that the cattle were issued to them by the Great Father and it is their right to do as they please with them. This evil is increasing daily and if not checked there will be but very few of this class of stock left on the reservation by spring. During the past week it is reported to me that two Indians in the Red Leaf Camp on Black White Creek had killed their cows for a feast at the ghost dance. I sent a policeman to bring them in; they refused to come.

The following day I sent two officers and eight policemen, and they returned without the men, reporting that after they arrived at the camp they were surrounded by seventy-five or more Indians, well armed and with plenty of ammunition, and they unanimously agreed that an attempt to arrest the offenders would have resulted in death to the entire posse. On Friday I sent the chief of police, with an interpreter, to explain matters and endeavor to bring the men in. They positively refused to come, and the chief of police reports that the matter is beyond the control of the police. This is one case which could be repeated indefinitely by attempting the arrest of parties guilty of the same offense.

The religious excitement aggravated by almost starvation is bearing fruits in this state of insubordination; Indians say they had better die fighting than to die a slow death of starvation, and as the new religion promises their return to earth, at the coming of the millennium, they have no great fear of death. To one not accustomed to the Indians, it is a hard matter to believe the confident assurance with which they look forward to the fulfillment of their Prophet's promise.

The time first set for the inauguration of the new era was next spring, but I am reliably informed that it has since and only lately been advanced to the new moon after the next one, or about December 11.

The indications are unmistakable; these Indians have within the past three weeks traded horses and everything else they could trade for arms and ammunition, and all the cash they became possessed of was spent in the same way.

One of the traders here reports that Indians within the last few days have come to his store and offered to sell receipts for wood delivered at the agency, and for which no funds are on hand to pay them for one-third the value *in cash*. When asked what urgent necessity there was for such a sacrifice of receipts for less than their face value, they answered that they wanted *the cash* to buy ammunition.

These are some of the signs of the times and strongly indicate the working of the Indian mind.

To me, there appears to be but one remedy (and all here agree with me) unless the old order of things (the Indians controlling the agency) is to be reestablished, and that is a sufficient force of troops to prevent the outbreak which is imminent, and which any one of a dozen unforeseen causes may precipitate.

Very respectfully, your obedient servant,
E. B. Reynolds
Special United States Indian Agent

The Commissioner of Indian Affairs
Washington, D.C.

United States Indian Service
Western Shoshone Agency, Nev., November 8, 1890

Sir:

The Indians of this reservation and vicinity have just concluded their second medicine dance, the previous one taking place in August last. They are looking for the coming of the Indian Christ, the resurrection of the dead Indians, and consequent supremacy of the Indian race. Fully one thousand people took part in the dance. While the best of order prevailed, the excitement was very great as morning approached, when the dancers were worn out mentally and physically. The medicine-men would shout that they could see the faces of departed friends and relatives moving about the circle. No pen can paint the picture of wild excitement that ensued; all shouted in a chorus, "Christ has come!" and then danced and sung until they fell in a confused and exhausted mass on the ground. The more intelligent ones freely admit that it is all foolishness, but dare not disobey the order of the medicine-men to attend. I apprehend no trouble beyond the loss of time and the general demoralizing effect of these large gatherings of people.

Several of the leading men have gone to Walker Lake to confer with a man that calls himself Christ; others have gone to Fort Hall to meet Indians from Montana and Dakota, to get the news from that section; in fact, the astonishing part of the business "is the fact that" all the Indians in the country seem to possess practically the same ideas and expect about the same result. So universal is this that I can not think but some designing white man or men are at the bottom of the whole matter, and yet there seems to be nothing beyond the merest suspicion to base that opinion on. . . .

Very respectfully,
William I. Plumb
United States Indian Agent

The Commissioner of Indian Affairs
Washington, D.C.

United States Indian Service, Office of Indian Agent
Pine Ridge Agency, S. Dak., November 12, 1890

Sir:

The condition of affairs at this agency when I took charge, whether intentional or not, were to render my administration a failure. Orders of constitutional authority are daily violated and defied, and I am powerless to enforce them. The condition of affairs is going from bad to worse. Yesterday in attempting to arrest an Indian for violation of regulations the offender drew a butcher knife on the police and in less than two minutes he was reënforced by two hundred ghost dancers all armed and ready to fight, consequently the arrest was not made. To-day I received a communication from the offender stating that the policeman who attempted to enforce my orders must be discharged or I could expect trouble, and I was given four weeks to do it.

The police force are overpowered and disheartened; we have no protection; are at the mercy of these crazy dancers.

The situation is serious. I urgently request that I be permitted to proceed to Washington at once and confer with you personally, as a correct idea of the situation can not be conveyed otherwise. The Indians have received their beef and rations, and are going home, and there is no immediate danger until next big issue (four weeks from to-day). I can leave now without the service being injured, and I do hope you will grant my request, or let the blame rest where it belongs. I have no other object in view save the best interest of the service.

Royer, Agent

Commissioner of Indian Affairs
Washington, D.C.

Pine Ridge Agency, S. Dak., November 15, 1890

Indians are dancing in the snow and are wild and crazy. I have fully informed you that employés and Government property at this agency have no protection and are at the mercy of these dancers. Why delay by further investigation? We need protection and we need it now. The leaders should be arrested and confined in some military post until the matter is quieted, and this should be done at once.

Royer, Agent

Introduction to Document 3

William T. Selwyn was a full-blooded Sioux who worked for the U.S. government on the Yankton reservation as a policeman. When he learned that a man named Kuwapi from the Rosebud reservation was at Yankton teaching the Ghost Dance, Selwyn arrested him. He then interviewed his prisoner and reported his findings to Colonel E. W. Foster on November 22, 1890.

 DOCUMENT 3   *". . . No White People in the Other World . . ."*

Selwyn's Interview with Kuwapi

Q. Do you believe in the new messiah?—A. I somewhat believe it.
Q. What made you believe it?—A. Because I ate some of the buffalo meat that he (the new messiah) sent to the Rosebud Indians through Short Bull.

Q. Did Short Bull say that he saw the living herd of roaming buffaloes while he was with the son of the Great Spirit?—A. Short Bull told the Indians at Rosebud that the buffalo and other wild game will be restored to the Indians at the same time when the general resurrection in favor of the Indians takes place.

Q. You said a "general resurrection in favor of the Indians takes place"; when or how soon will this be?—A. The father sends word to us that he will have all these caused to be so in the spring, when the grass is knee high.

Q. You said "father;" who is this father?—A. It is the new messiah. He has ordered his children (Indians) to call him "father."

Q. You said the father is not going to send the buffalo until the resurrection takes place. Would he be able to send a few buffaloes over this way for a sort of a sample, so as to have his children (Indians) to have a taste of the meat?—A. The father wishes to do things all at once, even in destroying the white race. . . .

Q. What other object could you come to by which you are led to believe that there is such a new messiah on earth at present?—A. The ghost dancers are fainted whenever the dance goes on.

Q. Do you believe that they are really fainted?—A. Yes.

Q. What makes you believe that the dancers have really fainted?—A. Because when they wake or come back to their senses they sometimes bring back some news from the unknown world, and some little trinkets, such as buffalo tail, buffalo meat, etc.

Q. What did the fainted ones see when they get fainted?—A. They visited the happy hunting ground, the camps, multitudes of people, and a great many strange people.

Q. What did the ghost or the strange people tell the fainted one or ones?—A. When the fainted one goes to the camp, he is welcomed by the relatives of the visitor (the fainted one), and he is also invited to several feasts.

Q. Were the people at Rosebud agency anxiously waiting or expecting to see all of their dead relatives who have died several years ago?—A. Yes.

Q. We will have a great many older folks when all the dead people come back, would we not?—A. The visitors all say that there is not a single old man nor woman in the other world—all changed to young.

Q. Are we going to die when the dead ones come back?—A. No; we will be just the same as we are today.

Q. Did the visitor say that there is any white men in the other world?—A. No; no white people.

Q. If there is no white people in the other world, where did they get their provisions and clothing?—A. In the other world, the messenger tells us that they have depended altogether for their food on the flesh of buffalo and other wild game; also, they were all clad in skins of wild animals.

Q. Did the Rosebud agency Indians believe the new messiah, or the son of the Great Spirit?—A. Yes.

Q. How do they show that they . . . believe in the new messiah?—A. They show themselves by praying to the father by looking up to heaven, and call him "father," just the same as you would in a church.

Q. Have you ever been in a church?—A. No.

Q. Do you faithfully believe in the new messiah?—A. I did not in the first place, but as I became more acquainted with the doctrines of the new messiah . . . I really believe in him.

Q. How many people at Rosebud, in your opinion, believe this new messiah?—A. Nearly every one.

Q. Did not the Rosebud people prepare to attack the white people this summer? While I was at Pine Ridge agency this summer the Oglalla Sioux Indians say they will resist against the government if the latter should try to put a stop to the messiah question. Did your folks at Rosebud say the same thing?—A. Yes. . . .

Q. You do not mean to say that the Rosebud Indians will try and cause an outbreak?—A. That seems to be the case. . . .

Introduction to Documents 4 and 5

The following petitions were submitted by citizens' committees to the federal government. The first, addressed to the president of the United States from Mandan, North Dakota, makes clear the contest over resources between white settlers and native peoples. How did the issues of safety, economics, race, and culture blur together? The second petition, from Chadron, Nebraska, insists that all Sioux be disarmed and that their horses be taken away. Under what justification did the citizens of these towns expect government intervention in their behalf?

DOCUMENT 4 *". . . Indians Armed to the Teeth . . ."*

Mandan, N. Dak., November 18, 1890

Dear Sir:

. . . The settlers who live in the country surrounding Mandan desire to urge strongly that the Indian Department from henceforth deny to Indians the right to carry arms or ammunition off their reservations. Game off the reservations belongs to the white men anyway. . . .

While this is being written there are camped within the city limits of Mandan over one hundred Indians, armed to the teeth, and our wives and our children are asking why these red men are allowed to molest and overawe and annoy us. Our people have stood the ravages of prairie fires, drought, and blizzards for a number of years and are still hopeful; but if, added to their other troubles, they are to be subjected to the depredations of Indians who are supposed to be under the control and subject to the Government they will have to leave the country.

The most conservative men in this community will be powerless to suppress the determination of the majority of the settlers to kill off every Indian that presents his face in this county in the future unless the Government does something to protect us. There are scores of men in this immediate neighborhood who were sufferers by the Minnesota massacres in 1862, and they don't propose to be annoyed and harassed any longer. Their property has been destroyed and their children and wives frightened by these worthless nomads, who are permitted by a lax Government to prowl over the country with arms that would not be allowed on the person of a white man. They will stand it no longer, and we ask that something be done to tighten the rules and regulations governing the actions of the Indians who are under the Indian agents of this locality.

R. M. Tuttle, Chairman
Jesse Ayers
P. B. Wickham
Joseph Miller

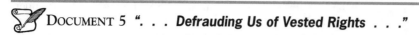

DOCUMENT 5 ". . . *Defrauding Us of Vested Rights* . . ."

Chadron, Nebr., November 26, 1890

Dear Sir:

I am instructed by a meeting of the citizens of this town and county, held last evening, to forward you a copy of resolutions unanimously adopted at that meeting, which copy I herewith respectfully submit in print.

Very obediently,
A. A. McFadon

Secretary of the Interior
Washington, D.C.

"*Resolved,* That we respectfully demand of the Government that such steps be taken at this opportune time as shall effectually dispose of the Indian outbreak subject on the Sioux Reservation, and restore to the citizens the confidence the Government may demand of him.

"*Resolved,* That the allowing of thousands of savages to be armed to the teeth in the center of a sparsely settled agrarian State is a condition improvident and unreasonable.

"*Resolved,* That the leaders and instigators of criminality in savages should receive at the hands of the Government the punishment the law provides for traitors, anarchists, and assassins.

"*Resolved,* That in our judgment the exigencies of the occasion demand nothing short of the complete disarming of the Indian and making it a crime for any person to furnish him with arms or implements of war, and we respectfully suggest that the shortest route to the satisfactory settlement of the question would be to deprive the savages of their horses, substituting therefor oxen trained to the plow.

<table>
<tr><td>"F. S. Little,</td><td>"A. C. Putnam,</td></tr>
<tr><td>"W. Rucker,</td><td>"A. Bartow,</td></tr>
<tr><td>"E. S. Ricker,</td><td>"Committee on Resolutions"</td></tr>
</table>

Introduction to Documents 6 through 8

The violence exploded as the year 1890 ended. Military forces that were sent to round up hostile Sioux engaged a band under Chief Big Foot camped at Wounded Knee Creek. Document 6 is an account taken from the Annual Report of the Commissioner of Indian Affairs for 1891. Document 7 is a set of three letters written by military leaders in the field; it is taken from the same congressional report as Document 2. Document 8 is a series of eyewitness reports from Indians who were interviewed by the Office of Indian Affairs. How do the accounts in Documents 6 through 8 differ? Which do you find most believable, and why? Were there white and Indian views?

DOCUMENT 6 *Annual Report of the Commissioner of Indian Affairs, 1891*

The "Messiah Craze"

Early in November reports received from the agents at Pine Ridge, Rosebud, and Cheyenne River showed that the Indians of those agencies, especially Pine Ridge, were arming themselves and taking a defiant attitude towards the Government and its representatives, committing depredations, and likely to go to other excesses, and November 13 this office recommended that the matter be submitted to the War Department, with request that such prompt action be taken to avert an outbreak as the emergency might be found by them to demand. . . .

DEATH OF SITTING BULL

At daybreak, December 15, 39 Indian police and 4 volunteers went to Sitting Bull's cabin and arrested him. He agreed to accompany them to the agency, but while dressing caused considerable delay, and during this time his followers began to congregate to the number of 150, so that when he was brought out of the house they had the police entirely surrounded. Sitting Bull then refused to go and called on his friends, the ghost dancers, to rescue him. At this juncture one of them shot Lieutenant Bullhead. The lieutenant then shot Sitting Bull, who also received another shot and was killed outright. Another shot struck Sergeant Shavehead and then the firing became general. In about two hours the police had secured possession of Sitting Bull's house and driven their assailants into the woods. Shortly after, when the United States troops, under command of Capt. Fechet reached the spot the police drew up in line and saluted. Their bravery and discipline received highest praise from Capt. Fechet. The ghost dancers fled from their hiding places to the Cheyenne River Reservation, leaving their families and dead behind them. Their women who had taken part in the fight had been disarmed by the police and placed under guard and were turned over to the troops when they arrived. The losses were six policemen killed (including Bullhead and Shavehead who soon died at the agency hospital) and one wounded. The attacking party lost eight killed and three wounded. . . .

INDIANS CONCENTRATE IN THE BAD LANDS

Groups of Indians from the different reservations had commenced concentrating in the "bad lands," upon or in the vicinity of the Pine Ridge Reservation. Killing of cattle and destruction of other property by these Indians almost entirely within the limits of Pine Ridge and Rosebud reservations occurred, but no signal fires were built, no warlike demonstrations were made, no violence was done to any white settler, nor was there cohesion or organization among the Indians themselves. Many of them were friendly Indians who had never participated in the ghost dance but had fled thither from fear of soldiers, in consequence of the Sitting Bull affair, or through the over persuasion of friends. The military gradually began to close in around them, and they offered no resistance, and a speedy and quiet capitulation of all was confidently expected.

FIGHT AT WOUNDED KNEE CREEK

Among them was Big Foot's band belonging to the Cheyenne River Agency, numbering with others who had joined him, about 120 men and 230 women and children. They had escaped to the bad lands, after arrest by the military at Cheyenne River, but soon started from the bad lands for the Pine Ridge Agency, and with a flag of truce advanced into the open country and proposed a parley with the troops whom they met. This being refused they surrendered unconditionally, remained in camp at Wounded Knee Creek over night, expecting to proceed next morning under escort of the troops to Pine Ridge, whither most of the quondam bad-land Indians were moving. The next day, December 29, when ordered to turn in their arms, they surrendered very few. By a search in the teepees 60 guns were obtained. When the military—a detachment of the Seventh Cavalry (Custer's old command), with other troops—began to take the arms from their persons a shot was fired and carnage ensued. According to reports of military officers, the Indians attacked the troops as soon as the disarmament commenced. The Indians claim that the first shot was fired by a half crazy, irresponsible Indian. At any rate, a short, sharp, indiscriminate fight immediately followed, and, during the fighting and the subsequent flight and pursuit of the Indians, the troops lost 25 killed and 35 wounded, and of the Indians, 84 men and boys, 44 women, and 18 children were killed and at least 33 were wounded, many of them fatally. Most of the men, including Big Foot, were killed around his tent where he lay sick. The bodies of women and children were scattered along a distance of two miles from the scene of the encounter.

Frightened and exasperated, again the Indians made for the bad lands. Indians en route thence to the agency turned back and others rushed away from Pine Ridge.

DOCUMENT 7 *Three Letters by Military Leaders*

Camp Pine Ridge Agency
December 31, 1890

Acting Assistant Adjutant General
Headquarters Department of the Platte
In the field

Sir:

I have the honor to report the following in connection with the movements of my command on the night of December 28th and during the following day. Pursuant to verbal orders from the Commanding General of the Department, I moved my command from this point to the crossing of the Wounded Knee by the main trail to the Rosebud Agency, leaving here at 4:40 P.M., and arriving there at about 8:30 P.M. Major Whitside's battalion of the 7th Cavalry and detachment Light Battery E, 1st Artillery, had that day captured Big Foot's band of Indians, and when I arrived had them in his camp. My command, consisting of Regimental Headquarters and the second battalion, detachment of Light Battery E, 1st Artillery, went into camp for the night. At about 7:30 the next morning, after considerable trouble, the bucks of Big Foot's band, numbering 106 were collected away from their camp, and after explaining to them that having surrendered they would be treated as prisoners of war, but that as such they must surrender their arms. Squads of twenty were cut off, and told to bring them to a designated place. The result of this was very unsatisfactory, but few arms being brought. Keeping the bucks collected, details of soldiers were made under officers to search the Indian camp. While this was in progress, one Indian separated a little from the rest, and in ghost dance costumes, began an address, to which I paid no attention, as the interpreter said he was telling the Indians to be quiet and submit. After a short while, however, the interpreter told me that he was talking of wiping out the whites. I then made him cease his address. Just after this, the search through their camp having proved almost fruitless, I gave orders to search the persons of the bucks, again telling them that they must do as white men always do when surrendering, that is, give up their arms.

At the first move to carry out the order last referred to, the bucks made a break, which at once resulted in terrific fire and a hot fight, lasting about twenty minutes, followed by skirmish firing of about one hour. From the first instant the squaws parted for the hills and it is my belief that comparatively few of them were injured. Some bucks succeeded in getting away and three troops were sent in pursuit. They overtook and captured five bucks (all badly wounded), nineteen squaws and children, and killed one buck. Very soon after the force was attacked by about 125 bucks, supposed to be from the agency. . . . As accurate estimate as could be made of the dead Indians, bucks in and near the camp, was 83, which added to the 7 before mentioned, makes 90 as the number of bucks killed. . . .

Chief Big Foot lying dead in the snow at Wounded Knee. (Smithsonian Institution National Anthropological Archives)

Our loss was one officer (Captain Wallace), six non-commissioned officers and eighteen privates killed, and two officers (Lieuts. Garlington and Gresham, the latter slightly, 7th Cavalry, and Lieut. Hawthorn, 2d Artillery), eleven non-commissioned officers and twenty-two privates wounded. . . .

In closing this report, I desire to express my admiration of the gallant conduct of my command in an engagement with a band of Indians in desperate condition, and crazed by religious fanaticism. . . .

Very respectfully,
Your obedient servant,
James W. Forsyth
Colonel 7th Cavalry Commanding

Headquarters Division of the Missouri
In the field, Pine Ridge, S.D.
January 21, 1891

To the Assistant Adjutant General
Headquarters Division of the Missouri
Pine Ridge, S.D.

Sir:

I have the honor to report that in obedience to verbal orders of the Division Commander, I proceeded this morning at 7 A.M., under escort of a detachment of the 1st Infantry, mounted, to White Horse Creek, about eleven miles distant, where I found the bodies of one woman, adult, two girls, eight and seven years old, and a boy of about ten years of age.

They were found in the valley of White Horse Creek, in the brush, under a high bluff, where they had evidently been discovered and shot. Each person had been shot once, the character of which was necessarily fatal in each case. The bodies had not been plundered or molested. The shooting was done at so close a range that the person or clothing of each was powder-burned.

The location of the bodies was about three miles westward of the scene of the Wounded Knee battle. All of the bodies were properly buried by the troops of my escort.

From my knowledge of the facts, I am certain that these people were killed on the day of the Wounded Knee fight, and no doubt by the troop of the 7th Cavalry, under command of Captain Godfrey. Tracks of horses shod with the Goodenough shoes were plainly visible and running along the road passing close by where the bodies were found. . . .

Very respectfully,
Your obedient servant,
Frank D. Baldwin
Captain 5th Infantry, A.A.I.G.

Headquarters Division of the Missouri
Chicago, Illinois, January 31, 1891

Respectfully forwarded to the Adjutant General of the Army . . .
Certain features of the affair at Wounded Knee Creek were so unusual and extraordinary, and such injurious reports were current immediately thereafter, so to imperatively demand an investigation in order to ascertain and record as accurately as possible all the facts, so that an intelligent opinion might guide in the bestowal of commendation or censure. The testimony elicited shows the following facts: First, that Colonel Forsyth had received repeated warnings as to the desperate and deceitful character of Big Foot's band of Indians, and repeated orders as to the exercise of constant vigilance to guard against surprise or disaster under all circumstances.

Secondly, that these warnings and orders were unheeded and disregarded by Colonel Forsyth, who seemed to consider an outbreak of the Indians as being beyond the pale of possibility, in the presence of the large force of troops at hand. The disasters that have occurred to our troops in the past from the desperation of the Indian nature are known to all who are familiar with our history. In addition to this it was well known and Colonel Forsyth had been warned that this particular band contained many of the most desperate and deceitful characters in the Sioux nation, and that a religious excitement nearly approaching frenzy had made them peculiarly dangerous. Under these circumstances the apparent indifference and security of the officer in command of the troops at Wounded Knee Creek is incomprehensive and inexcusable.

Thirdly. An examination of the accompanying map and testimony shows conclusively that at the beginning of the outbreak not a single company of the troops was so disposed as to deliver its fire upon the warriors without endangering the lives of some of their own comrades. It is in fact difficult to conceive how a worse disposition of the troops could have been made. It will be noticed that it would have been perfectly practicable for the entire command of upwards of four hundred and fifty men to have been placed between the warriors and the women and children, with their backs toward the latter and their faces toward the warriors, where they might have used their weapons effectively if required. The testimony goes to show that most of the troops were forced to withhold their fire, leaving the brunt of the affair to fall upon two companies until such warriors as had not been killed broke through or overpowered the small force directly about them and reached the camp occupied by their women and children. The battery of four Hotchkiss guns had until then been useless, the friction primers having been removed from the guns by order of the Captain commanding the battery, lest the gunners might in their excitement discharge the pieces and destroy their own comrades. These guns were now opened upon the Indian camp, even at that time placing in peril Troops C and D,

7th Cav., which were obliged to retreat for some distance owing to the fire from these guns and from the small arms of other portions of the command. The fact that a large number of the one hundred and six warriors were without fire arms when the outbreak occurred is shown by the evidence that forty-eight guns had been taken from the tepees and that a personal search of twenty or more warriors resulted in finding them unarmed. This fact taken in connection with the extremely injudicious disposition of the troops, and the large number of casualties among them, constrains the belief that some of these casualties were suffered at the hands of our own men. The fatal disposition of the troops was such as at the outset to counteract in great measure the immense disparity of strength, and would have been inexcusable in the face of an armed and desperate foe, even had no special warnings and orders been received from higher authority. . . .

Nelson A. Miles

DOCUMENT 8 *Eyewitness Reports of Indians Interviewed by the Office of Indian Affairs*

Turning Hawk, Pine Ridge (Mr. Cook, interpreter). . . . In the course of time we heard that the soldiers were moving toward the scene of trouble. After awhile some of the soldiers finally reached our place and we heard that a number of them also reached our friends at Rosebud. Of course, when a large body of soldiers is moving toward a certain direction they inspire a more or less amount of awe, and it is natural that the women and children who see this large moving mass are made afraid of it and be put in a condition to make them run away. At first we thought that Pine Ridge and Rosebud were the only two agencies where soldiers were sent, but finally we heard that the other agencies fared likewise. We heard and saw that about half our friends at Rosebud agency, from fear at seeing the soldiers, began the move of running away from their agency toward ours (Pine Ridge), and when they had gotten inside of our reservation they there learned that right ahead of them at our agency was another large crowd of soldiers, and while the soldiers were there, there was constantly a great deal of false rumor flying back and forth. The special rumor I have in mind is the threat that the soldiers had come there to disarm the Indians entirely and to take away all their horses from them. That was the oft-repeated story. . . .

They were met by the soldiers and surrounded and finally taken to the Wounded Knee creek, and there at a given time their guns were demanded. When they had delivered them up, the men were separated from their families, from their tipis, and taken to a certain spot. When the guns were thus taken and the men thus separated, there was a crazy man, a young man of very bad influence and in fact a nobody, among that bunch of Indians fired his gun, and of course the firing of a gun must have been the breaking of a military rule of some sort, because immediately the soldiers returned fire and indiscriminate killing followed.

Spotted Horse. This man shot an officer in the army; the first shot killed this officer. I was a voluntary scout at that encounter and I saw exactly what was done, and that was what I noticed; that the first shot killed an officer. As soon as this shot was fired the Indians immediately began drawing their knives, and they were exhorted from all sides to desist, but this was not obeyed. Consequently the firing began immediately on the part of the soldiers.

Turning Hawk. All the men who were in a bunch were killed right there, and those who escaped that first fire got into the ravine, and as they went along up the ravine for a long distance they were pursued on both sides by the soldiers and shot down, as the dead bodies showed afterwards. The women were standing off at a different place from where the men were stationed, and when the firing began, those of the men who escaped the first onslaught went in one direction up the ravine, and then the women, who were bunched together at another place, went entirely in a different direction through an open field, and the women fared the same fate as the men who went up the deep ravine.

American Horse. The men were separated, as has already been said, from the women, and they were surrounded by the soldiers. Then came next the village of the Indians and that was entirely surrounded by the soldiers also. When the firing began, of course the people who were standing immediately around the young man who fired the first shot were killed right together, and then they turned their guns, Hotchkiss guns, etc., upon the women who were in the lodges standing there under a flag of truce, and of course as soon as they were fired upon they fled, the men fleeing in one direction and the women running in two different directions. So that there were three general directions in which they took flight.

There was a woman with an infant in her arms who was killed as she almost touched the flag of truce, and the women and children of course were strewn all along the circular village until they were dispatched. Right near the flag of truce a mother was shot down with her infant; the child not knowing that its mother was dead was still nursing, and that especially was a very sad sight. The women as they were fleeing with their babes were killed together, shot right through, and the women who were very heavy with child were also killed. All the Indians fled in these three directions, and after most all of them had been killed a cry was made that all those who were not killed or wounded should come forth and they would be safe. Little boys who were not wounded came out of their places of refuge, and as soon as they came in sight a number of soldiers surrounded them and butchered them there. . . .

Introduction to Document 9

The following two reports try to assess what happened at Wounded Knee Creek and why. Dr. V. T. McGillycuddy had been the agent at the Pine Ridge reservation but had left months before the bloodshed. He wrote his report two weeks after the incident as a letter to General L. W. Colby. General Nelson A. Miles was in charge of the overall military operation on the plains. His report was printed in the Annual Report of the Secretary of War for 1891. How do the two reports agree or disagree on what happened and why?

 DOCUMENT 9 *Government and Military Statements on Wounded Knee*

Ex-Agent McGillycuddy's Statement

Sir:

In answer to your inquiry of a recent date, I would state that in my opinion to no one cause can be attributed the recent so-called outbreak on the part of the Sioux, but rather to a combination of causes gradually cumulative in their effect and dating back through many years—in fact to the inauguration of our practically demonstrated faulty Indian policy.

There can be no question but that many of the treaties, agreements, or solemn promises made by our government with these Indians have been broken. Many of them have been kept by us technically, but as far as the Indian is concerned have been misunderstood by him through a lack of proper explanation at time of signing, and hence considered by him as broken.

It must also be remembered that in all of the treaties made by the government with the Indians, a large portion of them have not agreed to or signed the same. Noticeably was this so in the agreement secured by us with them the summer before last, by which we secured one-half of the remainder of the Sioux reserve, amounting to about 16,000 square miles. This agreement barely carried with the Sioux nation as a whole, but did not carry at Pine Ridge or Rosebud, where the strong majority were against it; and it must be noted that wherever there was the strongest opposition manifested to the recent treaty, there, during the present trouble, have been found the elements opposed to the government.

The Sioux nation, which at one time, with the confederated bands of Cheyennes and Araphahos, controlled a region of country bounded on the north by the Yellowstone, on the south by the Arkansas, and reaching from the Missouri river to the Rocky mountains, has seen this large domain, under the various treaties, dwindle down to their now limited reserve of less than 16,000 square miles, and with the land has disappeared the buffalo and other game. The memory of this, chargeable by them to the white man, necessarily irritates them.

There is back of all this the natural race antagonism which our dealings with the aborigine in connection with the inevitable onward march of civilization has in no degree lessened. It has been our experience, and the experience of other nations, that defeat in war is soon, not sooner or later, forgotten by the coming generation, and as a result we have a tendency to a constant recurrence of outbreak on the part of the weaker race. It is now sixteen years since our last war with the Sioux in 1876—a time when our present Sioux warriors were mostly children, and therefore have no memory of having felt the power of the government. It is but natural that these young warriors, lacking in experience, should require but little incentive to induce them to test the bravery of the white man on the war path, where the traditions of his people teach him is the only path to glory and a chosen seat in the "happy hunting grounds." For these reasons every precaution should be adopted by the government to guard against trouble with its disastrous results. Have such precautions been adopted? Investigation of the present trouble does not so indicate. . . .

By the fortunes of political war, weak agents were placed in charge of some of the agencies at the very time that trouble was known to be brewing. Noticeably was this so at Pine Ridge, where a notoriously weak and unfit man was placed in charge. His flight, abandonment of his agency, and his call for troops have, with the horrible results of the same, become facts in history.

Now, as for facts in connection with Pine Ridge, which agency has unfortunately become the theater of the present "war," was there necessity for troops? My past experience with those Indians does not so indicate. For seven long years, from 1879 to 1886, I, as agent, managed this agency without the presence of a soldier on the reservation, and none nearer than 60 miles, and in those times the Indians were naturally much wilder than they are to-day. To be sure, during the seven years we occasionally had exciting times, when the only thing lacking to cause an outbreak was the calling for troops by the agent and the presence of the same. As a matter of fact, however, no matter how much disturbed affairs were, no matter how imminent an outbreak, the progressive chiefs, with their following, came to the front enough in the majority, with the fifty Indian policemen, to at once crush out all attempts at rebellion against the authority of the agent and the government.

Why was this? Because in those times we believed in placing confidence in the Indians; in establishing, as far as possible, a home-rule government on the reservation. We established local courts, presided over by the Indians, with Indian juries; in fact, we believed in having the Indians assist in working out their own salvation. We courted and secured the friendship and support of the progressive and orderly element, as against the mob element. Whether the system thus inaugurated was practicable, was successful, comparison with recent events will decide. . . .

As for the ghost dance, too much attention has been paid to it. It was only the symptom or surface indication of deep-rooted, long-existing difficulty: as well treat the eruption of smallpox as the disease and ignore the constitutional disease.

As regards disarming the Sioux, however desirable it may appear, I consider it neither advisable nor practicable. I fear that it will result as the theoretical enforcement of prohibition in Kansas, Iowa, and Dakota; you will succeed in disarming the friendly Indians, because you can, and you will not so succeed with the mob element, because you can not. If I were again to be an Indian agent and had my choice, I would take charge of 10,000 armed Sioux in preference to a like number of disarmed ones: and, furthermore, agree to handle that number, or the whole Sioux nation, without a white soldier.

Respectfully, etc.
V. T. McGillycuddy

Statement of General Miles

Cause of Indian dissatisfaction. The causes that led to the serious disturbance of the peace in the northwest last autumn and winter were so remarkable that an explanation of them is necessary in order to comprehend the seriousness of the situation. The Indians assuming the most threatening attitude of hostility were the Cheyennes and Sioux. . . .

The commanding officer at Fort Yates, North Dakota, under date of December 7, 1890, at the time the Messiah delusion was approaching a climax, says, in reference to the disaffection of the Sioux Indians at Standing Rock agency, that it is due to the following causes:

1. Failure of the government to establish an equitable southern boundary of the Standing Rock agency reservation.
2. Failure of the government to expend a just proportion of the money received from the Chicago, Milwaukee and St. Paul railroad company, for right of way privileges, for the benefit of the Indians of said agency. Official notice was received October 18, 1881, by the Indian agent at the Standing Rock agency, that the said railroad company had paid the government under its agreement with the Sioux Indians, for right of way privileges, the sum of $13,911. . . . No portion of the money had been expended up to that time (December, 1890) for the benefit of the Indians of the agency, and frequent complaints had been made to the agent by the Indians because they had received no benefits from their concessions to the said railroad companies.
3. Failure of the government to issue the certificates of title to allotments, as required by article 6 of the treaty of 1868.
4. Failure of the government to provide the full allowance of seeds and agricultural implements to Indians engaged in farming, as required in article 8, treaty of 1868.
5. Failure of the government to issue to such Indians the full number of cows and oxen provided in article 10, treaty of 1876.
6. Failure of the government to issue to the Indians the full ration stipulated in article 5, treaty of 1876. (For the fiscal year beginning July 1, 1890, the following shortages in the rations were found to exist: 485,275 pounds of beef [gross], 761,212 pounds of corn, 11,937 pounds of coffee, 281,712 pounds of flour, 26,234 pounds of sugar, and 39,852 pounds of beans.) . . .
7. Failure of the government to issue to the Indians the full amount of annuity supplies to which they were entitled under the provisions of article 10, treaty of 1868.
8. Failure of the government to have the clothing and other annuity supplies ready for issue on the first day of August of each year. Such supplies have not been ready for issue to the Indians, as a rule, until the winter season is well advanced. . . . Such supplies for the present fiscal year, beginning July 1, 1890, had not yet reached

(December, 1890) the nearest railway station, about 60 miles distant, from which point they must, at this season of the year, be freighted to this agency in wagons. It is now certain that the winter will be well advanced before the Indians at this agency receive their annual allowance of clothing and other annuity supplies.)

9. Failure of the government to appropriate money for the payment of the Indians for the ponies taken from them, by the authority of the government, in 1876.

In conclusion, the commanding officer says: "It, however, appears from the foregoing, that the government has failed to fulfill its obligations, and in order to render the Indians law-abiding, peaceful, contented, and prosperous it is strongly recommended that the treaties be promptly and fully carried out, and that the promises made by the commission in 1889 be faithfully kept."

POSTSCRIPT

Ten days before the bloodletting at Wounded Knee, an editorial appeared in the Aberdeen, South Dakota, *Pioneer.* The author declared that Sitting Bull's death marked the final passing of the "proud spirit" of these "wild" and "untamed" people. The best thing for whites to do now was to exterminate the remaining thousands:

> . . . The nobility of the Redskin is extinguished, and what few are left are a pack of whining curs who lick the hand that smites them. The Whites, by law of conquest, by justice of civilization, are masters of the American continent, and the best safety of the frontier settlements will be secured by the total annihilation of the few remaining Indians. Why not annihilation? Their glory has fled, their spirit broken, their manhood effaced; better that they should die than live the miserable wretches that they are. History would forget these latter despicable beings, and speak, in latter ages of the glory of these grand Kings of the forest and plain. . . .

The author's belief in the Indians' nobility was no bar to his calling for their elimination. Rather, by romanticizing their past, he was able to condemn them in the present. Two weeks after the above editorial appeared, just four days after Wounded Knee, the editor concluded: "Having wronged them for centuries we had better, in order to protect our civilization, follow it up by one more wrong and wipe these untamed and untamable creatures from the face of the earth. . . . Otherwise, we may expect future years to be as full of trouble with the redskins as those have been in the past." The author of these editorials was L. Frank Baum, who in 1900 became famous for writing *The Wizard of Oz.*

QUESTIONS

Defining Terms

Identify in the context of the chapter each of the following:

George Custer	Messiah Craze
Wavoka	Sioux
Ghost Dance	revitalization movements
Pine Ridge Agency	William T. Selwyn
Sitting Bull	Wounded Knee Creek

Probing the Sources

1. Describe the "Messiah Craze" and the Ghost Dance.
2. What evidence is there that the Sioux were armed and preparing to attack? Do you think that they were purely victims?
3. Give a sense of the range of feelings that agents, military officials, and government employees felt toward the Sioux.
4. How do you think whites and Native Americans differed in their ideas about progress?
5. Recount the story of Wounded Knee.

Interpreting the Sources

1. Why do you think so many Indians became interested in the Ghost Dance?
2. How did various whites react to the new religion? Many whites feared that the new religion was a cover for a Sioux uprising. What do you think?
3. Could Wounded Knee have been avoided? How?
4. Can you identify messianic movements among Euro-Americans in the nineteenth and twentieth centuries?
5. Was Wounded Knee a battle or a massacre?

ADDITIONAL READING

For the Plains wars, see Dee Brown, *Bury My Heart at Wounded Knee* (1971). A Native American perspective is provided in John G. Neihardt, *Black Elk Speaks* (1932). On the history of white-Indian relations, see Wilcomb Washburn, *The Indian in America* (1975); and Robert M. Utley, *The Indian Frontier of the American West, 1846–1890* (1984). For the myths that whites constructed about their confrontations with the Indians, see Richard Slotkin, *Regeneration Through Violence: The Mythology of the American Frontier, 1600–1860* (1973); and Slotkin, *The Fatal Environment: The Myth of the Frontier in the Age of Industrialization, 1800–1890* (1985). Also see Richard White, *"It's your Misfortune and None of My Own" A New History of the American West* (1991); Donald Wonster, *Under Western Skies* (1992); Janet A. McDowell, *The Dispossession of the American Indian* (1991); and Patricia Limerick, *The Legacy of Conquest* (1987).

New Americans
The Immigrants

HISTORICAL CONTEXT

One day in August 1921, the artist Joseph Pennell was walking in the Lower East Side of New York City. He wandered into a street of houses that were trimmed with ornate carvings, mouldings, and ironwork, all products of old craft traditions. Pennell was at once taken with the beauty of the architecture and disturbed by the people in the neighborhood. He wrote to his friend Cass Gilbert, a renowned architect, that the beauty of the buildings was "destroyed by the tribe of mongrels, the spewings out of niggers, dagoes, Chinese, and Greeks who herd in them and make by millions the new Americans." Nonetheless, Pennell advised Gilbert to go there: "If you can stand the stink and sight of your fellow countrymen and women though they aren't mostly naturalized and can get a police permit to see the dens where they herd and breed, *you might get some marble pieces.*" An architect like Gilbert, in other words, could extract artwork from these people's homes and reuse it in buildings located in more respectable neighborhoods. Pennell added as an afterthought that there was no danger that anyone in the neighborhood might object; "as there are no Jews there, these people don't know the things have any value."

It was not uncommon for Americans around the turn of the century to think of those from other lands as "spewings," to comment on how they smelled, or to mention their herding and breeding, terms usually reserved for animals. The inscription on the newly erected Statue of Liberty, after all, referred to immigrants as "wretched refuse," hardly a compliment to the parents, grandparents, and great–grandparents of so many of us. Nativism, racism, and xenophobia have been long and enduring in American culture. Pennell's letter merely tapped into the pervasive prejudices.

Nevertheless, it would be a mistake to see such attitudes as fixed and immutable. Ethnic stereotypes may range from tasteless jokes to vicious images that are used to justify violence. The intensity of prejudice varies with such circumstances as economic conditions, competition for jobs, the degree of closeness in which people of different groups live to each other, and the amount of contact over time they share with each other. (By 1880, for example, few Americans had encountered Polish people, but nearly everyone was familiar with the racist stereotypes of African Americans that infused popular culture.) Prejudice may be enduring, but its pervasiveness, intensity, and consequences change dramatically across time and place.

To read Pennell's letter as part of an unvarying climate of hatred for strangers is to imply that there were no alternatives. The logic is circular: Everyone harbored ugly prejudices because that was how everyone felt. Such a position absolves individuals from responsibility, for it makes them seem powerless before the ideas that control them. But to say "everybody thought that way back then" simply is not true; the history of ideas is never so clear or uniform. For example, Pennell's last remark derives from the age-old stereotype of Jews' alleged obsession with money, their stinginess, wealth, power, and so forth. In the stereotype, an entire people's history, traditions, and religion are reduced to a simple and pernicious cluster of prejudices.

Not everyone believed such nonsense. To cite an alternative (and history is the study of alternatives, of roads taken and not taken), Hutchins Hapgood, a man from an old American family, wrote an extraordinarily sensitive and complex book about the cultural life of the Jewish neighborhoods of New York City. Hapgood walked on the same streets as Pennell (though he had walked through them twenty years earlier) and saw something very different. "The Jewish quarter of New York," Hapgood wrote in the preface to his *Spirit of the Ghetto* (1902), "is generally supposed to be a place of poverty, dirt, ignorance, and immorality. . . . But the unpleasant aspect is not the subject of the following sketches." Philanthropists, sociologists, and reformers might enter ethnic neighborhoods to document the immigrants' debasement, but Hapgood was attracted by "the charm [he] felt in men and things there." By not reducing Jewish immigrant culture to poverty, depravity, or stereotypes, Hapgood could sensitively and complexly explore the rich cultural life that Jews created in America.

The history of America, of course, might be said to be the history of immigrants. But the half century between about 1880 and 1930—by which date new legal restrictions and economic depression had ended the influx of foreign peoples—witnessed unprecedented immigration. Roughly twenty-seven million newcomers entered the country in those years, sometimes at a rate of over one million per year. They came less from western and northern Europe than from southern and eastern Europe, and they came too from Asia, so that, taken together, Italians, Jews, Poles, Russians, and other Slavic and Mediterranean peoples, as well as Chinese, arrived in numbers far exceeding the numbers of the Irish, Germans, and Scandinavians who had dominated earlier migrations.

The newcomers tended to settle north of the Ohio and east of the Mississippi in burgeoning urban centers like Chicago and New York. Industrialization and the expansion of the worldwide market economy caused massive shifts in the supply of goods and the demand for labor, so that millions found themselves in motion. Italian peasants, for example, might discover that an overproduction of citrus fruit left them without work, but the need for laborers to build roads and subways in New York City offered a chance to survive. If the efficiency of wheat production now drove prices so low that Slavic peasants could not earn enough to eat, the mines and mills of Pennsylvania needed their backs and hands. Some people migrated within their native countries; others moved through Europe or Asia; many went overseas to Latin America, Canada, or especially the United States; but immigration was an international phenomenon rooted in economic dislocations that left millions without the means to make a living.

The majority of the new immigrants were men; they came in search of jobs while their families stayed behind. (Jews, more than other ethnic groups, migrated as whole families because political persecution in eastern Europe gave them little hope of a decent life there; Chinese women, on the other hand, were forbidden to enter the United States, so the men settled in all-male work camps to mine gold or to build the railroads in the West.) Many intended to remain in America—or wherever they found work—only long enough to send money home to secure the survival of their families in the old country. In some years, half as many people returned to Europe as came to America. Moreover, immigrants tended to come in patterns that demographers call *chain migrations.* The decision to go was not made randomly by individuals; rather, extended families, neighbors, or townspeople migrated together, sold their labor together, and settled into new communities together. The Chinatowns, Little Italys, and other ethnic neighborhoods were the result of people's need to help one another economically, to maintain their language and culture, and to defend themselves from prejudice.

Despite occasional recessions, America's economy boomed during this era, providing plenty of work to lure the newcomers. But immigrants were exploitable labor, easily replaced by others if they started to organize and make demands. In New York sweatshops, Jews sewed garments for the ready-to-wear industry; in Pittsburgh mills, Poles poured steel; on California ranches, Mexicans picked the crops; in downtown Chicago, Greeks shined businessmen's shoes—and most worked brutally long hours to make a bit more or less than subsistence wages. All lived with the fear that new workers might undercut their wages, and they labored in horrid conditions that caused tens of thousands to die prematurely every year. Epidemics swept the crowded slums, mines caved in, explosions rocked the mills, construction workers fell from shoddy scaffoldings, and tenements burned to the ground. Prejudice prevented many Americans from recognizing the human tragedy before their eyes. The relative powerlessness of immigrants—their inability to communicate across ethnic boundaries, their need to keep jobs, their sheer exhaustion from overwork—too often kept them from organizing effectively to resist oppression.

All of their hardships notwithstanding, the immigrants made a life for themselves and their children. Perhaps it is more accurate to say that, in order to survive the hardships—the prejudice, poverty, disease, and death—they knew they must stick together and cling to their old ways. In ethnic communities, they sang the songs, played the games, and told the stories of the old country. Extended families reinforced distinctive gender roles, food ways, languages, and other cultural patterns. The new immigrants built churches, especially Catholic churches, since the majority of them were of that faith. They worshiped in their own unique ways; Polish Catholicism differed markedly from Italian Catholicism, as did the Greek Orthodox church from the Russian Orthodox church. Politics engaged many immigrants' attention, and community leaders helped to develop local resources, to accomplish goals for their people, and, in the process, to become powerful individuals. Many groups also came with well-developed traditions of economic protest, so socialist, communist, trade unionist, and anarchist organizations flourished.

But always there were tensions. The children of immigrants were divided in their loyalties between the ways of their parents and those of the American culture. Wealthier foreigners were embarrassed by their poor compatriots, but often not too embarrassed to exploit them. Patriotic feelings toward the new home that fed them vied with hatred of America's prejudice and exploitation. The experiences of migrating to a new land, settling, making a living, establishing communities, and deciding whether to stay or for how long were difficult challenges that individuals negotiated for themselves day by day.

THE DOCUMENTS
Introduction to Documents 1 through 6

The documents in this section give a sense of the complexity of the immigrant experience. There are interviews with three immigrants—one Italian, one Chinese, and one Jewish—that appeared in the reform magazine *The Independent* just after the turn of the nineteenth century. While we cannot know what questions were asked by the representative of the magazine or how the interviews were edited, these pieces give us the rare opportunity to hear the immigrants' own voices and to glimpse how they viewed themselves. Preceding each interview is a portion of Jacob Riis's famous book *How the Other Half Lives* (1890). Riis was a Danish immigrant who became a journalist and a social reformer. Before his success and fame in middle age, however, he had suffered severe poverty and alienation shortly after he migrated to America. During the economic depression of the 1870s, when he was in his twenties, Riis wandered around the streets of New York unemployed, homeless, and suicidal. He was saved by a job as a police reporter for the New York *Tribune*. For the rest of the century, he wrote about the city's impoverished lower Manhattan wards.

Despite his own experience of immigration and poverty, Riis was by no means wholly sympathetic to the people he wrote about and photographed. He hated the dirt and the anarchy, the stink and the poverty of lower Manhattan, but he hated these things as a man running from something in himself. He saw mostly the immigrants' degradation, barely the people themselves, so he readily fastened onto ethnic stereotypes to describe them. Compare Riis's characterization of the Chinese with what Lee Chew says about himself and his people. Are there similarities between Riis's description of Italians and the picture we get from Rocco Corresca? Can you square Riis's characterization of Jews as obsessed with money with Rose Schneiderman's commitment to labor organizing?

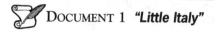

DOCUMENT 1   *"Little Italy"*

Jacob Riis

Certainly a picturesque, if not very tidy, element has been added to the population in the "assisted" Italian immigrant who claims so large a share of public attention, partly because he keeps coming at such a tremendous rate, but chiefly because he elects to stay in New York, or near enough for it to serve as his base of operations, and here promptly reproduces conditions of destitution and disorder which, set in the frame-work of Mediterranean exuberance, are the delight of the artist, but in a matter-of-fact American community become its danger and reproach. The reproduction is made easier in New York because he finds the material ready to hand in the worst of the slum tenements; but even where it is not he soon reduces what he does find to his own level, if allowed to follow his natural bent. The Italian comes in at the bottom, and in the generation that came over the sea he stays there. In the slums he is welcomed as a tenant who "makes less trouble" than the contentious Irishman or the order-loving German, that is to say: is content to live in a pig-sty and submits to robbery at the hands of the rent-collector without murmur. Yet this very tractability makes of him in good hands, when firmly and intelligently managed, a really desirable tenant. But it is not his good fortune often to fall in with other hospitality upon his coming than that which brought him here for its own profit, and has no idea of letting go its grip upon him as long as there is a cent to be made out of him.

Recent Congressional inquiries have shown the nature of the "assistance" he receives from greedy steamship agents and "bankers," who persuade him by false promises to mortgage his home, his few belongings, and his wages for months to come for a ticket to the land where plenty of work is to be had at princely wages. The padrone—the "banker" is nothing else—having made his ten per cent. out of him en route, receives him at the landing and turns him to double account as a wage-earner and a rent-payer. In each of these roles he is made to yield a profit to his unscrupulous countryman, whom he trusts implicitly with the instinct of utter helplessness. The man is so ignorant that, as one of the sharpers who prey upon him put it once, it "would be downright sinful not to take him in." His ignorance and unconquerable suspicion of strangers dig the pit into which he falls. He not only knows no word of English, but he does not know enough to learn. Rarely only can he write his own language. Unlike the German, who begins learning English the day he lands as a matter of duty, or the Polish Jew, who takes it up as soon as he is able as an investment, the Italian learns slowly, if at all. Even his boy, born here, often speaks his native tongue indifferently. He is forced, therefore, to have constant recourse to the middle-man who makes him pay handsomely at every turn. He hires him out to the railroad contractor, receiving a commission from the employer as well as from the laborer, and repeats the performance monthly, or as often as he can have him dismissed. In the city he contracts for his lodging, subletting to him space in the vilest tenements at extortionate rents, and sets an example that does not lack imitators. The "princely wages" have vanished with his coming, and in their place hardships and a dollar a day, [along] with the padrone's merciless mortgage, confront him. Bred to even worse fare, he takes both as a matter of course, and, applying the maxim that it is not what one makes but what he saves that makes him rich, manages to turn the very dirt of the streets into a hoard of gold, with which he either returns to his Southern home, or brings over his family to join in his work and in his fortunes the next season. . . .

Did the Italian always adapt himself as readily to the operation of the civil law as to the manipulation of political "pull" on occasion, he would save himself a good deal of unnecessary trouble. Ordinarily he is easily enough governed by authority—always excepting Sunday, when he settles down to a game of cards and lets loose all his bad passions. Like the Chinese, the Italian is a born gambler. His soul is in the game from the moment the cards are on the table, and very frequently his knife is in it too before the game is ended. No Sunday has passed in New York since "the Bend" became a suburb of Naples without one or more of these murderous affrays coming to the notice of the police. As a rule that happens only when the man the game went against is either dead or so badly wounded as to require instant surgical help. As to the other, unless he be caught red-handed, the chances that the police will ever get him are slim indeed. The wounded man can seldom be persuaded to betray him. He wards off all inquiries with a wicked "I fix him myself," and there the matter rests until he either dies or recovers. If the latter, the community hears after a while of another Italian affray, a man stabbed in a quarrel, dead or dying, and the police know that "he" has been fixed, and the account squared.

With all his conspicuous faults, the swarthy Italian immigrant has his redeeming traits. He is as honest as he is hot-headed. There are no Italian burglars in the Rogues' Gallery; the ex-brigand toils peacefully with pickaxe and shovel on American ground. His boy occasionally shows, as a pick-pocket, the results of his training with the toughs of the Sixth Ward slums. The only criminal business to which the father occasionally lends his hand, outside of murder, is a bunco game, of which his confiding countrymen, returning with their hoard to their native land, are the victims. The women are faithful wives and devoted mothers. Their vivid and picturesque costumes lend a tinge of color to the otherwise dull monotony of the slums they inhabit. The Italian is gay, lighthearted and, if his fur is not stroked the wrong way, inoffensive as a child. His worst offence is that he keeps the stale-beer dives. Where his headquarters is, in the Mulberry Street Bend, these vile dens flourish and gather about them all the wrecks, the utterly wretched, the hopelessly lost, on the lowest slope of depraved humanity. And out of their misery he makes a profit. . . .

 DOCUMENT 2   *"The Biography of a Bootblack"*

Rocco Corresca

[The story of Rocco Corresca is presented almost as he told it to a representative of *The Independent*. There are changes of language and some suppressions, but no change of meaning has been made. The ideas and statements of fact are all his, and, astonishing as it may seem to Americans, much of the experience is typical of thousands of Italians who come to this country penniless and make their fortunes, though beginning as low down in the scale as the narrator. Rocco is known to many people as "Joe." He claims that he has always been known as Rocco but that the name Corresca was given him when he went aboard the ship that brought him here. It was entered on the books. He has since kept it for official purposes and proposes to be known by it in the future.

—*Editor*.]

When I was a very small boy I lived in Italy in a large house with many other small boys, who were all dressed alike and were taken care of by some nuns. It was a good place, situated on the side of the mountain, where grapes were growing and melons and oranges and plums.

They taught us our letters and how to pray and say the catechism, and we worked in the fields during the middle of the day. We always had enough to eat and good beds to sleep in at night, and sometimes there were feast days, when we marched about wearing flowers.

Those were good times and they lasted till I was nearly eight years of age. Then an old man came and said he was my grandfather. He showed some papers and cried over me and said that the money had come at last and now he could take me to his beautiful home. He seemed very glad to see me and after they looked at his papers he took me away and we went to the big city—Naples. He kept talking about his beautiful house, but when we got there it was a dark cellar that he lived in and I did not like it at all. Very rich people were on the first floor. They had carriages and servants and music and plenty of good things to eat, but we were down below in the cellar and had nothing. There were four other boys in the cellar and the old man said they were all my brothers. All were larger than I and they beat me at first till one day Francisco said that they should not beat me any more, and then Paulo, who was the largest of all, fought him till Francisco drew a knife and gave him a cut. Then Paulo, too, got a knife and said that he would kill Francisco, but the old man knocked them both down with a stick and took their knives away and gave them beatings.

Each morning we boys all went out to beg and we begged all day near the churches and at night near the theatres, running to the carriages and opening the doors and then

"In the home of an Italian Ragpicker," photograph by Jacob Riis. (Museum of the City of New York)

getting in the way of the people so that they had to give us money or walk over us. The old man often watched us and at night he took all the money, except when we could hide something. . . .

Then the old man said to me: "If you don't want to be a thief you can be a cripple. That is an easy life and they make a great deal of money."

I was frightened then, and that night I heard him talking to one of the men that came to see him. He asked how much he would charge to make me a good cripple like those that crawl about the church. They had a dispute, but at last they agreed and the man said that I should be made so that people would shudder and give me plenty of money.

I was much frightened, but I did not make a sound and in the morning I went out to beg with Francisco. I said to him: "I am going to run away. I don't believe 'Tony is my grandfather . . . and I don't want to be a cripple, no matter how much money the people may give."

"Where will you go?" Francisco asked me.
"I don't know," I said; "somewhere."
He thought awhile and then he said: "I will go, too."

So we ran away out of the city and begged from the country people as we went along. We came to a village down by the sea and a long way from Naples and there we found some fishermen and they took us aboard their boat. We were with them five years, and tho it was a very hard life we liked it well because there was always plenty to eat. Fish do not keep long and those that we did not sell we ate.

The chief fisherman, whose name was Ciguciano, had a daughter, Teresa, who was very beautiful, and tho she was two years younger than I, she could cook and keep house quite well. She was a kind, good girl and he was a good man. When we told him about the old man who told us he was our grandfather, the fisherman said he was an old rascal who should be in prison for life. Teresa cried much when she heard that he was going to make me a cripple. Ciguciano said that all the old man had taught us was wrong—that it was bad to beg, to steal and to tell lies. He called in the priest and the priest said the same thing and was very angry at the old man in Naples, and he taught us to read and write in the evenings. He also taught us our duties to the church. . . .

We grew large and strong with the fisherman and he told us that we were getting too big for him, that he could not afford to pay us the money that we were worth. He was a fine, honest man—one in a thousand.

Now and then I had heard things about America—that it was a far off country where everybody was rich and that Italians went there and made plenty of money, so that they could return to Italy and live in pleasure ever after. One day I met a young man who pulled out a handful of gold and told me he had made that in America in a few days.

I said I should like to go there, and he told me that if I went he would take care of me and see that I was safe. I told Francisco and he wanted to go, too. So we said good-by to our good friends. Teresa cried and kissed us both and the priest came and shook our hands and told us to be good men, and that no matter where we went God and his saints were always near us and that if we lived well we should all meet again in heaven. We cried, too, for it was our home, that place. Ciguciano gave us money and slapped us on the back and said that we should be great. But he felt bad, too, at seeing us go away after all that time.

The young man took us to a big ship and got us work away down where the fires are. We had to carry coal to the place where it could be thrown on the fires. Francisco and I were very sick from the great heat at first and lay on the coal for a long time, but they threw water on us and made us get up. We could not stand on our feet well, for everything was going around and we had no strength. We said that we wished we had stayed in Italy no matter how much gold there was in America. We could not eat for three days and could not do much work. Then we got better and sometimes we went up above and looked about. There was no land anywhere and we were much surprised. How could the people tell where to go when there was no land to steer by? . . .

We were all landed on an island and the bosses there said that Francisco and I must go back because we had not enough money, but a man named Bartolo came up and told them that we were brothers and he was our uncle and would take care of us. He brought two other men who swore that they knew us in Italy and that Bartolo was our uncle. I had never seen any of them before, but even then Bartolo might be my uncle, so I did not say anything. The bosses of the island let us go out with Bartolo after he had made the oath.

We came to Brooklyn to a wooden house in Adams Street that was full of Italians from Naples. Bartolo had a room on the third floor and there were fifteen men in the room, all boarding with Bartolo. He did the cooking on a stove in the middle of the room and there were beds all around the sides, one bed above another. It was very hot in the room, but we were soon asleep, for we were very tired.

The next morning, early, Bartolo told us to go out and pick rags and get bottles. He gave us bags and hooks and showed us the ash barrels. On the streets where the fine houses are the people are very careless and put out good things, like mattresses and um-brellas, clothes, hats and boots. We brought all these to Bartolo and he made them new again and sold them on the sidewalk; but mostly we brought rags and bones. The rags we had to wash in the back yard and then we hung them to dry on lines under the ceiling in our room. The bones we kept under the beds till Bartolo could find a man to buy them.

Most of the men in our room worked at digging the sewer. Bartolo got them the work and they paid him about one quarter of their wages. Then he charged them for board and he bought the clothes for them, too. So they got little money after all.

Bartolo was always saying that the rent of the room was so high that he could not make anything, but he was really making plenty. He was what they call a padrone and is now a very rich man. The men that were living with him had just come to the country and could not speak English. They had all been sent by the young man we met in Italy. Bartolo told us all that we must work for him and that if we did not the police would come and put us in prison.

He gave us very little money, and our clothes were some of those that were found on the street. Still we had enough to eat and we had meat quite often, which we never had in Italy. Bartolo got it from the butcher—the meat that he could not sell to the other people—but it was quite good meat. Bartolo cooked it in the pan while we all sat on our beds in the evening. Then he cut it into small bits and passed the pan around, saying:

"See what I do for you and yet you are not glad. I am too kind a man, that is why I am so poor."

We were with Bartolo nearly a year, but some of our countrymen who had been in the place a long time said that Bartolo had no right to us and we could get work for a dollar and a half a day, which, when you make it *lire* (reckoned in the Italian currency) is very much. So we went away one day to Newark and got work on the street. Bartolo came after us and made a great noise, but the boss said that if he did not go away soon the police would have him. Then he went, saying that there was no justice in this country.

We paid a man five dollars each for getting us the work and we were with that boss for six months. He was Irish, but a good man and he gave us our money every Saturday night. We lived much better than with Bartolo, and when the work was done we each had nearly $200 saved. Plenty of the men spoke English and they taught us, and we taught them to read and write. That was at night, for we had a lamp in our room, and there were only five other men who lived in that room with us. . . .

When the Newark boss told us that there was no more work Francisco and I talked about what we would do and we went back to Brooklyn to a saloon near Hamilton Ferry, where we got a job cleaning it out and slept in a little room upstairs. There was a boot-black named Michael on the corner and when I had time I helped him and learned the business. Francisco cooked the lunch in the saloon and he, too, worked for the bootblack and we were soon able to make the best polish.

Then we thought we would go into business and we got a basement on Hamilton avenue, near the Ferry, and put four chairs in it. We paid $75 for the chairs and all the other things. We had tables and looking glasses there and curtains. We took the papers that have the pictures in and made the place high toned. Outside we had a big sign that said:

THE BEST SHINE FOR TEN CENTS

Men that did not want to pay ten cents could get a good shine for five cents, but it was not an oil shine. We had two boys helping us and paid each of them fifty cents a day. The rent of the place was $20 a month, so the expenses were very great, but we made money from the beginning. We slept in the basement, but got our meals in the saloon till we could put a stove in our place, and then Francisco cooked for us all. That would not do, tho, because some of our customers said that they did not like to smell garlic and onions and red herrings. I thought that was strange, but we had to do what the customers said. So we got the woman who lived upstairs to give us our meals and paid her $1.50 a week each. She gave the boys soup in the middle of the day—five cents for two plates. . . .

We had said that when we saved $1,000 each we would go back to Italy and buy a farm, but now that the time is coming we are so busy and making so much money that we think we will stay. We have opened another parlor near South Ferry, in New York. We have to pay $30 a month rent, but the business is very good. The boys in this place charge sixty cents a day because there is so much work.

At first we did not know much of this country, but by and by we learned. There are here plenty of Protestants who are heretics, but they have a religion, too. Many of the finest churches are Protestant, but they have no saints and no altars, which seems strange. . . .

There are plenty of rich Italians here, men who a few years ago had nothing and now have so much money that they could not count all their dollars in a week. The richest ones go away from the other Italians and live with the Americans. . . .

I am nineteen years of age now and have $700 saved. Francisco is twenty-one and has about $900. We shall open some more parlors soon. I know an Italian who was a boot-black ten years ago and now bosses bootblacks all over the city, who has so much money that if it was turned into gold it would weight more than himself. . . .

Brooklyn, N.Y.

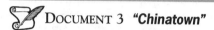

DOCUMENT 3 *"Chinatown"*

Jacob Riis

Between the tabernacles of Jewry and the shrines of the Bend, Joss has cheekily planted his pagan worship of idols, chief among which are the celestial worshippers' own gain and lusts. Whatever may be said about the Chinaman being a thousand years behind the age on his own shores, here he is distinctly abreast of it in his successful scheming to "make it pay." It is doubtful if there is anything he does not turn to a paying account, from his religion down, or up, as one prefers. At the risk of distressing some well-meaning, but, I fear, too trustful people, I state it in advance as my opinion, based on the steady observation of years, that all attempts to make an effective Christian of John Chinaman will remain abortive in this generation; of the next I have, if anything, less hope. Ages of senseless idolatry, a mere grub-worship, have left him without the essential qualities for appreciating the gentle teachings of a faith whose motive and unselfish spirit are alike beyond his grasp. He lacks the handle of a strong faith in something, anything, however wrong, to catch him by. There is nothing strong about him, except his passions when aroused. I am convinced that he adopts Christianity, when he adopts it at all, as he puts on American clothes, with what the politicians would call an ulterior motive, some sort of gain in the near prospect—washing, a Christian wife perhaps, anything he happens to rate for the moment above his cherished pigtail.

Stealth and secretiveness are as much part of the Chinaman in New York as the cat-like tread of his felt shoes. His business, as his domestic life, shuns the light, less because there is anything to conceal than because that is the way of the man. Perhaps the attitude of American civilization toward the stranger, whom it invited in, has taught him that way. At any rate, the very doorways of his offices and shops are fenced off by queer, forbidding partitions suggestive of a continual state of siege. The stranger who enters through the crooked approach is received with sudden silence, a sullen stare, and an angry "Vat you vant?" that breathes annoyance and distrust.

. . . The average Chinaman, the police will tell you, would rather gamble than eat any day, and they have ample experience to back them. Only the fellow in the bunk smokes away, indifferent to all else but his pipe and his own enjoyment. It is a mistake to assume that Chinatown is honeycombed with opium "joints." There are a good many more outside of it than in it. The celestials do not monopolize the pipe. In Mott Street there is no need of them. Not a Chinese home or burrow there but has its bunk and its lay-out, where they can be enjoyed safe from police interference. The Chinaman smokes opium as Caucasians smoke tobacco, and apparently with little worse effect upon himself. But woe unto the white victim upon which his pitiless drug gets its grip! . . .

From the teeming tenements to the right and left of [Chinatown] come the white slaves of its dens of vice and their infernal drug, that have infused into the "Bloody Sixth" Ward a subtler poison than ever the stale-beer dives knew, or the "sudden death" of the Old Brewery. There are houses, dozens of them, in Mott and Pell Streets, that are literally jammed, from the "joint" in the cellar to the attic, with these hapless victims of a passion which, once acquired, demands the sacrifice of every instinct of decency to its insatiate desire. . . . I came across a company of them [young Caucasian prostitutes] "hitting the pipe" together, on a tour through their dens one night with the police captain of the precinct. The girls knew him, called him by name, offered him a pipe, and chatted with him about the incidents of their acquaintance, how many times he had "sent them up," and their chances of "lasting" much longer. There was no shade of regret in their voices, nothing but utter indifference and surrender.

One thing about them was conspicuous: their scrupulous neatness. It is the distinguishing mark of Chinatown, outwardly and physically. It is not altogether by chance the Chinaman has chosen the laundry as his distinctive field. He is by nature as clean as the cat, which he resembles in his traits of cruel cunning and savage fury when aroused. On this point of cleanliness he insists in his domestic circle, yielding in others with crafty submissiveness to the caprice of the girls, who "boss" him in a very independent manner, fretting vengefully under the yoke they loathe, but which they know right well they can never shake off, once they have put the pipe to their lips and given Mott Street a mortgage upon their souls for all time. . . .

The frequent assertions of the authorities that at least no girls under age are wrecked on this Chinese shoal, are disproved by the observation of those who go frequently among these dens, though the smallest girl will invariably, and usually without being asked, insist that she is sixteen, and so of age to choose the company she keeps. Such assertions are not to be taken seriously. Even while I am writing, the morning returns from one of the precincts that pass through my hands report the arrest of a Chinaman for "inveigling little girls into his laundry," one of the hundred outposts of Chinatown that are scattered all over the city, as the outer threads of the spider's web that holds its prey fast. . . .

Withal the police give the Chinese the name of being the "quietest people down there," meaning in the notoriously turbulent Sixth Ward; and they are. The one thing they desire above all is to be let alone, a very natural wish perhaps, considering all the circumstances. If it were a laudable or even an allowable ambition that prompts it, they might be humored with advantage, probably, to both sides. But the facts show too plainly that it is not, and that in their very exclusiveness and reserve they are a constant and terrible menace to society, wholly regardless of their influence upon the industrial problems which their presence confuses. The severest official scrutiny, the harshest repressive measures are justifiable in Chinatown, orderly as it appears on the surface, even more than in the Bend, and the case is infinitely more urgent. To the peril that threatens there all the senses are alert, whereas the poison that proceeds from Mott Street puts mind and body to sleep, to work out its deadly purpose in the corruption of the soul. . . .

DOCUMENT 4   *"The Biography of a Chinaman"*

Lee Chew

[Mr. Lee Chew is a representative Chinese business man who expresses with much force views that are generally held by his countrymen throughout America. The interview that follows *is strictly as he gave it*, except as to detail of arrangement and mere verbiage. Mr. Lee was assisted by the well-known Chinese interpreter, Mr. Joseph M. Singleton, of 24 Pell Street.

—*Editor.*]

The village where I was born is situated in the province of Canton, on one of the banks of the Si-Kiang River. It is called a village, altho it is really as big as a city, for there are about 5,000 men in it over eighteen years of age—women and children and even youths are not counted in our villages.

All in the village belonged to the tribe of Lee. They did not intermarry with one another, but the men went to other villages for their wives and brought them home to their fathers' houses, and men from other villages—Wus and Wings and Sings and Fongs, etc.—chose wives from among our girls. . . .

My father's house is built of fine blue brick, better than the brick in the houses here in the United States. It is only one story high, roofed with red tiles and surrounded by a stone wall which also incloses the yard. There are four rooms in the house, one large living room which serves for a parlor and three private rooms, one occupied by my grandfather, who is very old and very honorable; another by my father and mother, and the third by my oldest brother and his wife and two little children. There are no windows, but the door is left open all day.

All the men of the village have farms, but they don't live on them as the farmers do here; they live in the village, but go out during the day time and work their farms, coming home before dark. My father has a farm of about ten acres, on which he grows a great abundance of things—sweet potatoes, rice, beans, peas, yams, sugar cane, pineapples, bananas, lychee nuts and palms. The palm leaves are useful and can be sold. Men make fans of the lower part of each leaf near the stem, and water proof coats and hats, and awnings for boats, of the parts that are left when the fans are cut out. . . .

We have our own Government, consisting of the elders of our tribe—the honorable men. When a man gets to be sixty years of age he begins to have honor and to become a leader, and then the older he grows the more he is honored. We had some men who were nearly one hundred years, but very few of them.

In spite of the fact that any man may correct them for a fault, Chinese boys have good times and plenty of play. We played games like tag, and other games like shinny and a sort of football called yin. . . . It was not all play for us boys, however. We had to go to school, where we learned to read and write and to recite the precepts of Kong-foo-tsze and the other Sages, and stories about the great Emperors of China, who ruled with the wisdom of gods and gave to the whole world the light of high civilization and the culture of our literature, which is the admiration of all nations.

I went to my parents' house for meals, approaching my grandfather with awe, my father and mother with veneration and my elder brother with respect. I never spoke unless spoken to, but I listened and heard much concerning the red haired, green eyed foreign devils with the hairy faces, who had lately come out of the sea and clustered on our shores. They were wild and fierce and wicked, and paid no regard to the moral precepts of Kong-foo-tsze and the Sages; neither did they worship their ancestors, but pretended to be wiser than their fathers and grandfathers. They loved to beat people and to rob and murder. In the streets of Hong Kong many of them could be seen reeling drunk. Their speech was a savage roar, like the voice of the tiger or the buffalo, and they wanted to take the land away from the Chinese. Their men and women lived together like animals, without any marriage or faithfulness, and even were shameless enough to walk the streets arm in arm in daylight. So the old men said.

All this was very shocking and disgusting, as our women seldom were on the street, except in the evenings, when they went with the water jars to the three wells that supplied all the people. Then if they met a man they stood still, with their faces turned to the

A scene from New York City's Chinatown around the turn of the century. (Museum of the City of New York)

wall, while he looked the other way when he passed them. A man who spoke to a woman on the street in a Chinese village would be beaten, perhaps killed.

My grandfather told how the English foreign devils had made wicked war on the Emperor, and by means of their enchantments and spells had defeated his armies and forced him to admit their opium, so that the Chinese might smoke and become weakened and the foreign devils might rob them of their land.

My grandfather said that it was well known that the Chinese were always the greatest and wisest among men. They had invented and discovered everything that was good. Therefore the things which the foreign devils had and the Chinese had not must be evil. Some of these things were very wonderful, enabling the red haired savages to talk with one another, tho they might be thousands of miles apart. They had suns that made darkness like day, their ships carried earthquakes and volcanoes to fight for them, and thousands of demons that lived in iron and steel houses spun their cotton and silk, pushed their boats, pulled their cars, printed their newspapers and did other work for them. They were constantly showing disrespect for their ancestors by getting new things to take the place of the old.

I heard about the American foreign devils, that they were false, having made a treaty by which it was agreed that they could freely come to China, and the Chinese as freely go to their country. After this treaty was made China opened its doors to them and then they broke the treaty that they had asked for by shutting the Chinese out of their country. . . .

I worked on my father's farm till I was about sixteen years of age, when a man of our tribe came back from America and took ground as large as four city blocks and made a paradise of it. He put a large stone wall around and led some streams through and built a palace and summer house and about twenty other structures, with beautiful bridges over the streams and walks and roads. Trees and flowers, singing birds, water fowl and curious animals were within the walls.

The man had gone away from our village a poor boy. Now he returned with unlimited wealth, which he had obtained in the country of the American wizards. After many amazing adventures he had become a merchant in a city called Mott Street, so it was said.

When his palace and grounds were completed he gave a dinner to all the people who assembled to be his guests. One hundred pigs roasted whole were served on the tables, with chickens, ducks, geese and such an abundance of dainties that our villagers even now lick their fingers when they think of it. He had the best actors from Hong Kong performing, and every musician for miles around was playing and singing. At night the blaze of the lanterns could be seen for many miles.

Having made his wealth among the barbarians this man had faithfully returned to pour it out among his tribesmen, and he is living in our village now very happy, and a pillar of strength to the poor.

The wealth of this man filled my mind with the idea that I, too, would like to go to the country of the wizards and gain some of their wealth, and after a long time my father consented, and gave me his blessing, and my mother took leave of me with tears, while my grandfather laid his hand upon my head and told me to remember and live up to the admonitions of the Sages, to avoid gambling, bad women and men of evil minds, and so to govern my conduct that when I died my ancestors might rejoice to welcome me as a guest on high.

My father gave me $100, and I went to Hong Kong with five other boys from our place and we got steerage passage on a steamer, paying $50 each. Everything was new to me. All my life I had been used to sleeping on a board bed with a wooden pillow, and I found the steamer's bunk very uncomfortable, because it was so soft. The food was different from that which I had been used to, and I did not like it at all. I was afraid of the stews, for the thought of what they might be made of by the wicked wizards of the ship made me ill. Of the great power of these people I saw many signs. The engines that moved the ship were wonderful monsters, strong enough to lift mountains. When I got to San Francisco, which was before the passage of the Exclusion act, I was half starved, because I was afraid to eat the provisions of the barbarians, but a few days' living in the Chinese quarter made me happy again. A man got me work as a house servant in an American family, and my start was the same as that of almost all the Chinese in this country.

The Chinese laundryman does not learn his trade in China; there are no laundries in China. The women there do the washing in tubs and have no washboards or flat irons. All the Chinese laundrymen here were taught in the first place by American women just as I was taught.

When I went to work for that American family I could not speak a word of English, and I did not know anything about housework. The family consisted of husband, wife and two children. They were very good to me and paid me $3.50 a week, of which I could save $3.

I did not know how to do anything, and I did not understand what the lady said to me, but she showed me how to cook, wash, iron, sweep, dust, make beds, wash dishes, clean windows, paint and brass, polish the knives and forks, etc., by doing the things herself and then overseeing my efforts to imitate her. She would take my hands and show them how to do things. She and her husband and children laughed at me a great deal, but it was all good natured. I was not confined to the house in the way servants are confined here, but when my work was done in the morning I was allowed to go out till lunch time. People in California are more generous than they are here.

In six months I had learned how to do the work of our house quite well, and I was getting $5 a week and board, and putting away about $4.25 a week. I had also learned some English, and by going to a Sunday school I learned more English and something about Jesus, who was a great Sage, and whose precepts are like those of Kong-foo-tsze.

It was twenty years ago when I came to this country, and I worked for two years as a servant, getting at the last $35 a month. I sent money home to comfort my parents, but tho I dressed well and lived well and had pleasure, going quite often to the Chinese theater and to dinner parties in Chinatown, I saved $50 in the first six months, $90 in the second, $120 in the third and $150 in the fourth. So I had $410 at the end of two years, and I was now ready to start in business.

When I first opened a laundry it was in company with a partner, who had been in the business for some years. We went to a town about 500 miles inland, where a railroad was building. We got a board shanty and worked for the men employed by the railroads. Our rent cost us $10 a month and food nearly $5 a week each, for all food was dear and we wanted the best of everything—we lived principally on rice, chickens, ducks and pork, and did our own cooking. The Chinese take naturally to cooking. It cost us about $50 for our furniture and apparatus, and we made close upon $60 a week, which we divided between us. We had to put up with many insults and some frauds, as men would come in and claim parcels that did not belong to them, saying they had lost their tickets, and would fight if they did not get what they asked for. Sometimes we were taken before Magistrates and fined for losing shirts that we had never seen. On the other hand, we were making money, and even after sending home $3 a week I was able to save about $15. When the railroad construction gang moved on we went with them. The men were rough and prejudiced against us, but not more so than in the big Eastern cities. It is only lately in New York that the Chinese have been able to discontinue putting wire screens in front of their windows, and at the present time the street boys are still breaking the windows of Chinese laundries all over the city, while the police seem to think it a joke.

We were three years with the railroad, and then went to the mines, where we made plenty of money in gold dust, but had a hard time, for many of the miners were wild men who carried revolvers and after drinking would come into our place to shoot and steal shirts, for which we had to pay. One of these men hit his head hard against a flat iron and all the miners came and broke up our laundry, chasing us out of town. They were going to hang us. We lost all our property and $365 in money, which members of the mob must have found.

Luckily most of our money was in the hands of Chinese bankers in San Francisco. I drew $500 and went East to Chicago, where I had a laundry for three years, during which I increased my capital to $2,500. After that I was four years in Detroit. I went home to China in 1897, but returned in 1898, and began a laundry business in Buffalo. But Chinese laundry business now is not as good as it was ten years ago. American cheap labor in the steam laundries had hurt it. So I determined to become a general merchant, and with this idea I came to New York and opened a shop in the Chinese quarter. . . .

The ordinary laundry shop is generally divided into three rooms. In front is the room where the customers are received, behind that a bedroom and in the back the work shop, which is also the dining room and kitchen. The stove and cooking utensils are the same as those of the Americans.

Work in a laundry begins early on Monday morning—about seven o'clock. There are generally two men, one of whom washes while the other does the ironing. The man who irons does not start in till Tuesday, as the clothes are not ready for him to begin till that time. So he has Sundays and Mondays as holidays. The man who does the washing finishes up on Friday night, and so he has Saturday and Sunday. Each works only five days a week, but those are long days—from seven o'clock in the morning till midnight.

During his holidays the Chinaman gets a good deal of fun out of life. There's a good deal of gambling and some opium smoking, but not so much as Americans imagine. Only a few of New York's Chinamen smoke opium. The habit is very general among rich men and the officials in China, but not so much among poor men. I don't think it does as much harm as the liquor that the Americans drink. There's nothing so bad as a drunken man. Opium doesn't make people crazy. . . .

The fights among the Chinese and the operations of the hatchet men are all due to gambling. Newspapers often say that there are feuds between the six companies, but that is a mistake. The six companies are purely benevolent societies, which look after the Chinaman when he first lands here. They represent the six southern provinces of China, where most of our people are from, and they are like the German, Swedish, English, Irish and Italian societies which assist emigrants. When the Chinese keep clear of gambling and opium they are not blackmailed, and they have no trouble with hatchet men or any others.

About 500 of New York's Chinese are Christians, the others are Buddhists, Taoists, etc., all mixed up. These haven't any Sunday of their own, but keep New Year's Day and the first and fifteenth days of each month, when they go to the temple in Mott Street.

In all New York there are only thirty-four Chinese women, and it is impossible to get a Chinese woman out here unless one goes to China and marries her there, and then he must collect affidavits to prove that she really is his wife. That is in case of a merchant. A laundryman can't bring his wife here under any circumstances, and even the women of the Chinese Ambassador's family had trouble getting in lately.

Is it any wonder, therefore, or any proof of the demoralization of our people if some of the white women in Chinatown are not of good character? What other set of men so isolated and so surrounded by alien and prejudiced people are more moral? Men, wherever they may be, need the society of women, and among the white women of Chinatown are many excellent and faithful wives and mothers. . . .

I have found out, during my residence in this country, that much of the Chinese prejudice against Americans is unfounded, and I no longer put faith in the wild tales that were told about them in our village, tho some of the Chinese, who have been here twenty years and who are learned men, still believe that there is no marriage in this country, that the land is infested with demons and that all the people are given over to general wickedness.

I know better. Americans are not all bad, nor are they wicked wizards. Still, they have their faults, and their treatment of us is outrageous.

The reason why so many Chinese go into the laundry business in this country is because it requires little capital and is one of the few opportunities that are open. Men of other nationalities who are jealous of the Chinese, because he is a more faithful worker than one of their people, have raised such a great outcry about Chinese cheap labor that they have shut him out of working on farms or in factories or building railroads or making streets or digging sewers. He cannot practice any trade, and his opportunities to do business are limited to his own countrymen. So he opens a laundry when he quits domestic service.

The treatment of the Chinese in this country is all wrong and mean. It is persisted in merely because China is not a fighting nation. The Americans would not dare to treat Germans, English, Italians or even Japanese as they treat the Chinese, because if they did there would be a war.

There is no reason for the prejudice against the Chinese. The cheap labor cry was always a falsehood. Their labor was never cheap, and is not cheap now. It has always commanded the highest market price. But the trouble is that the Chinese are such excellent and faithful workers that bosses will have no others when they can get them. If you look at men working on the street you will find an overseer for every four or five of them. That watching is not necessary for Chinese. They work as well when left to themselves as they do when some one is looking at them.

It was the jealousy of laboring men of other nationalities—especially the Irish—that raised all the outcry against the Chinese. No one would hire an Irishman, German, Englishman or Italian when he could get a Chinese, because our countrymen are so much more honest, industrious, steady, sober and painstaking. Chinese were persecuted, not for their vices, but for their virtues. There never was any honesty in the pretended fear of leprosy or in the cheap labor scare, and the persecution continues still, because Americans make a mere practice of loving justice. They are all for money making, and they want to be on the strongest side always. They treat you as a friend while you are prosperous, but if you have a misfortune they don't know you. There is nothing substantial in their friendship. . . .

Irish fill the almshouses and prisons and orphan asylums, Italians are among the most dangerous of men, Jews are unclean and ignorant. Yet they are all let in, while Chinese, who are sober, or duly law abiding, clean, educated and industrious, are shut out. There are few Chinamen in jails and none in the poor houses. There are no Chinese tramps or drunkards. Many Chinese here have become sincere Christians, in spite of the persecution which they have to endure from their heathen countrymen. More than half the Chinese in this country would become citizens if allowed to do so, and would be patriotic Americans. But how can they make this country their home as matters now are! They are not allowed to bring wives here from China, and if they marry American women there is a great outcry.

All Congressmen acknowledge the injustice of the treatment of my people, yet they continue it. They have no backbone.

Under the circumstances, how can I call this my home, and how can any one blame me if I take my money and go back to my village in China?

New York

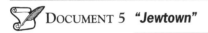

DOCUMENT 5 *"Jewtown"*

Jacob Riis

Thrift is the watchword of Jewtown, as of its people the world over. It is at once its strength and its fatal weakness, its cardinal virtue and its foul disgrace. Become an overmastering passion with these people who come here in droves from Eastern Europe to escape persecution, from which freedom could be bought only with gold, it has enslaved them in bondage worse than that from which they fled. Money is their God. Life itself is of little value compared with even the leanest bank account. In no other spot does life wear so intensely bald and materialistic an aspect as in Ludlow Street. Over and over again I have met with instances of these Polish or Russian Jews deliberately starving themselves to the point of physical exhaustion, while working night and day at a tremendous pressure to save a little money. An avenging Nemesis pursues this headlong hunt for wealth; there is no worse paid class anywhere. . . .

Penury and poverty are wedded everywhere to dirt and disease, and Jewtown is no exception. It could not well be otherwise in such crowds, considering especially their low intellectual status. The managers of the Eastern Dispensary, which is in the very heart of their district, told the whole story when they said: "The diseases these people suffer from are not due to intemperance or immorality, but to ignorance, want of suitable food, and the foul air in which they live and work." The homes of the Hebrew quarter are its workshops also. Reference will be made to the economic conditions under which they work in a succeeding chapter. Here we are concerned simply with the fact. You are made fully aware of it before you have travelled the length of a single block in any of these East Side streets, by the whir of a thousand sewing-machines, worked at high pressure from earliest dawn till mind and muscle give out together. Every member of the family, from the youngest to the oldest, bears a hand, shut in the qualmy rooms, where meals are cooked and clothing washed and dried besides, the live-long day. It is not unusual to find a dozen persons—men, women, and children—at work in a single small room. . . .

Oppression, persecution, have not shorn the Jew of his native combativeness one whit. He is as ready to fight for his rights, or what he considers his rights, in a business transaction—synonymous generally with his advantage—as if he had not been robbed of them for eighteen hundred years. One strong impression survives with him from his days of bondage: the power of the law. On the slightest provocation he rushes off to invoke it for his protection. . . .

In all matters pertaining to their religious life that tinges all their customs, they stand, these East Side Jews, where the new day that dawned on Calvary left them standing, stubbornly refusing to see the light. A visit to a Jewish house of mourning is like bridging the gap of two thousand years. The inexpressibly sad and sorrowful wail for the dead, as it swells and rises in the hush of all sounds of life, comes back from the ages like a mournful echo of the voice of Rachel "weeping for her children and refusing to be comforted, because they are not."

Attached to many of the synagogues, which among the poorest Jews frequently consist of a scantily furnished room in a rear tenement, with a few wooden stools or benches for the congregation, are Talmudic schools that absorb a share of the growing youth. The school-master is not rarely a man of some attainments who has been stranded there, his native instinct for money-making having been smothered in the process that has made of him a learned man. . . . But the majority of the children seek the public schools, where they are received sometimes with some misgivings on the part of the teachers, who find it necessary to inculcate lessons of cleanliness in the worst cases by practical demonstration with wash-bowl and soap. "He took hold of the soap as if it were some animal," said one of these teachers to me after such an experiment upon a new pupil, "and wiped three fingers across his face. He called that washing." . . .

As scholars, the children of the most ignorant Polish Jew keep fairly abreast of their more favored playmates, until it comes to mental arithmetic, when they leave them behind with a bound. It is surprising to see how strong the instinct of dollars and cents is in them. They can count, and correctly, almost before they can talk.

DOCUMENT 6 *"A Cap Maker's Story"*

Rose Schneiderman

[Miss Schneiderman led the women capmakers in their recent successful strike for the union shop. She is a small, quiet, serious, good looking young woman of twenty years, already a member of the National Board, and fast rising in the labor world.

—*Editor.*]

My name is Rose Schneiderman, and I was born in some small city of Russian Poland. I don't know the name of the city, and have no memory of that part of my childhood. When I was about five years of age my parents brought me to this country and we settled in New York.

Sweatshop in Ludlow Street tenement, photograph by Jacob Riis. (Museum of the City of New York)

So my earliest recollections are of living in a crowded street among the East Side Jews, for we also are Jews.

My father got work as a tailor, and we lived in two rooms on Eldridge Street, and did very well, though not so well as in Russia, because mother and father both earned money, and here father alone earned the money, while mother attended to the house. There were then two other children besides me, a boy of three and one of five.

I went to school until I was nine years old, enjoying it thoroughly and making great progress, but then my father died of brain fever and mother was left with three children and another one coming. So I had to stay at home to help her and she went out to look for work.

A month later the baby was born, and mother got work in a fur house, earning about $6 a week and afterward $8 a week, for she was clever and steady.

I was the house worker, preparing the meals and looking after the other children—the baby, a little girl of six years, and a boy of nine. I managed very well, tho the meals were not very elaborate. I could cook simple things like porridge, coffee and eggs, and mother used to prepare the meat before she went away in the morning, so that all I had to do was to put it in the pan at night. . . .

I was finally released by my little sister being taken by an aunt, and the two boys going to the Hebrew Orphan Asylum, which is a splendid institution, and turns out good men. One of these brothers is now a student in the City College, and the other is a page in the Stock Exchange.

When the other children were sent away mother was able to send me back to school, and I stayed in this school (Houston Street Grammar) till I had reached the Sixth Grammar Grade.

Then I had to leave in order to help support the family. I got a place in Hearn's as a cash girl, and after working there three weeks changed to Ridley's, where I remained for two and a half years. I finally left because the pay was so very poor and there did not seem to be any chance of advancement, and a friend told me that I could do better making caps.

So I got a place in the factory of Hein & Fox. The hours were from 8 A.M. to 6 P.M., and we made all sorts of linings—or, rather, we stitched in the linings—golf caps, yachting caps, etc. It was piece work, and we received from 3 1/2 cents to 10 cents a dozen, according to the different grades. By working hard we could make an average of about $5 a week. We would have made more but had to provide our own machines, which cost us $45, we paying for them on the installment plan. We paid $5 down and $1 a month after that.

I learned the business in about two months, and then made as much as the others, and was consequently doing quite well when the factory burned down, destroying all our machines—150 of them. This was very hard on the girls who had paid for their machines. It was not so bad for me, as I had only paid a little of what I owed.

The bosses got $500,000 insurance, so I heard, but they never gave the girls a cent to help them bear their losses. I think they might have given them $10, anyway.

Soon work went on again in four lofts, and a little later I became assistant sample maker. This is a position which, tho coveted by many, pays better in glory than in cash. It was still piece work, and tho the pay per dozen was better the work demanded was of a higher quality, and one could not rush through samples as through the other caps. So I still could average only about $5 per week.

After I had been working as a cap maker for three years it began to dawn on me that we girls needed an organization. The men had organized already, and had gained some advantages, but the bosses had lost nothing, as they took it out of us.

We were helpless; no one girl dare stand up for anything alone. Matters kept getting worse. The bosses kept making reductions in our pay, half a cent a dozen at a time. It did not sound important, but at the end of the week we found a difference.

We didn't complain to the bosses; we didn't say anything except to each other. There was no use. The bosses would not pay any attention unless we were like the men and could make them attend.

One girl would say that she didn't think she could make caps for the new price, but another would say that she thought she could make up for the reduction by working a little harder, and then the first would tell herself:

"If she can do it, why can't I?"

They didn't think how they were wasting their strength.

A new girl from another shop got in among us. She was Miss Bessie Brout, and she talked organization as a remedy for our ills. She was radical and progressive, and she stimulated thoughts which were already in our minds before she came.

Finally Miss Brout and I and another girl went to the National Board of United Cloth Hat and Cap Makers when it was in session, and asked them to organize the girls.

They asked us:

"How many of you are there willing to be organized?"

"In the first place about twelve," we said. We argued that the union label would force the bosses to organize their girls, and if there was a girls' union in existence the bosses could not use the union label unless their girls belonged to the union.

We were told to come to the next meeting of the National Board, which we did, and then received a favorable answer, and were asked to bring all the girls who were willing to be organized to the next meeting, and at the next meeting, accordingly, we were there twelve strong and were organized.

When Fox found out what had happened he discharged Miss Brout, and probably would have discharged me but that I was a sample maker and not so easy to replace. In a few weeks we had all the girls in the organization, because the men told the girls that they must enter the union or they would not be allowed to work in the shop.

Then came a big strike. Price lists for the coming season were given in to the bosses, to which they did not agree. After some wrangling a strike was declared in five of the biggest factories. There are 30 factories in the city. About 100 girls went out.

The result was a victory, which netted us—I mean the girls—$2 increase in our wages on the average.

All the time our union was progressing very nicely. There were lectures to make us understand what trades unionism is and our real position in the labor movement. I read upon the subject and grew more and more interested, and after a time I became a member of the National Board, and had duties and responsibilities that kept me busy after my day's work was done.

But all was not lovely by any means, for the bosses were not at all pleased with their beating and had determined to fight us again.

They agreed among themselves that after the 26th of December, 1904, they would run their shops on the "open" system.

This agreement was reached last fall, and soon notices, reading as follows, were hung in the various shops:

Notice

After the 26th of December, 1904, this shop will be run on the open shop system, the bosses having the right to engage and discharge employees as they see fit, whether the latter are union or nonunion.

Of course, we knew that this meant an attack on the union. The bosses intended gradually to get rid of us, employing in our place child labor and raw immigrant girls who would work for next to nothing.

On December 22d the above notice appeared, and the National Board, which had known about it all along, went into session prepared for action.

Our people were very restive, saying that they could not sit under that notice, and that if the National Board did not call them out soon they would go out of themselves.

At last word was sent out, and at 2:30 o'clock all the workers stopped, and, laying down their scissors and other tools, marched out, some of them singing the "Marseillaise."

We were out for thirteen weeks, and the girls established their reputation. They were on picket duty from seven o'clock in the morning till six o'clock in the evening, and gained over many of the nonunion workers by appeals to them to quit working against us.

Our theory was that if properly approached and talked to few would be found who would resist our offer to take them into our organization. No right thinking person desires to injure another. We did not believe in violence and never employed it.

During this strike period we girls each received $3 a week; single men $3 a week, and married men $5 a week. This was paid us by the National Board.

We were greatly helped by the other unions, because the open shop issue was a tremendous one, and this was the second fight which the bosses had conducted for it.

Their first was with the tailors, whom they beat. If they now could beat us the outlook for unionism would be bad.

Some were aided and we stuck out, and won a glorious victory all along the line. That was only last week. The shops are open now for all union hands and for them only. . . .

The bosses try to represent this open shop issue as tho they were fighting a battle for the public, but really it is nothing of the sort. The open shop is a weapon to break the unions and set men once more cutting each other's throats by individual competition.

Why, there was a time in the cap trade when men worked fourteen hours a day, and then took the heads of their machines home in bags and setting them up on stands, put mattresses underneath to deaden the sound and worked away till far into the morning.

We don't want such slavery as that to come back.

The shops are open now for all union people, and all nonunion people can join the union. In order to take in newcomer foreigners we have for them cut the initiation fees down to one-half what we Americans have to pay, and we trust them till they get work and their wages.

In order to give the newcomers a chance we have stopped night work, which doesn't suit the bosses, because it causes them to pay more rent when they can't use their buildings night and day. It costs them the price of another loft instead of costing the workers their health and lives as in the old days.

Our trade is well organized, we have won two victories and are not going backward.

But there is much to be done in other directions. The shop girls certainly need organization, and I think that they ought to be easy to organize, as their duties are simple and regular and they have a regular scale of wages.

Many saleswomen on Grand and Division streets, and, in fact, all over the East Side, work from 8 A.M. till 9 P.M. week days, and one-half a day on Sundays for $5 and $6 a week; so they certainly need organization.

The waitresses also could easily be organized, and perhaps the domestic servants. I don't know about stenographers. I have not come in contact with them.

Women have proved in the late strike that they can be faithful to an organization and to each other. The men give us the credit of winning the strike.

Certainly our organization constantly grows stronger, and the Woman's Trade Union League makes progress.

The girls and women by their meetings and discussions come to understand and sympathize with each other, and more and more easily they act together.

It is the only way in which they can hope to hold what they now have or better present conditions.

Certainly there is no hope from the mercy of the bosses.

Each boss does the best he can for himself with no thought of the other bosses, and that compels each to gouge and squeeze his hands to the last penny in order to make a profit.

So we must stand together to resist, for we will get what we can take—just that and no more.

New York

POSTSCRIPT

In 1921, 1924, and 1927, Congress passed a series of laws to restrict the flow of immigrants. The legislation targeted southern and eastern Europeans, as well as Asians. These laws were woven out of several ideological strands: resurgent fundamentalist Protestantism perceived Catholics as a major threat; immigrants were associated with important strikes and radical movements of the post-World War I period and so were targeted as un-American; and citizens from old families grew increasingly concerned about the so-called dilution of American stock, upholding their Anglo-Saxon ancestry as the key to national greatness. This last was a particularly insidious form of racism and was uppermost in Joseph Pennell's thinking. Whereas Jacob Riis would reform the immigrants into Americans, the new trend was toward exclusion. By the late 1920s, total immigration was capped at about one-quarter million per year, with western and northern Europe receiving much higher quotas than countries from the east or the south. Immigration did not reemerge as a vital factor in American life until the last decades of the twentieth century, when new migrants, especially from Latin America and Asia, poured in in numbers comparable to those of the late nineteenth and early twentieth centuries.

QUESTIONS

Defining Terms
Identify in the context of the chapter each of the following:

chain migrations   *How the Other Half Lives*
Little Italy   bootblack
padrone   Chinatown
Kong-foo-tsze   Rose Schneiderman
East Side Jews   Joseph Pennell

Probing the Sources

1. What was daily work like for the immigrants you have read about? Give details.
2. How did Riis describe the various immigrant groups? Did he use stereotypes that are still current today?
3. How did Corresca, Lee, and Schneiderman differ in their memories of their homelands? In their attitudes toward America? What do you think accounted for the differences?
4. What role did the family play in the lives of these people?
5. Compare Riis's depictions of immigrant groups with the interviews.

Interpreting the Sources

1. How do you think these three immigrants would have defined success? Had they achieved it by their own standards? By the standards of the larger society?
2. To what extent did the immigrants consider themselves American? To what extent Chinese, Italian, or Jewish?
3. How were the three immigrants whose life stories you read typical or atypical?
4. How and why did the lives of immigrant men and women differ?

ADDITIONAL READING

The classic work on nativism is John Higham's *Strangers in the Land: Patterns of American Nativism, 1860–1925* (1955). Oscar Handlin's *The Uprooted: The Epic Story of the Great Migration That Made the American People* (1951) remains a moving study of the pressures immigrants felt to abandon their native cultures. More recent studies, however, have emphasized ethnic groups' success in community building. For examples, see Irving Howe, *World of Our Fathers* (1976); and Ronald Takaki, *Strangers from a Different Shore: A History of Asian Americans* (1989). For a marvelous immigrant autobiography, try Marie Hall Ets, ed., *Rosa: The Life of an Italian Immigrant* (1970). For a survey of the diverse peoples' experiences, see Stephan Thernstrom, ed., *The Harvard Encyclopedia of American Ethnic Groups* (1980). For a fine anthology of women's writings, see Ellen Dubois and Vicki Ruiz, eds., *Unequal Sisters* (1990). A synthesis of multiculturalism is Ronald Takaki, *A Different Mirror* (1993). Finally, see Matthew Frye Jacobson, *Special Sorrows* (1992), and Jacobson, *Whiteness of a Different Color* (1999).

Building an Empire
America and the Philippines

HISTORICAL CONTEXT

Woodrow Wilson once declared Theodore Roosevelt "the most dangerous man of the age." Mark Twain called him "clearly insane," and added that Roosevelt was "insanest upon war and its supreme glories." Yet Roosevelt exercised an almost magical pull on the imagination of Americans. He was the very embodiment of energy. Even as president, he boxed and wrestled in the White House, took grueling cross-country hikes, and, after he stepped down from the presidency in 1909, went on a long hunting safari in Africa. Small and anemic as a child, he had whipped his body into shape with strenuous rounds of swimming, calisthenics, and gymnastics. At Harvard in the 1870s he was known for his sheer doggedness, if not his raw talent, as an athlete. Descriptions of his speeches as governor of New York in the 1890s refer endlessly to how his hands chopped the air, his body danced, his voice bristled, and his eyeglasses flashed. If, as the historian John Higham claims, there was a vigorous new spirit and an upbeat tempo in turn-of-the-century America, then Theodore Roosevelt was its embodiment.

One thing Roosevelt was not, however, was an example of the rags-to-riches mythology of American culture. He was born in 1858 to one of the wealthiest families in New York City, heirs to a Dutch fortune as old as the colony itself. Yet wealth did not confer ease. Like many men and women born to elite, or Brahmin, families, as they were known, privilege meant responsibility, a Calvinist sense of stewardship in which the "elect" must help take care of the less fortunate. Roosevelt grew up in a family of jurists, public servants, and philanthropists, and he was imbued early with a powerful sense of social duty.

The selections by Roosevelt in this chapter are from essays that he wrote in the years just before he became president. Read carefully, they give a sense of many of his underlying assumptions and values, what we might call his *ideology*. Ideology includes a person's or a society's fundamental beliefs about how the world is structured and what the relationship of individuals or nations to each other should be; it also includes their beliefs about the uses of power and the very nature of the social order.

For example, a simple statement such as "In America, any man can become president" is ideological. In the most literal sense, it is a true statement, for any native-born male who is not a felon and is over the age of thirty-five *can* run for the office of president; no legal barriers stand in his way. But usually when people use this phrase, they mean something more. They are expressing an ideal of equality, the faith that a person's own drive and talent are the keys to advancement in this society. To say that any man can become president is shorthand for the American dream, the belief that this nation offers equal and virtually unlimited opportunity for all and that such openness is one of the greatest things about our country.

Ideological statements, however, even as they purport to describe reality, tend to confuse the way things are with the way we would like them to be. For example, the phrase "any *man* can become president" already has inequality built into it, for it excludes women, over half of the population. This raises a question: Is the statement that any man can become president intended to be an expression of fact or of a hoped-for condition? Presidents have historically tended to be white males from upper-middle-class or wealthy families whose ethnic backgrounds were British and Protestant.

While America has provided considerable opportunity for social and economic mobility, that opportunity has never been equally distributed among all groups of citizens. Over the decades, some individuals have made dramatic leaps up and down in power and wealth, but recent research in social history shows that most Americans make only modest gains or losses in their class status across the generations. To put it concretely, the son of a small-town banker has a much better chance of becoming wealthy than the son of an Appalachian coal miner or the daughter of a black inner-city mail carrier. So the statement that any man can become president is an ideological one; behind its literal truth there is an *idealized* picture of the way American society works and a very loud silence about excluded groups. Ideological statements like this one invite us to question how closely historical reality approaches the social ideal.

American foreign policy at the end of the nineteenth century became a focus of deep ideological tensions. As the country grew increasingly involved in overseas business and military ventures, Americans debated the proper place of a democracy in a world divided between imperial powers and their colonies. Just as in the Mexican War a half century earlier, the conflicts at the end of the nineteenth century had grown out of the presence of the old Spanish Empire in the Western Hemisphere.

Cuba lies less than one hundred miles off the Florida coast. Before the Civil War, southerners coveted the island as an extension of the slave empire. For decades, the Cuban people had sought their independence from Spain in a series of rebellions, and a new round of insurgency and repression beginning in 1895 brought a wave of American sympathy for the rebels. American newspapers whipped up sentiment for the underdog Cubans, as Spain moved to crush the uprising. Moreover, large American companies had invested millions of dollars in Cuban sugar plantations, and these companies wanted to secure stable markets against political upheaval. President William McKinley resisted calls for American intervention until 1898. The revelation of a secret cable by the Spanish minister to the United States calling McKinley weak and hypocritical, followed by the mysterious blowing up of the United States battleship *Maine,* docked in Havana harbor (262 sailors perished on the ship sent to Cuba to protect Americans), made the pressure for American intervention irresistible. McKinley asked Congress for a declaration of war.

The war was popular, quick, and glorious. The Spanish colonies of Cuba, Guam, Puerto Rico, and the Philippines all fell with only a few hundred American battle deaths (though over five thousand died of tropical diseases). Naval confrontations in Santiago Bay and Manila Bay were even more decisive, as American ships destroyed the Spanish fleet while sustaining minimal damage and casualties.

With victory came controversy. By August 1898, an armistice had ended hostilities, but within half a year, Filipinos and Americans—former allies—were locked in war with each other. The Treaty of Paris between Spain and the United States ceded all seven thousand islands of the Philippine archipelago to the United States, in exchange for $20 million. Philippine rebels were not willing to trade Spain's domination for America's. By February 1899, Congress had approved the treaty with Spain, McKinley was on the verge of calling for Philippine annexation, and a bloody two-year struggle had begun. Before it was over, more than 100,000 Americans served in the Philippines; over 4,000 of them were killed, and another 3,000 were wounded. Nearly 20,000 Filipinos were killed in combat, and ten times that number died of starvation and disease, as the American military pursued a policy of burning villages and destroying farms.

Those Americans who opposed annexation were never a majority, but they were very vocal and included such diverse people as Andrew Carnegie, Jane Addams, William Jennings Bryan, Mark Twain, Samuel Gompers, and former presidents Harrison and Cleveland. Their arguments ranged widely. Friends of unions worried that new territories would only supply a cheap source of labor that would undercut American workers. Racists like Senator Ben Tillman of South Carolina argued that freeing Spain's colonies was a patriotic act, but that annexing those territories to the United States would not only defy our democratic principles but contaminate American blood with inferior racial stock. Still others argued that an empire would overextend an already troubled American economy, or that it would dangerously expand the powers of the presidency, or that a colonial empire simply could not be reconciled with deep American principles of freedom and self-determination. Proponents of overseas expansion argued that other imperial powers would seize the islands if we failed to, that America was obliged to civilize and Christianize "inferior" peoples, that an empire would open new markets and bring prosperity to all, and that overseas expansion would bring glory and honor to the military.

THE DOCUMENTS

The following documents are filled with ideological positions on politics, foreign policy, labor, gender, race, and ethnicity. As you read these selections, try to uncover their authors' underlying ideological assumptions. What were their social ideals? How did they believe groups interacted or ought to interact? With what tone did they address their audience, and who was that audience?

Introduction to Documents 1 and 2

Albert J. Beveridge was elected Republican senator from Indiana in 1898, when he was just thirty-six years old. The following speech, "The March of the Flag," was delivered first in Indianapolis in September 1898, after the victory over Spain but before the Treaty of Paris ceding the Philippines to the United States. Beveridge's speech became a kind of manifesto of American expansionism during this era; it was widely reprinted. Note how seamlessly he merged America's God-given mission in the world to elevate those less "civilized" than ourselves, the almost mystical spread of freedom wherever the American flag waved, the need for the United States to compete with other imperial powers, and the benefits (moral as well as economic) of opening up new overseas markets. And all were part of a historical pageant of progress from Bunker Hill to Manila Bay. Beveridge gave this speech countless times.

William Graham Sumner, on the contrary, viewed recent events as a betrayal of all that America stood for. Sumner was a professor of sociology at Yale and one of the best-known intellectuals of his day. He had popularized the concept of social Darwinism in America, which held that social groups—nations, classes, businesses—competed for resources, and that, on balance, the most fit among them lived and the weakest perished, ensuring progress through the survival of the strong. Sumner's assumption was that social evolution, like natural selection, created the greatest good for the greatest number, cruel as that process might appear.

Sumner's was an austere view of history's unfolding, but since he assumed that people would wield force in hurtful ways, he advocated limiting the power of institutions. He believed that different peoples had their own values, beliefs, and patterns of interacting—their own folkways, as he called them—and that social life ran as smoothly as possible when these local ways were respected and kept uncontaminated by others. Sumner's ideas could lead in two directions: to an acceptance of provincialism, and even racism and nativism, but also to a hands off policy toward foreign lands. We are not like other people, he declared; we do not understand them and cannot improve them; colonization could only contaminate both cultures and bring on the hatred of those whom we subjugate. Sumner was deeply suspicious of government's tendency to acquire more and more power, and many conservative politicians, especially in the South and the West, agreed with him. The speech "The Conquest of the United States by Spain" was a Phi Beta Kappa address at Yale given in 1898, almost simultaneously with Beveridge's address. What might these two men have said to each other in a debate?

DOCUMENT 1 *"The March of the Flag"*

Albert J. Beveridge

It is a noble land that God has given us; a land that can feed and clothe the world; a land whose coastlines would inclose half the countries of Europe; a land set like a sentinel between the two imperial oceans of the globe, a greater England with a nobler destiny.

It is a mighty people that He has planted on this soil; a people sprung from the most masterful blood of history; a people perpetually revitalized by the virile, man-producing working-folk of all the earth; a people imperial by virtue of their power, by right of their institutions, by authority of their Heaven-directed purposes—the propagandists and not the misers of liberty.

It is a glorious history our God has bestowed upon His chosen people; a history heroic with faith in our mission and our future. . . .

. . . Shall the American people continue their march toward the commercial supremacy of the world? Shall free institutions broaden their blessed reign as the children of liberty wax in strength, until the empire of our principles is established over the hearts of all mankind?

Have we no mission to perform, no duty to discharge to our fellow-man? Has God endowed us with gifts beyond our deserts and marked us as the people of His peculiar favor, merely to rot in our own selfishness, as men and nations must, who take cowardice for their companion and self for their deity—as China has, as India has, as Egypt has? . . .

The Opposition tells us that we ought not to govern a people without their consent. I answer, The rule of liberty that all just government derives its authority from the consent of the governed, applies only to those who are capable of self-government. We govern the Indians without their consent, we govern our territories without their consent, we govern our children without their consent. How do they know that our government would be without their consent? Would not the people of the Philippines prefer the just, humane, civilizing government of this Republic to the savage, bloody rule of pillage and extortion from which we have rescued them?

And, regardless of this formula of words made only for enlightened, self-governing people, do we owe no duty to the world? Shall we turn these peoples back to the reeking hands from which we have taken them? Shall we abandon them, with Germany, England, Japan, hungering for them? Shall we save them from those nations, to give them a self-rule of tragedy? . . .

The march of the flag! In 1789 the flag of the Republic waved over 4,000,000 souls in thirteen states, and their savage territory which stretched to the Mississippi, to Canada, to the Floridas. The timid minds of that day said that no new territory was needed, and, for the hour, they were right. But Jefferson, through whose intellect the centuries marched; Jefferson, who dreamed of Cuba as an American state; Jefferson, the first Imperialist of the Republic—Jefferson acquired that imperial territory which swept from the Mississippi to the mountains, from Texas to the British possessions, and the march of the flag began!

The infidels to the gospel of liberty raved, but the flag swept on! The title to that noble land out of which Oregon, Washington, Idaho and Montana have been carved was uncertain; Jefferson, strict constructionist of constitutional power though he was, obeyed the Anglo-Saxon impulse within him, whose watchword then and whose watchword throughout the world to-day is, "Forward!": another empire was added to the Republic, and the march of the flag went on!

Those who deny the power of free institutions to expand urged every argument, and more, that we hear, to-day; but the people's judgment approved the command of their blood, and the march of the flag went on!

A screen of land from New Orleans to Florida shut us from the Gulf, and over this and the Everglade Peninsula waved the saffron flag of Spain; Andrew Jackson seized both, the American people stood at his back, and, under Monroe, the Floridas came under the dominion of the Republic, and the march of the flag went on! The Cassandras prophesied every prophecy of despair we hear, to-day, but the march of the flag went on!

Then Texas responded to the bugle calls of liberty, and the march of the flag went on! And, at last, we waged war with Mexico, and the flag swept over the southwest, over peerless California, past the Gate of Gold to Oregon on the north, and from ocean to ocean its folds of glory blazed.

And, now, obeying the same voice that Jefferson heard and obeyed, that Jackson heard and obeyed, that Monroe heard and obeyed, that Seward heard and obeyed, that Grant heard and obeyed, that Harrison heard and obeyed, our President to-day plants the flag over the islands of the seas, outposts of commerce, citadels of national security, and the march of the flag goes on! . . .

But the Opposition is right—there is a difference. We did not need the western Mississippi Valley when we acquired it, nor Florida, nor Texas, nor California, nor the royal provinces of the far northwest. We had no emigrants to people this imperial wilderness, no money to develop it, even no highways to cover it. No trade awaited us in its savage fastnesses. Our productions were not greater than our trade. There was not one reason for the land-lust of our statesmen from Jefferson to Grant, other than the prophet and the

Saxon within them. But, to-day, we are raising more than we can consume, making more than we can use. Therefore we must find new markets for our produce.

And so, while we did not need the territory taken during the past century at the time it was acquired, we do need what we have taken in 1898, and we need it now. The resources and the commerce of these immensely rich dominions will be increased as much as American energy is greater than Spanish sloth. In Cuba, alone, there are 15,000,000 acres of forest unacquainted with the ax, exhaustless mines of iron, priceless deposits of manganese, millions of dollars' worth of which we must buy, to-day, from the Black Sea districts. There are millions of acres yet unexplored.

The resources of Porto Rico have only been trifled with. The riches of the Philippines have hardly been touched by the finger-tips of modern methods. And they produce what we consume, and consume what we produce—the very predestination of reciprocity—a reciprocity "not made with hands, eternal in the heavens." They sell hemp, sugar, co-coanuts, fruits of the tropics, timber of price like mahogany; they buy flour, clothing, tools, implements, machinery and all that we can raise and make. Their trade will be ours in time. Do you endorse that policy with your vote?

Cuba is as large as Pennsylvania, and is the richest spot on the globe. Hawaii is as large as New Jersey; Porto Rico half as large as Hawaii; the Philippines larger than all New England, New York, New Jersey and Delaware combined. Together they are larger than the British Isles, larger than France, larger than Germany, larger than Japan. . . .

So Hawaii furnishes us a naval base in the heart of the Pacific; the Ladrones another, a voyage further on; Manila another, at the gates of Asia—Asia, to the trade of whose hundreds of millions American merchants, manufacturers, farmers, have as good right as those of Germany or France or Russia or England; Asia, whose commerce with the United Kingdom alone amounts to hundreds of millions of dollars every year; Asia, to whom Germany looks to take her surplus products; Asia, whose doors must not be shut against American trade. Within five decades the bulk of Oriental commerce will be ours. . . .

Wonderfully has God guided us. Yonder at Bunker Hill and Yorktown His providence was above us. At New Orleans and on ensanguined seas His hand sustained us. Abraham Lincoln was His minister and His was the altar of freedom the Nation's soldiers set up on a hundred battle-fields. His power directed Dewey in the East and delivered the Spanish fleet into our hands, as He delivered the elder Armada into the hands of our English sires two centuries ago. . . . We can not fly from our world duties; it is ours to execute the purpose of a fate that has driven us to be greater than our small intentions. We can not re-treat from any soil where Providence has unfurled our banner; it is ours to save that soil for liberty and civilization.

DOCUMENT 2 *"The Conquest of the United States by Spain"*

William Graham Sumner

. . . Spain was the first, for a long time the greatest, of the modern imperialistic states. The United States, by its historical origin, its traditions, and its principles, is the chief representative of the revolt and reaction against that kind of state. I intend to show that, by the line of action now proposed to us, which we call expansion and imperialism, we are throwing away some of the most important elements of the American symbol and are adopting some of the most important elements of the Spanish symbol. We have beaten Spain in a military conflict, but we are submitting to be conquered by her on the field of ideas and policies. Expansionism and imperialism are nothing but the old philosophies of national prosperity which have brought Spain to where she now is. Those philosophies appeal to national vanity and national cupidity. They are seductive, especially upon the first view and the most superficial judgment, and therefore it cannot be denied that they are very strong for popular effect. They are delusions, and they will lead us to ruin unless we are hard-headed enough to resist them. . . .

There is not a civilized nation which does not talk about its civilizing mission just as grandly as we do. The English, who really have more to boast of in this respect than anybody else, talk least about it, but the Phariseeism with which they correct and instruct other people has made them hated all over the globe. The French believe themselves the guardians of the highest and purest culture, and that the eyes of all mankind are fixed on Paris, whence they expect oracles of thought and taste. The Germans regard themselves as charged with a mission, especially to us Americans, to save us from egoism and materialism. . . . Now each nation laughs at all the others when it observes these manifestations of national vanity. You may rely upon it that they are all ridiculous by virtue of these pretensions, including ourselves. The point is that each of them repudiates the standards of the others, and the outlying nations, which are to be civilized, hate all the standards of civilized men. We assume that what we like and practice, and what we think better, must come as a welcome blessing to Spanish-Americans and Filipinos. This is grossly and obviously untrue. They hate our ways. They are hostile to our ideas. Our religion, language, institutions, and manners offend them. They like their own ways, and if we appear amongst them as rulers, there will be social discord in all the great departments of social interest. The most important thing which we shall inherit from the Spaniards will be the task of suppressing rebellions. If the United States takes out of the hands of Spain her mission, on the ground that Spain is not executing it well, and if this nation in its turn attempts to be school-mistress to others, it will shrivel up into the same vanity and self-conceit of which Spain now presents an example. To read our current literature one would think that we were already well on the way to it. Now, the great reason why all these enterprises which begin by saying to somebody else, "We know what is good for you better than you know yourself and we are going to make you do it," are false and wrong is that they violate liberty; or, to turn the same statement into other words, the reason why liberty, of which we Americans talk so much, is a good thing is that it means leaving people to live out their own lives in their own way, while we do the same. If we believe in liberty, as an American principle, why do we not stand by it? Why are we going to throw it away to enter upon a Spanish policy of dominion and regulation? . . .

There are plenty of people in the United States to-day who regard negroes as human beings, perhaps, but of a different order from white men, so that the ideas and social arrangements of white men cannot be applied to them with propriety. Others feel the same way about Indians. This attitude of mind, wherever you meet with it, is what causes tyranny and cruelty. . . . The doctrine that all men are equal has come to stand as one of the corner-stones of the temple of justice and truth. It was set up as a bar to just this notion that we are so much better than others that it is liberty for them to be governed by us.

The Americans have been committed from the outset to the doctrine that all men are equal. We have elevated it into an absolute doctrine as a part of the theory of our social and political fabric. It has always been a domestic dogma in spite of its absolute form, and as a domestic dogma it has always stood in glaring contradiction to the facts about Indians and negroes and to our legislation about Chinamen. In its absolute form it must, of course, apply to Kanakas, Malays, Tagals, and Chinese just as much as to Yankees, Germans, and Irish. It is an astonishing event that we have lived to see American arms carry this domestic dogma out where it must be tested in its application to uncivilized and half-civilized peoples. At the first touch of the test we throw the doctrine away and adopt the Spanish doctrine. We are told by all the imperialists that these people are not fit for liberty and self-government; that it is rebellion for them to resist our beneficence; that we must send fleets and armies to kill them if they do it; that we must devise a government for them and administer it ourselves; that we may buy them or sell them as we please, and dispose of their "trade" for our own advantage. What is that but the policy of Spain to her dependencies? What can we expect as a consequence of it? Nothing but that it will bring us where Spain is now.

But then, if it is not right for us to hold these islands as dependencies, you may ask me whether I think that we ought to take them into our Union, at least some of them, and let them help to govern us. Certainly not. . . . It is unwisdom to take into a State like this any foreign element which is not congenial to it. Any such element will act as a solvent upon it. Consequently we are brought by our new conquests face to face with this dilemma: we must either hold them as inferior possessions, to be ruled and exploited by us after the fashion of the old colonial system, or we must take them in on an equality with ourselves, where they will help to govern us and to corrupt a political system which they do not understand and in which they cannot participate. From that dilemma there is no escape except to give them independence and to let them work out their own salvation or go without it. . . .

Everywhere you go on the continent of Europe at this hour you see the conflict between militarism and industrialism. You see the expansion of industrial power pushed forward by the energy, hope, and thrift of men, and you see the development arrested, diverted, crippled, and defeated by measures which are dictated by military considerations. . . . It is militarism which is eating up all the products of science and art, defeating the energy of the population and wasting its savings. It is militarism which forbids the people to give their attention to the problems of their own welfare and to give their strength to the education and comfort of their children. It is militarism which is combating the grand efforts of science and art to ameliorate the struggle for existence. . . .

Now what will hasten the day when our present advantages will wear out and when we shall come down to the conditions of the older and densely populated nations? The answer is: war, debt, taxation, diplomacy, a grand governmental system, pomp, glory, a big army and navy, lavish expenditures, political jobbery—in a word, imperialism. . . .

Expansion and imperialism are at war with the best traditions, principles, and interests of the American people. . . . They will plunge us into a network of difficult problems and political perils, which we might have avoided, while they offer us no corresponding advantage in return. . . . Three years ago we were on the verge of a law to keep immigrants out who were not good enough to be in with us. Now we are going to take in eight million barbarians and semi-barbarians, and we are paying twenty million dollars to get them. . . . That is the great fundamental cause of what I have tried to show throughout this lecture, that we cannot govern dependencies consistently with our political system, and that, if we try it, the State which our fathers founded will suffer a reaction which will transform it into another empire just after the fashion of all the old ones. That is what imperialism means. That is what it will be; and the democratic republic, which has been, will stand in history, like the colonial organization of earlier days, as a mere transition form. . . .

My patriotism is of the kind which is outraged by the notion that the United States never was a great nation until in a petty three months' campaign it knocked to pieces a poor, decrepit, bankrupt old state like Spain. To hold such an opinion as that is to abandon all American standards, to put shame and scorn on all that our ancestors tried to build up here, and to go over to the standards of which Spain is a representative.

Introduction to Document 3

Theodore Roosevelt was one of the most aggressive advocates of overseas empire. He was part of a group of like-minded men who pushed for expansion, men such as Senator Henry Cabot Lodge, Admiral Alfred Thayer Mahan, and Brooks Adams, all from powerful and wealthy families. Not only did Roosevelt become the most prominent spokesman for freeing Cuba and the Philippines from Spanish rule, annexing Hawaii, and asserting American military might around the world, but as assistant secretary of the Navy in the late 1890s, he was in a position to build up American sea power and beat the drums of war from inside the government. When the Spanish-American War began, Roosevelt resigned his job, obtained a commission as colonel, raised a regiment known as the Rough Riders, and led his men in a bloody charge up San Juan Hill in Cuba. Document 3 is taken from Roosevelt's speech "The Strenuous Life," given to an audience of businessmen and local leaders at the Hamilton Club in Chicago on April 10, 1899. The very phrase "the strenuous life" became an emblem for the age of Roosevelt.

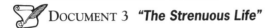 DOCUMENT 3 *"The Strenuous Life"*

Theodore Roosevelt

In speaking to you, men of the greatest city of the West, men of the State which gave to the country Lincoln and Grant, men who preeminently and distinctly embody all that is most American in the American character, I wish to preach, not the doctrine of ignoble ease, but the doctrine of the strenuous life, the life of toil and effort, of labor and strife; to preach that highest form of success which comes, not to the man who desires mere easy peace, but to the man who does not shrink from danger, from hardship, or from bitter toil, and who out of these wins the splendid ultimate triumph.

A life of slothful ease, a life of that peace which springs merely from lack either of desire or of power to strive after great things, is as little worthy of a nation as of an individual. I ask only that what every self-respecting American demands from himself and from his sons shall be demanded of the American nation as a whole. Who among you would teach your boys that ease, that peace, is to be the first consideration in their eyes—to be the ultimate goal after which they strive? . . . We do not admire the man of timid peace. We admire the man who embodies victorious effort; the man who never wrongs his neighbor, who is prompt to help a friend, but who has those virile qualities necessary to win the stern strife of actual life. . . . A mere life of ease is not in the end a very satisfactory life, and, above all, it is a life which ultimately unfits those who follow it for serious work in the world.

In the last analysis a healthy state can exist only when the men and women who make it up lead clean, vigorous, healthy lives; when the children are so trained that they shall endeavor, not to shirk difficulties, but to overcome them; not to seek ease, but to know how to wrest triumph from toil and risk. The man must be glad to do a man's work, to dare and endure and to labor; to keep himself, and to keep those dependent upon him. The woman must be the housewife, the helpmeet of the homemaker, the wise and fearless mother of many healthy children. . . . When men fear work or fear righteous war, when women fear motherhood, they tremble on the brink of doom; and well it is that they should vanish from the earth, where they are fit subjects for the scorn of all men and women who are themselves strong and brave and high-minded.

As it is with the individual, so it is with the nation. It is a base untruth to say that happy is the nation that has no history. Thrice happy is the nation that has a glorious history. Far better it is to dare mighty things, to win glorious triumphs, even though checkered by failure, than to take rank with those poor spirits who neither enjoy much nor suffer much, because they live in the gray twilight that knows not victory nor defeat. If in 1861 the men who loved the Union had believed that peace was the end of all things, and war and strife the worst of all things, and had acted up to their belief, we would have saved hundreds of thousands of lives, we would have saved hundreds of millions of dollars. Moreover, besides saving all the blood and treasure we then lavished, we would have prevented the heartbreak of many women, the dissolution of many homes, and we would have spared the country those months of gloom and shame when it seemed as if our armies marched only to defeat. We could have avoided all this suffering simply by shrinking from strife. And if we had thus avoided it, we would have shown that we were weaklings, and that we were unfit to stand among the great nations of the earth. Thank God for the iron in the blood of our fathers, the men who upheld the wisdom of Lincoln, and bore sword or rifle in the armies of Grant! Let us, the children of the men who proved themselves equal to the mighty days, let us, the children of the men who carried the great Civil War to a triumphant conclusion, praise the God of our fathers that the ignoble counsels of peace were rejected; that the suffering and loss, the blackness of sorrow and despair, were unflinchingly faced, and the years of strife endured; for in the end the slave was freed, the Union restored, and the mighty American republic placed once more as a helmeted queen among nations.

We of this generation do not have to face a task such as that our fathers faced, but we have our tasks, and woe to us if we fail to perform them! We cannot, if we would, play the part of China, and be content to rot by inches in ignoble ease within our borders, taking no interest in what goes on beyond them, sunk in a scrambling commercialism; heedless of the higher life, the life of aspiration, of toil and risk, busying ourselves only with the wants of our bodies for the day, until suddenly we should find, beyond a shadow of question, what China has already found, that in this world the nation that has trained itself to a career of unwarlike and isolated ease is bound, in the end, to go down before other nations which have not lost the manly and adventurous qualities. If we are to be a really great people, we must strive in good faith to play a great part in the world. We cannot avoid meeting great issues. All that we can determine for ourselves is whether we shall meet them well or ill. In 1898 we could not help being brought face to face with the problem of war with Spain. All we could decide was whether we should shrink like cowards from the contest, or enter into it as beseemed a brave and high-spirited people; and, once in, whether failure or success should crown our banners. So it is now. We cannot avoid the responsibilities that confront us in Hawaii, Cuba, Porto Rico, and the Philippines. All we can decide is whether we shall meet them in a way that will redound to the national credit, or whether we shall make of our dealings with these new problems a dark and shameful page in our history. To refuse to deal with them at all merely amounts to dealing with them badly. We have a given problem to solve. If we undertake the solution, there is, of course, always danger that we may not solve it aright; but to refuse to undertake the solution simply renders it certain that we cannot possibly solve it aright. The timid man, the lazy man, the man who distrusts his country, the over-civilized man, who has lost the great fighting, masterful virtues, the ignorant man, and the man of dull mind, whose soul is incapable of feeling the mighty lift that thrills "stern men with empires in their brains"—all these, of course, shrink from seeing the nation undertake its new duties; shrink from seeing us build a navy and an army adequate to our needs; shrink from seeing us do our share of the world's work, by bringing order out of chaos in the great, fair tropic islands from which the valor of our soldiers and sailors has driven the Spanish flag. These are the men who fear the strenuous life, who fear the only national life which is really worth leading. They believe in that cloistered life which saps the hardy virtues in a nation, as it saps them in the individual; or else they are wedded to that base spirit of gain and greed which recognizes in commercialism the be-all and end-all of national life, instead of realizing that, though an indispensable element, it is, after all, but one of the many elements that go to make up true national greatness. No country can long endure if its foundations are not laid deep in the material prosperity which comes from thrift, from business energy and enterprise, from hard, unsparing effort in the fields of industrial activity; but neither was any nation ever yet truly great if it relied upon material prosperity alone. All honor must be paid to the architects of our material prosperity, to the great captains of industry who have built our factories and our railroads, to the strong men who toil for wealth with brain or hand; for great is the debt of the nation to these and their kind. But our debt is yet greater to the men whose highest type is to be found in a states-man like Lincoln, a soldier like Grant. They showed by their lives that they recognized the law of work, the law of strife; they toiled to win a competence for themselves and those dependent upon them; but they recognized that there were yet other and even loftier duties—duties to the nation and duties to the race.

We cannot sit huddled within our own borders and avow ourselves merely an assem-blage of well-to-do hucksters who care nothing for what happens beyond. Such a policy would defeat even its own end; for as the nations grow to have ever wider and wider in-terests, and are brought into closer and closer contact, if we are to hold our own in the struggle for naval and commercial supremacy, we must build up our power without our own borders. We must build the isthmian canal, and we must grasp the points of vantage which will enable us to have our say in deciding the destiny of the oceans of the East and the West.

So much for the commercial side. From the standpoint of international honor the ar-gument is even stronger. The guns that thundered off Manila and Santiago left us echoes of glory, but they also left us a legacy of duty. If we drove out a mediæval tyranny only to make room for savage anarchy, we had better not have begun the task at all. It is worse than idle to say that we have no duty to perform, and can leave to their fates the islands we have conquered. Such a course would be the course of infamy. It would be followed at once by utter chaos in the wretched islands themselves. Some stronger, manlier power would have to step in and do the work, and we would have shown ourselves weaklings, unable to carry to successful completion the labors that great and high-spirited nations are eager to undertake. . . .

The problems are different for the different islands. Porto Rico is not large enough to stand alone. We must govern it wisely and well, primarily in the interest of its own peo-ple. Cuba is, in my judgment, entitled ultimately to settle for itself whether it shall be an independent state or an integral portion of the mightiest of republics. But until order and stable liberty are secured, we must remain in the island to insure them, and infinite tact, judgment, moderation, and courage must be shown by our military and civil representa-tives in keeping the island pacified, in relentlessly stamping out brigandage, in protecting all alike, and yet in showing proper recognition to the men who have fought for Cuban liberty. The Philippines offer a yet graver problem. Their population includes half-caste and native Christians, warlike Moslems, and wild pagans. Many of their people are utterly unfit for self-government, and show no signs of becoming fit. Others may in time become fit but at present can only take part in self-government under a wise supervision, at once firm and beneficent. We have driven Spanish tyranny from the islands. If we now let it be replaced by savage anarchy, our work has been for harm and not for good. I have scant pa-tience with those who fear to undertake the task of governing the Philippines, and who openly avow that they do fear to undertake it, or that they shrink from it because of the expense and trouble; but I have even scanter patience with those who make a pretense of humanitarianism to hide and cover their timidity, and who cant about "liberty" and the "consent of the governed," in order to excuse themselves for their unwillingness to play the part of men. Their doctrines, if carried out, would make it incumbent upon us to leave the Apaches of Arizona to work out their own salvation, and to decline to interfere in a single Indian reservation. Their doctrines condemn your forefathers and mine for ever having settled in these United States.

England's rule in India and Egypt has been of great benefit to England, for it has trained up generations of men accustomed to look at the larger and loftier side of public life. It has been of even greater benefit to India and Egypt. And finally, and most of all, it has advanced the cause of civilization. So, if we do our duty aright in the Philippines, we will add to that national renown which is the highest and finest part of national life, will greatly benefit the people of the Philippine Islands, and, above all, we will play our part well in the great work of uplifting mankind. But to do this work, keep ever in mind that we must show in a very high degree the qualities of courage, of honesty, and of good judgment. Resistance must be stamped out. The first and all-important work to be done is to establish the supremacy of our flag. We must put down armed resistance before we can accomplish anything else, and there should be no parleying, no faltering, in dealing with our foe. As for those in our own country who encourage the foe, we can afford contemptuously to disregard them; but it must be remembered that their utterances are not saved from being treasonable merely by the fact that they are despicable. . . .

I preach to you, then, my countrymen, that our country calls not for the life of ease but for the life of strenuous endeavor. The twentieth century looms before us big with the fate of many nations. If we stand idly by, if we seek merely swollen, slothful ease and ignoble peace, if we shrink from the hard contests where men must win at hazard of their lives and at the risk of all they hold dear, then the bolder and stronger peoples will pass us by, and will win for themselves the domination of the world. Let us therefore boldly face the life of strife, resolute to do our duty well and manfully; resolute to uphold righteousness by deed and by word; resolute to be both honest and brave, to serve high ideals, yet to use practical methods. Above all, let us shrink from no strife, moral or physical, within or without the nation, provided we are certain that the strife is justified, for it is only through strife, through hard and dangerous endeavor, that we shall ultimately win the goal of true national greatness.

Introduction to Document 4

Although most newspapers supported government policy, there was dissent. Document 4 consists of five newspaper articles that appeared in the summer of 1899, shortly after Roosevelt's "Strenuous Life" speech, during the height of the controversy following President McKinley's decision to annex the Philippines. The first, an editorial from the *New York Evening Post,* directly challenged Roosevelt's ideas. The second piece is from the *New Orleans Times Democrat,* and it suggested that the war threatened to become more costly and difficult than its supporters had admitted.

The article from the *Baltimore Sun* contains an interview with an American naval commander newly returned from the Philippines who denied that the Filipinos were either "barbaric" or "uncivilized." "The True American," which appeared in the *Springfield Republican,* again challenged Roosevelt and condemned expansion as a violation of American democratic ideals. The last article is actually an anonymous letter from a black soldier to the editor of the *New York Age*—an African-American newspaper—which expressed anger at the racism of white American troops toward the Filipinos. Taken together, these pieces give a good sense of how controversial the question of empire had become.

DOCUMENT 4 *Press Opposition to the War*

New York Evening Post

. . . Governor Roosevelt's recent speech in Chicago . . . glorified war and fighting as the only remedies of a nation against what he is fond of calling on all occasions "ignoble peace." . . . This is the gospel of war for the sake of war, of fighting, not merely or necessarily for a just and righteous and inevitable cause, but for the effect upon your own virility. Whatever you do, you must fight. The worst thing that can happen to a man or a nation is to remain long in peace. That is to become "despicable," "ignoble," "slothful," an object of contempt to yourself and to the world. This is the view of the savage, the barbarian. . . .

The Roosevelt view of life is essentially a boy's view, and if it were to become the permanent basis of a national policy would make us the most turbulent people the world has ever seen. Our national life would become one perpetual Donnybrook fair, with "rows" with every power that got within range of us, for no other purpose than the development of our "virile strength," lest we become a nation of sloths.

Happily there is no danger of such a future for us. Our governor is not taken seriously by anybody except himself when he talks "war." . . . So long as he insists upon favoring war as the chief end of man, without which the human race can make no progress towards what Admiral Sampson so well calls the "true living which we all long for," the people of this country will never trust him in a station in which he can carry out his views. . . .

New Orleans Times-Democrat

We are beginning to realize the fact—even the imperialists—that we have bought from Spain a very disagreeable guerilla war, in which there are no honors to win, but much loss, expense, and vexation of spirit. . . . As [the Philippines] is a land of swamps and mountains, an ideal country for guerilla warfare, with a malarial tropical climate disastrous to Americans, we can realize the bargain we bought from Spain. . . . It is time for us to count up the cost and see whether our Philippine bargain is worth what we are likely to pay for it before we get through, and then determine whether it would not be better to cease this war of McKinley's, which has accomplished so very little beyond showing the courage and fighting quality of our soldiers, and restore peace in the islands so as to allow their development, retaining such control over them that the United States would share in the prosperity and commerce that would come with peace and order.

Baltimore Sun

Commander John D. Ford, fleet engineer of the Asiatic station, reached his home, No. 1522 West Lanvale street, on Saturday morning before noon, after an absence of a year and a half, most of which period he spent on board the cruiser "Baltimore," in the bay of Manila. . . .

"The Filipinos pictured in the sensational papers are not the men we are fighting. They are entirely distinct and separate. The fellows we deal with out there are not ignorant savages, fighting with bows and arrows, but an intelligent, liberty-loving people, full of courage and determination. The idea that the Filipino is an uncivilized being is a mistaken one. Originally the natives of those islands sprang from Japanese stock, and are identically the same race, with a change of language and customs. There was a time when the feudal system prevailed in Manila, but no vestige now remains, and the savagery of the people is found only in the very lowest class. . . .

"What they are fighting for now is absolute and entire liberty. They don't want us there or over them, and in the course of time might wear out our patience entirely. An excellent postal and telegraph system is in existence, which we wish very much we could get hold of. While they fight for entire freedom, all they ask is a chance for life, liberty, and the pursuit of happiness, and they care not whether it be a republic of their own or some form devised for them by the great United States of North America. I see nothing promising in the struggle now or any hope of speedy success on our part, unless many more troops are sent out. . . .

Springfield [Massachusetts] Republican

What is an American—a true American? It is to be first of all, we conceive, a friend of liberty and self-government at home and abroad. . . . There is not only open and brazen renunciation of the fundamental doctrines which make a republic, but there is the assertion, no longer thinly disguised, that our democracy is called of God to police the world—and that in order to do this we must doff the garments of peaceful republicanism, put on an old-world uniform, and, in the graphic language of Governor Roosevelt, "see that the outburst of savagery" (that we have stirred up by outraging the spirit of liberty) "is repressed once for all." It is a relentless programme, and one impossible of execution. Repression of that sort never represses—but we need not discuss that now.

Our firm belief and expectation is that the people of the United States will, soon or late, stand where they always have stood—with Lincoln and not with Roosevelt. The one is an American and the other represents Anglo-Americanism, and there is not room here for both. We shall stick to the new-world type. As it was in 1776, it must be now, else we shall recant and fall away from the simple yet prophetic and sufficient faith of Washington and Lincoln. Shall we exalt militarism more than struggling freedom, power more than principle, and hold physical dominion higher than the moral sway and helpfulness that has made liberty, as we have practised it with all our imperfections, the light of the world?

New York Age

Editor, New York Age

I have mingled freely with the natives and have had talks with American colored men here in business and who have lived here for years, in order to learn of them the cause of their (Filipino) dissatisfaction and the reason for this insurrection, and I must confess they have a just grievance. All this never would have occurred if the army of occupation would have treated them as people. The Spaniards, even if their laws were hard, were polite and treated them with some consideration; but the Americans, as soon as they saw that the native troops were desirous of sharing in the glories as well as the hardships of the hard-won battles with the Americans, began to apply home treatment for colored peoples: curse them as damned niggers, steal [from] and ravish them, rob them on the street of their small change, take from the fruit vendors whatever suited their fancy, and kick the poor unfortunate if he complained, desecrate their church property, and after fighting began, looted everything in sight, burning, robbing the graves.

This may seem a little tall—but I have seen with my own eyes carcasses lying bare in the boiling sun, the results of raids on receptacles for the dead in search of diamonds. The [white] troops, thinking we would be proud to emulate their conduct, have made bold of telling their exploits to us. One fellow, member of the 13th Minnesota, told me how some fellows he knew had cut off a native woman's arm in order to get a fine inlaid bracelet. On upbraiding some fellows one morning, whom I met while out for a walk (I think they belong to a Nebraska or Minnesota regiment, and they were stationed on the Malabon road) for the conduct of the American troops toward the natives and especially as to raiding, etc., the reply was: "Do you think we could stay over here and fight these damn niggers without making it pay all it's worth? The government only pays us $13 per month: that's starvation wages. White men can't stand it." Meaning they could not live on such small pay. In saying this they never dreamed that Negro soldiers would never countenance such conduct. They talked with impunity of "niggers" to our soldiers, never once thinking that they were talking to home "niggers" and should they be brought to remember that at home this is the same vile epithet they hurl at us, they beg pardon and make some effeminate excuse about what the Filipino is called.

I want to say right here that if it were not for the sake of the 10,000,000 black people in the United States, God alone knows on which side of the subject I would be. And for

Wounded Filipinos in a U.S. army camp. (Library of Congress)

the sake of the black men who carry arms and pioneer for them as their representatives, ask them to not forget the present administration at the next election. Party be damned! We don't want these islands, not in the way we are to get them, and for Heaven's sake, put the party [Democratic] in power that pledged itself against this highway robbery. Expansion is too clean a name for it.

[Unsigned]

Introduction to Document 5

Document 5 is an address called "National Duties" given by Theodore Roosevelt at the Minnesota State Fair on September 2, 1901. Four days later, just six months after Roosevelt had assumed the vice presidency, President William McKinley was assassinated. In this speech, Roosevelt asserted America's obligation as a powerful democratic nation to bring civilization to others. What were Roosevelt's views on the role of war, the responsibilities of wealthy and powerful people like himself, and the limits of acceptable dissent? *Wounded Filipinos in a U.S. army camp. (Library of Congress)*

 Document 5 *"National Duties"*

Theodore Roosevelt

. . . Our country had been populated by pioneers, and therefore it has in it more energy, more enterprise, more expansive power than any other in the wide world. . . . The men who with ax in the forests and pick in the mountains and plow on the prairies pushed to completion the dominion of our people over the American wilderness have given the definite shape to our nation. They have shown the qualities of daring, endurance, and far-sightedness, of eager desire for victory and stubborn refusal to accept defeat, which go to make up the essential manliness of the American character. Above all, they have recognized in practical form the fundamental law of success in American life—the law of worthy work, the law of high, resolute endeavor. . . .

In the Philippines we have brought peace, and we are at this moment giving them such freedom and self-government as they could never under any conceivable conditions have obtained had we turned them loose to sink into a welter of blood and confusion, or to become the prey of some strong tyranny without or within. The bare recital of the facts is sufficient to show that we did our duty; and what prouder title to honor can a nation have than to have done its duty? We have done our duty to ourselves, and we have done the higher duty of promoting the civilization of mankind. The first essential of civilization is law. Anarchy is simply the handmaiden and forerunner of tyranny and despotism. Law and order enforced with justice and by strength lie at the foundations of civilization . . . There can be no weakening of the law-abiding spirit here at home, if we are permanently to succeed; and just as little can we afford to show weakness abroad. Lawlessness and anarchy were put down in the Philippines as a prerequisite to introducing the reign of justice.

Barbarism has, and can have, no place in a civilized world. It is our duty toward the people living in barbarism to see that they are freed from their chains, and we can free them only by destroying barbarism itself. The missionary, the merchant, and the soldier may each have to play a part in this destruction, and in the consequent uplifting of the people. Exactly as it is the duty of a civilized power scrupulously to respect the rights of all weaker civilized powers and gladly to help those who are struggling toward civilization, so it is its duty to put down savagery and barbarism . . . Not only in our own land, but throughout the world, throughout all history, the advance of civilization has been of incalculable benefit to mankind, and those through whom it has advanced deserve the highest honor. All honor to the missionary, all honor to the soldier, all honor to the merchant who now in our own day have done so much to bring light into the world's dark places.

Let me insist again, for fear of possible misconstruction, upon the fact that our duty is twofold, and that we must raise others while we are benefiting ourselves. In bringing order to the Philippines, our soldiers added a new page to the honor-roll of American history, and they incalculably benefited the islanders themselves. Under the wise administration of Governor Taft the islands now enjoy a peace and liberty of which they have hitherto never even dreamed. But this peace and liberty under the law must be supplemented by material, by industrial development. Every encouragement should be given to their commercial development, to the introduction of American industries and products; not merely because this will be a good thing for our people, but infinitely more because it will be of incalculable benefit to the people in the Philippines.

We shall make mistakes; and if we let these mistakes frighten us from our work we shall show ourselves weaklings. Half a century ago Minnesota and the two Dakotas were Indian hunting-grounds. We committed plenty of blunders, and now and then worse than blunders, in our dealings with the Indians. But who does not admit at the present day that we were right in wresting from barbarism and adding to civilization the territory out of which we have made these beautiful States? And now we are civilizing the Indian and putting him on a level to which he could never have attained under the old conditions.

In the Philippines let us remember that the spirit and not the mere form of government is the essential matter. The Tagalogs have a hundredfold the freedom under us that they would have if we had abandoned the islands. We are not trying to subjugate a people; we are trying to develop them and make them a law-abiding, industrious, and educated people, and we hope ultimately a self-governing people. In short, in the work we have done we are but carrying out the true principles of our democracy. . . . We gird up our loins as a nation, with the stern purpose to play our part manfully in winning the ultimate triumph; and therefore we turn scornfully aside from the paths of mere ease and idleness, and with unfaltering steps tread the rough road of endeavor, smiting down the wrong and battling for the right, as Greatheart smote and battled in Bunyan's immortal story.

Introduction to Document 6

The public debate over American annexation of the Philippines proved so heated that a special congressional committee was appointed to investigate the conduct of the war. Although the Committee on the Philippines (chaired by Senator Henry Cabot Lodge) was established in January 1900, hearings did not begin until two years later. The following two interviews, part of the investigation, give a sense of the conduct of the war, and of why it was so controversial. Robert P. Hughes was a brigadier general who commanded American troops in the Philippines at the turn of the century. Charles S. Riley had risen from private to first sergeant; he had served in the Philippines from October 1899 through March 1901.

 DOCUMENT 6   *Proceedings of the Congressional Committee on the Philippines*

Testimony of Robert P. Hughes

Sen. Rawlins: In burning towns, what would you do? Would the entire town be destroyed by fire or would only offending portions of the town be burned?

Gen. Hughes: I do not know that we ever had a case of burning what you would call a town in this country, but probably a barrio or a sitio; probably a half a dozen houses, native shacks, where the insurrectos would go in and be concealed, and if they caught a detachment passing they would kill some of them.

Sen. Rawlins: What did I understand you to say would be the consequences of that?

Gen. Hughes: They usually burned the village.

Sen. Rawlins: All of the houses in the village?

Gen. Hughes: Yes; every one of them.

Sen. Rawlins: What would become of the inhabitants?

Gen. Hughes: That was their lookout. . . . The destruction was as a punishment. . . .

Sen. Rawlins: The punishment in that case would fall, not upon the men, who could go elsewhere, but mainly upon the women and little children.

Gen. Hughes: The women and children are part of the family, and where you wish to inflict a punishment you can punish the man probably worse in that way than in any other.

Sen. Rawlins: But is that within the ordinary rules of civilized warfare? Of course you could exterminate the family, which would be still worse punishment.

Gen. Hughes: These people are not civilized.

Sen. Rawlins: But is that within the ordinary rules of civilized warfare?

Gen. Hughes: No; I think it is not.

Sen. Rawlins: You think it is not?

Sen. Dietrich: In order to carry on civilized warfare both sides have to engage in such warfare. . .

Testimony of Charles S. Riley

Q. During your service there [in the Philippine Islands] did you witness what is generally known as the water cure?—A. I did.

Q. When and where?—A. On November 27, 1900, in the town of Igbaras, Iloilo Province, Panay Island. . . .

The burning of civilian homes in Manila, 1899. (Library of Congress)

Q. You may state what you saw.—A. I saw the *presidente* standing in the—
Q. Whom do you mean by the presidente?—A. The head official of the town.
Q. The town of Igbaras?—A. Yes, sir.
Q. A Filipino?—A. Yes, sir.
Q. How old was he?—A. I should judge that he was a man of about forty or forty-five years.
Q. When you saw him, what was his condition?—A. He was stripped to the waist; he had nothing on but a pair of white trousers, and his hands were tied behind him. . . . He was then taken and placed under the tank, and the faucet was opened and a stream of water was forced down or allowed to run down his throat; his throat was held so he could not prevent swallowing the water, so that he had to allow the water to run into his stomach. . . .
Q. Was anything done besides forcing his mouth open and allowing the water to run down?—A. When he was filled with water it was forced out of him by pressing a foot on his stomach or else with their hands. . . .
Q. What had been his crime?—A. Information had been obtained from a native source as to his being an insurgent officer. After the treatment he admitted that he held the rank of captain in the insurgent army—an active captain. His police force, numbering twenty-five, were sworn insurgent soldiers. He was the *presidente* of the town and had been for a year, and he always showed himself to be friendly on the outside to the officers, and the men the same way.
Sen. Beveridge: But in reality—
The Witness: He was an insurgent officer and his men were insurgent soldiers. He acknowledged that, and his police acknowledged the same thing. When they took the oath as police they took the oath of an insurgent soldier.
The Chairman: Were they supposed to be friendly to the United States?
The Witness: They were; yes, sir.
Sen. Beveridge: That was a pretense?—A. Yes, sir.

Q. And this was during the time of active warfare?—A. Yes, sir; during the entire time he held the place as the *presidente* in that town.

Sen. Burrows: His offense was treachery to the American cause?—A. Yes, sir. . . .

POSTSCRIPT

Mark Twain returned to the United States in October 1900, after nearly a decade overseas. He had supported American intervention in Cuba, for he believed the war against Spain to be a selfless act of a free people intent on helping a neighbor gain its liberty. Yet as the new century approached, he looked with growing horror on America's ongoing presence in Cuba and its ugly guerrilla war in the Philippines. Twain became an outspoken anti-imperialist.

The cause elicited some of the most scathing words from his "pen warmed-up in hell," for Twain viewed imperial expansion, especially by America, as a betrayal of Christian and democratic ideals. On December 30, 1900, in the pages of the New York *Herald,* he greeted the new century with an attack on the role of churches and missionaries: "I bring you the stately matron named Christendom, returning bedraggled, besmirched and dishonored from pirate raids in Kiao-Chow, Manchuria, South Africa and the Philippines, with her soul full of meanness, her pockets full of boodle, and her mouth full of pious hypocrisies. Give her soap and a towel, but hide the looking glass."

For the next several years, Twain wrote a series of articles, open letters, and reviews condemning American overseas expansion. He turned away from his original notion of the Spanish-American War as a good cause gone bad and came to see expansionist rhetoric as a cynical cover for avarice. Soon imperialist spokesmen accused Twain of treason, a charge that redoubled his activities. Patriotism, he argued, consisted of following one's own conscience; Filipinos resisting the American invasion were patriots, while American jingoists were traitors to their own ideals.

One of Twain's angriest attacks on American policy in the Philippines came in the article, "To the Person Sitting in Darkness" (*North American Review,* February 1901):

> . . . We have crushed a deceived and confiding people; we have turned against the weak and the friendless who trusted us; we have stamped out a just and intelligent and well-ordered republic; we have stabbed an ally in the back and slapped the face of a guest . . . we have robbed a trusting friend of his land and his liberty; we have invited our clean young men to shoulder a discredited musket and do bandit's work under a flag which bandits have been accustomed to fear, not to follow; we have debauched America's honor and blackened her face before the world. . . .

Perhaps Twain's most despairing antiwar statement was published posthumously. "I have told the whole truth," he declared, "and only dead men can tell the truth in this world. It can be published after I am dead." "The War-Prayer" appeared six years after he died, in the November 1916 issue of *Harper's Monthly.* Twain describes a community preparing for war, with bands and parades swelling the patriotic fervor. On

Sunday before the troops leave for the front, the church is filled, and the preacher offers a prayer asking the Lord to bless the soldiers' efforts with victory.

Just as the minister finishes his supplication, an aged stranger with long white hair and robes that reach to the floor ascends the pulpit. He motions the preacher aside and addresses the congregation. He bears a message from the Almighty. God has heard their words and will grant their wishes, but they must know that with their spoken prayer has gone an unspoken one. ". . . O Lord, our God," he prays,

> "help us to tear their soldiers to bloody shreds with our shells; help us to cover their smiling fields with the pale forms of their patriot dead; help us to drown the thunder of the guns with shrieks of their wounded, writhing in pain; help us to lay waste their humble homes with a hurricane of fire; help us to wring the hearts of their unoffending widows with unavailing grief; help us to turn them out roofless with their little children to wander unfriended the wastes of their desolated land. . . . For our sakes who adore Thee, Lord, blast their hopes, blight their lives, protract their bitter pilgrimage, make heavy their steps, water their way with their tears, stain the white snow with the blood of their wounded feet! We ask it in the spirit of love, of Him Who is the Source of Love, . . . Amen.

> "[*After a Pause.*] Ye have prayed it; if ye still desire it, speak!—The messenger of the Most High waits."

> It was believed afterwards, that the man was a lunatic, because there was no sense in what he said.

QUESTIONS

Defining Terms

Identify in the context of the chapter each of the following:

rags to riches	"the most dangerous man of the age"
ideology	Albert Beveridge
social Darwinism	folkways
imperialism	Henry Cabot Lodge
"The Strenuous Life"	water cure

Probing the Sources

1. What was the fighting like in the Philippines? How did the nature of the war itself relate to people's characterization of the Philippine people?

2. What ideas about racial groups do you find in Beveridge, Sumner, and Roosevelt? What was the relationship of those ideas to their views on overseas expansion?

3. What did Sumner mean by Spain's conquest of the United States? Why did he believe an overseas empire would make America weaker?

4. Why did Roosevelt believe foreign territories would make America stronger? How did his ideas about citizenship relate to foreign policy?

5. How did ideas about "manhood" enter the debates on overseas expansion?

6. Describe Beveridge's belief about America's special mission to the world.

Interpreting the Sources

1. The selections by Roosevelt, Beveridge, and Sumner all contain a sense that American life was threatened at the turn of the century. What did they fear in the future, and why?

2. What was meant by phrases like "true Americanism," "national duties," and the "strenuous life"? In what ways did the anti-imperialists express alternatives to these concepts?

3. How did assumptions about gender influence ideology in these selections? What about race?

4. Do you think that ideologies operate more as a system of lies or as a system of metaphors? Select passages from this chapter to argue your case.

5. How did the various participants in this debate view the role of business government, and the military in American foreign policy?

ADDITIONAL READING

On America's emergence as a world power in the late nineteenth century, see Walter La Feber, *The New Empire: An Interpretation of American Expansion, 1860–1898* (1963); and Charles Campbell, *The Transformation of American Foreign Relations, 1865–1900* (1976). The role of racial beliefs in foreign policy is discussed in Rubin Weston, *Racism in U.S. Imperialism: The Influence of Racial Assumptions on American Foreign Policy, 1893–1946* (1972). For the ideological bases of the new foreign policy, see Emily Rosenberg, *Spreading the American Dream: American Economic and Cultural Expansion, 1890–1945* (1982). On Roosevelt, see Frederick Marks II, *Velvet on Iron: The Diplomacy of Theodore Roosevelt* (1979). For those who opposed the aggressive new tone in late-nineteenth-century foreign policy, see Robert Beisner, *Twelve Against Empire: The Anti-Imperialists, 1898–1900* (1975). For an important interpretation of American diplomatic history, see Walter La Feber, *The American Age: United States Policy at Home and Abroad Since 1750* (1989). For American relations with the Philippines, see Stanley Karnow, *In Our Image: America's Empire in the Philippines* (1989). Finally, see Kristin L. Hoganson, *Fighting for American Manhood* (1998). Gail Bederman, *Manliness and Civilization* (1996) and Matthew Frye Jacobson, *Barbarian Virtues* (2000).

The Woman Rebel
Margaret Sanger and the Birth Control Movement

Historical Context

The use of contraceptive devices for family planning has become so common that it is difficult to imagine a time when it was controversial. Yet in 1914, when Margaret Sanger began to speak and write openly in behalf of birth control, she put herself in jeopardy of prosecution under the so-called Comstock Law of 1873, which prohibited mailing, importing, or selling materials of an "obscene, lewd, or lascivious" nature. Indeed, both she and her husband, William Sanger, were indicted under the law for distributing birth control information.

The irony is that family planning had been practiced in America for a century. (Indeed, ancient Greek and Roman doctors had prescribed a variety of contraceptive methods.) Couples limited their offspring by simply abstaining from sexual contact and by practicing coitus interruptus. Equally important, a variety of contraceptive devices, including forerunners of modern condoms, diaphragms, and douches, had been available since at least the early nineteenth century. Not only were such items occasionally advertised in popular magazines, but retailers of contraceptive paraphernalia mailed printed circulars advertising their wares to couples whose wedding announcements appeared in the newspapers. One bit of indirect evidence that the use of such devices was widespread is to be found in declining birthrates: in 1800, families averaged slightly over 7 children, under 6 by 1825, 5.4 in 1850, 4.24 by 1880, and 3.54 in 1900. In other words, the overall fertility rate declined by half in a century, with most urban middle-class families having no more than two children.

The declining birthrate was not simply a matter of new technology changing peoples' lives. Couples' willingness to use contraceptive devices or to otherwise limit the size of their families had social, economic, and cultural origins. As Americans left the countryside for the city, and as the old artisan system of manufacture declined, large numbers of children usually became a hindrance rather than an aid to a family's economic well-being; in a modern urban setting, children entered a family more as mouths to feed than as hands to labor. A cash-based economy (in which people exchanged goods and labor for money) rather than a subsistence one (where work produced items for home consumption) made raising a child very costly and made the "return" on parents' "investment" in their children very slow.

Other important social changes encouraged the use of birth control. The turn of the century witnessed a new emphasis on sexuality as an expression of passion, love, and intimacy. Contraception liberated these feelings from the fear of unwanted pregnancy. This was especially true for women, who had always borne the burden of child rearing. Birth control was part of a larger transformation of women's position in society. Important female voices were raised during the nineteenth and early twentieth century demanding new roles for women, roles apart from the home-centered ones of wife and mother, roles that placed women in the practical worlds of politics, business, and reform. Needless to say, the average of seven children per family in 1800, had it continued, would have made education and careers impossible for most women.

Even though contraception had been practiced for a century when Margaret Sanger began to champion the cause in the years straddling World War I, her crusade generated great controversy. Part of the reason was that she was so open in her advocacy. The genteel Victorian code still held sway sufficiently so that sex remained a subject most people preferred not to talk about in public; even couples who practiced birth control—a criminal act, after all—were silent. Their open discussion of sexuality made birth control advocates harbingers of the freer, less morally rigid styles of living and speaking that we associate with the 1920s.

But it was more than a matter of style alone. At the beginning of her crusade, Sanger allied herself with a variety of radical thinkers—feminists, socialists, labor militants (such as the Industrial Workers of the World), and others—and it was out of the creative, avant-garde ferment of New York City in the prewar era that she forged her ideas. Birth control was not merely a technique; it grew out of a radical political ideology, and Sanger believed it would contribute to the liberation of women, especially working-class women. She did not argue for the open distribution of contraceptive information and devices in order simply to expand the realm of personal freedom. She believed that limitation of family size was the key to freeing women from the physical dangers of continual childbearing and to giving them the opportunity to become active outside the home.

Nineteenth-century feminists often opposed the use of contraception, believing that birth control would make women more vulnerable to male sexual aggressiveness. In this way of thinking, abstinence and self-control became a form of sexual liberation because women rejected male desires.

Contraceptive devices and literature were illegal in most states for years after Sanger began her crusade. They remained a delicate subject until birth control pills became widely available in the 1960s; the Catholic Church prohibits their use today. Feminists point out that the burden of contraception still falls on women. Nonetheless, Margaret Sanger succeeded in opening the *public* debate that led to eventual legalization. Although she was forced to flee the country in 1914 for distributing literature about family limitation, she returned a few years later and founded the National Birth Control League, an organization supported by doctors, social workers, and other professionals from the mainstream of American life.

There were ironies on the road to victory. Those who believed contraception to be against the laws of God and nature were eventually marginalized and often dismissed as prudes or fanatics. But Margaret Sanger's morally earnest campaign to uplift the downtrodden through family planning moved onto a side-rail of history, too. The birth control campaign succeeded when it became a movement by and for the middle class; family planning grew acceptable not because of some new passion for the plight of the poor, but because it was indispensable to middle-class families balancing growing expenses, careers for both parents, the allures of consumer life, and the difficulties of raising children in urban or suburban nuclear families.

THE DOCUMENTS

The debate over birth control takes us into a variety of important issues. These include the right of individuals to privacy versus the right of a community to regulate moral behavior; the ethnic makeup of the American people; the ability of women to control their own physical destinies by limiting family size; and the feeling of many people that opportunities for advancement were shrinking and that small families were one way to keep the American dream alive.

As you read these documents, ask yourself about the connections between personal issues and political ones. Was birth control merely a matter of individual choice, or was it about power, wealth, opportunity, and similar questions? How did gender, ethnicity, and social class figure in the debate?

Introduction to Document 1

Margaret Sanger burst on the scene in 1914 with the publication of the first issue of *The Woman Rebel*. The tabloid described itself as "A Monthly Paper of Militant Thought." Testimony to the editor's radical political commitments was the reprinting of the Preamble to the Charter of the Industrial Workers of the World: "The working class and the employing class have nothing in common. . . . Between these two classes a struggle must go on until the workers of the world organize as a class, take possession of the earth and the machinery of production, and abolish the wage system. . . . It is the historic mission of the working class to do away with capitalism." Making contraceptive devices available, then, was part of a much larger project of radical social change, embracing the liberation of women and of the working class.

In the very first issue, Sanger explained herself in an essay entitled "Why the Woman Rebel?" Later on the same page, in an article entitled "The Prevention of Conception," Sanger made it clear that she would defy the laws against distributing birth control information.

 DOCUMENT 1 *From* **The Woman Rebel**

Margaret Sanger

Why the Woman Rebel?

Because I believe that deep down in woman's nature lies slumbering the spirit of revolt.

Because I believe that woman is enslaved by the world machine, by sex conventions, by motherhood and its present necessary child-rearing, by wage slavery, by middle-class morality, by customs, laws and superstitions.

Because I believe that woman's freedom depends upon awakening that spirit of revolt within her against these things which enslave her.

Margaret Sanger with her son Stuart in 1904. (Sophia Smith Collection, Smith College, Northampton, MA)

Because I believe that these things which enslave woman must be fought openly, fearlessly, consciously.

Because I believe she must consciously disturb and destroy and be fearless in its accomplishment.

Because I believe in freedom, created through individual action.

Because I believe in the offspring of the immigrant, the great majority of whom make up the unorganized working class to-day. . . .

Because I believe that through the efforts of the industrial revolution will woman's freedom emerge.

Because I believe that not until wage slavery is abolished can either woman's or man's freedom be fully attained.

The Prevention of Conception

Is there any reason why women should not receive clean, harmless, scientific knowledge on how to prevent conception? Everybody is aware that the old, stupid fallacy that such knowledge will cause a girl to enter into prostitution has long been shattered. Seldom does a prostitute become pregnant. Seldom does the girl practicing promiscuity become pregnant. The woman of the upper middle class has all available knowledge and implements to prevent conception. The woman of the lower middle class is struggling for this knowledge. She tries various methods of prevention, and after a few years of experience plus medical advice succeeds in discovering some method suitable to her individual self. The woman of the people is the only one left in ignorance of this information. Her neighbors, relatives and friends tell her stories of special devices and the success of them all.

They tell her also of the blood-sucking men with M.D. after their names who perform operations for the price of so-and-so. But the working woman's purse is thin. It's far cheaper to have a baby, "though God knows what it will do after it gets here." Then, too, all other classes of women live in places where there is at least a semblance of privacy and sanitation. It is easier for them to care for themselves whereas the large majority of the women of the people have no bathing or sanitary conveniences. This accounts too for the fact that the higher the standard of living, the more care can be taken and fewer children result. No plagues, famines or wars could ever frighten the capitalist class so much as the universal practice of the prevention of conception. On the other hand no better method could be utilized for increasing the wages of the workers.

As is well known, a law exists forbidding the imparting of information on this subject, the penalty being several years' imprisonment. Is it now time to defy this law! And what fitter place could be found than in the pages of the WOMAN REBEL!

Introduction to Document 2

The second issue of *The Woman Rebel* announced that the United States postmaster had declared the newspaper unmailable under section 211 of the United States Criminal Code. Copies of that issue and subsequent ones were confiscated. The man most responsible for marshaling support for such legislation, then seeing it enforced, was Anthony Comstock, who had a long career during the late nineteenth and early twentieth centuries as a crusader against vice.

Violation of the law carried a maximum five-year prison sentence or a $5,000 fine. Comstock had waged a forty-year-long personal crusade to pass and enforce such laws. Since 1873 he had made it his career to eliminate "smut" from American culture. He founded the Society for the Suppression of Vice, which drew financial backing from some of America's wealthiest men, and he was appointed special agent of the Post Office Department. On his fortieth anniversary, Comstock reminded his followers why their work was so essential:

In an interview with Mary Alden Hopkins, who wrote a series of articles on the birth control controversy for *Harper's Weekly* in Spring 1915, Comstock justified the laws against publicizing contraception:

 DOCUMENT 2   *Anthony Comstock's Views on Birth Control*

The law under which *The Woman Rebel* was confiscated read, in part:

Every obscene, lewd, or lascivious and every filthy book, pamphlet, picture, paper, letter, writing, print, or other publication of an indecent character, and every article or thing designated, adapted or intended for preventing conception or procuring abortion, or for any indecent or immoral use; and every article, instrument, substance, drugs, medicine, or thing which is advertised or described in a manner calculated to lead another to use or apply it for preventing conception or producing abortion, or for any indecent or immoral purpose; and every written or printed card, circular, book, pamphlet, advertisement or notice or any kind giving information, directly, or indirectly, where or how, or by what means any of the hereinbefore mentioned matters, articles or things may be obtained or made; . . . and every description calculated to induce or incite a person to so use or apply any such article, instrument, substance, drug, medicine or thing, is hereby declared to be non-mailable matter, and shall not be conveyed in the mails or delivered from any post office or by any letter carrier. . . .

THE WOMAN REBEL

NO GODS NO MASTERS

The masthead of Margaret Sanger's radical newspaper.

The three great crime-breeders of today are intemperance, gambling, and evil reading. The devil is sowing his seed for his future harvest. There is no foe so much to be dreaded as that which perverts the imagination, sears the conscience, hardens the heart, and damns the soul.

If you allow the devil to decorate the Chamber of Imagery in your heart with licentious and sensual things, you will find that he has practically thrown a noose about your neck and will forever after exert himself to draw you away from the "Lamb of God which taketh away sins of the world." You have practically put rope on memory's bell and placed the other end of the rope in the devil's hands, and, though you may will out your mind, the memory of some vile story or picture that you may have looked upon, be assured that even in your most solitary moments the devil will ring memory's bell and call up the hateful thing to turn your thoughts away from God and undermine all aspirations for holy things.

. . . My experience leads me to the conviction that once these matters enter through the eye and ear into the chamber of imagery in the heart of the child, nothing but the grace of God can ever erase or blot it out. . . .

Brethren, "let us not be weary in well doing, for in due season we shall reap if we faint not." Raise over each of your heads the banner of the Lord Jesus Christ. Look to Him as your Commander and Leader. . . .

"Do the laws never thwart the doctor's work; in cases, for instance, where pregnancy would endanger a woman's life?"

Mr. Comstock replied with the strongest emphasis:

"A doctor is allowed to bring on an abortion in cases where a woman's life is in danger. And is there anything in these laws that forbids a doctor's telling a woman that pregnancy must not occur for a certain length of time or at all? Can they not use self-control? Or must they sink to the level of the beast?"

"But," I protested, . . . "if the parents lack that self-control the punishment falls upon the child."

"It does not," replied Mr. Comstock. "The punishment falls upon the parents. When a man and woman marry they are responsible for their children. You can't reform a family in any of these superficial ways. You have to go deep down into their minds and souls. The prevention of conception would work the greatest demoralization. God has set certain natural barriers. If you turn loose the passions and break down the fear you bring worse disaster than the war. It would debase sacred things, break down the health of women and disseminate a greater curse than the plagues and diseases of Europe."

Introduction to Document 3

Just before she was to be arrested for distributing contraceptive information, Sanger fled America for England, where she spent her time among European radicals, reformers, and family-planning professionals. But a few months later, her husband, William Sanger, was arrested by Anthony Comstock in New York City, then imprisoned for purveying lewd materials (he gave a copy of his wife's little book, *Family Limitation,* to one of Comstock's undercover agents). Margaret Sanger returned to New York, where she knew she would face trial. She was eventually acquitted, but in the meantime, she lectured, wrote essays, and opened the nation's first family-planning clinic.

Document 3 comes from the introduction to a book Sanger edited called *The Case for Birth Control* (1917). In this brief essay, she summarized much of the argument she had been promulgating since returning to the United States. While her commitment to poor and working women is still evident here, her style had changed considerably since *The Woman Rebel.* Sanger was in the midst of concentrating all of her efforts on birth control, distancing herself from the radical positions she had staked out earlier. Perhaps she though this was the practical way to achieve her one important goal. Or maybe the experience of exile had tempered her ardor. Certainly Sanger now spent more time among wealthy women who helped finance both her trial defense and the birth control movement. Note how the tone of this essay differs from that of *The Woman Rebel;* the radical passion is now obscured somewhat by the Progressive Era style of fact-laden analysis in the name of practical reform.

 DOCUMENT 3 *From* **The Case for Birth Control**

Margaret Sanger

Before I attempt to refute the arguments against birth control. I should like to tell you something of the conditions I met with as a trained nurse and of the experience that convinced me of its necessity and led me to jeopardize my liberty in order to place this information in the hands of the women who need it.

My first clear impression of life was that large families and poverty went hand in hand. I was born and brought up in a glass factory town in the western part of New York

State. I was one of eleven children—so I had some personal experience of the struggles and hardships a large family endures.

When I was seventeen years old my mother died from overwork and the strain of too frequent child bearing. I was left to care for the younger children and share the burdens of all. When I was old enough I entered a hospital to take up the profession of nursing.

In the hospital I found that seventy-five percent of the diseases of men and women are the result of ignorance of their sex functions. I found that every department of life was open to investigation and discussion except that shaded valley of sex. . . .

So great was the ignorance of the women and girls I met concerning their own bodies that I decided to specialize in woman's diseases and took up gynecological and obstetrical nursing.

A few years of this work brought me to a shocking discovery—that knowledge of the methods of controlling birth was accessible to the women of wealth while the working women were deliberately kept in ignorance of this knowledge!

I found that the women of the working class were as anxious to obtain this knowledge as their sisters of wealth, but that they were told that there are laws on the statute books against imparting it to them. And the medical profession was most religious in obeying these laws when the patient was a poor woman.

For the laws against imparting this knowledge force these women into the hands of the filthiest midwives and the quack abortionists—unless they bear unwanted children—with the consequence that the deaths from abortions are almost wholly among the working-class women.

No other country in the world has so large a number of abortions nor so large a number of deaths of women resulting therefrom as the United States of America. Our law makers close their virtuous eyes. A most conservative estimate is that there are 250,000 abortions performed in this country every year.

How often have I stood at the bedside of a woman in childbirth and seen the tears flowing in gladness and heard the sigh of "Thank God" when told that her child was born dead! What can man know of the fear and dread of unwanted pregnancy? What can man know of the agony of carrying beneath one's heart a little life which tells the mother every instant that it cannot survive? Even were it born alive the chances are that it would perish within a year.

Do you know that three hundred thousand babies under one year of age die in the United States every year from poverty and neglect, while six hundred thousand parents remain in ignorance of how to prevent three hundred thousand more babies from coming into the world the next year to die of poverty and neglect?

I found from records concerning women of the underworld that eighty-five per cent of them come from parents averaging nine living children. And that fifty percent of these are mentally defective.

We know, too, that among mentally defective parents the birth rate is four times as great as that of the normal parent. Is this not cause for alarm? Is it not time for our physicians, social workers and scientists to face this array of facts and stop quibbling about woman's morality? I say this because it is these same people who raise objection to birth control on the ground that it *may* cause women to be immoral.

Solicitude for woman's morals has ever been the cloak Authority has worn in its age-long conspiracy to keep woman in bondage. . . .

Is woman's health not to be considered? Is she to remain a producing machine? Is she to have time to think, to study, to care for herself? Man cannot travel to his goal alone. And until woman has knowledge to control birth she cannot get the time to think and develop. Until she has the time to think, neither the suffrage question nor the social question nor the labor question will interest her, and she will remain the drudge that she is and her husband the slave that he is just as long as they continue to supply the market with cheap labor. . . .

Am I to be classed as immoral because I advocate small families for the working class while Mr. [Theodore] Roosevelt can go up and down the length of the land shouting and urging these women to have large families and is neither arrested nor molested but considered by all society as highly moral?

But I ask you which is the more moral—to urge this class of women to have only those children she desires and can care for, or to delude her into breeding thoughtlessly. Which is America's definition of morality?

You will agree with me that a woman should be free.

Yet no adult woman who is ignorant of the means to prevent conception can call herself free.

No woman can call herself free who cannot choose the time to be a mother or not as she sees fit. This should be woman's first demand. . . .

I saw that fortunes were being spent in establishing baby nurseries, where new babies are brought and cared for while the mothers toil in sweatshops during the day. I saw that society with its well-intentioned palliatives was in this respect like the quack, who cures a cancer by burning off the top while the deadly disease continues to spread underneath. I never felt this more strongly than I did three years ago, after the death of the patient in my last nursing case.

This patient was the wife of a struggling working man—the mother of three children—who was suffering from the results of a self-attempted abortion. I found her in a very serious condition, and for three weeks both the attending physician and myself labored night and day to bring her out of the Valley of the Shadow of Death. We finally succeeded in restoring her to her family.

I remember well the day I was leaving. The physician, too, was making his last call. As the doctor put out his hand to say "Good-bye," I saw the patient had something to say to him, but was shy and timid about saying it. I started to leave the room, but she called me back and said:

"Please don't go. How can both of you leave me without telling me what I can do to avoid another illness such as I have just passed through?"

I was interested to hear what the answer of the physician would be, and I went back and sat down beside her in expectation of hearing a sympathetic reply. To my amazement, he answered her with a joking sneer. We came away.

Three months later, I was aroused from my sleep one midnight. A telephone call from the husband of the same woman requested me to come immediately as she was dangerously ill. I arrived to find her beyond relief. Another conception had forced her into the hands of a cheap abortionist, and she died at four o'clock the same morning, leaving behind her three small children and a frantic husband.

I returned home as the sun was coming over the roofs of the Human Bee-Hive, and I realized how futile my efforts and my work had been. I, too, like the philanthropists and social workers, had been dealing with the symptoms rather than the disease. I threw my nursing bag into the corner and announced to my family that I would never take another case until I had made it possible for working women in America to have knowledge of birth control.

Introduction to Document 4

Michael P. Dowling was a member of the Society of Jesus, and as a Jesuit, he articulated a position familiar to the Catholic church and its followers. Document 4 is excerpted from his pamphlet *Race-Suicide* (1915), which couched arguments against birth control in the language of duty, self-sacrifice, religious obligation, and family values. Whereas Sanger argued for the right of women and the poor to make individual decisions about contraception, Dowling appealed to the good of the community, which he asserted took precedence over personal needs or desires. Note that the phrase "race-suicide" was highly charged. These could become code words meaning that the white race—and therefore civilization itself—was in jeopardy.

DOCUMENT 4 *From Race-Suicide*

Michael P. Dowling

The subject which we propose to discuss under this title has engaged the attention of the thinking men of our country for many years. The grave offense it connotes against morality and social order has been aptly described by Colonel [Theodore] Roosevelt as race-suicide. Some thoughtless people have made the expression a target for sneer and ridicule, have held up to contempt those who agree with the views of the ex-President, but in their hearts the great mass of God-fearing persons admit that there is in what the phrase stigmatizes, an imminent danger to society. . . .

At three different epochs in human history, the Creator made known His will. Just as to the first man, He said: "Increase and multiply," so a thousand years later to the second father of humanity, to Noe [Noah], and to his sons, He spoke a pregnant word, and it bore the same burden, "Increase and multiply and fill the earth"; for so we read in Genesis. Still another thousand years rolled on and the same blessing was repeated, for the word of the Lord came to Abraham: "Fear not; I am thy protector and thy reward exceeding great." The patriarch answered: "What wilt Thou give me; behold, I have no child." Then God brought him forth out of the tent, saying: "Look up to the heavens and number the stars, if thou canst; so shall thy seed be." The reward of Abraham's faith is paternity.

And after that, from Abraham to the last of the prophets, text on text and example after example, confirm the doctrine that children are the blessing of marriage, no matter what the new gospel of selfishness may proclaim. In the Old Testament curse alternates with blessing: "He who is blessed shall be a father, the cursed shall stand alone." If it is said to the just, "Thy wife shall be like a fruitful vine," (*Ps.* 127); to the wicked man and the sinner comes the sentence: "In a single generation his name will be blotted out." (*Ps.* 108). . . .

God said: "Increase and multiply"; man says: "Let us fear to increase and multiply; the earth might become too narrow; the fewer there are to share the good things of life the more there will be for each. . . .

. . . Malthus, in his book entitled "Principles of Population As It Affects the Future Improvement of Society," gave the impetus to the movement. He held that the population of the earth increases more rapidly than the means of subsistence, because population advances almost in a geometrical proportion, as two, four, eight, sixteen, while the fertility of the land increases approximately only in an arithmetical proportion, as one, two, three, four, five and so on. Hence, the continually increasing population must eventually exceed the capacity of the earth to supply food. . . .

But the facts are against the theory that the earth is inadequate to support the growth of population. The United States, even with the wasteful methods of farming now in vogue, could feed hundreds of millions. Under different conditions even little Ireland would be capable of supporting three times its present population. Brazil, Peru, Mexico have room for teeming millions within their borders. Portions of the dark continent of Africa were once densely peopled; so was Asia Minor; and they might become garden spots of the earth once more. There is still plenty of elbow room on the globe. . . .

God makes no mistakes, and for every soul He creates and infuses into a mortal body, He furnishes what is needful for its well-being. History may be reviewed in vain for an instance of any considerable country wherein poverty and want can be fairly traced to the increase of the number of mouths beyond the power of the accompanying hands to fill them. In most cases they can, more properly, be attributed to unjust laws, misgovernment, destructive warfare, decadent commerce, a disregard of the Divine law, vice and crime. . . .

Can it be possible that wealth is the natural enemy of infancy and childhood? And is the instinct of reproduction weaker in the privileged classes, the spirit of self-denial more pronounced? Is it not rather that large families are looked upon with disdain as a plebeian institution, entailing too much sacrifice, debarring the mother from many pleasures she is unwilling to forgo? Is it not because every new birth requires the expense account to be overhauled, several chapters of travel to be blotted out, transfers to be made to the side of the nurse and the governess, balls and parties and receptions to be given up?

People sin today by excessive prudence. If families are growing smaller, it is not because there is less natural fruitfulness; if the births do not keep pace with the deaths, it is not because men and women are attracted by a life of voluntary chastity or are deeply in love with the Evangelical Counsels; but because the designs of God are frustrated by the prosperous classes; and that a period of moral decay is begun. It is because the warm stream of infant life is kept back. It is because instead of guardian spirits parents become the exterminating angels of their offspring. In rigorous simplicity of language, it must be said that too many are engaged in a systematic and deliberate opposition to God, in as far as they can thwart His designs and impede His providential dispensations. Practically, they say to Him: "Let us make a compact; in the law You place before me are certain things which I accept; but the consequences I decline; I will embrace pleasure but reject duty; what agrees with my inclinations and the ideas and decrees of contemporary society, I will obey, but I will carry no cross, make no sacrifices." . . .

We must get back to Christian principles and mold Christian lives, till the humblest sees that life is not all for pleasure, self-ease and enjoyment, that duty and conscience must play a great part and march in the vanguard of true progress.

Introduction to Document 5

In its series of articles by Mary Alden Hopkins on contraception, *Harper's Weekly* published the thoughts of several doctors. While we cannot assume that the following statements represented the opinions of the entire medical profession, they do give a sense of the arguments offered by physicians who opposed birth control. The only doctor who spoke unequivocally in favor of contraception to *Harper's* (the first interview here) was Dutch, not American, and a woman, not a man.

 DOCUMENT 5 *Physicians' Statements about Birth Control*

Dr. Aletta Jacobs

Very often the mothers in this hospital did not want the babies that were born to them. They were actually glad when the babies were born dead. No, they were not bad women—just ordinary, every-day women. Sometimes it was because they already had enough babies, sometimes because the previous baby was still so little, sometimes because they were so very poor, sometimes for other reasons. But whether the reason was a good one or a bad one, the fact remained that the baby was not desired. Now it seemed to me that a baby should not be a punishment. If a woman does not want a child it is better both for her and for the child that she should not have one.

Moreover, I noticed that many of the sickly children born in the hospital were children that had been born against their mothers' wishes. The mothers' state of mind during pregnancy had affected the baby. Besides this there were many children with very bad heredity—mental sickness and physical sickness in the parents, which would very probably appear in the offspring. These children should never have been born.

Sometimes a mother would say to me. "No wonder the baby is puny and sick. Why, when this child was conceived my husband was as drunk as could be." For reasons like these I decided that mothers should be taught how to prevent conception.

Children should be born not oftener than once in three years. For the first year the mother should devote herself to caring for the child. The second year she should have to get back her vitality and strength. The third year she may again become pregnant.

Dr. Howard A. Kelly

Let me enunciate these fundamental principles which must control my judgment:

1. That the medical profession must continually deal with the moral aspects of a case, and today our great loss is the unwillingness of some doctors to have anything to do with morals, because they have had no moral training and have done no moral thinking . . .

2. That in times of great decadence we are not to try to accommodate ourselves to decadent conditions by temporizing expedients, but by the highest moral remedies and by righteousness—*at whatever cost*. Practically I find that the people who came to me having used various mechanical means of preventing conception, have lost something in their married life which ought to have been more precious to them than life itself. All meddling with the sexual relation to secure facultative sterility degrades the wife to the level of a prostitute.

Therefore there is no right or decent way of controlling births but by total abstinence. . . .

Dr. John W. Williams

I make it a rule to refuse to discuss the question with perfectly healthy, normal persons. On the other hand, if I find that a wife is steadily losing ground as the result of rapidly recurring pregnancies, I send for the husband and say that in my opinion as a medical man it is highly advisable that his wife should not have another child for a specified length of time. In that event I advise him as to the most efficacious method of preventing conception; as I consider it more intelligent to prevent a breakdown than to treat it after it has occurred.

I give the same advice after certain serious obstetrical complications, and in women who are suffering from tuberculosis, certain forms of heart disease and other serious chronic diseases, in which I know by experience that another pregnancy will subject the patient to serious danger. In such cases I consider it more conservative to give such advice than to be obliged to perform a therapeutic abortion after pregnancy has occurred.

Finally, in the presence of certain chronic diseases, which to my mind will always complicate the occurrence of pregnancy, and in which therapeutic abortion is necessary to relieve immediate danger to the patient's life, I hold that it is justifiable to render the patient sterile by operative means. In this event the desired result should be attained, not by the removal of the ovaries, but by a procedure which will temporarily prevent conception, and at the same time make it possible to restore the child-bearing function by a second operation should it appear desirable in the future.

In other words, I do not believe that the physician is justified in giving advice as to the prevention of conception solely for the convenience of his patients, but should limit it entirely to those cases which present a definite medical indication for the temporary or permanent avoidance of pregnancy. To my mind any other course practically places the physician in the same class as the professional abortionist.

Dr. R. C. Brannon

I beg to take issue with you, in regard to your propaganda for the control of births, as being subversive to religion, morals, and health of both men and women. This, when you come to sift the matter down to its final analysis, is what is shortening the lives of the human race, making weaklings in mind and body the children of strong men, and wrecking the nerves and bodies of women who ought to be the proud and happy mothers of a dozen healthy children.

The prevention of large families has caused an increase in insanity, tuberculosis, Bright's disease, diabetes and cancer, and I am willing to submit the proposition to the judgment of three of the greatest gynecologists in the United States. I have stepped in the breach and used my influence to curtail the bad practice of limiting the size of the family, as my experience as a physician of twenty years' practise has proven to my mind that it is the most hurtful, and wicked sin that was ever indulged in since the world was created. It is a swift and sure road to the grave.

Man was put here to multiply and replenish the earth. How terrible has been the punishment of many a rich man I have known—perhaps poor and struggling in early life, who decided he would escape the responsibility of rearing a large family, with the result when a little past life's prime his wife died of a cancer, and what enjoyment did either of them derive from his fortune of more than a half million dollars; filthy lucre begotten by miserly habits, that rightly should have been expended unselfishly in bringing up a large family that would have blessed the earth.

Introduction to Document 6

The following debate took place in New York City in 1920. Margaret Sanger and Winter Russell addressed the issue: "Resolved, that the spreading of birth control knowledge is injurious to the welfare of humanity." Pay attention to the assumptions each debater made in arguing his or her case: How were "facts" tied to a "higher morality" for both speakers? What were the ultimate values each espoused? Note that the debate turned on the issue of free speech, for the question to be resolved was the spreading of *information* about birth control, not birth control technologies.

Freedom of speech was an issue that had got Winter Russell, a New York City attorney, in trouble on the eve of World War I. His disavowal of military preparedness and his espousal of pacifism on Christian grounds were cause for considerable official and public censure. Yet, when it came to contraception, he implied that restricting the flow of information served a higher good. While Russell's rhetoric is more emotional than Sanger's, they both asserted "scientific" claims. Russell declared it a "law of nature" that there could be no pleasure without cost, and that it was akin to alchemy to think otherwise. Moreover, Russell depicted a world of Darwinian struggle that limited human freedom and happiness. Sanger appealed less to scientific metaphors and more to scientific method. She argued her case fully in the style of the Progressive Era: fact-laden, scientific, analytical. She now spoke in terms of middle-class reform, not working-class or feminist rebellion.

DOCUMENT 6 *Debate between Margaret Sanger and Winter Russell*

Winter Russell

FIRST SPEECH

Ladies and gentlemen. I am very glad to have this opportunity of speaking to you this afternoon, and I may say at the outset that it is obvious that my adversary and I agree upon one thing, and that is that we are discussing what is absolutely the most vital question before the American people today. (*Applause.*) We are absolutely in accord on that, and we are just as far opposed in our method of approach as it is [possible] to be. . . .

I propose that we should meet this problem by the measure of self-control. I believe by that means that we can solve the problem thusly, and at the same time we gain one of the greatest advantages that you can possibly win on the face of the earth. Sex control is the best path to self-control and to self-discipline. It is the key to wisdom. It is the key to power. It is the key to intellectual and mental development; indeed, [Sanger] has once stated that only those people who are mentally developed are capable of self-control, and I want to say that they got a large measure of their mental development by self-control. She is looking through the wrong end of the telescope.

And so we come to this method. I want as another part of my platform upon which I am to stand to say that I conceive and hold marriage to be more than physical. It is not a purely sensual relationship. It borders on the aesthetic, spiritual, mental and modern aspects of life, and when you try to take the physical by itself you find a condition of naked sensuality, which is disastrous in the extreme. . . . I believe it is disastrous, intellectually, mentally, and spiritually. It is disastrous and it perpetrates a great wrong upon the unborn millions who are waiting for entrance upon this great amphitheatre of life. It is disastrous physically, mentally, and spiritually upon the future. It is disastrous to the same degree upon the people who practice it—the husbands and the wives who resort to these measures, and then I hold that it perpetrates the greatest crime of all the ages, namely, race suicide.

Let me approach the first method, and that is this question of whether it is right from the point of view of the philosophy of man, if you will, and I want you to consider it simply from the practical living point of view. I want to lay down this proposition—it is that you can't have pleasure in this world without paying for it—that there are certain laws that sweep through the entire universe from the furtherest star to the tiniest atom and molecule that you can find in existence.

I am a member of the bar of the State of New York. I trust that I have due regard and respect for the statutes, the constitution, and the laws of this great city, state and nation. But I hold them as the veriest trash when they come up against the laws of Nature. The laws of Nature cannot be revised. They cannot be repealed. There is no power in this whole universe that can change these laws, and you have to deal with that.

That means you can't get pleasure without paying for it. Nature is inexorable in bringing about her retribution. It does not need any balance book. You can never embezzle. You can't cheat. You can't get away from it. . . .

You must pay at last for your own debt. Those are the laws. Now we recognize it in physics. Energy cannot be annihilated. Birth control says "yes." You shall pay the price. You can annihilate that energy and drink from the cup of pleasure, but you don't take the responsibility—the duty and the care. . . . It is along the lines of the people who are alchemists, who think they can turn the baser metals into gold. It is an age-long dream. It is a belief that has been held from the beginning of time. That thing cannot be done. That is the law of life—of God—that you have to pay. . . .

Margaret Sanger

FIRST SPEECH

. . . As usual with most of the opponents of birth control, they have absolutely no intelligent argument. . . .

The only weapon that women have and the most uncivilized weapon that they have to use if they will not submit to having children every year or every year and a half, the weapon they use is abortion. We know how detrimental abortion is to the physical side as well as to the psychic side of the woman's life, and yet there are in this nation, because of these generalities and opinions that are here before us, that are stopping the tide of progress, we have more than one million women with abortions performed on them each year. . . . We speak of the rights of the unborn. I say that it is time to speak of those who are already born. . . .

We find in the South that where children come according to Nature, every year and one-half, that as soon as they are able, they are shuffled and hustled on in to take the place and compete with their father in the factories. That is the place that society has for the children of the poor. We find in other States, too, where it is only a question of a few years later that also the children, as soon as they are able to take their place in industry, are pushed out of the home, not because the mothers of these children are not just as anxious to see them in the universities and colleges, but because of the pitiless earnings that she must have to support those who are coming behind them.

Most of us know this. We know something about the actual conditions of life as it is among us. In some of the factories of Lowell and Fall River, Mass., it was found that of the children who work and toil there, under ten years of age, that 85% of them come from families of eight—their mothers have given birth to eight children—and we find in the South very much the same thing, excepting a higher percentage of 90 to 93% of the children there.

That is not the only thing. We have a condition not only as these that I have related, but we have a condition again that is more disastrous to the race than child labor or infant mortality, and that is the transmission of venereal disease to the race that is to come. . . . We know, too, that out of this terrible scourge of venereal disease that we have 90% of the insanity in this country, due to syphilis. Anyone who is dealing with fundamentals would know that these people should use means to protect themselves against having children. They should absolutely in due regard to themselves, to their children and to the race, not allow a child to be born while that disease is running riot in the system, and then we have that terrible consequence which is insanity. . . .

We have here 400,000 feeble-minded people in the United States, that any authority on this subject would say to you, "Not one of them should have been born." They never should have been born and sometimes these parents are perfectly normal, and yet this taint has gone through the blood and has left this perfectly normal, physical person, who arrives at the adult age with all its physical functions, and yet it has the mentality of a child eight years of age. The feeble-minded man or woman is of no use to itself or society, and it would be better if we were living in a real civilization that they should not have been born. Only 40,000 of this 400,000 are entered in institutions, and the others are living among us, producing and reproducing their progeny and providing abundant material and opportunity for the continuance of charities and other institutions for ages and generations more to come.

We found also in one institution—a so-called reformatory where they take the girls of the underworld—prostitutes—in Geneva, Ill., they find that 50% of these girls coming into the underworld—the prostitutes—was of this cause, that she belonged to the feeble-minded, and again we find that 89% of these came from large families. . . .

Also our child labor—we make laws in Washington against child labor, hoping we will wipe that out of existence. For fifty years they have been trying to wipe child labor off the books in the United States, but they have not succeeded and they will never succeed until they establish birth control clinics in those districts where these women are, where they put in birth control clinics, like they have in Holland—in every industrial section in the United States where women can come to trained nurses and physicians and get from them scientific information whereby they may control birth. . . .

Now, Mr. Russell has said some things that are very interesting to me, He tells us that we cannot have pleasure without pain. It is a man who is speaking. (*Laughter and applause.*) It is very peculiar that Nature only works on the one side of the human family when it comes to that law. She applies all the pain to the woman. It is absurd—a perfectly absurd argument in the face of rational intelligence (*applause*) to talk about marriage being for one purpose. . . .

Winter Russell
SECOND SPEECH

May I say at the outset that I did not say we could not have pleasure without pain. I said we could not have pleasure without paying for it and the man has to pay. (*Laughter.*) . . . Mrs. Sanger sees poverty, she sees misery and she sees unwanted children. To be sure, there are many thousands of these homes where, sad to say, the children are unwanted, but they have made this devout prayer to God, I believe, for children, and they have gotten them. They have gotten what I believe to be the greatest wealth and treasure of the Kingdom of Heaven that there is on the face of the earth, and when they get that, they have to pay for it. They have to pay and take the responsibility. . . .

Then she says that here is where we get our prostitution. Yes, again she is right; a large number of the poor and unfortunate girls who walk the streets do come from these homes. For every girl who walks the street in that condition—I believe there are 100 who have a wedding certificate and who live in a home—they are worse than prostitutes—they are worse prostitutes than any who walk upon streets (*applause*)—they want somebody to be their meal ticket. They want somebody that will support them. They want respectability. They want all the joy that they haven't got. You men have to pay and you assume the responsibility. Before these poor girls upon the street I take off my hat and before these I can't express my detestation. (*Applause.*) . . .

I am going to give you a picture of the block on which I was born and brought up, that I have watched for 30 years. Thirty years ago I began to watch the block. There were 17 families, 34 people at the start; 34 people who were successful, they believe, in this little town of 3,500 people. It had a fine high school, a State Normal School—one of the foremost in the State. It had a Boys' School known nationally, if not internationally, and they were 34 people in 17 homes. . . .

Out of . . . 17 families, 9 are extinct. Nine are dead and gone. They have passed away. Is that race suicide? Out of the 8 who remain, out of the 34 people, out of these 8 families, there are 26 grandchildren. My father's family produced 12 of the 26. Out of 33 of the families, there are 14 grandchildren if you except mine. I think I am an exception. There is race suicide. Don't tell me that that is one exceptional block. I can duplicate that block on every street in that town except one blessed community, Little Canada. They were not Americans. They were vulgar. They were poor. They want big families, but from these poor families in Little Canada, there have come the French Canadians. From them come doctors, lawyers, and teachers, and they are inheriting the town. There is race suicide.

I can duplicate that block in practically every American city in this country. I can duplicate that block in every apartment house on the west side.

America is dying today—the America that we know. I wish that it weren't. I wish that it could get a cleaner and better ideal, but it hasn't got it. That is the tragedy of it all. . . .

Margaret Sanger
SECOND SPEECH

. . . Again I say, Mr. Russell tells us that he was quite sick when he heard me tell about women who had tuberculosis and heart disease and other ailments, and should have been prevented from becoming pregnant. He said the man who did not have self-control was not worth much. I wonder if Mr. Russell knows—he is a lawyer, and I wonder if he knows what the laws of this State are as far as you men are concerned. The Bible states "wives, submit yourselves unto your husbands." It is one of the things put into our laws, and the woman who does not submit to her husband—he does not have to support her. I wonder if Mr. Russell knows that. . . .

I am speaking for the millions of women who are crushed with over child-bearing, whose lives are broken and who have become drudges in the family today. I am speaking for the mothers and the individual here and there does not concern me in the least. They may be an exception, but I know there are millions and millions of women who are married, who are just as self-controlled as anyone Mr. Russell can show us, who are living in a terror of pregnancy, and they have men who are just as good to them. Men are not all beasts. These people give you an idea that men are a lustful, beastly creature, looking to violate some woman's virtue. I wonder why a man does not stand up against that. They never do. It takes a woman to stand up for them. I know that most of the women that I have lived with—their husbands are men who are just as considerate and decent as anyone you can find. They are trapped in this ignorance. That is what is the matter. . . .

I am not going to take up all the time I have been allotted because I am quite through. I want to say in the first place birth control joins the fight against the transmission of venereal disease to the next generation. Birth control is the pivot around which every movement must swing making for race betterment. Birth control does not act as a substitute for any social scheme or other ideal system. But it must be the base and serve them as a foundation.

Birth control will free the mother from the trap of pregnancy. It will save the child from that procession of coffins, as well as from the toil of mill and factory.

Birth control will make parenthood a voluntary function instead of an accident as it is today. When motherhood and childhood is free, we then can go hand in hand with man, to remake the world, for the glorification as well as the emancipation of the human race. (*Applause.*) . . .

Winter Russell
THIRD SPEECH

. . . We are misled on this matter of quality—this matter of accomplishments. I don't know how I can possibly impress this any better than this. I believe that a woman who comes into Ellis Island and can neither read or write, and has seven to eight children, is worth more to the United States of America than a graduate of Vassar University. I will go further. I say this, that if I had not been blessed with a wife and a mother such as Mrs. Russell is, that I would choose for a wife today—I would rather have a girl that cooks and can't read nor write, who loves children than some of these graduates with accomplishments.

We have four sons, and I hope and I pray that instead of getting as a wife an educated rag and a bone and a hank of hair with accomplishments, that they will get some of these women that want and love a big family of children. I believe that their life will be richer, nobler, and fuller. I have a daughter. I hope and I devoutly pray that instead of any person who is so utterly absorbed in this volunteer practice and they think that after some years that they will have one or two children—I would not say a common working man—I would say a divine working man—I would rather she have one of those and have a big family of children rather than she should have one of the other kind.

Introduction to Document 7

Margaret Sanger's commitment to freeing women from domestic entrapment never wavered. Yet by the 1920s, her language tilted increasingly toward depicting birth control as a means of reducing "undesirable" populations. Note here how her empathy for working people gave way to disturbing fears of convicts, prostitutes, the insane, and other "defectives."

DOCUMENT 7 *From* **Woman and the New Race**

Margaret Sanger

The creators of over-population are the women, who, while wringing their hands over each fresh horror, submit anew to their task of producing the multitudes who will bring about the *next* tragedy of civilization.

While unknowingly laying the foundations of tyrannies and providing the human tinder for racial conflagrations, woman was also unknowingly creating slums, filling asylums with insane, and institutions with other defectives. She was replenishing the ranks of the prostitutes, furnishing grist for the criminal courts and inmates for prisons. Had she planned deliberately to achieve this tragic total of human waste and misery, she could hardly have done it more effectively.

Woman's passivity under the burden of her disastrous task was almost altogether that of ignorant resignation. She knew virtually nothing about her reproductive nature and less about the consequences of her excessive childbearing. It is true that, obeying the inner urge of their natures, *some* women revolted. They went even to the extreme of infanticide and abortion. Usually their revolts were not general enough. They fought as individuals, not as a mass. In the mass they sank back into blind and hopeless subjection. They went on breeding with staggering rapidity those numberless, undesired children who become the clogs and the destroyers of civilizations.

To-day, however, woman is rising in fundamental revolt. Even her efforts at mere reform are, as we shall see later, steps in that direction. Underneath each of them is the feminine urge to complete freedom. Millions of women are asserting their right to voluntary motherhood. They are determined to decide for themselves whether they shall become mothers, under what conditions and when. This is the fundamental revolt referred to. It is for women the key to the temple of liberty.

Even as birth control is the means by which woman attains basic freedom, so it is the means by which she must and will uproot the evil she has wrought through her submission. As she has unconsciously and ignorantly brought about social disaster, so must and will she consciously and intelligently *undo* that disaster and create a new and a better order. . . .

From Margaret Sanger, *Woman and the New Race* (NY, 1920) pp. 4–6

POSTSCRIPT

Margaret Sanger's drift toward intolerance grew more pronounced as the years passed. In 1922 she published *The Pivot of Civilization,* in which she argued that the "overfecundity" of the "degenerate classes" was responsible for poverty and crime. She used phrases like "human waste," "human weeds," the "unfit," and "dead weight" to describe the poor and the disabled; she argued that charity only encouraged overbreeding; she advocated that the state administer IQ tests to identify "degenerates" and prevent them from breeding uncontrollably. By 1932, she advocated in *The Birth Control Review* segregating or even sterilizing people deemed by the government to be genetically inferior.

Thus, birth control's gradual acceptance under the law was accompanied by a shift away from its radical beginnings. The legal barriers against transmitting contraceptive information and devices were gradually repealed, overturned, or ignored. Conservative women, even members of elite women's clubs, had generally opposed birth control because it seemed to assault motherhood, which had become both a hallowed role for women and a safeguard against male selfishness (men, after all, were still the prime breadwinners). Many women on the left also opposed birth control. They argued that the movement did not promise radical change, and some even claimed that contraceptives would only make women more vulnerable to sexual exploitation by men, who could now escape the consequences of their acts.

Still, a growing number of women insisted on having command over their own reproductive lives. In the 1920s and after, the birth control movement became thoroughly the creature of middle-class professionals: doctors, nurses, social workers, and public health administrators. Moreover, the movement grew quite bureaucratized, as activities were directed from central institutions, Margaret Sanger's American Birth Control League being prime among them. With bureaucratization and professionalization from the 1920s onward, the tone and goals of the movement changed profoundly. One result was a distinctly elitist shift in direction. When the early opponents of contraception spoke of "race suicide," they meant that "inferior" peoples—immigrants, the poor, and blacks—would outbreed and overwhelm old-stock, respectable white people. Sanger herself drifted toward that position, and by the 1920s, birth controllers often allied themselves with eugenicists.

Eugenics is the "science" of human engineering. While men like Theodore Roosevelt had argued that the "best" people—white, successful, and respectable—were breeding in numbers insufficient to keep up with more "virile" races, birth control advocates now claimed that legalization would help curb the masses' tendency to produce retarded, diseased offspring. Contraceptives, in other words, might limit the "breeding" of "racially inferior" peoples. The eugenics movement had powerful supporters, and the elitist tendencies of professionalization gave birth controllers a common cause with those who wished to engineer human population. Emblematic of the movement increasingly abandoning its working-class sympathies during the 1920s, the Sanger clinics began to keep records showing the nationality, religion, heredity, occupation, and union affiliation of patients. In her *Autobiography* (1938), Sanger even argued that the eugenics and birth control movements needed each other: "The eugenists wanted to shift the birth-control emphasis from less children for the poor to more children for the rich. We went back of that and sought first to stop the multiplication of the unfit." She no longer saw the poor as those who might be empowered to resist their oppression, but as the source for the "unfit" on the road to elimination.

QUESTIONS

Defining Terms

Identify in the context of the chapter each of the following:

contraceptive devices	birth control
Comstock Law of 1873	feminists
The Woman Rebel	Society for the Suppression of Vice
Michael Dowling	Winter Russell
"race suicide"	"Sex control is the best path to self control"

Probing the Sources

1. Recount the main arguments against birth control. In favor of birth control.

2. Why did Margaret Sanger become an advocate of birth control? Why did she believe that the issue was so important?

3. What religious reasons were given for opposing the use of birth control devices and information? How did birth control advocates respond?

4. What dangers did Michael Dowling, Winter Russell, Anthony Comstock, and some doctors see in the legalization of birth control?

5. How did Sanger's ideas change with time?

Interpreting the Sources

1. What moral or ethical claims did Sanger and Russell make in their debate? How would you characterize the ideological division between these two?

2. To what extent was birth control a women's issue? What do you think each side in the debate would have said to Italian, Chinese, or Jewish women?

3. What similarities or differences do you see between the debate over birth control and the current debate over abortion?

4. Does Winter Russell's call for self-control remind you of other documents you have read in this collection? How is such a belief related not just to personal values, but to larger social ideologies?

5. Why were issues of class, race, and ethnicity so important to opponents and proponents of family planning?

ADDITIONAL READING

The best general history of sexual behavior and ideology in America is Estelle Friedman and John D'Emilio, *Intimate Matters, A History of Sexuality in America* (1988). On the subject of birth control, see Elen Chesler, *Woman of Valor: Margaret Sanger and the Birth Control Movement in America* (1992); James Reed, *From Private Vice to Public Virtue* (1978); David M. Kennedy, *Birth Control in America: The Career of Margaret Sanger* (1970); and Linda Gordon, *Woman's Body, Woman's Right: A Social History of Birth Control in America* (1976). For discussions of related topics, see Allan M. Brandt, *No Magic Bullet: A Social*

History of Venereal Disease in the United States Since 1880 (1985); Elaine Tyler May, *Great Expectations: Marriage and Divorce in Post-Victorian America* (1980); Kathy Peiss, *Cheap Amusements: Working Women and Leisure in Turn-of-the-Century New York* (1986); Mary E. Odem, *Delinquent Daughters: Protecting and Policing Adolescent Sexuality* (1996); and Janet Farrell Brodie, *Contraception and Abortion in Nineteenth Century America* (1994).

Selling the War
Recruitment Posters of World War I

HISTORICAL CONTEXT

If you have watched a televised sporting event—or any other program aimed at an eighteen- to thirty-five-year-old age group—you have seen commercials designed to encourage young men and women to enlist in one or another of the armed services. The commercials are slick and professional; they feature attractive, well-conditioned young people and promise a better life replete with friends, adventure, and perhaps a touch of romance. They also appeal to values that Americans hold most dear. What are those values? And how do the commercials address them? These are the central questions that may be asked about such promotional campaigns, and though the values and forms of the commercials may change over the years, the ultimate object—the encouragement of enlistments—remains the same.

Take, for example, two popular marines commercials from the 1980s. The first begins with a scene from the court of King Arthur. Arthur, with his sword, Excalibur, in his hands, prepares to knight a young, handsome, physically ideal man. The knight-to-be dismounts from his powerful steed—the universal symbol in Western culture of nobility and masculine virility—and walks toward Arthur. The young man kneels, his head slightly bowed. Arthur lowers Excalibur to the man's shoulder, proclaiming him a knight. With a flash of lightning, the medieval knight is transformed into a modern marine. A voice and the on-screen message announce simply that the marines are "looking for a few good men." The second commercial centers on the process of forging and crafting a fine sword. It is filled with images of molten steel, a blacksmith forming a sword on his anvil, and an experienced craftsman finishing and polishing the sword. In the end, the sword finds its way into the hand of a marine, who demonstrates that he is trained fully in the handling of the weapon. Again a voice asserts that the marines are "looking for a few men with the mettle to be Marines."

Together the two commercials drive home the point of yet another marine slogan: "The few, the proud, the Marines." But what are the values to which these commercials appeal? Patriotism? At no point is patriotism mentioned or scenes of defending the United States shown. Upward mobility? Again, not really. Although many armed-forces commercials promise technical training or the opportunity of future education, here the images of horses, swords, and knights have an anachronistic appeal. Few modern soldiers would care to go into battle mounted on a horse and armed only with a sword. Rather, these effective appeals are narcissistic. Not unlike the commercials for health spas or gymnasiums, they attempt to enlist those who believe (or would like to believe) that they are the physical elite who may join a highly selective club. The commercials traffic in self-image.

The army, the air force, and, most recently, the navy have chosen to appeal to other values. The air force officially counsels, "Aim high." The army suggests, "Be all you can be, . . . and get an edge on life." The navy used to emphasize adventure with the slogan "It's not just a job, . . . it's an adventure." But beginning in 1988, its official slogan became, "You are tomorrow. . . . You are the Navy." All these slogans contain the same appeal—service in the armed forces is "a great place to start" a lucrative career. In one army commercial, a high school senior announces to his friends, while they engage in a late-night snack, that he has found a way to go to college; he will enlist in the army, and it will provide him with the opportunity to get a college education. Another army commercial shows a man and a woman meeting after a university class. To their mutual interest, they discover that the army provided them with a chance to attend college, and, of course, to meet. Here the promise of upward mobility is mixed with the promise of romance. It is important to note, however, that, once again, there are no overt appeals to patriotism or service to one's country, and, if military scenes are pictured at all, they are scenes of training and not of combat.

Self-image and self-advancement—both values are important to modern American culture. A nation at war presents a different problem to armed forces recruiters. The army in a time of war might be "a great place to begin" one's career, but it may also be the place where one's life ends. Therefore recruiters have to emphasize different values. World War I presented a series of difficult problems. Unlike World War II, there was no Pearl Harbor in World War I. The United States was not attacked, and millions of Americans—especially those with familial or emotional ties to Germany, Austria-Hungary, or Ireland—opposed the United States' entry into the war. For example, journalist H. L. Mencken openly defended Germany during the early years of the war. He ended letters to his German-American friends with "May all Englishmen roast forever in hell! A pox upon the English!" or "The Kaiser must and shall win!" And Mencken ended pro-German newspaper columns with "In Paris by Thanksgiving!" or "In Paris by Christmas!" Even people who did not cheer on the German war machine as Mencken did opposed President Woodrow Wilson's decision in April 1917 to involve the United States in the conflict. Intellectual Randolph Bourne clearly expressed his reasons for opposing America's decision to go to war. Far from being a noble struggle—"a war to end all wars" as Wilson phrased it—Bourne predicted that the war would become an imperialistic grab bag. In addition, at home it would foster the growth of governmental power, the suppression of civil liberties, and the curtailment of the free expression of ideas. War, Bourne wrote, "automatically sets in motion throughout society those irresistible forces of uniformity, for passionate cooperation with the Government in coercing into obedience the minority groups and individuals which lack the larger herd sense."

Bourne defined patriotism as "merely the emotion that fills the herd when it imagines itself engaged in mass defense or massed attack." And more than anything, he feared the mass herd instinct of people. Bourne's fear was fully justified. Moved to a frenzied sense of anti-Germanicism, the "herd" was capable of tragic and great harm. It cried for "100 percent Americanism." It demanded that hamburger and sauerkraut be renamed liberty sandwich and liberty cabbage, that the German language and literature no longer be taught in public schools, that all things German be viewed with suspicion and disgust. Along with mindless hate came mindless violence. In Wyoming, a man who exclaimed "Hoch der Kaiser" on the day that Wilson delivered his war message was hanged, cut down while still alive, and forced to kneel and kiss the American flag. Near St. Louis, a mob attacked Robert Prager, a German-American who had actually tried to enlist in the United States Navy, bound him in an American flag, dragged him through the streets, and lynched him before a cheering crowd of five hundred "patriots." For this crime, the leaders of the mob were tried and found not guilty. After the trial, one jury member remarked, "Well, I guess nobody can say we aren't loyal now." Such episodes would lead social critic Walter Lippmann to write in his influential essay *Public Opinion* (1922) that most American citizens are "mentally children or barbarians. . . . The stream of public opinion is stopped by them in little eddies of misunderstanding, where it is discolored with prejudices and farfetched analogy."

Bourne particularly dreaded the role the government would play in creating this sense of mass conformity. "It will be coercion from above that will do the trick rather than patriotism from below," he cautioned. True to his prediction, soon after America's entry into the war, the government officially began to shape the public's attitude toward the war effort and Germany. During the first month of the war, Wilson and his military leaders organized the Committee on Public Information (CPI) and placed George Creel, a Progressive supporter of Wilson and a muckraker journalist, at the head of the agency. At first, the CPI was no crude propaganda mill. In the early months of the CPI, Creel saw his duty as providing information that enlightened Americans, not propaganda and censorship that altered or hid the truth. Like Wilson, Creel believed in the essential righteousness of the American cause, and he insisted that a mere recitation of "the facts" would be enough to convince anyone. As the war went on, however, the CPI engaged in an ever-increasing amount of propaganda. Its Four-Minute Men, speakers who sang the praises of America's war effort, began to dwell more on German atrocities and less on American war aims; and upbeat films such as *Pershing's Crusaders* and *Old Colored Fighters* gave way to such hate productions as *Prussian Cur* and *The Kaiser, the Beast of Berlin.*

The American war message was spread in a number of ways. The CPI tirelessly pumped out propaganda—75 million pamphlets, 6,000 press releases, and 14,000 drawings. Some 75,000 speakers stumped for their country. Certainly words—written or spoken—were important, but equally as important were the posters that supported America's war effort. Posters were employed, noted one authority on the subject, "to call for recruits . . . , to request war loans, to make national policies acceptable, to spur industrial effort, to channel emotions such as courage or hate, to urge conservation of resources and inform the public of food and fuel substitutes." Often posters were used as part of some larger campaign and were augmented with personal appearances by celebrities, popular songs, press releases, flag ceremonies, and patriotic badges. Altogether, millions of posters were printed. For example, in the First Liberty Bond campaign, two million posters were printed; this number increased to five million for the Second Liberty Bond campaign and nine million for the Third Liberty Bond campaign.

To understand the impact of these posters, one has to try to imagine a time before television or even the mass use of radio. Although newspapers informed—or misinformed—the literate public, posters supplied a primary means of mass communication. Industries used posters to hawk their goods; newspapers and magazines used posters to entice readers; circuses and motion picture theaters used posters to attract spectators. Posters were everywhere—on the fences of baseball parks, on the sides of public and private buildings, and on the wooden sandwich boards that men and boys wore to advertise some product or event. When the British passenger liner the *Lusitania* was sunk by a German U-boat on May 7, 1915, the United States exploded with anger. Newspapers mourned the 128 Americans lost in the tragedy, and Wilson threatened war. But perhaps the horror and meaning of the event was most fully portrayed in a poster released by the Boston Committee of Public Safety in June of 1915. The crude but powerful image drawn by Fred Spear shows a drowning woman clothed in a gossamer gown sinking to the bottom of the sea. In her arms she maternally holds an infant. It is an almost surreal scene, both sensual and familial at the same time. "ENLIST" is the poster's simple message. The impact of the poster was felt across the nation.

Spear's poster—like the millions that would follow it—was "the weapon on the wall." Although it looked like art, in the fullest sense it was not art. Art seeks to extend the viewer's understanding of nature and life. War posters attempt to restrict the viewer's understanding. Peter Stanley, a historian of the subject, observed, "A successful poster was one capable of only one interpretation. Most of the posters . . . did not seek a dialogue: they imposed, imparted, and impelled, but did not inquire. They sought to persuade the viewer, and then to have him or her act in ways regarded as useful by the sponsors of the posters." To do this, they dealt with slogans and basic, easily comprehensible visual images. To strike the proper response, however, those images had to be part of the viewer's cultural baggage, and they had to speak to the viewer's deepest needs, desires, or fears.

A number of important illustrators and artists turned their talents to poster making during the war. In mid-April 1917, Charles Dana Gibson, creator of the Gibson Girl and the editor of the original *Life* magazine, called upon artists to enlist their creativity in the war effort. The result was the Division of Pictorial Publicity, which offered its services free of charge to the government. Such famous artists as James Montgomery Flagg, Howard Chandler Christy, and Joseph Pennell contributed to the output of the Division of Pictorial Publicity. Each artist brought to his work a distinctive style, and each labored to strike a particular chord in the viewer. James Montgomery Flagg appealed to simple, sentimental patriotism. In his most famous poster, a deadly serious Uncle Sam, modeled after himself, aims a pointed finger at the viewer and announces "I WANT <u>YOU</u> for the U.S. ARMY." Another poster, which pictures a sleeping woman dressed in the Stars and Stripes, reads, "WAKE UP, AMERICA! CIVILIZATION CALLS EVERY MAN WOMAN AND CHILD!" Howard Chandler Christy employed sex to make his point. The Christy Girl exuded a wholesome sex appeal. In one Navy recruitment poster, a Christy Girl exclaims, "<u>GEE</u>! I WISH I WERE <u>A MAN</u> . . . <u>I'd</u> JOIN The NAVY." In another, a more sultry Christy Girl says, "<u>I WANT YOU</u> for <u>THE NAVY.</u>" F. Strothman produced an effective Liberty Bond poster by portraying the Germans as Huns bent on destroying civilization. One of his posters shows a satan-eyed, spike-helmeted German, his bayonet and hands dripping blood, staring at the viewer over the smoldering rubble of a destroyed city. "Beat Back the HUN with LIBERTY BONDS," reads the poster.

THE DOCUMENTS
Recruitment Posters

The following posters proved effective during World War I. They managed to create a world without complexity, a world that was two-dimensional. By stereotyping Germans, women, and their fellow Americans, the artists were able to inflame emotions and bend reality. What appeals did they make? What fears were aroused? What values are embedded in these images?

Remember, war poster art is political in that it attempts to arouse a civic response. The challenge of such visual documents is the act of interpretation. Each poster can be "read." For example, Germans in American World War I posters are often portrayed as faceless or apelike, giving rise to the visual impression that they represent a subhuman enemy. As another example, the eyes of the central figure in the posters can also be read. What do the eyes say to each viewer? Do they seek to elevate or denigrate, challenge or flirt with the viewer? Eyes that look up often increase the viewer's estimation of the subject, and ennoble the cause that is being advanced. Eyes that look directly at the viewer are often meant to be threatening. To read the posters intelligently, you have to examine the small as well as the large details and constantly ask yourself, "What response is this meant to arouse?" Finally, since the posters are reprinted here in black and white, try to imagine what colors were used in the originals, for color is also political. Some colors, like primary red and black, are threatening and foreboding; others, like green, light blue, and silver, are uplifting.

Poster by James Montgomery Flagg. (National Archives)

Poster by Howard Chandler Christy. (National Archives)

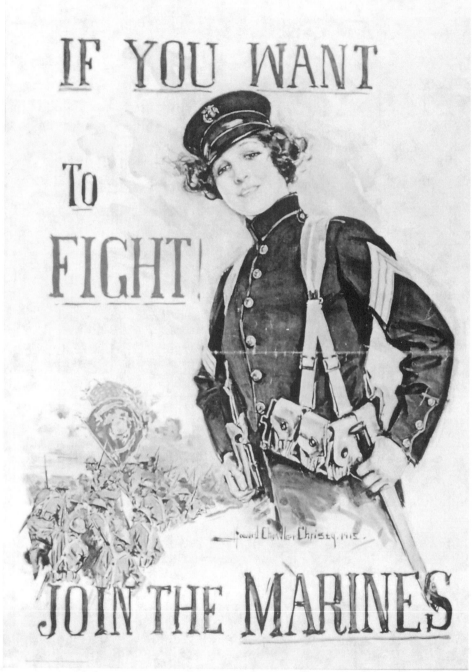

Poster by Howard Chandler Christy. (National Archives)

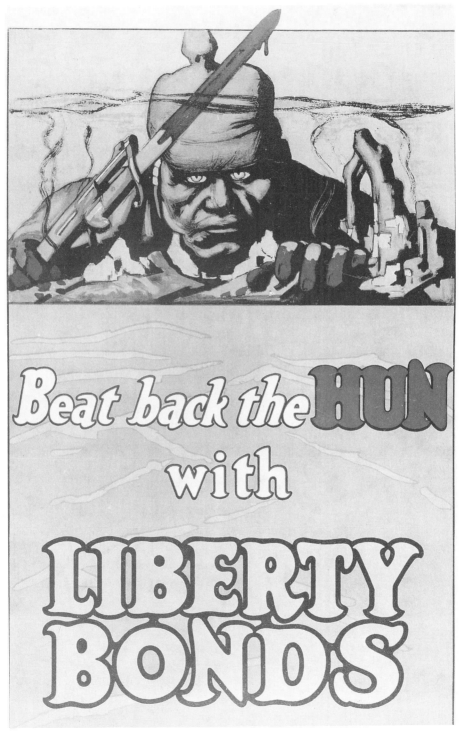

Poster by F. Strothmann. (National Archives)

Poster by James Montgomery Flagg. (National Archives)

Poster by James Montgomery Flagg. (National Archives)

(National Archives)

(National Archives)

Poster by Sidney H. Rosenberg.

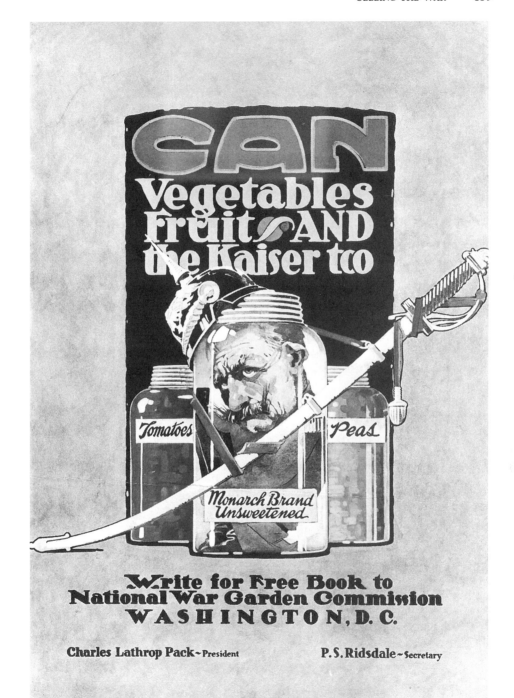

Poster by J. Paul Verrees. (West Point Museum)

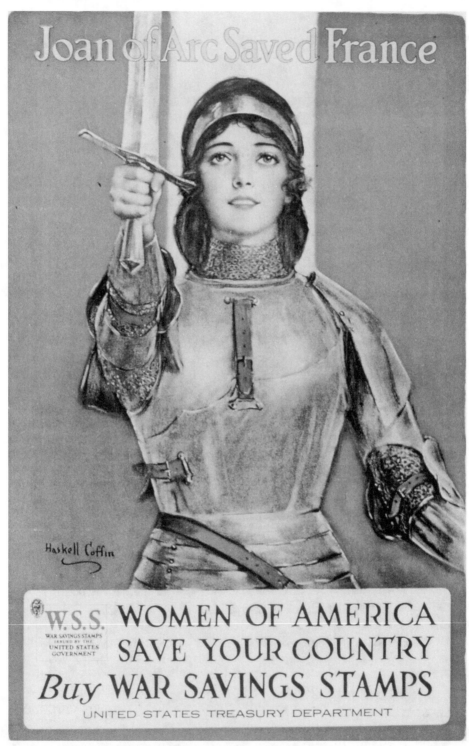

Poster by Haskell Coffin. (National Archives)

QUESTIONS

Defining Terms

Identify in the context of the chapter each of the following:

patriotism	"Be all you can be"
"100 percent Americanism"	George Creel
CPI	Fred Spear
the Gibson Girl	Liberty Bonds
James Montgomery Flagg	"GEE! I WISH I WERE A MAN"

Probing the Sources

1. What are the core values to which the posters speak? How do they compare to recruitment efforts that you have seen?

2. How are women portrayed in the posters?

3. How are Germans portrayed in the posters?

4. What emotions do the posters arouse?

5. According to the posters, why did America fight?

Interpreting the Sources

1. What advantages do visual appeals have over written appeals?

2. What similarities are there between the posters and such provocative writings as *The Jungle* and *How the Other Half Lives*?

3. How do you feel about the use of propaganda in a democracy?

4. Do you think advertising is a source of knowledge or deception? Give examples from your own experience.

5. How does World War I advertising differ from today's advertising for the military?

ADDITIONAL READING

Poster art and propaganda appeals are considered in George Creel, *How We Advertised America* (1920); Joseph Darracott and Belinda Loftus, *First World War Posters* (1972); Philipp Fehl and Patricia Fenix, *World War I Propaganda Posters* (1969); Maurice Richards, *Posters of the First World War* (1969); and E. McNight Kauffer, *The Art of the Poster* (1924). David M. Kennedy, *Over Here: The First World War and American Society,* (1980), explores the impact of the war on American society. Opposition to the war is discussed in H. C. Peterson and Gilbert C. Fite, *Opponents of War, 1917–1918* (1957), and William Preston, Jr., *Aliens and Dissenters: Federal Suppression of Radicals, 1903–1933* (1953). For the views of Randolph S. Bourne, see James R. Vitelli, *Randolph Bourne* (1981). Other works on the war include James Joll, *The Origins of the First World War* (1992); and Thomas Knock, *To End All Wars: Woodrow Wilson and the Quest for a New World Order* (1992).

Science on Trial
Tennessee versus John Thomas Scopes

HISTORICAL CONTEXT

During the 1920s, America was in many ways divided into two nations, one urban and one rural. Economic dynamism reigned in the cities.Business, particularly consumer industries, flourished. Urban Americans purchased cars and radios, vacuum cleaners, and other electrical appliances as never before. In rural America, however, there was no pronounced prosperity. Low prices for rural commodities stretched the financial resources of millions of farmers and took their toll on the small towns that depended on the business of farmers. Electrical lines had still not reached much of rural America, which remained as isolated as it had been in the nineteenth century. But more than economics divided urban and rural life. While many urban Americans reconciled their religious beliefs with scientific advancements in biology and geology, large numbers of rural Americans held to a strict Fundamentalist interpretation of the Bible. They insisted that the Rock of Ages was much younger than such scientists as Charles Darwin claimed. To be sure, Fundamentalism was not restricted just to rural America. But cultural and religious conservatism combined with economic stasis made the urban-rural division seem very wide.

Adherence to "that old-time religion" in small, rural Dayton, Tennessee, led to the decade's greatest showdown between the values of rural and urban America. Dayton lived in the shadow of urban prosperity. To its southwest, Chattanooga served as the hub of the region, attracting northern investment capital and surplus population. As for Dayton—the "other Dayton," people called it, referring to the bigger Dayton, Ohio—it enjoyed only modest, fitful growth and prosperity. To be sure, some citizens saw hopeful signs of a better future for Dayton. Most of its major streets were paved; a few automobiles navigated those streets; trains and buses made regular stops; and the tax rate was one of the lowest in the state. And Dayton was the county seat of a thriving farm region. But with all this, the town's business section was small and the town's prospects for the future were not great. To most outsiders, Dayton seemed—and largely was—a quiet, sleepy southern town where little changed but the seasons. Commenting on the lack of social experimentation in the town, historian Ray Ginger noted:

> Whiskey had been banned by local option since 1903. Dayton had no gamblers and no abandoned women—unless one chooses to think that all of its women had been

abandoned. They did not smoke cigarettes, wear cosmetics, or bob their hair. They never attended trials. No woman had ever served on a jury in the county. The women's clubs stayed out of civic affairs. That was men's business. White men. The town's two hundred Negroes observed the law and stayed in their prescribed place.

In 1925, it was not just Dayton that seemed backward; the entire state of Tennessee appeared behind the times to liberal-thinking, religiously progressive Americans. In that year, John Washington Butler, a decent, respected forty-nine-year-old farmer who had been elected to the Tennessee legislature the previous year, introduced a bill to make it illegal to teach the theory of evolution in the state's public schools. Butler's crusade was fired by passionate intensity, and those who opposed the bill were paralyzed by a lack of conviction. The faculty of the University of Tennessee maintained a deafening public silence, although in private many opposed the bill. The officials of the state's department of education were similarly mute, and the leaders of the Tennessee Academy of Science joined the silent chorus. As for the legislators themselves, they sat back and hoped that the entire embarrassment would go away. Describing the curious legislative process, William Manchester wrote:

> The House of Representatives—believing, its leaders claimed, that the Senate would kill it—passed the bill overwhelmingly. The Senate, thinking the governor would veto it, did likewise, and the governor, to the astonishment of that body, signed it on March 21, 1925. Butler's theology . . . had been translated into law by the irresponsible canons of political chance.

The passage of the antievolution law did not end the public debate over the issue. In fact, it did just the opposite. In Dayton, George Rappelyea, a native of New York who was the manager of the Cumberland Coal and Iron Company of Dayton, expressed the opinion that the law was bunk. Down at Robinson's Drug Store, several natives of Dayton disagreed. Both sides discussed the merits of their case, but getting nowhere, they called in an outside opinion. Rappelyea summoned John Scopes, the local biology teacher, from the tennis courts and asked his opinion of the law. Scopes remarked that it would be impossible to teach biology without breaking the new law and that he had already broken the antievolution law in the classroom. The discussion—the heat it generated and the passions it inflamed—gave Rappelyea an idea. Why not have a test case for the law in Dayton? Scopes could teach a class on evolution, the police could arrest him for breaking the Butler law, and a trial could be staged in Dayton. It would put Dayton on the map and be good for local business at the same time. The trial will be "a big sensation," Rappelyea said. "Why not bring a lot of doctors and preachers here? Let's get H. G. Wells and a lot of big fellows." At first Scopes declined the offer. The thought of having an arrest and conviction on his record did not sit well with him. But eventually, he relented. "It was just a drugstore discussion that got past control," he later remarked.

H. G. Wells did not travel to Dayton, but a lot of other "big fellows" did. William Jennings Bryan quickly offered his services to the Christian defenders of the Butler law. Bryan was nearing the end of a long, industrious, and distinguished, if a bit disappointing, career. In 1896, he had exploded on the national scene with his "Cross of Gold" speech at the Democratic Presidential Convention in Chicago.

Claiming to represent the toiling masses—the American producers—Bryan had generated support for the free silver cause and won the Democratic nomination for the presidency. A great orator and a passionate believer, Bryan threw his heart and mouth into the campaign, but he lost the election. Only thirty-six years of age in 1896, he was young enough to try again. In 1900, he was nominated by the Democratic party to run once more for the presidency; again he lost. In 1908, the Democrats again chose Bryan to carry their standard, and for the third time he lost. After the 1908 election, he became increasingly involved in social crusades. In 1909, he announced his conversion to the prohibitionist cause and joined the fight for a national prohibition amendment. For a brief time before World War I, he served as Woodrow Wilson's secretary of state, resigning over a moral dispute. After the Great War ended, Bryan became an antievolutionist. With the same passion with which he had once embraced free silver, he latched onto the idea that Darwinism was the root of the world's troubles. People had to shun liberal modernism and return to the teachings of the Bible. "You believe in the ages of rocks: I believe in the Rock of Ages," he told his opponents. For Bryan it was a simple issue of good and evil. He did not see—or refused to acknowledge—the complexity of the issue. As Ray Ginger observed, "His perception changed every shade of gray into a dismal black or a dazzling white. He saw no object as it really was. The people were an Absolute Good, the gold power was an Absolute Evil, as was Darwinism." Consistent with this view, in 1924 Bryan drafted the text of an antievolution resolution passed by the Florida legislature, which made it illegal "to teach as true Darwinism or any other hypothesis that links man in blood relationship to any other form of life." Thus, when the call came from Dayton to stand witness for his beliefs, Bryan hurried to Tennessee to defend the Butler law.

Clarence Seward Darrow ventured to Dayton to defend Scopes and the Darwinian view of evolution. Like Bryan, Darrow was a product of rural America. He had been born and reared in Kinsman, Ohio, the son of a man who had attended Meadville Theological Seminary, preached for a short time, and then undergone a crisis in faith from which he emerged an agnostic. Clarence Darrow was clearly his father's son. He was skeptical of philosophical and religious absolutes, and he placed more faith in scientific rationalism than the untested teachings of the would-be guardians of public and private morality. Although he loved rural America—and held dear the independent rural ideal—he had made his reputation in Chicago and is most closely identified with urban society. And like the urban society of his day, Darrow presented a mass of contradictions: He started his career as a railroad lawyer but became the country's leading defense attorney; he passionately defended the rights of blacks but scoffed at equal rights for women; and he lived well and spent lavishly but harbored a belief in socialism. Yet of one thing he was certain: The state should defend, not restrict, a person's right of self-expression, and free speech was the foremost example of self-expression. It was this principle that drew Darrow from Chicago to Dayton. Scopes had the right to teach the theory of evolution even if the Tennessee legislature said he could not.

Joining Darrow and Bryan in Dayton were journalists, preachers, and an odd assortment of curious spectators. There was the white-haired, wild-eyed T. T. Martin, field secretary for the Anti-Evolution League, who urged all who would listen to "Drive Hell out of the high Schools." There was a party of Seventh Day Adventists who drove around Dayton in an automobile that proudly displayed a sign

Clarence Darrow and William Jennings Bryan at the Scopes trial. (AP/Wide World)

proclaiming, "Get Right with God." There were the many mountaineers who came into Dayton to see what all the commotion was about. One of the mountain people explained his position and that of many of Butler's defenders: "Well, brother, my way's the safest; just believe what the Bible says and quit trying to figure out something different."

Of all the reporters who traveled to Dayton, H. L. Mencken was the most notorious. He was the consummate cynic. A newspaperman from Baltimore, he was opposed to all that was smug and confident in the American character. He attacked American puritanism, decried the country's worship of business, and lambasted conventional morality and religion. For Mencken, Bryan represented the worst side of the American character. Bryan's confident refusal to subject any of his beliefs to questioning and his willingness to use the power of the federal government to make other people live by his rules repelled Mencken. And in the *Scopes* trial, Mencken saw repressive Bryanism writ large. On the day the trial began, Mencken wrote:

> The trial of the infidel Scopes . . . will greatly resemble, I suspect, the trial of a prohibition agent accused of mayhem in Union Hill, New Jersey. That is to say, it will be conducted with the most austere regard for the highest principles of jurisprudence. Judge and jury will go to extreme lengths to assure the prisoner the last and least of his rights. He will be protected in his person and feelings by the full military and naval power of the State of Tennessee. No one will be permitted to pull his nose, to pray publicly for his condemnation or even to make a face at him. But all the same he will

be bumped off inevitably when the time comes, and to the applause of all right-thinking men.

The *Scopes* trial dominated the public's interests. Indeed, in the still, intense summer heat of Dayton, Bryan and Darrow defended two different worldviews, one rooted in America's rural past and the other based on the tenets of scientific modernism. For Americans in 1925, the *Scopes* trial symbolized their country in transition. When Darrow and Bryan engaged in their famous confrontation, two worlds collided.

THE DOCUMENTS
Introduction to Documents 1 through 3

Document 1 is an excerpt from George William Hunter's *Civic Biology,* the textbook, published in 1914, that John Scopes used to teach evolution. Note the racial and class attitudes in this "scientific" text.

Document 2, Clarence Darrow's examination of William Jennings Bryan in the case of *Tennessee v. John Thomas Scopes,* has been edited to highlight the conflict between the two men. Most of the normal legal objections and rulings have been removed. Because of the extreme heat of the day, the examination was moved outdoors, and it lasted all day.

Five days after the end of the Scopes trial, Bryan suffered a cerebral hemorrhage and died. Document 3, H. L. Mencken's "In Memoriam: W. J. B.," was published in the Baltimore *Evening Sun* on July 27, 1925, the day after Bryan's death. Mencken rewrote the piece for the October 1925 issue of the *American Mercury.* Document 3 is selected from the second version. It, more than any other document, suggests the level of hostility between urban and rural America.

DOCUMENT 1 *From Civic Biology*

George William Hunter

The Doctrine of Evolution.—We have now learned that animal forms may be arranged so as to begin with very simple one-celled forms and culminate with a group which contains man himself. This arrangement is called the *evolutionary series.* Evolution means change, and these groups are believed by scientists to represent stages in complexity of development of life on the earth. Geology teaches that millions of years ago, life upon the earth was very simple, and that gradually more and more complex forms of life appeared, as the rocks formed latest in time show the most highly developed forms of animal life. The great English scientist, Charles Darwin, from this and other evidence, explained the theory of evolution. This is the belief that simple forms of life on the earth slowly and gradually gave rise to those more complex and that thus ultimately the most complex forms came into existence. . . .

Evolution of Man.—Undoubtedly there once lived upon the earth races of men who were much lower in their mental organization than the present inhabitants. If we follow the early history of man upon the earth, we find that at first he must have been little better than one of the lower animals. He was a nomad, wandering from place to place, feeding upon whatever living things he could kill with his hands. Gradually he must have learned to use weapons, and thus kill his prey, first using rough stone implements for this purpose. As man became more civilized, implements of bronze and of iron were used. About this time the subjugation and domestication of animals began to take place. Man then began to cultivate the fields, and to have a fixed place of abode other than a cave. The beginnings of civilization were long ago, but even to-day the earth is not entirely civilized.

The Races of Man.—At the present time there exist upon the earth five races or varieties of man, each very different from the other in instincts, social customs, and, to an extent, in structure. These are the Ethiopian or negro type, originating in Africa; the Malay or brown race, from the islands of the Pacific; the American Indian; the Mongolian or yellow race, including the natives of China, Japan, and the Eskimos; and finally, the highest type of all, the Caucasians, represented by the civilized white inhabitants of Europe and America. . . .

Improvement of Man.—If the stock of domesticated animals can be improved, it is not unfair to ask if the health and vigor of the future generations of men and women on the earth might not be improved by applying to them the laws of selection. This improvement of the future race has a number of factors in which we as individuals may play a part. . . .

Eugenics.—When people marry there are certain things that the individual as well as the race should demand. The most important of these is freedom from germ diseases which might be handed down to the offspring. Tuberculosis, syphilis, that dread disease which cripples and kills hundreds of thousands of innocent children, epilepsy, and feeble-mindedness are handicaps which it is not only unfair but criminal to hand down to posterity. The science of being well born is called *eugenics*.

The Jukes.—Studies have been made on a number of different families in this country, in which mental and moral defects were present in one or both of the original parents. The "Jukes" family is a notorious example. The first mother is known as "Margaret, the mother of criminals." In seventy-five years the progeny of the original generation has cost the state of New York over a million and a quarter of dollars, besides giving over to the care of prisons and asylums considerably over a hundred feeble-minded, alcoholic, immoral, or criminal persons. Another case recently studied is the "Kallikak" family. This family has been traced back to the War of the Revolution, when a young soldier named Martin Kallikak seduced a feeble-minded girl. She had a feeble-minded son from whom there have been to the present time 480 descendants. Of these 33 were sexually immoral, 24 confirmed drunkards, 3 epileptics, and 143 *feeble-minded*. The man who started this terrible line of immorality and feeble-mindedness later married a normal Quaker girl. From this couple a line of 496 descendants have come, with *no* cases of feeble-mindedness. The evidence and the moral speak for themselves!

Parasitism and Its Cost of Society.—Hundreds of families such as those described above exist to-day, spreading disease, immorality, and crime to all parts of this country. The cost to society of such families is very severe. Just as certain animals or plants become parasitic on other plants or animals, these families have become parasitic on society. They not only do harm to others by corrupting, stealing, or spreading disease, but they are actually protected and cared for by the state out of public money. Largely for them the poorhouse and the asylum exist. They take from society, but they give nothing in return. They are true parasites.

The Remedy.—If such people were lower animals, we would probably kill them off to prevent them from spreading. Humanity will not allow this, but we do have the remedy of separating the sexes in asylums or other places and in various ways preventing intermarriage and the possibilities of perpetuating such a low and degenerate race. Remedies of this sort have been tried successfully in Europe and are now meeting with success in this country.

Blood Tells.—Eugenics show us, on the other hand, in a study of the families in which are brilliant men and women, the fact that the descendants have received the *good* inheritance from their ancestors. The following, taken from Davenport's *Heredity in Relation to Eugenics*, illustrates how one family has been famous in American History.

In 1667 Elizabeth Tuttle, "of strong will, and of extreme intellectual vigor, married Richard Edwards of Hartford, Conn., a man of high repute and great erudition. From their one son descended another son, Jonathan Edwards, a noted divine, and president of Princeton College. Of the descendants of Jonathan Edwards much has been written; a brief catalogue must suffice: Jonathan Edwards, Jr., president of Union College; Timothy Dwight, president of Yale; Sereno Edwards Dwight, president of Hamilton College; Theodore Dwight Woolsey, for twenty-five years president of Yale College; Sarah, wife of Tapping Reeve, founder of Litchfield Law School, herself no mean lawyer; Daniel Tyler, a general in the Civil War and founder of the iron industries of North Alabama; Timothy Dwight, second, president of Yale University from 1886 to 1898; Theodore William Dwight, founder and for thirty-three years warden of Columbia Law School; Henrietta Frances, wife of Eli Whitney, inventor of the cotton gin, who, burning the midnight oil by the side of her ingenious husband, helped him to his enduring fame; Merrill Edwards Gates, president of Amherst College; Catherine Maria Sedgwick of graceful pen; Charles Sedgwick Minot, authority on biology and embryology in the Harvard Medical School; Edith Kermit Carow, wife of Theodore Roosevelt; and Winston Churchill, the author of *Coniston* and other well-known novels."

Of the daughters of Elizabeth Tuttle distinguished descendants also came: Robert Treat Paine, signer of the Declaration of Independence; Chief Justice of the United States Morrison R. Waite; Ulysses S. Grant and Grover Cleveland, presidents of the United States. These and many other prominent men and women can trace the characters which enabled them to occupy the positions of culture and learning they held back to Elizabeth Tuttle.

Euthenics.—Euthenics, the betterment of the environment, is another important factor in the production of a stronger race. The strongest physical characteristics may be ruined if the surroundings are unwholesome and unsanitary. The slums of a city are "at once symptom, effect, and cause of evil." A city which allows foul tenements, narrow streets, and crowded slums to exist will spend too much for police protection, for charity, and for hospitals.

Every improvement in surroundings means improvement of the chances of survival of the race. In the spring of 1913 the health department and street-cleaning department of the city of New York cooperated to bring about a "clean up" of all filth, dirt, and rubbish from the houses, streets, and vacant lots in that city. During the summer of 1913 the health department reported a smaller percentage of deaths of babies than ever before. We must draw our own conclusions. Clean streets and houses, clean milk and pure water, sanitary housing, and careful medical inspection all do their part in maintaining a low rate of illness and death, thus reacting upon the health of the citizens of the future. . . .

DOCUMENT 2 *Darrow versus Bryan*

Mr. Hays	[defense attorney]: The defense desires to call Mr. Bryan as a witness. . . .
Darrow:	You have given considerable study to the Bible, haven't you, Mr. Bryan?
Bryan:	Yes, sir, I have.
D:	Well, we all know you have; we are not going to dispute that at all. But you have written and published articles almost weekly, and sometimes have made interpretations of various things?

B: I would not say interpretations, Mr. Darrow, but comments on the lesson.

D: If you comment to any extent, these comments have been interpretations.

B: I presume that my discussion might be to some extent interpretations, but they have not been primarily intended as interpretations. . . .

D: Do you claim that everything in the Bible should be literally interpreted?

B: I believe everything in the Bible should be accepted as it is given there; some of the Bible is given illustratively. For instance: "Ye are the salt of the earth." I would not insist that man was actually salt, or that he had flesh of salt, but it is used in the sense of salt as saving God's people.

D: But when you read that Jonah swallowed the whale—or that the whale swallowed Jonah—excuse me, please—how do you literally interpret that?

B: When I read that a big fish swallowed Jonah—it does not say whale.

D: Doesn't it? Are you sure?

B: That is my recollection of it. A big fish, and I believe it, and I believe in a God who can make a whale and can make a man and make both do what He pleases . . .

B: Yes, sir. Let me add: one miracle is just as easy to believe as another.

D: It is for you.

B: It is for me.

D: Just as hard?

B: It is hard to believe for you, but easy for me. A miracle is a thing performed beyond what man can perform. When you get beyond what man can do, you get within the realm of miracles; and it is just as easy to believe in the miracle of Jonah as any other miracle in the Bible.

D: Perfectly easy to believe that Jonah swallowed the whale?

B: If the Bible said so; the Bible doesn't make as extreme statements as evolutionists do. . . .

D: Do you believe Joshua made the sun stand still?

B: I believe what the Bible says. I suppose you mean that the earth stood still?

D: I don't know. I am talking about the Bible now.

B: I accept the Bible absolutely.

D: The Bible says Joshua commanded the sun to stand still for the purpose of lengthening the day, doesn't it; and you believe it?

B: I do.

D: Do you believe at that time the sun went around the earth?

B: No, I believe that the earth goes around the sun.

D: Do you believe that the men who wrote it thought that the day could be lengthened or that the sun could be stopped?

B: I don't know what they thought.

D: You don't know?

B: I think they wrote the fact without expressing their own thoughts. . . .

D: Have you an opinion as to whether—whoever wrote the book, I believe Joshua, the Book of Joshua, thought the sun went around the earth or not? . . .

B: I believe that the Bible is inspired, with an inspired author. Whether one who wrote as he was directed to write understood the things he was writing about, I don't know.

D: Whoever inspired it? Do you think whoever inspired it believed that the sun went around the earth?

B: I believe it was inspired by the Almighty, and He may have used language that could be understood at that time.

D: Was—

B: Instead of using language that could not be understood until Darrow was born. (*Laughter and applause*)

D: So, it might have been subject to construction, might it not? . . .

B: He was using language at that time the people understood. . . .

D: You believe the story of the flood to be a literal interpretation?

B: Yes, sir.

D: When was that flood?

B: I would not attempt to fix the date. The date is fixed, as suggested this morning.

D: About 4004 B.C.?

B: That has been the estimate of a man that is accepted today. I would not say it is accurate.

D: That estimate is printed in the Bible?

B: Everybody knows, at least, I think most of the people know, that was the estimate given.

D: But what do you think the Bible itself says? Don't you know how it was arrived at?

B: I never made a calculation.

D: A calculation from what?

B: I could not say.

D: From the generations of man?

B: I would not want to say that.

D: What do you think?

B: I do not think about things I don't think about.

D: Do you think about things you do think about?

B: Well, sometimes. (*Laughter*)

Policeman: Let us have order. . . .

B: These gentlemen have not had much chance—they did not come here to try this case. They came here to try revealed religion. I am here to defend it, and they can ask me any question they please.

The Court: All right. (*Applause*)

D: Great applause from the bleachers.

B: From those whom you call "yokels."

D: I have never called them yokels.

B: That is the ignorance of Tennessee, the bigotry.

D: You mean who are applauding you? (*Applause*)

B: Those are the people whom you insult.

D: You insult every man of science and learning in the world because he does not believe in your fool religion.

The Court: I will not stand for that. . . .

D: How long ago was the flood, Mr. Bryan?

B: Let me see Usher's calculation about it?

D: Surely. (*He hands a Bible to the witness*)

B: It is given here as 2348 years B.C.

D: Well, 2348 years B.C. You believe that all the living things that were not contained in the ark were destroyed?

B: I think the fish may have lived.

D: Outside of the fish?

B: I cannot say.

D: You cannot say?

B: No, except that just as it is, I have no proof to the contrary.

D: I am asking you whether you believe?

B: I do.

D: That all living things outside of the fish were destroyed?

B: What I say about the fish is merely a matter of humor.

D: I understand. . . .

B: I accept that, as the Bible gives it, and I have never found any reason for denying, disputing, or rejecting it. . . .

D: Don't you know there are any number of civilizations that are traced back to more than 5000 years?

B: I know we have people who trace things back according to the number of ciphers they have. But I am not satisfied they are accurate.

D: You are not satisfied there is any civilization that can be traced back 5000 years?

B: I would not want to say there is because I have no evidence of it that is satisfactory.

D: Would you say there is not?

B: Well, so far as I know, but when the scientists differ, from 24,000,000 to 306,000,000 in their opinion, as to how long ago life came here, I want them nearer, to come nearer together before they demand of me to give up my belief in the Bible. . . .

D: Let me make this definite. You believe that every civilization on the earth and every living thing, except possibly fishes, that came out of the ark were wiped out by the flood?

B: At that time.

D: At that time. And then, whatever human beings, including all the tribes, that inhabited the world, and have inhabited the world, and who run their pedigree straight back, and all the animals, have come onto the earth since the flood?

B: Yes.

D: Within 4200 years. Do you know a scientific man on the face of the earth that believes any such thing?

B: I cannot say, but I know some scientific men who dispute entirely the antiquity of man as testified to by other scientific men.

D: Oh, that does not answer the question. Do you know of a single scientific man on the face of the earth that believes any such thing as you stated, about the antiquity of man?

B: I don't think I have ever asked one the direct question.

D: Quite important, isn't it?

B: Well, I don't know as it is.

D: It might not be?

B: If I had nothing else to do except speculate on what our remote ancestors were and what our remote descendants may be—but I have been more interested in Christians living right now, to make it much more important than speculation on either the past or the future.

D: You have never had any interest in the age of the various races and people and civilization and animals that exist upon the earth today? Is that right?

B: I have never felt a great deal of interest in the effort that has been made to dispute the Bible by the speculations of men, or the investigations of men. . . .

D: . . . Now, I ask you if you know if it was interesting enough, or important enough for you to try to find out about how old these ancient civilizations were?

B: No; I have not made a study of it.

D: Don't you know that the ancient civilizations of China are 6000 or 7000 years old, at the very least?

B: No; they would not run back beyond the creation, according to the Bible, 6000 years.

D: You don't know how old they are, is that right?

B: I don't know how old they are, but probably you do. I think you would give the preference to anybody who opposed the Bible, and I give the preference to the Bible.

D: I see. Well, you are welcome to your opinion. Have you any idea how old the Egyptian civilization is?

B: No.

D: Do you know of any record in the world, outside of the story of the Bible, which conforms to any statement that it is 4200 years ago or thereabouts that all life was wiped off the face of the earth?

B: I think they have found records. . . .

D: Mr. Bryan, don't you know that there are many old religions that describe the flood?

B: No, I don't know.

D: You know there are others besides the Jewish?

B: I don't know whether there are records of any other religion which refer to this flood.

D: Don't you ever examine religion so far as to know that?

B: Outside of the Bible?

D: Yes.

B: No; I have not examined to know that, generally.

D: You have never examined any other religions?

B: Yes, sir.

D: Have you ever read anything about the origins of religions?

B: Not a great deal.

D: You have never examined any other religion?

B: Yes, sir.

D: And you don't know whether any other religion ever gave a similar account of the destruction of the earth by the flood?

B: The Christian religion has satisfied me, and I have never felt it necessary to look up some competing religions. . . .

D: Mr. Bryan, am I the first man you ever heard of who has been interested in the age of human societies and primitive man?

B: You are the first man I ever heard speak of the number of people at those different periods.

D: Where have you lived all your life?

B: Not near you. (*Laughter and applause*)

D: Nor near anybody of learning?

B: Oh, don't assume you know it all.

D: Do you know there are thousands of books in our libraries on all those subjects I have been asking you about?

B: I couldn't say, but I will take your word for it.

D: Did you ever read a book on primitive man? Like Tyler's *Primitive Culture*, or Boas, or any of the great authorities?

B: I don't think I ever read the ones you have mentioned.

D: Have you read any?

B: Well, I have read a little from time to time. But I didn't pursue it, because I didn't know I was to be called as a witness.

D: You have never in all your life made any attempt to find out about the other peoples of the earth—how old their civilizations are—how long they had existed on earth, have you?

B: No, sir; I have been so well satisfied with the Christian religion that I have spent no time trying to find arguments against it. . . .

Stewart: I want to interpose another object. What is the purpose of this examination?

B: The purpose is to cast ridicule on everybody who believes in the Bible, and I am perfectly willing that the world shall know that these gentlemen have no other purpose than ridiculing every Christian who believes in the Bible.

D: We have the purpose of preventing bigots and ignoramuses from controlling the education of the United States and you know it, and that is all.

B: I am glad to bring out that statement. I want the world to know that this evidence is not for the view Mr. Darrow and his associates have filed affidavits here stating, the purpose of which, I understand, is to show that the Bible story is not true.

Malone: Mr. Bryan seems anxious to get some evidence in the record that would tend to show that those affidavits are not true.

B: I am not trying to get anything into the record. I am simply trying to protect the Word of God against the greatest atheist or agnostic in the United States. (Prolonged applause) I want the papers to know I am not afraid to get on the stand in front of him and let him do his worst. I want the world to know. (Prolonged applause)

D: I wish I could get a picture of these clackers. . . .

D: Mr. Bryan, do you believe that the first woman was Eve?

B: Yes.

D: Do you believe she was literally made out of Adam's rib?

B: I do.

D: Did you ever discover where Cain got his wife?

B: No, sir; I leave the agnostics to hunt for her.

D: You have never found out?

B: I have never tried to find out.

D: You have never tried to find out?

B: No.

D: The Bible says he got one, doesn't it? Were there other people on the earth at that time?

B: I cannot say.

D: You cannot say. Did that ever enter your consideration?

B: Never bothered me.

D: There were no others recorded, but Cain got a wife.

B: That is what the Bible says.

D: Where she came from you do not know. All right. Does the statement, "The morning and the evening were the first day," and "The morning and the evening were the second day," mean anything to you?

B: I do not think it necessarily means a twenty-four-hour day.

D: You do not?

B: No.

D: What do you consider it to be?

B: I have not attempted to explain it. If you will take the second chapter— let me have the book. (Examines the Bible) The fourth verse of the second chapter says: "These are the generations of the heavens and of the earth, when they were created in the day that the Lord God made the earth and the heavens." The word "day" there in the very next chapter is used to describe a period. I do not see that there is any necessity for construing the words, "the evening and the morning," as meaning necessarily a twenty-four-hour day, "in the day when the Lord made the heaven and the earth."

D: Then, when the Bible said, for instance, "and God called the firmament heaven. And the evening and the morning were the second day," that does not necessarily mean twenty-four hours?

B: I do not think it necessarily does.

D: Do you think it does or does not?

B: I know a great many think so.

D: What do you think?

B: I do not think it does.

D: You think those were not literal days?

B: I do not think they were twenty-four-hour days.

D: What do you think about it?

B: That is my opinion—I do not know that my opinion is better on that subject than those who think it does.

D: You do not think that?

B: No. But I think it would be just as easy for the kind of God we believe in to make the earth in six days as in six years or in 6,000,000 years or in 600,000,000 years. I do not think it important whether we believe one or the other.

D: Do you think those were literal days?

B: My impression is they were periods, but I would not attempt to argue as against anybody who wanted to believe in literal days.

D: Have you any idea of the length of the periods?

B: No; I don't.

D: Do you think the sun was made on the fourth day?

B: Yes.

D: And they had evening and morning without the sun?

B: I am simply saying it is a period.

D: They had evening and morning for four periods without the sun, do you think?

B: I believe in creation as there told, and if I am not able to explain it I will accept it. Then you can explain it to suit yourself.

D: Mr. Bryan, what I want to know is, do you believe the sun was made on the fourth day?

B: I believe just as it says there.

D: Do you believe the sun was made on the fourth day?

B: Read it.

D: I am very sorry; you have read it so many times you would know, but I will read it again:
"And God said, let there be lights in the firmament of the heaven, to divide the day from the night; and let them be for signs, and for seasons, and for days, and years. And let them be for lights in the firmament of the heaven, to give light upon the earth; and it was so. And God made two great lights; the greater light to rule the day, and the lesser light to rule the night; He made the stars also. And God set them in the firmament of the heaven, to give light upon the earth, and to rule over the day and over the night, and to divide the light from the darkness; and God saw that it was good. And the evening and the morning were the fourth day."
Do you believe, whether it was a literal day or a period, the sun and the moon were not made until the fourth day?

B: I believe they were made in the order in which they were given there. . . .

D: Cannot you answer my question?

B: I have answered it. I believe that it was made on the fourth day, in the fourth day.

D: And they had the evening and the morning before that time for three days or three periods. All right, that settles it. Now, if you call those periods, they may have been a very long time. . . .

B: Your Honor, I think I can shorten this testimony. The only purpose Mr. Darrow has is to slur at the Bible, but I will answer his question. I will answer it all at once, and I have no objection in the world, I want the world to know that this man, who does not believe in a God, is trying to use a court in Tennessee—

D: I object to that.

B: (*Continuing*)—to slur at it, and while it will require time. I am willing to take it.

D: I object to your statement. I am examining you on your fool ideas that no intelligent Christian on earth believes.

The Court: Court is adjourned until tomorrow morning.

Document 3   *"In Memoriam: W. J. B."*

H. L. Mencken

Has it been duly marked by historians that William Jennings Bryan's last secular act on this globe of sin was to catch flies? A curious detail, and not without its sardonic overtones. He was the most sedulous fly-catcher in American history, and in many ways the most successful. His quarry, of course, was not *Musca domestica* but *Homo neandertalensis*. For forty years he tracked it with coo and bellow, up and down the rustic backways of the Republic. Wherever the flambeaux of Chautauqua smoked and guttered, and the bilge of idealism ran in the veins, and Baptist pastors dammed the brooks with the sanctified, and men gathered who were weary and heavy laden, and their wives who were full of Peruna and as fecund as the shad (*Alosa sapidissima*), there the indefatigable Jennings set up his traps and spread his bait. He knew every country town in the South and West, and he could crowd the most remote of them to suffocation by simply winding his horn. The city proletariat, transiently flustered by him in 1896, quickly penetrated his buncombe and would have no more of him; the cockney gallery jeered him at every Democratic national convention for twenty-five years. But out where the grass grows high, and the horned cattle dream away the lazy afternoons, and men still fear the powers and principalities of the air—out there between the corn-rows he held his old puissance to the end. There was no need of beaters to drive in his game. The news that he was coming was enough. For miles the flivver dust would choke the roads. And when he rose at the end of the day to discharge his Message there would be such breathless attention, such a rapt and enchanted ecstasy, such a sweet rustle of amens as the world had not known since Johann fell to Herod's ax.

There was something peculiarly fitting in the fact that his last days were spent in a one-horse Tennessee village, beating off the flies and gnats, and that death found him there. The man felt at home in such simple and Christian scenes. He liked people who sweated freely, and were not debauched by the refinements of the toilet. Making his progress up and down the Main street of little Dayton, surrounded by gaping primates from the upland valleys of the Cumberland Range, his coat laid aside, his bare arms and hairy chest shining damply, his bald head sprinkled with dust—so accoutred and on display, he was obviously happy. He liked getting up early in the morning, to the tune of cocks crowing on the dunghill. He liked the heavy, greasy victuals of the farmhouse kitchen. He liked country lawyers, country pastors, all country people. He liked country sounds and country smells.

I believe that this liking was sincere—perhaps the only sincere thing in the man. His nose showed no uneasiness when a hillman in faded overalls and hickory shirt accosted him on the street, and besought him for light upon some mystery of Holy Writ. The simian gabble of the cross-roads was not gabble to him, but wisdom of an occult and superior sort. In the presence of city folks he was palpably uneasy. Their clothes, I suspect, annoyed him, and he was suspicious of their too delicate manners. He knew all the while that they were laughing at him—if not at his baroque theology, then at least at his alpaca pantaloons. But the yokels never laughed at him. To them he was not the huntsman but the prophet, and toward the end, as he gradually forsook mundane politics for more ghostly concerns, they began to elevate him in their hierarchy. When he died he was the peer of Abraham. His old enemy, Wilson, aspiring to the same white and shining robe, came down with a thump. But Bryan made the grade. His place in Tennessee hagiography is secure. If the village barber saved any of his hair, then it is curing gall-stones down there today.

But what label will he bear in more urbane regions? One, I fear, of a far less flattering kind. Bryan lived too long, and descended too deeply into the mud, to be taken seriously hereafter by fully literate men, even of the kind who write schoolbooks. There was a scattering of sweet words in his funeral notices, but it was no more than a response to conventional sentimentality. The best verdict the most romantic editorial writer could dredge up, save in the humorless South, was to the general effect that his imbecilities were excused by his earnestness—that under his clowning, as under that of the juggler of Notre Dame, there was the zeal of a steadfast soul. But this was apology, not praise; precisely the same thing might be said of Mary Baker G. Eddy. The truth is that even Bryan's sincerity will probably yield to what is called, in other fields, definitive criticism. . . .

This talk of sincerity, I confess, fatigues me. If the fellow was sincere, then so was P. T. Barnum. The word is disgraced and degraded by such uses. He was, in fact, a charlatan, a mountebank, a zany without sense or dignity. His career brought him into contact with the first men of his time; he preferred the company of rustic ignoramuses. It was hard to believe, watching him at Dayton, that he had traveled, that he had been received in civilized societies, that he had been a high officer of state. He seemed only a poor clod like those around him, deluded by a childish theology, full of an almost pathological hatred of all learning, all human dignity, all beauty, all fine and noble things. He was a peasant come home to the barnyard. Imagine a gentleman, and you have imagined everything that he was not. What animated him from end to end of his grotesque career was simply ambition—the ambition of a common man to get his hand upon the collar of his superiors, or, failing that, to get his thumb into their eyes. He was born with a roaring voice, and it had the trick of inflaming half-wits. His whole career was devoted to raising those half-wits against their betters, that he himself might shine.

His last battle will be grossly misunderstood if it is thought of as a mere exercise in fanaticism—that is, if Bryan the Fundamentalist Pope is mistaken for one of the bucolic Fundamentalists. There was much more in it than that, as everyone knows who saw him on the field. What moved him, at bottom, was simply hatred of the city men who had laughed at him so long, and brought him at last to so tatterdemalion an estate. He lusted for revenge upon them. He yearned to lead the anthropoid rabble against them, to punish them for their execution upon him by attacking the very vitals of their civilization. He went far beyond the bounds of any merely religious frenzy, however inordinate. When he began denouncing the notion that man is a mammal even some of the hinds at Dayton were agape. And when, brought upon Clarence Darrow's cruel hook, he writhed and tossed in a very fury of malignancy, bawling against the veriest elements of sense and decency like a man frantic—when he came to that tragic climax of his striving there were snickers among the hinds as well as hosannas.

Upon that hook, in truth, Bryan committed suicide, as a legend as well as in the body. He staggered from the rustic court ready to die, and he staggered from it ready to be forgotten, save as a character in a third-rate farce, witless and in poor taste. It was plain to everyone who knew him, when he came to Dayton, that his great days were behind him—that, for all the fury of his hatred, he was now definitely an old man, and headed at last for silence. There was a vague, unpleasant manginess about his appearance; he somehow seemed dirty, though a close glance showed him as carefully shaven as an actor, and clad in immaculate linen. All the hair was gone from the dome of his head, and it had begun to fall out, too, behind his ears, in the obscene manner of Samuel Gompers. The resonance had departed from his voice; what was once a bugle blast had become reedy and quavering. Who knows that, like Demosthenes, he had a lisp? In the old days, under the magic of his eloquence, no one noticed it. But when he spoke at Dayton it was always audible.

When I first encountered him, on the sidewalk in front of the office of the rustic lawyers who were his associates in the Scopes case, the trial was yet to begin, and so he was still expansive and amiable. I had printed in the *Nation*, a week or so before, an article arguing that the Tennessee anti-evolution law, whatever its wisdom, was at least constitutional—that the yahoos of the State had a clear right to have their progeny taught whatever they chose, and kept secure from whatever knowledge violated their superstitions. The old boy professed to be delighted with the argument, and gave the gaping bystanders to understand that I was a publicist of parts. Not to be outdone, I admired the preposterous country shirt that he wore—sleeveless and with the neck cut very low. We parted in the manner of two ambassadors.

But that was the last touch of amiability that I was destined to see in Bryan. The next day the battle joined and his face became hard. By the end of the week he was simply a walking fever. Hour by hour he grew more bitter. What the Christian Scientists call malicious animal magnetism seemed to radiate from him like heat from a stove. From my place in the courtroom, standing upon a table, I looked directly down upon him, sweating horribly and pumping his palm-leaf fan. His eyes fascinated me; I watched them all day long. They were blazing points of hatred. They glittered like occult and sinister gems. Now and then they wandered to me, and I got my share, for my reports of the trial had come back to Dayton, and he had read them. It was like coming under fire.

Thus he fought his last fight, thirsting savagely for blood. All sense departed from him. He bit right and left, like a dog with rabies. He descended to demagogy so dreadful that his very associates at the trial table blushed. His one yearning was to keep his yokels heated up—to lead his forlorn mob of imbeciles against the foe. That foe, alas, refused to be alarmed. It insisted upon seeing the whole battle as a comedy. Even Darrow, who knew better, occasionally yielded to the prevailing spirit. One day he lured poor Bryan into the folly I have mentioned: his astounding argument against the notion that man is a mammal. I am glad I heard it, for otherwise I'd never believe it. There stood the man who had been thrice a candidate for the Presidency of the Republic—there he stood in the glare of the world, uttering stuff that a boy of eight would laugh at. The artful Darrow led him on: he repeated it, ranted for it, bellowed it in his cracked voice. So he was prepared for the final slaughter. He came into life a hero, a Galahad, in bright and shining armor. He was passing out a poor mountebank.

POSTSCRIPT

After nine minutes of deliberation, the jury found Scopes guilty of violating the Butler law, and the court fined him $100. The verdict was later reversed on a technical defect in the trial.

QUESTIONS

Defining Terms

Identify in the context of the chapter each of the following:

Fundamentalism   Darwinism

John Butler   George Rappelyea

John Scope   William J. Bryan

Clarence Darrow   H. L. Mencken

Civic Biology   eugenics

Probing the Sources

1. What was the purpose of Darrow's examination of Bryan? How did Darrow characterize Bryan? How did Bryan characterize Darrow?

2. Bryan was the self-proclaimed defender of rural values and Fundamentalist beliefs. H. L. Mencken opposed Bryan and those who blindly followed him. What social and class tensions boil beneath Mencken's bilious obituary of Bryan?

3. Darrow placed his faith in science, but science had its own prejudices. What class and racial prejudices were being taught under the guise of science?

4. As a representative of urban America, how did Mencken regard rural America?

Interpreting the Sources

1. What issues and tensions were highlighted by the *Scopes* trial?

2. Are any of the larger issues that were debated in the *Scopes* trial still important today? Which ones? Why? How?

3. During which periods in American history has religious Fundamentalism been particularly strong? In what ways does Fundamentalism represent a social as well as a religious movement?

4. What was at stake for men like Darrow and Bryan in the trial?

ADDITIONAL READING

Ray Ginger, *Six Days or Forever* (1958), tells the story of the *Scopes* trial in all its detail and with all its color. Also see Edward J. Larson, *Summer for the Gods: The Scopes Trial and America's Continuing Debate over Science and Religion* (1997); and Ronald L. Numbers, *Darwinism Comes to America* (1998). For the religious issues involved, see Norman F. Furniss, *The Fundamentalist Controversy, 1918–1933* (1958). Bryan's last years are covered in Lawrence Levine, *Defender of the Faith* (1965). Clarence Darrow told his own story in *The Story of My Life* (1932). For Mencken, see William Manchester, *Disturber of the Peace* (1952), and Mencken's own *Heathen Days* (1943). The classic study of the 1920s is Frederick Lewis Allen, *Only Yesterday* (1931). Very good more recent treatments of the decade include Roderick Nash, *The Nervous Generation: American Thought, 1917–1930* (1970); William Leuchtenburg, *The Perils of Prosperity* (1958); Geoffrey Perrett, *America in the Twenties* (1982); and two books by Paul A. Carter, *The Twenties in America* (1969) and *Another Part of the Twenties* (1977).

Writing the Great Depression

HISTORICAL CONTEXT

Great literature, we like to believe, is timeless, so Shakespeare's works will endure forever. No doubt he gave voice to emotional truths that touch very diverse people. But interpretations of the meanings of Shakespeare's plays have varied widely over the years, and these interpretations have been shaped by events taking place in the interpreters' own times. Shakespeare himself was enmeshed in the social, religious, and political issues of Elizabethan England, and his plays are full of direct and indirect references to those issues. To give another example, from American literary history, Herman Melville's *Moby Dick* (1851) was mostly ignored during the nineteenth century; it became acknowledged as great literature only in the 1920s, long after the author's death. The reason was that Melville's work tended to be very skeptical of human perfectibility and social progress, and such skepticism resonated more for the intellectuals of the early twentieth century than for those in the nineteenth century.

Artists and writers always are influenced by the context of their times, and how their works are received depends on the historically shaped beliefs of those who behold them. This was especially true during the 1930s. Of course, the descent into economic depression that began with the stock market crash of October 1929 was felt most directly in material life. The previous decade had brought prosperity for middle- and upper-class Americans. True, the twenties were hard times for farmers and the urban poor, but a larger number of Americans than ever before had more income and could afford more consumer goods than at any time in U.S. history. With the Great Depression, however, came massive cuts in wages and employment. Per capita disposable income dropped about one-third, while the unemployment rate reached 25 percent in the early thirties. Working-class people were hit hardest, for they had few resources to fall back on, but the downward spiral of the economy tugged at almost everyone. To put it simply, most families still had the necessities of life, and even some luxuries, but most families also had less than before. More important, the number of families slipping into impoverishment grew dramatically.

Beyond the shrinkage of material resources, Americans' confidence was shaken. No one seemed to know when, how, or if the crisis would end; Franklin Roosevelt's New Deal helped some, but politicians and economists had no permanent solutions. The depression made people question the most fundamental tenets of the

American creed: that our economy and society ensured a brighter future for all, that equality of opportunity was the American way, that hard work would be rewarded, and that the American dream of prosperity still worked. How could they believe such things when the leaders and heroes of the twenties—businessmen, financiers, and great captains of wealth—seemed as confused as everyone else, when bread-lines grew ever longer, and when unemployment and poverty wore the familiar faces of family members and friends?

Much of the art and literature of the era reflected these changed perceptions. It was not as if the writers and artists of the twenties had been celebrants of American culture. On the contrary, the carnage of World War I, the meanness of the Ver-sailles treaty, the postwar era's gaudy materialism—these all alienated many tal-ented people, making them a "lost generation" of American writers. Several exiled themselves to Paris (Ernest Hemmingway and F. Scott Fitzgerald among them), but even those who stayed in the United States wrote with a bitterness born of betrayal. John Dos Passos captured his generation's loathing of the money grubbing, the spir-itual emptiness, and the unseemly hedonism just behind the espousal of democratic ideals. Most writers would have agreed with H. L. Mencken that the more a man declared his own honesty, patriotism, or piety, the more likely he was to be a scoundrel or a thief. Above all, the literature of the twenties stressed the individual's need to make a separate peace with the world; each person must suffer his or her pain alone and must find his or her own joy or community, but all must know that God, human society, and money could not save them.

Ironically, the literature of the Great Depression contained less of this cynicism. In the midst of the crisis, writers and artists no longer felt so peripheral to their culture. The worship of money that characterized most of the twenties culture marginalized all who felt that the life of the mind—scholarship, artistic creation, the humanities—counted for more than mere dollars. As the Great Depression ground on, Ameri-cans' belief that millionaires were heroes worthy of emulation grew shaky. For some intellectuals, there was a strange exhilaration in others' loss of faith in the American dream. If the competitive economy had atomized people, the depression could bring them together as each others' keepers, and there is no doubt that the redis-covery of communities—of workers, regions, and racial or ethnic groups—was an important theme of the writing of the decade.

Moreover, the crisis called for new *ideas*, intellectuals' specialty. On the most functional level, this meant the channeling of university people like economists and sociologists into the government. But even novelists and painters became tied to the Roosevelt administration. The New Deal appropriated funds for agencies like the Federal Writers Project (in which the government underwrote the creation of plays, oral histories, and travel guides), the Works Progress Administration (which hired unemployed artists to paint murals on new federal buildings), and the Farm Security Administration (in which unemployed photographers—including such respected camera artists as Dorothea Lange, Walker Evans, and Ansel Adams—documented the lives of homeless families, unemployed workers, and southern tenant farmers). So a small amount of government aid and, more important, a sense of being socially useful made the Great Depression a period of great energy and excitement in the arts.

This notion of being socially useful took highly political forms. For some, the crisis intensified a hatred of modernity, including cities, factories, and all that was progressive. This tendency was exemplified by the southern agrarians, a group of fiction writers, poets, and historians who self-consciously rejected the booming growth and power of the twentieth century to extol the virtues of small-scale life on the land, more particularly in the rural South. The agrarians were fundamentally conservative and nostalgic, and certainly they were blind to the poverty and racism of the southern past. Still, theirs was a powerful critique of the aggrandizing, money-worshiping, progress-loving elements of American culture.

More commonly, artists and writers turned to the left. Many believed that capitalism, with its enormous concentrations of private wealth and power, made a few rich while it impoverished the masses, and the Great Depression certainly seemed to offer evidence. Their political and economic solutions varied widely, from New Deal reforms through socialism, communism, and anarchism. What united them, however, was their commitment to depicting common folk struggling against the system that exploited them. Much of the cynicism of the twenties was gone, for the new literature sought to be a tool of empowerment. Rather than maintaining a detached and critical distance from America, intellectuals now strove to make the arts and humanities instruments of change by depicting ordinary people in their daily struggles, sometimes being overwhelmed, and sometimes winning symbolic or real triumphs.

Poverty, exploitation, disease—the arts revealed life in all of its grimness. Indeed, the primary task of creative expression, many would have argued, was to expose human misery and to unmask the evil system that caused it. However, it was at this historical moment of crisis that glimmers of hope also appeared in literature, hope arising from a renewed faith that masses of men and women could be makers of their own destinies, that they might seize as their birthright America's unfulfilled democratic promise.

Such an environment was not congenial to "art for art's sake," the belief that creativity was pure mental work that soared above the "real world." The view was that artists and intellectuals must never again become mere aesthetes, escaping from daily life to challenge themselves only by creating beautiful, if empty, works. They had an obligation to engage the issues confronting people. One can even see this shift in the styles of artistic expression: a renewed emphasis on realism and naturalism in fiction, less stress on abstraction in painting, and, above all, a shift to the documentary style, a mode of expression that seemed to deny the presence of the artist altogether. Documentary style pretends to be artless: the camera just records what is going on; the writer merely reports what she sees. The documentary style—seemingly objective, dispassionate, and factually accurate—became very common in fiction and nonfiction and in film and photography, for it appeared to reveal human suffering in the most clear and unmediated way and by so doing, sounded an unmistakable call for reform.

"Migrant Mother," by Dorothea Lange, 1936. (Library of Congress)

Homeless family in Oklahoma in 1938, by Dorothea Lange. (© 1982, The Oakland Museum, The City of Oakland)

Photographers working for New Deal agencies, most notably the Farm Security Administration, produced powerful images of the victims of the Great Depression. While the program provided employment for the artists, their photographs helped engender support for New Deal relief agencies.

Rural family during the depression, by Ben Shahn. (Library of Congress)

THE DOCUMENTS

Introduction to Document 1

During the Great Depression, Franklin and Eleanor Roosevelt and other members of the government received thousands of letters, some asking for assistance, others applauding the New Deal, still others condemning it. Document 1 gives a sense of the range of opinions expressed by citizens, including racist and nativist attacks on the poor, warnings that the New Deal smacked of communism, and declarations that, if something more was not done soon, revolution was inevitable. But above all, there were pleas for help from the poor.

DOCUMENT 1 *Americans Write to Their Leaders*

ElKader Iowa Sep the 11 1934

Mr. FranKlin Roosevelt
Dear President Roosevelt

I am in a terrible perdicament So I thought of you to send my plea of trouble to you because I drempt the other night that I Should write to you thinking that may = be I could get Some help from you as long as no one els will help me out I am an old woman Seventy two years old and an invalid that is the worst of it I can't get around at all. I bin Sitting in a chair for years already if I am not in bed I can't walk alone atall So that makes it pretty hard fore me to be put out of my home the one I worked so hard for over forty-Six years, So please help me Some way or I will half to Sine my last bit away if I could only raise thirteen Hundred Dollars than I could Stay in my home Oh. So please help me Mr. Roosevelt and answer right away or els it will be to late if I ever get onto my feet I Sure will try and pay you back. I helped So many out but it Seems now that I am in the grattes trouble no = body will help me So please Mr. Roosevelt help me Sincerly Mrs. A. M. U.

February 1936

Mr. and Mrs. Roosevelt
Wash. D.C.
Dear Mr. President:

I'm a boy of 12 years. I want to tell you about my family My father hasn't worked for 5 months He went plenty times to relief, he filled out application. They won't give us anything. I don't know why. Please you do something. We haven't paid 4 months rent, Everyday the landlord rings the door bell, we don't open the door for him. We are afraid that will be put out, been put out before, and don't want to happen again. We haven't paid the gas bill, and the electric bill, haven't paid grocery bill for 3 months. My brother goes to Lane Tech. High School. he's eighteen years old, hasn't gone to school for 2 weeks because he got no carfare. I have a sister she's twenty years, she can't find work. My father he staying home. All the time he's crying because he can't find work. I told him why are you crying daddy, and daddy said why shouldn't I cry when there is nothing in the house. I feel sorry for him. That night I couldn't sleep. The next morning I wrote this letter to you, in my room. Were American citizens and were born in Chicago, Ill. and I don't know why they don't help us Please answer right away because we need it. will starve Thank you.

God bless you.

Anonymous
Chicago, Ill.

Fayetteville, W.Va.
Nov. 4, 1936

[Dear Mrs. Roosevelt,]

. . . Personally I have found that the more you give the lower classes the more they want. Never satisfied. In my charitable work I become discouraged and it makes me know what your husband is up against. The people (some) are so simple-minded. They think the President is going to keep on giving. My gardener (White) and my maid (col.) voted democratic this election, not from coercion on my part but because "Roosevelt will take care of us." . . .

I am very sincerely yours,
Mrs. N. J. S.

New York, N.Y.
October 1939

Mr. Harry Hopkins
Washington, D.C.
Dear Mr. Hopkins:

Will you please investigate the various relief agencies in many cities of the United States. The cities where there are a large foreign and jewish population. No wonder the cities are now on the verge of bankruptcy because we are feeding a lot of ignorant foreigners by giving them relief. And, they are turning against us every day. I would suggest to deport all foreigners and jews who are not citizens over the United States back to any land where they choose to go and who will admit them. As America is now over crowded with too much immigration and it can not feed even its own citizens without feeding the citizens of other foreign nations. I have found out after careful investigation that we are feeding many foreigners who send out their wives to work and who have money in the bank. While the men drink wine and play cards in saloons and cafes. I have spoken to one Italian whom I met. And I ask him what he was doing for a living. He said me drinka da dago red wine and play cards and send the wife out to work. Isn't a very good thing for us to support them. No wonder the taxpayers are grumbling about taxes. Most of them are a race of black hands murders boot leggers bomb throwers. While most of the sheeney jews as they are called are a race of dishonest people who get rich by swindling, faking and cheating the poor people. Besides the jews are responsible by ruining others in business by the great amount of chisling done. And selling even below the cost prices, in order to get all the others business. The foreigners and jews spend as little as they can to help this country. And, they live as cheap as they can. And, work as cheap as they can, and save all the money they can. And when they have enough they go back to their country. Why don't we deport them under the section of the United States Immigration Laws which relates to paupers and those who become a public charge. The Communist Party is composed mostly by foreigners and jews. The jews are the leaders of the movement and urge the downfall of this government. . . .

A Taxpayer

Hornell, New York
March 7, 1934

U.S. Senator Robert F. Wagner
Senate Building,
Washington, D.C.

My Dear Senator:

It seems very apparent to me that the Administration at Washington is accelerating its pace towards socialism and communism. Nearly every public statement from Washington is against stimulation of business which would in the end create employment.

Everyone is sympathetic to the cause of creating more jobs and better wages for labor; but, a program continually promoting labor troubles, higher wages, shorter hours, and less profits for business, would seem to me to be leading us fast to a condition where the Government must more and more expand it's relief activities, and will lead in the end to disaster to all classes. . . .

I am not addicted to annoying public office holders with correspondence but if there are any private rights left in this country, then I would appreciate an early reply to this letter, so that I may take such action as is still possible to protect myself and family.

With kindest personal regards,
Yours truly,
W. L. C. [male]

Nashville, Tenn.
8/15/36

Mrs. Franklin D. Roosevelt,
Dear Lady

Will you please warn the people of whats going to happen in America if these property owners dont quit making industrial slaves out of their laborers and working them on starvation wages, paying them a wage whereby they cannot obtain the desires of life, or else installing machinery and laying the common laborer off of his job to starve to death.

We dont want a revolution in this country where innocent men, women, and children will be shot down without mercy like they are doing in spain and also like they did in Russia. We want peace on earth good will toward men. You know mrs. Roosevelt with the majority of us poor people we desire good things as well as the higher classes of society. For instance we desire a nice home to live in with sanitary surroundings. we desire a nice refrigadaire, electric stove, fan, nice furniture, radio, a nice car with money to take a vacation, but one cannot have these desires of life at a wage of 8.00 10.00 or $12.00 per week, and if we could, we could not accumalate no money and would have to go on being industrial slaves and our children would fall under the same yoke of bondage that we and our fore parents were under. And never be considered no more than an ordinary slaves. . . .

Mrs. Roosevelt this nation is hanging over a giant powder keg just waiting for someone to light a match. You see I am forced to mingle with the poorer classes and I hear what they have to say. As far as I am concerned I dont believe in taking the carnal weapon against my fellow man. Therefore all I can do is stand still and see the salvation of the lord. I am thirty four years old married and have one daughter. I have a eighth grade education. I got a job last week as labourer on the new courthouse here, although I am a painter by trade, and just because I am a little crippled on my right side the contractor would not work me, he said the insurance company would not allow him to.

And so I cannot see a very bright prospect in life. Although my wife slaves in a cotton mill but I want a job so as I can get her out of it, for I am afraid she has contracted tuburcolosis, hoping an answer I remain

Yours,
Sincerely,
D. B. P. [male]

Introduction to Document 2

Tom Kromer grew up in West Virginia, where his father had been a coal miner and then a glassblower. Tom was a talented student, and he enrolled at Marshall College, but the death of his father and his own lack of funds caused him to drop out before finishing a degree. The Great Depression soon followed, and Kromer was left a vagrant. For a few years, he rode freight trains across the country. Finally, he was able to join the Civilian Conservation Corps, which afforded him the time and money to write his autobiographical *Waiting for Nothing* (1935). The author Lincoln Steffens assisted Kromer in having the manuscript published by Alfred A. Knopf. Perhaps more than any other depression-era book, this one gave a sense, not only of hopeless wandering, but also of the terror of being homeless. Kromer left nothing out: the alcoholism, the cruelty of the police and the middle class, the violence of "stiffs" against each other, and the ever-pressing need for "three hots and a flop"—food and shelter.

DOCUMENT 2 *From* Waiting for Nothing

Tom Kromer

I crouch here in this doorway of the blind baggage. For five hours I have huddled here in the freezing cold. My feet dangle down beneath the car. The wind whistles underneath and swings them back and forth. The wheels sing over the rails. Up in front of me the engine roars through the blackness, that is blacker than the night. The smoke and the fire belch into the sky and scatter into scorching sparks that burn my back and neck. I do not feel the wind that swings my legs. They are frozen. I have no feeling in them. I slink far back in this door and put my hands over my face. Great God, but I am miserable. I cannot stand this much longer. I was a fool for nailing the blind baggage of this passenger. I was a fool, and now I am freezing to death.

I think. How am I ever going to get off this drag if it ever does stop? I can't walk. My feet, that are frozen, will not hold me up. I sit here and think, and I doze. I awake with a jerk.

"You damn fool," I say, "you can't go to sleep here. You will fall under those wheels that sing beneath you. Those wheels would make quick work of you, all right. Those wheels would make mincemeat of you. You would not be cold any more."

I begin to sing. I sing loud. I yell at the top of my voice, because of the roar of the wheels and the sound of the wind underneath me. I don't want to fall under those wheels. I am only a stiff, and I know that a stiff is better off dead, but I don't want to fall under those wheels. I can feel myself getting dopey. I try to sing louder. I try to hear my voice over the sound of the wind and the cars, but I cannot. I cannot keep awake. I can see that I cannot keep awake. I am falling asleep. I wonder if this is the way a guy freezes to death. I am not so cold now. I am almost warm. The wind roars just as loud as before. It must be just as cold as it was before. But I am not cold. I am warm. Great Christ, I must not let myself freeze to death. I swing my arms. I reach my head far out over the side of the car. The wind tears at my face, but I keep it there until the tears run down my cheeks. Oh, Christ, won't this drag never stop?

I feel the buckle of this drag beneath me. I feel it jerk and throw me forward. I hear the whine of air for brakes. I grab the sides of this car with all my might. My frozen fingers slip, then hold. I am not scared. I am not afraid. I just grab the sides of the car and hold. I feel this train slacken speed. I see the scattered lights of a town. Only a few lights, but I see that this drag is going to stop. I begin to laugh. I laugh like a crazy man when I see that this drag is going to stop.

I hang on with all my might. There will be a jerk when this drag stops. I do not want to go under those wheels. We pull to a stop in front of this jerk-water station. There will be no bulls [police] in this place. The thing to do is to get off this drag before it starts again. It will not stay here long. How am I going to reach the ground? My legs are numb. They are frozen. They will not hold me up. I rub them fast and hard. I feel them sting and burn as the blood begins to run. I try to move them. I can move them. I can see them move. But I feel nothing when they move. I pull myself to my feet. I am standing. I can see that I am standing, but I cannot feel the car beneath my feet. I reach out over the side of the car and grab the ladder. I climb down. I hold with one hand and guide my legs with the other, but I climb down. I stop at this last step. It is a long way to the ground for my frozen feet. I jump. I fall face-down in the cinders at the side of the track. This drag whistles the high ball. She pulls out. I lie here in the cinders with my bleeding face and watch the coaches go by. I lie here in the cinders with my frozen legs that have no feeling in them. I shiver as I think of that blind baggage with the roar of the wheels and the sound of the wind underneath. I push my fists into the ground and get to my feet. I grimace at the pain that shoots through my legs, but I grit my teeth and walk.

What I want right now is a cup of coffee. A cup of good hot coffee will always warm a guy up. I am too cold to want to eat. I make it to the main stem of this town. There are lights in the few stores that are still open. I pass a restaurant. There is a sign in the window. It says: "Try our ten-cent hamburgers." I wonder if they would let a frozen stiff try their ten-cent hamburgers. I walk in. There are two customers eating. I walk up to this bird behind the counter. He backs away. He glances at his cash register. He has a scared look on his face. I look in the mirror that lines the wall. I do not blame this guy for being scared. What I see scares me, too. My face is as black as the ace of spades. It is smeared with blood from the cuts of the cinders as they scraped my face. I hit those cinders hard.

"Buddy," I say, "I am broke. Could you spare me a cup of coffee?"

"I can't spare you nothin'," he says. "Beat it before I throw you out."

Imagine this bastard. I am half starved and half froze, and he turns me down for a lousy cup of coffee. I am too cold to even cuss him out. I want to cuss him out, but I am too cold. I walk down the street and hit these other two restaurants. They turn me down flat. I can't get me anything to warm me up. But there is one thing I will have to get, and that is a flop. In weather like this a stiff has got to have a flop.

"Where is the town bull?" I say to this guy on the corner.

"You will find him in the garage," he says. "He will be shootin' the bull by the stove in the garage."

I walk over to this garage and find this hick cop by the stove in the office.

"Chief," I say, "I want to get locked up in the can. I am on the fritz with no place to flop."

"The jail ain't no hotel," he says. "I can't lock you up. I can't louse the jail up by locking you up."

Well, if this is not a hell of a note! A stiff can't even break into a lousy can. They call this a free country, and a stiff can't even break into jail to get away from the cold and the wind.

"Can I warm up a little by your fire?" I say. "I am froze."

"Get this straight," this bull says; "we have no use for lousy stiffs in this town. The best thing you can do is to hit the highway away from here."

"What is a stiff supposed to do, shoot himself?" I say.

"If I catch you in this town tomorrow, it will be a good thing if you do shoot yourself," he says.

I go out to the street and walk. I walk fast. I do not feel like walking fast, but I have to to keep from freezing to death. That's how cold I am. I pass a pecan grove. Over away from the road I can see a shack with a light in it. I knock on the door. An old man comes to the door with a lantern in his hand.

"Hello," I say. "Have you got somewhere a guy could flop for the night around here? I am freezing to death, with no place to flop."

He puts his hand on the top of my head.

"Son, do you believe in Christ?" he says.

"Sure," I say, "I believe in Christ. Have you got some place I could flop around here?"

"The last days are upon us," he says. "The sound of the trumpet is soon upon us. Repent or you burn in everlasting flame."

This guy is as batty as a loon. I can see that.

"Have you got some place I could flop outside?" I say. "An old shed or something?"

Outside will not be too far away from this guy. He is ready for the booby-hatch.

"The lamb that is lost is the care of the Lord," he says.

He leads the way to this building where they store the pecans. It is a big place. The floor is covered with piles of these pecans. He takes a shovel and digs a hole down in one of these piles, he puts two burlap sacks in the bottom of it.

"Son," he says, "lay down in this hole and rest."

I get in.

He covers me up with pecans, and piles sacks on top of me. My face is all that is sticking out of the hole. He puts a sack over my face.

"Rest that you may better fight the battles of the Lord," he says.

He takes his lantern and goes back to his shack.

It is pitch-dark in here now. I lie under these pecans and think. Here I am lying down in a hole. Here I am covered up with pecans. Before I went on the fritz, I was lying nights in a feather bed. I thought I was hard up then. I had a decent front. I had my three hots and a flop. Can you imagine a guy thinking he is hard up when he has his three hots and a flop? That was two years ago, but two years are ten years when you are on the fritz. I look ten years older now. I looked like a young punk then. I was a young punk. I had some color in my cheeks. I have hit the skids since then. This is as low down as a guy can get, being down in a hole with pecans on top of him for covers. If a guy had any guts, he wouldn't put up with this. I think. Why should one guy have a million dollars, and I am down in a hole with pecans on top of me for covers? Maybe that guy has brains. Maybe he works hard. I don't know. What is that to me if he is there and I am here? Religion, they say in the missions. Religion and morals. What are religion and morals to me, if I am down in a hole with pecans on top of me? Who is there to say that this world belongs to certain guys? What right has one guy to say: This much of the world is mine; you can't sleep here?

I lie here in the darkness and think. It is too cold to sleep. On the blind baggage of the drag I could not keep my eyes open. Now I cannot close them. I listen to these rats that rustle across the floor. I pull this sack off my face and strain my eyes through the blackness. I am afraid of rats. Once in a jungle [hobo camp] I awoke with two on my face. Since then I dream of rats that are as big as cats, who sit on my face and gnaw at my nose and eyes. I cannot see them. It is too dark. I cannot lie here and wait with my heart thumping against my ribs like this. I cannot lie here and listen to them patter across the floor, and me not able to see them. I pull myself out of these pecans and get to my feet. I tiptoe out to the road. I do not want to wake this crazy old codger who dug the hole for me. I do not want to hurt his feelings, and besides, he might go off his nut.

I walk. I lower my head far down to keep the whistling wind from cutting my face like a knife. I listen to the creak of the trees as the wind tears through them. I keep to the left of the road. I cannot hear the sounds of the cars as they come up behind me. You can hear nothing for the roar of the wind. From time to time I turn my head to stare through the night for signs of a headlight. When I see one, I stop in my tracks and hold out my hand for a ride. They do not stop when they see me raise my hand. They step on the gas and go faster. They do not care to pick up a worn-out stiff with blisters on his feet. It is night. They are afraid. They are afraid of being knocked in the head. I do not blame them for being afraid. You cannot tell what a stiff might do when he is as cold and fagged as I am. A stiff is not himself when he is as cold as I am.

I reach the town and skirt it. I am afraid of rats, and this town bull has a face like a rat. I reach the yards and crawl into one of these cars that line the tracks. I shove the doors almost shut. I do not shut it tight. If they start moving these cars during the night, I want to be ready for a quick get-away. I take this newspaper out of my pocket and spread it on the floor. I take off my shoes and use them for a pillow. I lie down, I am all in. I am asleep in a minute.

I do not know how long I am asleep. I awake with a jerk. Something has awakened me. All at once I am wide-eyed and staring. There is a feeling of queerness in the top of my head. I know that feeling. I get that feeling when there is something wrong. I had that feeling once when a drag I was on went over the ditch. That feeling was in the top of my head just before a guy I was talking to on the street dropped dead. My breath comes in short gasps. There is a crawling feeling all over me. A tingle starts at my feet and runs to my hair. I feel a chill in the roots of my hair. I know what that is. My hair is standing up. I raise up on my elbow. The rustle I make as I move on the paper sounds like thunder in the quietness of the car. A ray of light comes through the opening in the door. It is not strong enough to reach to the other end of the car, but I know that there is nothing there. It is in back of me. Whatever it is that is in this car is in back of me. . . .

Then, through the dark, comes this squeal. It is a wild squeal. A squeal like something is mad and crazy. It is like something that has lost its mind. I feel it bound through the air and land on my back. It knocks me down to the floor. These sharp claws bite into the nape of my neck. The long fingers grip my throat so that my breath comes in sobs. I am strangling. I grab at these claws. I feel a man's wrist. A strong wrist. A wrist that is all covered with hair like an animal's. I am down on my belly on the floor of the car. These fingers like hot iron press tighter and tighter. I feel these knees that bore into the small of my back. My neck wrenches backward. So far back I wait to hear it snap. Dizzier I get, and dizzier. Like in a dream I know that these claws that bite into my neck are trying to kill me, to choke me to death. I struggle blindly in the darkness.

I throw myself to my back. I feel the claws loosen their grip. I feel them slide off my neck and tear the flesh off in strips. I feel the burn on my throat and the moistness that I know is blood. I stumble to my feet as he sprawls on the floor. I am facing him now in the dark. He scrambles to his feet. He is only a shapeless mass in front of me. It is a shapeless mass that wants to kill me, to choke me till there is no life in me. I see it hurl itself through the air. I brace myself against the side of the car and kick out with my foot with all my might. I feel it hit, hard. I hear a grunt, a squeally grunt that a pig might give. My foot is buried in his belly. He thuds to the floor. He rolls over and over, but he is up again in a second. There is a flash in his hand. Through the ray of light that comes through the door I see this flash. My spine creeps. I know what that flash is. It is a knife. I cannot let him get at me with the knife. I cannot let him rip me open with the knife. He is going to murder me with the knife. I have to get out of here. Great Christ, I have to get out of here. I leap towards the door and reach it. I claw at it and try to pry it open. It is caught. The splinters bury themselves in my finger-nails. I do not notice the pain. I am too afraid to notice the pain of a splinter in my nails. Again behind me I hear that scream.

I swing around. The knife flashes through the air above my head. I grab at the hairy wrist that holds the knife. The razor-sharp edge slashes my arms. I know it slashes my arms because of the scorched feeling and the wet that spurts against my face. I struggle with the wrist that holds the knife and the arm that clubs at my head. I am getting weak. The loss of blood has made me weak. I cannot hold the arm that clutches the knife. I glue my eyes to this flash that quivers and shakes over my head as we strain in the ray that comes through the door from the moonlight. Nearer it comes and nearer. I twist the wrist with all my strength. I twist till I hear the snap of it through our panting and scuffling. I hear this scream again as the arm goes limp and the knife clatters to the box-car floor. I start to dive for the knife on the floor and feel this fist that smashes to my face. I sprawl to the other end of the car. I grope in the dark and try to get up. I cannot. I am too weak to get to my feet. I lie here and tremble on the floor.

Through the ray of light that comes from the door I see this guy stand and stare at the floor. The gleam of the knife is there. He does not pick it up. He is not looking at the knife. It is this pool of blood from my slashed-up arm he is staring at. He stares like a guy in a trance at this blood. He flops to his knees and splashes his hands in the blood and screams. He splashes his hands in the pool of blood and smears it all over his face. I can see him quiver and shake and hear his jabber as he smears the blood. I lie here and wait for the flash of the knife, but it does not come. He leaps to his feet and jumps towards the door of the car. He jabbers and babbles as he shoves against it. He slides it open and leaps to the tracks. I can hear his screams as he crashes through the thickets.

I lie in the darkness with my bloody arm and shiver and sob in my breath.

Introduction to Documents 3 and 4

In the following two pieces, Meridel Le Sueur offers us chilling visions of how women were affected by the depression. "Women on the Breadlines" (1932), from which Document 3 is excerpted, captures some of the same wandering, hopeless quality of Kromer's novel. As Le Sueur points out, however, many vagrant women would rather have starved alone than face the shame of asking for help. "Women on the Breadlines" appeared in *New Masses,* the cultural organ of the Communist Party of America. The editors appended a note criticizing the article for its despairing tone. In Document 4, "I Was Marching," which appeared in *New Masses* two years later, Le Sueur took a much more affirmative position. The immediate subject was the 1934 Minneapolis Teamsters strike. Here Le Sueur captured the terrors of the strike; this time, however, collective resistance triumphed over individual hopelessness.

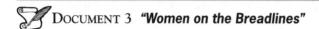 DOCUMENT 3   *"Women on the Breadlines"*

Meridel Le Sueur

I am sitting in the city free employment bureau. It's the woman's section. We have been sitting here now for four hours. We sit here every day, waiting for a job. There are no jobs. Most of us have had no breakfast. Some have had scant rations for over a year. Hunger makes a human being lapse into a state of lethargy, especially city hunger. Is there any place else in the world where a human being is supposed to go hungry amidst plenty without an outcry, without protest, where only the boldest steal or kill for bread, and the timid crawl the streets, hunger like the beak of a terrible bird at the vitals?

We sit looking at the floor. No one dares think of the coming winter. There are only a few more days of summer. Everyone is anxious to get work to lay up something for that long siege of bitter cold. But there is no work. Sitting in the room we all know it. That is why we don't talk much. We look at the floor dreading to see that knowledge in each other's eyes. There is a kind of humiliation in it. We look away from each other. We look at the floor. It's too terrible to see this animal terror in each other's eyes.

So we sit hour after hour, day after day, waiting for a job to come in. There are many women for a single job. A thin sharp woman sits inside the wire cage looking at the book. For four hours we have watched her looking at the book. She has a hard little eye. In the small bare room there are half a dozen women sitting on the benches waiting. Many come and go. Our faces are all familiar to each other, for we wait here every day.

This is a domestic employment bureau. Most of the women who come here are middle aged, some have families, some raised their families and are now alone, some have men who are out of work. Hard times and the man leaves to hunt for work. He doesn't find it. He drifts on. The woman probably doesn't hear from him for a long time. She expects it. She isn't surprised. She struggles alone to feed the many mouths. Sometimes she gets help from the charities. If she's clever she can get herself a good living from the charities, if she's naturally a lick spittle, naturally a little docile and cunning. If she's proud then she starves silently, leaving her children to find work, coming home after a day's searching to wrestle with her house, her children.

Some such story is written on the faces of all these women. There are young girls too, fresh from the country. Some are made brazen too soon by the city. There is a great exodus of girls from the farms into the city now. Thousands of farms have been vacated completely in Minnesota. The girls are trying to get work. The prettier ones can get jobs in the stores when there are any, or waiting on table but these jobs are only for the attractive and the adroit, the others, the real peasants, have a more difficult time. . . .

It's one of the great mysteries of the city where women go when they are out of work and hungry. There are not many women in the bread line. There are no flop houses for women as there are for men, where a bed can be had for a quarter or less. You don't see women lying on the floor at the mission in the free flops. They obviously don't sleep in the jungle or under newspapers in the park. There is no law I suppose against their being in these places but the fact is they rarely are.

Yet there must be as many women out of jobs in cities and suffering extreme poverty as there are men. What happens to them? Where do they go? Try to get into the Y.W.C.A. without any money or looking down at heel. Charities take care of very few and only those that are called "deserving." The lone girl is under suspicion by the virgin women who dispense charity.

I've lived in cities for many months broke, without help, too timid to get in bread lines. I've known many women to live like this until they simply faint on the street from privations, without saying a word to anyone. A woman will shut herself up in a room until it is taken away from her, and eat a cracker a day and be as quiet as a mouse so there are no social statistics concerning her.

I don't know why it is, but a woman will do this unless she has dependents, will go for weeks, verging on starvation, crawling in some hole, going through the streets ashamed, sitting in libraries, parks, going for days without speaking to a living soul like some exiled beast, keeping the runs mended in her stockings, shut up in terror in her own misery, until she becomes too super sensitive and timid to even ask for a job.

Bernice says even strange men she has met in the park have sometimes, that is in better days, given her a loan to pay her room rent. She has always paid them back.

In the afternoon the young girls, to forget the hunger and the deathly torture and fear of being jobless, try and pick up a man to take them to a ten cent show. They never go to more expensive ones, but they can always find a man willing to spend a dime to have the company of a girl for the afternoon.

Sometimes a girl facing the night without shelter will approach a man for lodging. A woman always asks a man for help. Rarely another woman. I have known girls to sleep in men's rooms for the night, on a pallet without molestation, and given breakfast in the morning.

It's no wonder these young girls refuse to marry, refuse to rear children. They are like certain savage tribes, who, when they have been conquered refuse to breed.

Not one of them but looks forward to starvation, for the coming winter. We are in a jungle and know it. We are beaten, entrapped. There is no way out. Even if there were a job, even if that thin acrid woman came and gave everyone in the room a job for a few days, a few hours, at thirty cents an hour, this would all be repeated tomorrow, the next day and the next.

Not one of these women but knows, that despite years of labour there is only starvation, humiliation in front of them. . . .

So we sit in this room like cattle, waiting for a non existent job, willing to work to the farthest atom of energy, unable to work, unable to get food and lodging, unable to bear children; here we must sit in this shame looking at the floor, worse than beasts at a slaughter.

It is appalling to think that these women sitting so listless in the room may work as hard as it is possible for a human being to work, may labour night and day, like Mrs. Gray wash street cars from midnight to dawn and offices in the early evening, scrubbing for fourteen and fifteen hours a day, sleeping only five hours or so, doing this their whole lives, and never earn one day of security, having always before them the pit of the future.

The endless labour, the bending back, the water soaked hands, earning never more than a week's wages, never having in their hands more life than that.

It's not the suffering, not birth, death, love that the young reject, but the suffering of endless labour without dream, eating the spare bread in bitterness, a slave without the security of a slave.

Editorial Note: This presentation of the plight of the unemployed woman, able as it is, and informative, is defeatist in attitude, lacking in revolutionary spirit and direction which characterize the usual contribution to *New Masses*. We feel it our duty to add, that there is a place for the unemployed woman, as well as man, in the ranks of the unemployed councils and in all branches of the organized revolutionary movement. Fight for your class, read *The Working Woman*, join the Communist Party.

DOCUMENT 4 *"I Was Marching"*

Meridel Le Sueur

I have never been in a strike before. It is like looking at something that is happening for the first time and there are no thoughts and no words yet accrued to it. If you come from the middle class, words are likely to mean more than an event. You are likely to think about a thing, and the happening will be the size of a pin point and the words around the happening very large, distorting it queerly. It's a case of "Remembrance of things past." When you are in the event, you are likely to have a distinctly individualistic attitude, to be only partly there, and to care more for the happening afterwards than when it is happening. That is why it is hard for a person like myself and others to be in a strike.

Besides, in American life, you hear things happening in a far and muffled way. One thing is said and another happens. Our merchant society has been built upon a huge hypocrisy, a cut-throat competition which sets one man against another and at the same time an ideology mouthing such words as "Humanity," "Truth," the "Golden Rule," and such. Now in a crisis the word falls away and the skeleton of that action shows in terrific movement.

For two days I heard of the strike. I went by their headquarters, I walked by on the opposite side of the street and saw the dark old building that had been a garage and lean, dark young faces leaning from the upstairs windows. I had to go down there often. I looked in. I saw the huge black interior and live coals of living men moving restlessly and orderly, their eyes gleaming from their sweaty faces.

I saw cars leaving filled with grimy men, pickets going to the line, engines roaring out. I stayed close to the door, watching. I didn't go in. I was afraid they would put me out. After all, I could remain a spectator. A man wearing a polo hat kept going around with a large camera taking pictures.

I am putting down exactly how I felt, because I believe others of my class feel the same as I did. I believe it stands for an important psychic change that must take place in all. I saw many artists, writers, professionals, even business men and women standing across the street, too, and I saw in their faces the same longings, the same fears.

The truth is I was afraid. Not of the physical danger at all, but an awful fright of mixing, of losing myself, of being unknown and lost. I felt inferior. I felt no one would know me there, that all I had been trained to excel in would go unnoticed. I can't describe what I felt, but perhaps it will come near it to say that I felt I excelled in competing with others and I knew instantly that these people were NOT competing at all, that they were acting in a strange, powerful trance of movement *together*. And I was filled with longing to act with them and with fear that I could not. I felt I was born out of every kind of life, thrown up alone, looking at other lonely people, a condition I had been in the habit of defending with various attitudes of cynicism, preciosity, defiance and hatred.

Looking at that dark and lively building, massed with men, I knew my feelings to be those belonging to disruption, chaos and disintegration and I felt their direct and awful movement, mute and powerful, drawing them into a close and glowing cohesion like a powerful conflagration in the midst of the city. And it filled me with fear and awe and at the same time hope. I knew this action to be prophetic and indicative of future actions and I wanted to be part of it.

Our life seems to be marked with a curious and muffled violence over America, but this action has always been in the dark, men and women dying obscurely, poor and poverty marked lives, but now from city to city runs this violence, into the open, and colossal happenings stand bare before our eyes, the street churning suddenly upon the pivot of mad violence, whole men suddenly spouting blood and running like living sieves, another holding a dangling arm shot squarely off, a tall youngster, running, tripping over his intestines, and one block away, in the burning sun, gay women shopping and a window dresser trying to decide whether to put green or red voile on a mannikin.

In these terrible happenings you cannot be neutral now. No one can be neutral in the face of bullets.

The next day, with sweat breaking out on my body, I walked past the three guards at the door. They said, "Let the women in. We need women." And I knew it was no joke. . . .

I found the kitchen organized like a factory. Nobody asks my name. I am given a large butcher's apron. I realize I have never before worked anonymously. At first I feel strange and then I feel good. The forewoman sets me to washing tin cups. There are not enough cups. We have to wash fast and rinse them and set them up quickly for buttermilk and coffee as the line thickens and the men wait. . . .

Then I am changed and put to pouring coffee. At first I look at the men's faces and then I don't look any more. It seems I am pouring coffee for the same tense, dirty sweating face, the same body, the same blue shirt and overalls. Hours go by, the heat is terrific. I am not tired. I am not hot. I am pouring coffee. I am swung into the most intense and natural organization I have ever felt. I know everything that is going on. These things become of great matter to me.

Eyes looking, hands raising a thousand cups, throats burning, eyes bloodshot from lack of sleep, the body dilated to catch every sound over the whole city. Buttermilk? Coffee?

"Is your man here?" the woman cutting sandwiches asks me.

"No," I say, then I lie for some reason, peering around as if looking eagerly for someone, "I don't see him now."

But I was pouring coffee for living men. . . .

That night at eight o'clock a mass-meeting was called of all labor. It was to be in a parking lot two blocks from headquarters. All the women gather at the front of the building with collection cans, ready to march to the meeting. I have not been home. It never occurs to me to leave. The twilight is eerie and the men are saying that the chief of police is going to attack the meeting and raid headquarters. The smell of blood hangs in the hot, still air. Rumors strike at the taut nerves. The dusk looks ghastly with what might be in the next half hour.

"If you have any children," a woman said to me, "you better not go." I looked at the desperate women's faces, the broken feet, the torn and hanging pelvis, the worn and lovely bodies of women who persist under such desperate labors. I shivered, though it was 96 and the sun had been down a good hour.

The parking lot was already full of people when we got there and men swarmed the adjoining roofs. An elegant café stood across the street with water sprinkling from its roof and splendidly dressed men and women stood on the steps as if looking at a show.

The platform was the bullet riddled truck of the afternoon's fray. We had been told to stand close to this platform so we did, making the center of a wide massed circle that stretched as far as we could see. We seemed buried like minerals in a mass, packed body to body. I felt again that peculiar heavy silence in which there is the real form of the happening. My eyes burn. I can hardly see. I seem to be standing like an animal in ambush. I have the brightest, most physical feeling with every sense sharpened peculiarly. The movements, the masses that I see and feel I have never known before. I only partly know what I am seeing, feeling, but I feel it is the real body and gesture of a future vitality. I see that there is a bright clot of women drawn close to a bullet riddled truck. I am one of them, yet I don't feel myself at all. It is curious. I feel most alive and yet for the first time in my life I do not feel myself as separate. I realize then that all my previous feelings have been based on feeling myself separate and distinct from others and now I sense sharply faces, bodies, closeness and my own fear is not my own alone, nor my hope. . . .

[THE NEXT DAY.]

The strikers keep moving up cars. We keep moving back together to let cars pass and form between us and a brick building that flanks the parking lot. . . . We all watched carefully the placing of the cars. Sometimes we looked at each other. I didn't understand that look. I felt uneasy. It was as if something escaped me. And then suddenly, on my very body, I knew what they were doing, as if it had been communicated to me from a thousand eyes, a thousand silent throats, as if it had been shouted in the loudest voice.

THEY WERE BUILDING A BARRICADE.

Two men died from that day's shooting. Men lined up to give one of them a blood transfusion, but he died. Black Friday men called the murderous day. Night and day workers held their children up to see the body of Ness who died. Tuesday, the day of the funeral, one thousand more militia were massed downtown.

It was still over ninety in the shade. I went to the funeral parlors and thousands of men and women were massed there waiting in the terrific sun. One block of women and children were standing two hours waiting. I went over and stood near them. I didn't know whether I could march. I didn't like marching in parades. Besides, I felt they might not want me.

I stood aside not knowing if I would march. I couldn't see how they would ever organize it anyway. No one seemed to be doing much.

At three-forty some command went down the ranks. I said foolishly at the last minute, "I don't belong to the auxiliary—could I march?" Three women drew me in. "We want all to march," they said gently. "Come with us."

The giant mass uncoiled like a serpent and straightened out ahead and to my amazement on a lift of road I could see six blocks of massed men, four abreast, with bare heads, moving straight on and as they moved, uncoiled the mass behind and pulled it after them, I felt myself walking, accelerating my speed with the others as the line stretched, pulled taut, then held its rhythm.

Not a cop was in sight. The cortege moved through the stop-and-go signs, it seemed to lift of its own dramatic rhythm, coming from the intention of every person there. We were moving spontaneously in a movement, natural, hardy and miraculous.

We passed through six blocks of tenements, through a sea of grim faces and there was not a sound. There was the curious shuffle of thousands of feet, without drum or bugle, in ominous silence, a march not heavy as the military, but very light, exactly with the heart beat.

I was marching with a million hands, movements, faces and my own movement was repeating again and again, making a new movement from the many gestures, the walking, falling back, the open mouth crying, the nostrils stretched apart, the raised hand, the blow falling, and the outstretched hand drawing me in.

I felt my legs straighten. I felt my feet join in that strange shuffle of thousands of bodies moving with direction, of thousands of feet and my own breath with the gigantic breath. As if an electric charge had passed through me, my hair stood on end. I was marching.

Introduction to Document 5

Like Kromer's *Waiting for Nothing*, Michael Gold's *Jews Without Money* (1930) might best be called documentary fiction. Gold reveals how many Jews of his own American-born generation remained victims of poverty and discrimination. Gold was a member of the Communist party, indeed a leader in the move to radicalize art and literature during the depression. *Jews Without Money* did not romanticize poverty, nor did it dwell on a particular political agenda; Gold was content to dramatize people's sense of being locked into a system that promised prosperity, but delivered despair. Although Gold grew up before the Great Depression, his book came out during the crisis. His description of his own youth spoke with passion to readers about the devastation wrought on families during the 1930s.

 DOCUMENT 5 *From* **Jews Without Money**

Michael Gold

The neighbors were talking about us. They were worrying. In the tenement each woman knew what was cooking for supper in her neighbor's pot. Each knew the cares, too, that darkened a neighbor's heart.

One night a neighbor called. He kissed the *mezzuzah* over the door, and wiped his feet on the burlap rags. Then he timidly entered our kitchen like an intruder.

"Good evening, Mr. Lipzin," said my mother. "Please sit down."

"Good evening," he stammered, seating himself. "It was raining to-day, and I did not sell many bananas, so I brought you some. Maybe your children like bananas."

He handed my mother a bunch of bananas, and she took them, saying, "Thanks, Mr. Lipzin."

The pot-bellied little peddler shyly fingered his beard. He had come for a purpose, but was too embarrassed to speak. . . .

My father fidgeted uneasily. He was about to say something to break the spell cast by the tongue-tied peddler, when Mr. Lipzin became articulate. "Excuse me, but my wife nagged me into coming here," he stammered. "She is worrying about you. Excuse me, but they say you have been out of work a long time and can find nothing to do, Mr. Gold."

"Yes, Mr. Lipzin, why should one conceal it?" said my father. "Life is dark for us now."

"*Nu*," said the little peddler, as he wiped his forehead, "so that is why my wife nagged me to see you. If there is nothing else, one can at least make a kind of living with bananas. I have peddled them, with God's help, for many years. It is a hard life, but one manages to live. . . ."

My father stood up and folded his arms haughtily.

"And you are suggesting, Mr. Lipzin, that I, too, should go out peddling bananas?" he asked.

The peddler sweated like a runner with embarrassment. He stood up and edged toward the door to make his escape.

"No, no, God forbid," he stammered. "Excuse me, it was my wife who nagged me to come here. No, no, Mr. Gold! Good evening to you all; may God be with you!"

He went out, mopping his fiery face with a bandanna. My father stared after him, his arms still folded in that fierce, defiant attitude.

"What a gall! What meddling neighbors we have! To come and tell me that I ought to peddle these accursed bananas! After my fifteen years in America, as if I were a greenhorn! I, who once owned a suspender shop, and was a foreman of house painters! . . ."

Two weeks after Mr. Lipzin's visit [my father] was in the street with a pushcart, peddling the accursed bananas.

He came back the first night, and gave my mother a dollar bill and some silver. His face was gray; he looked older by ten years; a man who had touched bottom. My mother tried to comfort him, but for days he was silent as one who has been crushed by a calamity. Hope died in him; months passed, a year passed; he was still peddling bananas.

I remember meeting him one evening with his pushcart. . . . I recognized him, a hunched, frozen figure in an old overcoat standing by a banana cart. He looked so lonely, the tears came to my eyes. Then he saw me, and his face lit with his sad, beautiful smile— Charlie Chaplin's smile.

"Ach, it's Mikey," he said. "So you have sold your papers! Come and eat a banana."

He offered me one. I refused it. I was eleven years old, but poisoned with a morbid proletarian sense of responsibility. I felt it crucial that my father *sell* his bananas, not give them away. He thought I was shy, and coaxed and joked with me, and made me eat the banana. It smelled of wet straw and snow.

"You haven't sold many bananas to-day, pop," I said anxiously.

He shrugged his shoulders.

"What can I do? No one seems to want them."

It was true. The work crowds pushed home morosely over the pavements. The rusty sky darkened over New York buildings, the tall street lamps were lit, innumerable trucks, street cars and elevated trains clattered by. Nobody and nothing in the great city stopped for my father's bananas. . . .

"Look at me," he said. "Twenty years in America, and poorer than when I came. A suspender shop I had, and it was stolen from me by a villain. A house painter foreman I became, and fell off a scaffold. Now bananas I sell, and even at that I am a failure. It is all luck." He sighed and puffed at his pipe.

"Ach, Gott, what a rich country America is! What an easy place to make one's fortune! Look at all the rich Jews! Why has it been so easy for them, so hard for me? I am just a poor little Jew without money."

"Poppa, lots of Jews have no money," I said to comfort him.

"I know it, my son," he said, "but don't be one of them. It's better to be dead in this country than not to have money. Promise me you'll be rich when you grow up, Mikey!"

"Yes, poppa."

"Ach," he said fondly, "this is my one hope now! This is all that makes me happy! I am a greenhorn, but you are an American! You will have it easier than I; you will have luck in America!"

"Yes, poppa," I said, trying to smile with him. But I felt older than he; I could not share his naïve optimism; my heart sank as I remembered the past and thought of the future. . . .

At the age of twelve I carried in my mind a morbid load of responsibility.

I had been a precocious pupil in the public school, winning honors not by study, but by a kind of intuition. I graduated a year sooner than most boys. At the exercises I was valedictory orator.

My parents were proud, of course. They wanted me to go on to high school, like other "smart" boys. They still believed I would be a doctor.

But I was morbid enough to be wiser than my parents. Even then I could sense that education is a luxury reserved for the well-to-do. I refused to go to high school. More than half the boys in my graduating class were going to work; I chose to be one of them.

It was where I belonged. I figured it out on paper for my parents. Four years of high school, then six years of college before one could be a doctor. Ten years of study in all, with thousands of dollars needed for books, tuition, and the rest.

There were four of us in my family. My mother seemed unable to work. Would my father's banana peddling keep us alive during those ten years while I was studying?

Of course not. I was obstinate and bitter; my parents wept, and tried to persuade me, but I refused to go to high school.

Miss Barry, the English teacher, tried to persuade me, too. She was fond of me. She stared at me out of wistful blue eyes, with her old maid's earnestness, and said:

"It would be a pity for you to go into a factory. I have never seen better English compositions than yours, Michael."

"I must work, Miss Barry," I said. I started to leave. She took my hand. I could smell the fresh spring lilacs in the brass bowl on her desk.

"Wait," she said earnestly, "I want you to promise me to study at night. I will give you a list of the required high school reading; you can make up your Regents' counts that way. Will you do it?"

"Yes, Miss Barry," I lied to her sullenly.

I was trying to be hard. For years my ego had been fed by every one's praise of my precocity. I had always loved books; I was mad about books; I wanted passionately to go to high school and college. Since I couldn't, I meant to despise all that nonsense.

"It will be difficult to study at night," said Miss Barry in her trembly voice, "but Abraham Lincoln did it, and other great Americans."

"Yes, Miss Barry," I muttered.

She presented me with a parting gift. It was a volume of Emerson's Essays, with her name and my name and the date written on the flyleaf.

I thanked her for the book, and threw it under the bed when I got home. I never read a page in it, or in any book for the next five years. I hated books; they were lies, they had nothing to do with life and work.

It was not easy to find my first job. I hunted for months, in a New York summer of furnace skies and fogs of humidity. I bought the *World* each morning, and ran through the want ads:

Agents Wanted—Addressers Wanted—Barbers Wanted—Bushelmen Wanted—Butchers Wanted—Boys Wanted—

That fateful ad page brings news of life and death each morning to hundreds of thousands. How often have I read it with gloomy heart. Even to-day the sight of it brings back the ache and hopelessness of my youth.

There was a swarm of boys pushing and yapping like homeless curs at the door of each job. I competed with them. We scrambled, flunkeyed and stood at servile attention under the boss's eye, little slaves on the block.

No one can go through the shame and humiliation of the job-hunt without being marked for life. I hated my first experience at it, and have hated every other since. There can be no freedom in the world while men must beg for jobs.

I rose at six-thirty each morning, and was out tramping the streets at seven. There were always hundreds of jobs, but thousands of boys clutching after them. The city was swarming with these boys, aimless, bewildered and as hungry for work as I was.

I found a job as errand boy in a silk house. But it was temporary. The very first morning the shipping clerk, a refined Nordic, suddenly realized I was a Jew. He politely fired me. They wanted no Jews. In this city of a million Jews, there was much anti-Semitism among business firms. Many of the ads would read: Gentile Only. Even Jewish business houses discriminated against Jews. How often did I slink out of factory or office where a foreman said Jews were not wanted. How often was I made to remember I belonged to the accursed race, the race whose chief misfortune it is to have produced a Christ.

At last I found a job. It was in a factory where incandescent gas mantles were made, a dark loft under the elevated trains on the Bowery near Chatham Square.

This was a spectral place, a chamber of hell, hot and poisoned by hundreds of gas flames. It was suffocating with the stink of chemicals.

I began to sweat immediately. What was worse, I could not breathe. The place terrified me. The boss came up and told me to take off my coat. He was a grim little man, thick as a cask about the middle, and dressed in a gaudy pink silk shirt. He chewed a cigar.

His face was morbid and hard like a Jewish gangster's.

"Monkey Face," he called, "show this new kid what to do."

An overgrown Italian boy approached, in pants and undershirt streaked with sweat. His slit nose, ape muzzle, and tiny malicious eyes had earned him his appropriate nickname.

"Come here, kid," he said. I followed him down the loft. There were thirty unfortunate human beings at work. Men sat at a long table testing mantles. Their faces were death masks, fixed and white. Great blue spectacles shielded their eyes.

Little Jewish and Italian girls dipped racks of mantles in chemical tanks. Boys stood before a series of ovens in which sixty gas jets blazed. They passed in the racks for the chemicals to burn off. Every one dripped with sweat; every one was haggard, as though in pain.

"Where did yuh work last?" growled Monkey Face.

"It's my first job. I'm just out of school."

"Yeh?" he snickered. "Just out of school, huh? Well, yuh struck a good job, kid; it'll put hair on your chest. Here, take dis."

I took the iron rack he gave me, and dropped it at once. It scorched my hand. Monkey Face laughed at the joke.

"You son-of-a-bitch!" I said, "it's hot."

He pushed his apish face close to mine.

"Yuh little kike, I'll bite your nose off if yuh get fresh wit' me! I'm your boss around here."

He went away. I worked. Racks of mantles were brought me, and I burned them off. Hell flamed and stank around me. At noon the boss blew a whistle. We sat on benches for our half-hour lunch. I could not eat for nausea. I wanted air, air, but there was no time for air.

There was no time for anything but work in that evil hell-hole. I sweated there for six months. Monkey Face tortured me. I lost fifteen pounds in weight. I raged in nightmares in my sleep. I forgot my college dreams; I forgot everything, but the gas mantles.

My mother saw how thin I was becoming. She forced me to quit that job. I was too stupefied to have done this myself. Then I read the Want Ads for another month. I found a job in a dark Second Avenue rat-hole, a little printing shop. Here I worked for another five months until I injured my hand in a press.

Another spell of job-hunting. Then a brief interval in a matzoth bakery. Job in an express company. Job in a mail order house. Job in a dry goods store.

Jobs, jobs. I drifted from one to the other, without plan, without hope. I was one of the many. I was caught like my father in poverty's trap. I was nothing, bound for nowhere. . . .

And I worked. And my father and mother grew sadder and older. It went on for years. I don't want to remember it all; the years of my adolescence. Yet I was only one among a million others.

QUESTIONS

Defining Terms

Identify in the context of the chapter each of the following:

New Deal   the American Dream
socialism   southern agrarians
Tom Kromer   Communist Party
Meridel Le Sueur   1934 Minneapolis Teamsters Strike
New Masses   Mike Gold

Probing the Sources

1. Why did people write to President and Mrs. Roosevelt? What did they ask for, and what opinions did they express about the origins and solution of the economic crisis?

2. In what sense were these pieces hopeful or despairing? Did any of them offer a vision of collective over individual action?

3. According to these accounts, in what specific ways did the Great Depression affect people in their daily lives?

4. How did the letters to the president compare to the fiction you read?

5. What impact did the depression have on women?

Interpreting the Sources

1. Why did Kromer and Gold blur the line between fiction and autobiography?

2. Why are images of strikes and unions so powerful in Le Sueur's writings? Do you think she responded to the editor's criticism at the end of "Women on the Breadlines"?

3. What did Mike Gold mean by "Jews without money"?

4. While they certainly hated human misery, in what sense did these writers welcome the crisis?

5. What are the advantages and disadvantages of using fiction to study history?

ADDITIONAL READING

On the economic aspects of the crisis, see Lester V. Chandler, *America's Greatest Depression* (1970). For an account of the Roosevelt administration, try William E. Leuchtenburg's *The FDR Years: On Roosevelt and His Legacy* (1995). The flavor of the times is captured in Studs Terkel's oral history *Hard Times* (1970) and Ann Banks's *First Person America* (1981). In *Voices of Protest* (1982), Alan Brinkley discusses the popular appeal of two depression-era demagogues, Huey Long and Father Coughlin. For artistic and intellectual trends of the era, see Richard Pells, *Radical Visions and American Dreams* (1973); and William Stott, *Documentary Expression and 30's America* (1973). For Oklahoma and Arkansas migrants, see James Gregory, *American Exodus: The Dust Bowl Migration and California Okie Subculture* (1989). On workers' response to the crisis, see Lizabeth Cohen, *Making a New Deal* (1991). On the depression and race, see Patricia Sullivan, *Days of Hope: Race and Democracy in the New Deal Era* (1996). And see Michael Denning's *The Cultural Front* (1996).

In Love and War
Exploring World War II
through Family History

Historical Context

One of the most basic facts of war is that it separates families—children from parents and husbands from wives. The moment of parting has a special poignancy because there is always the chance that it will become permanent. This was certainly true for World War II. In the United States alone, 16 million men and women left their families to serve in the armed services. Some 320,000 of these Americans never returned. Another 800,000 were wounded in action. Every month for three and a half years, families across America mourned for loved ones declared killed or missing. And for the relatives of soldiers who survived, there was always the dread that the next day would bring the fateful telegram beginning, "We are saddened to inform you. . . ."

Popular World War II songs spoke to this pain of separation. "White Christmas" expressed the soldiers' desire to return to the familiar comforts and joys of home. "I'll Be Seeing You" was written by Irving Kahad for the 1938 musical *Right This Way*, a Broadway failure. In 1943, "I'll Be Seeing You" was revived and became one of the most popular ballads of World War II. It aroused the longing for "old familiar places"—small cafes, carousels, chestnut trees, wishing wells, and many others. By combining small-town and large-city images, it spoke to every American couple separated by the war. Its last line—"I'll be looking at the moon, but I'll be seeing you"—captured perfectly the mood of wartime separations.

Letters to the front echoed the same refrain. They were the tissue that connected relatives in the United States with loved ones in Europe and the Pacific. To be sure, Americans followed the reports of the war in newspapers and magazines; they listened to the radio commentaries and watched the newsreels at the local movie theaters. They plastered maps of Europe and the Pacific on their walls and followed the paths of the war, marking with pins the location of their sons, husbands, lovers, and friends. But letters were so much more personal than newspapers, newsreels, or maps. Letters kept love—and, perhaps even more important, hope—alive.

Millions of letters were sent to and from American soldiers and sailors overseas. Letters from home carefully recorded everyday life and changes wrought by war. They noted wartime shortages and the details of family gossip. Letters from the front required monitoring. Censorship regulations prohibited soldiers from providing details regarding time and place or from including stories that could produce negative troop morale. Despite these restrictions, news poured into the states from the pens of soldiers in every theater of the war. Parents and spouses read and reread these messages, and then carefully placed them into treasure boxes for safe storage.

In the decades since these notes were written, millions of letters have been destroyed, yet millions more remain in dusty attics scattered across the nation. Some letters were opened and read one final time, and then burned by their creators to ensure the privacy of their intimate words. Other letters remain in their envelopes, unopened for more than five decades. Among the war letters recently disclosed is a collection that tells the story of Skipper and Joy Bilhartz.

This chapter draws upon those letters and upon the memories of a sailor who served with Skipper on the USS *Arenac*. The stories told in the letters are special, not because they are extraordinary, but because they are ordinary. The stories are of common people in extraordinary times. The letters relate tales of a wartime marriage and the birth of a first child, commonplace happenings during a four-year period when 13 million Americans were married and 12 million children were born. The letters describe everyday personal reactions to national events such as the reelection and death of President Roosevelt, VE Day, the use of an atomic weapon and the surrender of Japan. They disclose private attitudes about moral issues of the day, including the appropriateness of wartime strikes, divorce, alcohol abuse, and extramarital sexual relationships. They contain candid observations about the defeated enemy and about the U.S. government and military that brought about its defeat.

As you read these intimate letters and the oral history transcript, remember that your primary goal is not to piece together the story of one family. Rather, your task is to search the documents for insights into the daily activities and concerns of the 16 million American families that were broken apart by the war. How did Americans cope with the pains of wartime separation? In what ways did the intensity of these years shape the lives and influence the attitudes of the generation that fought the war?

To find answers to these questions, you must continuously make assessments about how the concerns of this family intersect with the sentiments of other groups of Americans. Note that the following letters were written by young, white, middle-class, Protestant, college-educated Texans. Skipper was a navy man of German descent; Joy was a homemaker and mother who lived with her parents during the time of separation from her husband. As you read about these ordinary people, reflect upon how other everyday Americans—middle-aged adults, nonwhites, northerners, working women, Jews, and blue-collar workers—would have reacted to the events of the times. More specifically, speculate about and begin to investigate your own family history. In what ways would the activities and concerns of your relatives have paralleled the experiences of this household? Finally, compare the sentiments expressed in these documents with contemporary American attitudes. Have attitudes about war, patriotism, gender roles, race, sex, marriage, parenting, and work changed significantly in the last half century? If so, why? If not, why not? Although it will not provide answers to all of these questions, the story contained in these documents should give you greater understanding of an age that demonstrated humankind's capacity for both intensive love and hate.

THE DOCUMENTS

Introduction to Document 1

The following selections represent less than ten percent of the letters between Skipper and Joy Bilhartz. The selections are arranged chronologically and grouped into four subject headings: Courtship and Marriage, Separation and Parenthood, War News from Home and Abroad, and Demobilization Days. Look for the major themes discussed in each section. What does the expression of these concerns tell us about the impact of World War II upon the American family?

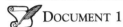 DOCUMENT 1   *The War Letters of Skipper and Joy Bilhartz*

Courtship and Marriage

On the day that Japan invaded Pearl Harbor, Skipper Bilhartz was a 19-year-old junior at Southwestern University in Georgetown, Texas. At this time, Joy Coleman, the future Mrs. Bilhartz, was an 18-year-old freshman at Southwestern. Following the attack, Skipper along with tens of thousands of other students across the nation inquired about his options for military service. After studying the various plans, Skipper committed himself to the V-7 Program, a plan that would allow him to continue schooling on his own until graduation, at which time he would be eligible to enter a Navy Officers Training Program.

Despite the shock of war, college life at Southwestern continued largely uninterrupted. Students attended classes, studied and partied, joined fraternities and sororities, made lasting memories, and worried about their futures. Three semesters later, Skipper graduated, and gathered the nerve to propose to his college sweetheart. Although only 19 years old, Joy already had turned away two marriage suitors. However, she said yes to Skipper. In the summer of 1943, Skipper left Texas for the U.S. Naval Midshipman's School at Columbia University in New York City. Between August and November 1943, the engaged couple carried on a long-distance romance. The following letters are among the few surviving letters written during Skipper's stay in New York. Although lonesome for Joy, Skipper was upbeat about his future. Above all, he was anticipating his upcoming marriage, an event he assumed would take place in Dallas a few days after his graduation from Midshipman's School.

28 September 1943

My very dearest Joy,

I just got back from a trip to the Brooklyn Navy yard. We went aboard a destroyer for quite a while, and also saw the battleship "Texas." Don't mention that too much as it is more or less confidential. At least so we are told. We have strict orders against telling a lot of things we learn yet often times the very same things are published in "Life" or some other magazine.

Your letter yesterday asked me to tell you what type of ring I wanted. It really makes no difference. I will like anything from you. I think the one with all the rims is very pretty, but it may be hard to keep clean. You go ahead and surprise me with anything you want to get.

Your letter today said something about getting married as soon as possible. Joy, that is the one thing I want more than anything else. It can't possibly happen too soon for me. Every day I get more impatient to be with you. It has seemed years since we were together. I don't see how I can wait 7 more weeks to see you. Joy, no one has ever loved anyone more than I love you. My love for you will last as long as I live. I'll love you forever,

SKIPPER

14 November 1943

My very dearest Joy,

Another weekend is just about gone now. I only have one more in New York. There are a million things I haven't seen yet, but I will still be plenty glad to see graduation day come around. . . . Joy, it is only ten days until graduation and then our marriage. If I get to Texas Friday afternoon when will we be married? By the way when is the latest that it would be proper for me to arrange for a best man? I hate to say anything until I am sure I can come home. If we have even a semi-formal wedding we will have to have a rehearsal. How long will that take? Will it be on the same day as the wedding? I suppose you think I am terribly dumb asking so many questions don't you. Well, I am afraid I am. At least when it comes to weddings. I suppose I should read up on them before getting married, but since I haven't time for that I am afraid I will have to depend upon suggestions from you. Do you mind an awful lot? Joy, I love you more than I can ever tell you. . . .

I'll love you forever,

SKIPPER

Separation and Parenthood

Time and transportation problems prevented Skipper's return to Texas. Joy, however, secured a rail ticket, said good-bye to her parents, and boarded a train for New York, arriving several hours before Skipper's graduation from Midshipman's School. After the graduation ceremony, Joy and Skipper were married in a 20-minute service in New York's Riverside Church on 24 November 1943. Following a brief honeymoon in the city, the newlyweds spent nine months together in Cambridge, Massachusetts. During this period Skipper studied radar technology and electronics at Harvard University and the Massachusetts Institute of Technology. Upon completion of his course work, Skipper was ordered to report to San Diego.

On 31 August 1944, Skipper and Joy left Cambridge by train for Texas, where they spent several final days together visiting their families in Dallas and Breckenridge. On 10 September, after a departing kiss, Skipper boarded a train for San Diego, and Joy, at this time seven months pregnant, returned to Dallas to live with her parents and two younger brothers. The following letters were written during this period of separation.

Sept 22 [1944]

My very dearest Joy,

I had two letters today. One from you and one from the folks. They certainly made me feel good too. A letter from you means more than anything that could happen to me here.

You ask if I knew how long I am going to be here. It is all very uncertain. It has varied with everyone. I may get orders from here direct to the South Pacific this week or again I may be assigned to a new ship that isn't completed yet and be around several months. In

This photograph of an anonymous couple captures a commonplace World War II image. (Frederic Lewis/Archive Photos)

the case of the latter I am certainly going to do my very best to come home in November [when our baby is to be born]. As far as your coming here, I am afraid that is impossible. There is no place at all to stay. It is much more crowded than Boston. One boy here with me brought his wife. They are staying in a tourist camp about 12 miles from here. He is going to have to send her back home. I hate to say all that, because there is nothing in this world that I want more than being with you. You know how I have always wanted sea duty so bad. Now I have changed my mind, at least until after November, because I want to come home then so bad that I can "taste" it. I can't bear to leave without seeing our baby. After that I want to ship out for a while anyway. My only hope though is that there is a very slight possibility that I may get a new ship that isn't yet commissioned. Keep your fingers crossed anyway. . . .

Joy, I'll love you forever, I love you

SKIPPER

September 23, 1944

My very dearest Skipper,

This morning there were two letters from you and they surely made me happy. Getting a letter from you in the morning is the very best part of the day. I'm so lucky to be married to such a wonderful boy. You are my ideal in everything Skipper—I wouldn't change a single little thing about you if I could change you into the ideal man—you are just that already. Emerson & Lyman [Joy's younger brothers] keep asking how you did certain things and I guess I sound like you are Superman. . . . I've really gone into the pie baking business since I've been home. I just love to make pies and everyone loves to eat them here too so I have appreciation. . . . Wish I were baking for you—then I'd really enjoy it.

Tomorrow it will be 2 weeks since we saw each other—seems a lot longer to me. I sure wish I were in San Pedro with you now Skipper but I know I shouldn't be anyway. I still miss you more & more each day. It will be so wonderful when we can go to bed together again. I won't ever feel lonesome when I can reach over and kiss you and put my arms around you. I'll never quit loving you. . . .

Joy

[undated letter on
San Pedro YMCA stationary,
probable date 3 October 1944]

My very dearest Joy,

I was planning to go to bed early tonight, but somehow or other I ended up in a big bull session with Dressler and Kelly. As is always the case our topic was wholly political. Dressler is a staunch Republican or maybe I should say Anti-Roosevelt while Kelly and I are just as much pro-Roosevelt. We can always manage to get into interesting discussions. . . . Tomorrow I am going to sea for the first time. For several weeks now the weather has been very foggy. As these big ships go on their test runs they only have skeleton crews. In the fog the other day one almost hit a tanker so now they won't go out without radar. So tomorrow I have to operate the radar on board a big transport over its trial run as a representative of the Consolidated Steel Company. That is really getting into something with responsibility [for] as far as I know I will be the only man with radar knowledge aboard and when fog wets in they are almost entirely dependent upon radar for safe navigation. Here's hoping my gear stays in working order. . . .

Joy, I'll love you always. . . .

SKIPPER

The following letter was written by one of Skipper's Southwestern classmates and navy buddies after he learned of Joy's pregnancy.

20 October 1944

Dear Skip,

. . . You knocked me off with the statement about little Skip (or Joy). . . . I'm very mad at you for waiting so long to tell me. Now I will have to speed up my treatise on how to bring up Skip's and Joy's children. Of course the little tot will be jerked up according to my specifications. Yes, there will be great benefits for the youngster to sit in on bull sessions with his wise old uncle. . . .

Your encouragement [about me finding a girlfriend] is to no avail. It seems I am destined to go through life as a bastard [the next word is blacked out with a note in Skipper's handwriting "Censored by me"] bachelor. The only ones up here who would have me are Jews, Catholics and little tramps. Most fun is had with the little tramps. Maybe I should go to more churches and fewer bars. Except for a bit of loneliness for something a little more stable I am having a pretty good time. Too good considering the fact that several million other guys are doing all the fighting and suffering all the hardships.

1953 [10 year reunion] is reserved. Give Joy my love. . . .

Dana

October 26, 1944

My very, very dearest Skipper,

I finally got to see the doctor today and he said he was just about sure we were going to have a boy. I asked him to really make sure & he listened again & said he was quite

Along with the writing of letters, the taking and exchanging of photographs helped to sustain morale during the periods of prolonged separation. These photos from the Bilhartz family album portray Skipper, dressed in his military garb, and Joy, with baby Linda. What values are expressed in these commonplace World-War-II-era photographs?

sure. Two nurses that always help him kind of laughed & said he missed two last week & he was really taking the razzing. But anyway, his guess ought to be better than anyone's so you can start looking forward to a son, Skipper. I really hope the doctor is right and our little boy is just like you. . . .

Skipper, I still miss you more every day. Sept. 10th seems so long ago now. Telling you good-bye that day was the worse thing I've ever had to do. I hope it won't be long until we can say hello again in person & I can kiss you a million times and be near you every minute of the day & night. Your letter this morning said how you remember every minute of those last days we spent in Breckenridge. I do too Skipper, and every time I think of how we cried when we turned out the lights & held each other so tight—I cry again but it's not because I'm unhappy, just because I love you so very, very much. I'll love you forever,

Joy

7 November 1944

My very, very, dearest Joy,

Well today is election day. Maybe now some of these arguments will stop. The papers here (Los Angeles) are absolutely the worst I have ever read. . . . Two of them hear really hate Roosevelt and it is sickening to read them sometimes. I guess that is because I hate to read what they say about a man I like.

Our commissioning date has been changed officially to 5 December now because of the strike. The strike is over now, so I guess they can get back to work. . . . Joy, I love you so very, very much. . . .

SKIPPER

November 7, 1944

My very, very dearest Skipper,

Tonight I went down town and met Viola Dare, girl friend of mine. She works for Paramount Motion Pictures here in Dallas and every Tuesday & Friday they have screening of the newest shows and they get around to Dallas about 2 or 3 months later. She invited me to come down & be her guest tonight. . . . We went to a drug store & had toasted cheese sandwiches and Dr. Peppers and talked—then came home and have been listening to the election returns. I wonder if you are listening. Is there a radio in the Y.M.C.A? It is 11:15 now and Roosevelt seems to just about have it cinched. I just finished listening to the sounds of Times Square in N.Y. City and all the description of the crowd. I tried to picture in my mind what it was like by remembering the night we walked down the street on a Saturday night . . . wish we were both there together tonight and would be going pretty soon to that apartment on 116th St. that we spent 5 wonderful days in. I can remember every day we have spent together Skipper and they were all so wonderful. They are what keep me going. . . . I love you,

Joy

14 November 1944
[San Francisco]

To the very sweetest wife in the world,

Well, this is your birthday. Was it a happy one? I certainly hope so. I wish we could be together, then it would have been perfect, at least for me any way. . . . Joy, today has been one of the most lonesome days I have ever spent. This town [San Francisco] is so much like New York. At least every time I turn around something reminds me of New York, and New York reminds me of you and our wedding. I was walking down the brightly lighted streets tonight and it seemed as though you should be with me. Every thing was just like it was last year about this time when we wondered down the streets of New York. I was so happy then I could hardly think and now my happiness and my love for you has grown a million times. . . . I'll love you forever. . . .

SKIPPER

19 November 1944
[San Francisco]

To the sweetest wife in the world,

I hardly know how to start this letter. It is the first one since our baby came. Last night when I called, your father said that you were in the hospital. The wire that our baby was here didn't get here until this morning. I don't think I have ever spent a more "worrisome" night than last night. It so happens that my captain lives in this same hotel, so last night after talking to your father I went to his room and asked his permission for leave. He was very nice, much nicer than my executive officer in San Pedro, and said he would O.K. my leave and would help me write my request. I can't do anything until Monday morning. Here's hoping everything works out. I don't think I could stand leaving without seeing Linda. That is what we are going to name her, isn't it? Or have you found a name you like better? If my leave comes through I probably won't be able to leave here until Tuesday at the earliest. If I do get to come home I may beat this letter and in that case I will tell you all this in person. I will wire you as soon as I find out for sure. . . . I'll love you forever and ever, I love you,

SKIPPER

Skipper received his requested leave and spent ten days in Dallas with Joy and baby Linda. The following letters were written after his departure.

November 30, 1944

My very dearest & sweetest Skipper,

You haven't been gone from the house long enough yet to have hardly gotten to the airport, but already I feel like an empty shell. Linda is sound asleep—everyone has come in and looked at her. I keep seeing you in my mind holding her up close to your face and kissing her. I'll keep that picture in my mind for the rest of my life as the sweetest picture in the world. . . . I'll tell her about how wonderful a Daddy she has everyday so that she will grow up hearing it. She is the luckiest little baby there is to have you for her daddy. . . . I'll love you forever.

Joy

5 December 1944

My very dearest, sweetest Joy,

. . . This morning something happened that made me "madder" than I have ever been in all my life. While I was on the ship the welders and burners staged an unauthorized walkout strike. I was standing at the gang way as they left the ship. I do believe that I could have shot each one as he went over the side. I could have easily tortured the fat slicked up guy standing there telling all the welders to leave the ship. You don't know how disgusting it is to stand by and see something like that happen. They are still out tonight and almost everything is held up while they are gone. Our ship is already two months behind the original plan and here they are pulling stunts like that. I don't see how a single one of them can sleep a wink tonight. They walked out over the silliest thing too. The shipwrights claim that part of their job is to spot weld studs on bulkheads while the welders claim that they aren't allowed to weld at all because they don't belong to a welders union. I was standing only two feet from a welder when two others came up and told him to quit working. If I can get tonight's paper I will send you the big red headlines telling of the walk out. The fellow on watch with me tonight from the APA 125 just read in paper (just under those red headlines telling of the walk out) about the loss of the ammunitions ship the USS Mount Hood. He helped commission her and was detached from her only a short time ago. He knew most of the men and their families. It is really disgusting to read about so many men being killed while these ignorant so called patriots sitting over here making fortunes and being home with their families every night go on strikes. If they could only realize what it means to be away from their family, maybe they would act differently. Joy, I am sorry to have raved on like this. . . . I'll love you forever. . . .

SKIPPER

December 17,—44

To the very sweetest husband in the world,

. . . Yesterday afternoon at 2 o'clock Fred phoned me and asked me for a date. He said he & Marie had an extra ticket to the Sunset—Highland Park football game and would I like to go. So I did. Sunset really got cleaned up on—it was pitiful 20 to 0, but I have never had any more fun at a football game. . . . There was a big fight right near us between 3 men & a high school boy & 3 policemen had to stop it & they almost got killed themselves. An old man who tried to take up for the hi. school boy got his nose broken. I saw more people that I use to go to high school with and most of the girls looked so sophisticated that I felt like a baby and hardly any of them were married & here I am already a mother. But I'm really the lucky one. . . . I'll love you forever I love you,

Joy

31 December 1944

To the very sweetest and most wonderful wife,

I wish that I were a writer of some ability, so I could describe Market Street of San Francisco tonight. It is just about the wildest place I have ever seen in all my life. If you were to take all of the frenzied football fans that you have seen in your whole life and put them all together you wouldn't have half the excitement there is on one block of Market Street right now. It is only 8:00 o'clock too. I am afraid to think what it will be like at midnight when the new year is really ushered in. Already confetti completely covers the whole street. Every one has a horn and no one has any scruples against making a lot of noise, so let your imagination run wild when you try to think of Market Street.

I just came from seeing the show "Hollywood Canteen." It was the best show I have seen since coming to California. I almost enjoyed it and that is more than I can say about any other show I have seen, because I always get so lonesome for you sitting in a theater by myself. My mind always goes back to Boston where we would go to the show so often. Then I could sit next to you, hold your hand, and then really enjoy the picture. Now all a picture brings is lots of extra loneliness. . . .

I'll love you always,

SKIPPER

War News from Home and Abroad

On January 8, 1945, Skipper's ship, the USS *Arenac* was commissioned into service. The *Arenac* was an attack transport ship designed to deliver combat teams to beachheads during amphibious operations. Following a brief training period along the coast of California, the ship left the states for the Pacific theater on March 11. Before departure, Joy made a trip to Long Beach, California to see Skipper. Twelve months would pass before their next visit. During this time, they would exchange more than 500 letters. The following are selections from these letters.

March 23, 1945

My dearest and sweetest Skipper,

It was one month ago today that we were together. You met me at the train station and we went to Long Beach to the Hilton Hotel and you weren't hungry & neither was I, and my hair was straight and you introduced me to a lot of people. Isn't it funny what you remember about things. How long ago does it seem to you that we were together. A short time away from you always seems like ages but when we see each other again I forget all the time we were apart and start right where we left off. . . . Bobby Hopkings, a boy down the street, was reported missing today in the S.W. Pacific. He is 19, a navigator (Lt.). He spent most of the time at our house for years playing with Emerson. . . . I love you so much. . . .

Joy

8 April 1945

My sweet and wonderful wife,

. . . We had church today out on the open deck again. This was more or less Easter service for us because on Easter Sunday we did not have services. We did have a very nice Palm Sunday service though. . . . The news release was just brought in from the radio shack. The news in Germany looks pretty good now, doesn't it? Speaking of the war in Europe my technician for radar received word at our last port that his brother was missing in action in France. I certainly hope that he turns up in a prison. . . . I'll love you forever. . . .

SKIPPER

April 12, 1945

My dearest, darling Skipper,

Today has been almost too much for us. . . . First it was the news that Franscine Maldin's husband, Davis, was killed in Germany on Easter Sunday. Franscine knows you well, she was in your graduating class. They have a little boy nine months old. . . . Leora, Jean & Mildred went over to see her this afternoon for a few minutes. Then when we heard that the President had died. . . . I love you so much

Joy

15 April 1945

My very dearest, sweetest sweetheart,

. . . This morning we had memorial services for President Roosevelt. I am enclosing the program. I wish you would keep it for our scrap book.

This afternoon I went swimming at an officers club. . . . After swimming a couple of hours I decided to join the rest of the officers of our dear ship. I knew, of course, exactly where to find them. Yes, almost all of them were in . . . the bar room. Those fellows can't seem to think of anything but sex and drink and out here the former is almost nonexistent, so they proceeded to drown all sorrows. I did enjoy in a gruesome sort of way watching them one by one get terribly drunk. . . .

I'll love you always. . . .

SKIPPER

April 23, 1945

My dearest & sweetest Skipper,

For the past 30 minutes I have just sat here & read your last four letters over & over. When I read your letters I get even more lonesome for you than the rest of the time. Sometimes I almost cry but it is a happy cry because I love you so much. When the war is over & you are home nothing will ever keep us apart again, will it Skipper? I want to be close enough to touch you every single minute. . . . I never think of anything now without thinking how you would like it—food, clothes, houses, flowers, books, people— everything I think or wish for has you in it. I want you to come home too so that Linda will know what a sweet Daddy she has. I try to imagine how you would be playing with her and carrying her. It hardly fits in my mind now because I never saw you that way except for a few days with Bobby [Skipper's nephew]. That picture taken of you & Bobby I still have in my purse & I look at it just about every day—wish I had one of you & Linda too. But when you get home we will fill our days with so much fun & happiness that we will make up for all this separation. . . .

Emerson has offers to go to either Baylor or A&M on a track scholarship. He wanted to go to Southwestern but they don't have a track team so I think he may go to Baylor, now. Skipper, dream about me in your dreams. I'll be dreaming of you in mine. I'll love you always. . . .

Joy

2 May 1945

My very dearest sweetest Joy,

. . . I just heard a news broadcast telling of the Berlin surrender. It also told about the unconditional surrender of the Germans in Italy. This has been an exciting day in Europe. It looks very much like the war on that continent is almost over. I hope the USS Arenac makes Europe one of its stops before this is all over. I would love to see what that part of the world looks like. I have seen enough here and am more than willing to "head" back the other way now. . . .

I can tell you, because thirty days have passed, where my first excursion to the Pacific took me. We, of course, made our first stop Pearl Harbor. From there we took another long hop westward to the Marshall Is. and the Marianas. I have seen both Eniwetok and Guam. That brings me up to exactly 30 days ago so the rest of the story of our "pleasure" yacht will have to remain secret for a while. Look those places up on the map some time, and you will realize just how far they are from home. . . . Joy, I will love you forever. . . .

SKIPPER

May 8, 1945

My dearest and sweetest Skipper,

This is VE Day in Europe and that's all that has been on the radio all day. Some places the people are just about going mad with happiness & drinking but in Dallas everything was quiet and large crowds at church tonight. Both papers put out extras but the news over the radio came out much sooner. It wasn't a surprise to anyone of course. Hope this good news in Europe will help the war to be over sooner in the Pacific. . . .

Do you feel any different now that you are a father, Skipper. I'll be glad when I can watch you play with Linda. You will make the best dad any girl ever had. I still tell Linda about you every day. . . . I love you so much. . . .

Joy

23 May 1945

My most wonderful wife,

I have an hour before going on watch, so maybe that will give me time to finish a letter. It may be my last chance to write for quite a while, so if there aren't many letters in this bunch please don't think that I haven't been thinking of you. If you only knew what is happening I know you would understand. Someday, not too far off I hope, I will tell you about it. . . .

How is Linda now? She is over six months old now. It doesn't seem, in a way, that long since I knocked nervously on the captain's hotel room door to ask him for a leave. I will remember that leave all my life. I was never before so afraid as I was then. I remember now how I was scared to even touch Linda for days. I wouldn't be now though. I want to hold her and play with her more than anything. . . . Joy, I love you so very much. . . .

SKIPPER

May 24, 1945

To my darling husband,

We have been married a year and a half today. Seems like much longer to me because I've lived most of my life in that time—the best part. The last nine months haven't been as pleasant as the first except for a few weeks but when this war is over we will make up double for every day we spent away from each other. I remember all the things that happened around this time last year. You fitted a dress form on me one night; Mary used to eat lunch with me just about every day & you & Dick had the same lunches because we bought our things together; we got a wedding present from Aunt Alice. . . . I can think of a jillion little things that happened about this time last year. . . . I'll get out of the past as soon as you get home to get me out. Then I'll live in the present. I haven't lost my power of imagining the future though. . . . You will be my sweetheart forever. . . .

Joy

1 June 1945

To the most wonderful wife in the world,

Well, I am finally going to write a letter to you regardless of what happens.—On second thought I had better say I will start one because here things can happen mighty fast—This is my second letter to you in eight days.—I hope you can understand the reason although I know you can't really know until I can explain it to you and that will have to wait quite a while. I doubt very much if I can write the folks, so will you tell them I'm fine. . . . I will be glad when I can come home to you. . . . I'll love you forever, I love you

SKIPPER

June 8, 1945

To my darling husband,

I've sure been missing my letters from you. I'm so anxious to know where you are now. Are you in a lot of fighting now Skipper, guess you are. It seems like most of the hardest fighting is being done now. . . . Emerson is trying to teach Linda to call him Pop. I told him he might be terribly embarrassed someday. He took her buggy riding the other night by himself while I washed & rolled my hair. That was mighty nice of him & I thought strange too for a teen age boy to want to be nurse maid to a baby. . . . Come home to us soon. . . .

Joy

13 June 1945

To the sweetest sweetheart in the world,

. . . At 5 minutes until sunset every ship in the harbor raises "Prep" (that is an alphabet flag "P") at the signal yard room. At sunset exactly the ensign is lowered slowly and every ship hauls down prep at exactly the same time. Tonight as I stood saluting the flag while it came down I was looking right into a beautiful sunset. There were just enough clouds in the sky to make it perfect. You can probably tell from this letter that things have "cooled" off considerably. It is probably only very temporary but certainly appreciated by every one any way. Joy, I'll love you forever. . . .

SKIPPER

June 18, 1945

My dearest, darling Skipper,

Tonight I talked to your Mother. She wanted to know if Linda & I could come to see them next Sunday and spend a week in Breckenridge before we went on our vacation and I said we could and would enjoy it if they didn't get tired of us. . . .

Skipper, I do remember all our mornings together in Cambridge and how hard it was for us to get up—to stop our loving each other in time for breakfast. . . . I haven't forgotten our days & nights together at your house or here when Linda was born & our two weeks in Long Beach and the weekends before we were married and all our dates together at Southwestern & our morning walk to town for an ice cream cone. Everything wonderful in life has happened to me since I've known you and you have done it all. I know there are few people who ever are as happy as I am with you. I'll love you forever & ever. . . .

Joy

20 June 1945

To my most wonderful wife,

. . . Every island in the Pacific regardless of how isolated and desolate has an officers "club." It seems that is just about the first establishment set up after an invasion. . . . Absolutely the only reason for such places is for drinking purposes. . . . This afternoon the other fellows gave me quite a hard time. It seems as though they still want to see me drunk. . . . In fact this afternoon I added another $10 bet to my other $20 that I would go back to the states without getting drunk. . . . Do you remember my telling you there was only one other officer aboard that didn't drink. I was wrong; there were actually two but the one I was telling you about has become one of the "boys," so there are really only two of us now out of 62. . . . some day I am going to "found" an officers club that gives recreational facilities to fellows who might enjoy something besides liquor. Then I can enjoy a shore liberty now and then. . . . I'll love you forever. . . .

SKIPPER

22 June 1945

To my wonderful wife,

. . . I heard today that Okinawa had been secured. That is good, because from all hearsay that was a slaughter. If "Oki" could possibly be so bad, I hate to even think of the next one that we all know must come. Unless I am very wrong, and I hope I am, the worst part of America's war is still ahead. I am afraid too many people are being led to believe that this mess is already over. That all sounds awful of me doesn't it. I am praying my ideas are all wrong, because I want to come home so very much. . . . I love you.

SKIPPER

25 June 1945

To my most wonderful wife,

Tonight I am writing after the movie. We saw "Casa Blanca." It was good, but it is getting a little tiresome seeing movies over and over again. . . . There is a big poker game going on at the end of this table. We have quite a gang of poker players aboard. That is one thing I stay clear of. The best way to stay clear is to leave the money with the disbursing officer. I only draw enough to pay my mess bill. The rest I will collect when the *Arenac* heads "East." Have you bought anymore extra bonds for us? I think it would be a good idea. We have enough cash on hand now. . . . I'll love you forever, I love you,

SKIPPER

July 4, 1945
[on the family farm near San Antonio]

To my darling husband,

Sure missed you today—so did everyone else here. They said until last year you had never missed a summer in your life coming to the farm. . . . Linda made it down her first summer & they said you did your first summer. . . .

Leora [Skipper's sister] got a letter from Cecil today that made her awfully unhappy. He said it would probably be the first of September now before he would get to start home. New equipment has been issued to him & he is now having to make German prisoners of war work for him. He must be feeding war prisoners—3,200 of them. Leora had thought it would only be a few days before he would be on his way and she had gotten just lots of new summer clothes but now he won't be here until later. September won't be so far away though now. Sure wish you were coming home then or even by Christmas. I keep thinking about what a wonderful Christmas we could have this year if we were all together. Santa Claus will really be someone to Linda this year. . . . All my love all my life. . . .

Joy

7 July 1945

My darling wife,

. . . They haven't cleared any more news that I would like to tell. That 30 day limit is a minimum subject to change by the commanding officer. You know, Joy, a guy sees some mighty sobering sights aboard a transport. You can see troops just before they land on a beach and then what is always more pleasant you can see the change of expression when they are loading getting ready to go back home or at least back to some friendly island. So far we have been awfully lucky ourselves. We have always been very well protected. I'll love you forever. . . .

SKIPPER

July 19, 1945

My darling Skipper,

Today Linda is eight months old. Can you imagine her that old already? I believe she is going to have another tooth through in a day or so. . . . Leora didn't get a letter again from Cecil. Your mother and I both had dreams of him being here at nap today. We hope that maybe it really meant something. I wish your chances were as good as his of getting home soon. . . . I'll love you forever. . . .

Joy

22 July 1945

My dearest darling wife,

. . . This morning I attended church service. . . . Joy, every Sunday during church I spend almost the whole time thinking of home—you and Linda. I always figure the time difference and know exactly how long ago you were at Tyler Street [Methodist Church]. I often wonder what it will be like when Linda is Christened. Are you still waiting for me for that? I know I will be about the proudest father in the world that day, because I can show off my wife and baby to everyone. I still think about Harvard Epworth in Cambridge. We had some swell times there, didn't we? Joy, every minute that I have ever spent with you has given me that much more to live for. . . . I'll love you forever. . . .

SKIPPER

August 6, 1945

My darling Skipper,

. . . I have just been listening to the radio about the atomic energy bomb and what it cost in materials and labor to discover and all the possibilities it has for future power. I was just thinking what the next war would be if there were one, but so much good could come out of the same discovery. Maybe this war will be over a lot sooner now—I hope so. Linda may not be so old when her Daddy comes home.

I'll love you forever. . . .

Joy

August 8, 1945

My darling Skipper,

The way the news sounds tonight it won't be long until the war will be over. I hope and pray it won't be much longer. I've been listening to reports for an hour and a half on the destruction the atomic bomb on Japan caused. It frightens me to think of its power—seems like too much for man to be in control of. But if Japan has sense they can still save lives of everyone by surrendering. Maybe I'll still get to see you in just a few months and it will be for good. If the war should end how long do you think you would have to stay in the Pacific before you got to come home. I'm not trying to cross my bridge before I get to it but just dreaming and hoping. . . . I love you so much.

Joy

15 August 1945

My darling wife,

Well, the war is finally over. How did Dallas take the big news? We were in one heck of a spot for celebrating—right out in the middle of the Pacific with nothing in sight but water—but an awful lot of that. That was really wonderful news, but today the bad news came. The navy announced its demobilization plan and it doesn't do me very much good. They allow 1/2 point for each year of age and 1/2 point for each month of active duty, plus 10 points for dependents. It takes 49 points for a discharge and my total is 34. According to that plan I need 15 more points and that as you can figure out means 30 months. . . . This point system has been the sole topic of discussion all day. Only a very few reserve men have enough points now. I expect the drop in points within six months, but I'm afraid the first drop still won't catch me. Joy, I want out of the navy so we can be together more than anything else in the world. . . .

I have just been talking to one of my radarmen that has had a bit of tough luck. When we got back to the states, he went to San Diego on his 72 hours pass. That is his home, or was his home. This time he found that his wife had left town with one of their "friends." His parents knew what had happened but did not write him because his wife told them they had separated, but this poor guy knew nothing of it until he went "home." He is only one of four aboard our ship that found the same thing when we arrived in the states this time. I do believe that fully 10% of our men have had their homes broken since we left the states last March. I felt funny talking to the kid tonight. You could tell he had been hurt, but was trying to cover it up. Something like that would mean the end of the world to me. Things like that happening all the time make me realize more and more that our love is something very special, Joy. . . . How is Linda now? The last pictures make me realize that my baby is really beginning to grow up. I hope that I can see her real soon. Joy, you have all my love forever. . . .

SKIPPER

Demobilization Days

VJ Day brought Americans great joy, but it did not immediately unite all separated American households. For Skipper and Joy, this reunion was delayed until February 1946. During these final months apart, they continued to write their daily letters to each other. The following excerpts are taken from Skipper's letters during these days of demobilization. The letters include Skipper's observations about places and peoples devastated by the war. They also reflect Skipper's evolving attitudes toward his former enemies and toward his own government. How would you describe Skipper's morale during these days of waiting?

24 August 1945

My darling wife,

. . . How is Dallas enjoying peace time living? From all news things must be in quite an "uproar" back in the states. I read in our news sheet yesterday that over 1,000,000 people had been laid off since the surrender of Japan. How are the products that were formally rationed holding out now that every thing is open for purchase? I imagine everything will be "fouled up" for a while yet.

In one of your last letters you said maybe I would be home in time to start Linda to school. Don't feel too pessimistic. I don't think it will be too long until we can be together. When I do get back, Joy, we will make up in every way for all this time that we have been apart. . . . I'll love you forever and ever. . . .

SKIPPER

4 September 1945

My darling wife,

This navy is certainly going "peace-time" in a hurry. Today we received a message eliminating all censorship. That means I can maybe write more interesting letters. A message also came saying that civilian clothes can be worn now by naval personnel when on liberty. We are at Ulithi now but are getting underway for Manila. . . . From Manila we aren't sure where we are going, but everyone is hoping it will be Japan. I want to see China and Japan as long as I have to be away from home anyway. . . . I'll love you forever. . . .

SKIPPER

P.S. This letter was scribbled in just exactly 8 minutes, because the mail is leaving right now. I just told all the confidential material that has always been forbidden.

15 September 1945

My darling Joy,

. . . Joy, I am awfully confused. If only we could talk everything over together. I received your letter today telling me you liked the idea of navy life. I like it a lot too in many ways, but there are so many catch's. I talked to Dr. Finch [a former professor at Southwestern University] and he is against the idea. In fact he was very emphatic. Then tonight I mustered up courage enough to talk to the commodore asking for personal advice. He has been a navy man 30 years and has a son that is a Lt. Cmdr. too. He was very frank and gave me both sides with nothing held back. . . . He said that Navy life was necessarily not a home life. He mentioned many advantages, but said that a navy man is definitely limited in almost every way. He stressed the same points that Dr. Finch did in saying that in the navy almost all initiative and ambition is lost. I suppose he is right at that, because advancements aren't always as much a sign of ability as of politics. He said there were many disappointments and I can understand that easily. All of that coming from a regular navy ranking officer whose whole life has been navy should mean something. He said a young man who liked uniforms, social life, adventures around the world and also one who didn't mind being away from home should make the navy a career, but a fellow that wanted home life and had any ideas of his own should stay out. I'm afraid my status comes under the home loving type. This was all concerning transfer to USN; however, he said that remaining in Reserves might be different. He recommended . . . finishing school under the G.I. Bill of Rights. Under that I can go to any college for any course with all school expenses paid plus $85 a month to live on. Besides that I would be allowed a part time job. This letter sort of gives you an idea of how things stand on both sides. However I am still undecided. There is one thing I know for sure though and that is if any job takes me away from you for any length of time I will refuse it to start with, because I can never again stand to be away from my wife. . . . I'll love you forever. . . .

SKIPPER

7 October 1945

My darling Joy,

We have been in Wakayama Harbor Japan now for a couple of days. . . . Every one is talking tonight about the friendliness of the Japanese people. I am afraid the sense of forgiveness of the American people is going to be bad. I can't seem to hold a grudge even when I know how awful they were during the war. Everyone seems of the same opinion. The Japs are probably smart enough to play up to that attitude too. . . . I'll love you forever. . . .

SKIPPER

12 October 1945

My darling Joy,

. . . More about Japan—The women here still carry the babies on their backs Indian style. The little kids hung like rags some times. . . . I was more than a little disappointed in the town. It seems strange that an enemy that is seemingly so backward in all respects could possibly prove to be so dangerous. . . .

I love you,

SKIPPER

23 October 1945

My *darling Joy*,

. . . I suppose there isn't much use to keep telling you that we still haven't any mail. It has been one month now since I've had a letter. I hope you are getting my letters. We keep hearing in the news that Congress is keeping heat on the navy for their slowness in demobilization. At first I believed they were doing the best possible, but after sitting in Wakayama harbor 3 weeks when every one is crying for transportation, I am inclined to think some one is just a little fouled up. What do you think?

. . . I have definitely given up the navy idea for our future. . . . My other plans are just tentative. I can't decide anything definite until I get back. Anyway, I have thought of going back to some school where we can live fairly reasonably. . . . What school would you suggest? I have considered only one seriously so far. That is the University of Texas. Can you think of any others? SMU might be OK, but I have never been there. Let me know what you would like. . . .

I'll love you all my life. . . .

SKIPPER

14 November 1945

My *darling Joy*,

Happy Birthday!!!! I wish I were there to kiss you and wish you many happy returns of the day. When I see you again you can bet your everything that I'm going to make up to you in kisses for all the time we have been apart. It seems awful to let my own wife's birthday pass without a gift, but it is out of my hands this year. . . . On Nov. 19 I want you to kiss Linda for me and tell her that her "Dad" is thinking of her and wishing her a happy first birthday. Joy, make Linda love me. I want to make you two the happiest home in all the world. Your happiness is all that matters to me. On Nov. 24 [our anniversary] I want you to remember more than ever my love for you. . . . You will be my sweetheart forever. . . .

SKIPPER

19 November 1945

My *darling Joy*,

Will you tell Linda Happy Birthday for me? I have thought of you both today an awful lot trying to visualize my daughter on her first birthday. . . . I have missed something that can never be regained. It has been unfair to me in many ways, but more than any thing it has been hard for you. I wasn't there during the time you most needed someone to help you. I will make it up for it as much as possible when the time comes for us to together again. I will certainly be there to see our next baby through "its" first year, that is if a year as a mother hasn't changed your mind about children. . . . I'll love you forever. . . .

SKIPPER

26 November 1945

My darling Joy

. . . When I sat down to write this letter I was in a fair frame of mind—now I am disgusted. The chaplain has been carrying on a conversation with one of the enlisted men just across the table. I couldn't help but over hear the conversation. This fellow went to a phone as soon as we landed just like a lot of the rest of us to call his wife and boy. To his surprise, the wife had moved from his home and was living with another man. When he finally did talk to her, she out right demanded a divorce. He is worried sick. He is through with her, but he wants to keep the boy. That is what I call a real "surprise" to find waiting back in the states. I can't even comprehend such a thing. . . . I love you,

SKIPPER

CHRISTMAS DAY
Latitude—36 degrees 50′ North
Longitude—152 degrees 00′ East
Weather—Storming with snow and sheet
25 December 1945

My darling Joy,

This Christmas Day isn't exactly the happiest I've ever spent. Last night I opened my presents after our Christmas Eve church service. We did have service even though the sea was mighty rough. I had quite a few packages to open. Thanks a lot for every thing Joy. . . .

I haven't written for two days, but it has been almost impossible. You see night before last this old ship almost took her last roll. We were fighting a full gale with winds over 56 miles an hour (knots) and the waves were averaging 70 feet in height. You can't imagine what a 70 foot roller looks like until you have been through an ocean storm. I had the 20–24 watch on deck and the ship seemed to be riding it out OK when I went off watch at midnight. Of course we were taking a beating but nothing that couldn't be expected. About 0130 I was awakened by a series of awful rolls. Every one thought we were going over. We got out of bed to see what was the matter. Well, the worst had happened, the engine plant had failed. Here we were trying to ride out a gale with no power. You see it takes an awful lot of power to help a ship heading into the wind in a storm, so without power the ship was troughed immediately. A ship can last only about 15–20 minutes like that, so you can see the predicament we were in. Each roll of the ship got worse. We finally rolled over 41 degrees or 82 degrees both ways—our critical or danger angle is only 37 degrees so we were not just a little bit scared. Finally after what seemed hours the engine room rang up 1/3 speed and the screw began to turn. You could feel the ship begin to take hold, and you can take my word for it that was about the best feeling I can remember. That was as close as I ever want to come to seeing the Arenac go down. We are still in a storm, but not nearly so bad.

Joy, I have tried to imagine what Linda was like on her second Christmas. I have wondered what you are like taking care of her. I will be the happiest man alive when I can live in my own home with the sweetest family in the world. . . .

Joy, I'll love you forever. . . .

SKIPPER

1 January 1946

My darling Joy,

. . . I was shore patrol officer during liberty yesterday in Sasebo. In pre-war days it was a city of 500,000 people and the third largest naval base in Japan, but the buildings were so leveled by bombing that what was formerly the main business section is now supply dumps. . . . It is impossible to tell that only a short time ago the whole area was a Jap business district. . . . From the looks of things this is going to be a hard winter for many people here. Jap laborers raid Army garbage cans and eat the scraps. . . . Darling, I'll love you forever. . . .

SKIPPER

9 January 1946

My darling Joy,

This is our last night in Japan. . . . I have seen all of Japan I want to see for a long time. Don't ever let anyone say that these people live at all like Americans. Their standards more nearly approach an American dogs. . . . Joy, as the time gets closer I get more and more anxious. I can hardly stand being away any longer. . . .

I'll love you forever. . . .

SKIPPER

Introduction to Document 2

The above letters provide us with anecdotal information about American life during World War II. The following tables give us with information about changes taking place in American society during the 1940s. These tables are derived from data contained in the readily available government source, *Historical Statistics of the United States*. What historical patterns are reflected in these numbers? How do you explain these patterns? In what ways do these statistics enlighten the anecdotal sources contained in the chapter?

DOCUMENT 2 *Historical Statistics of the United States, 1940–1950**

U.S. Population		Live Births	Deaths	Marriages	Divorces	Unemployed
1940	132,122	2,559	1,417	1,596	264	8,120
1941	133,402	2,703	1,398	1,696	293	5,560
1942	134,860	2,989	1,385	1,772	321	2,660
1943	136,739	3,104	1,460	1,577	359	1,070
1944	138,397	2,939	1,411	1,452	400	670
1945	139,928	2,858	1,402	1,613	485	1,040
1946	141,389	3,411	1,396	2,291	610	2,270
1947	144,126	3,817	1,445	1,992	483	2,142
1948	146,631	3,637	1,444	1,811	408	2,064
1949	149,188	3,649	1,444	1,580	397	3,395
1950	151,683	3,632	1,452	1,667	385	3,142

	Average Annual Earnings (AAE)		Inflation Adjusted AAE (in 1940 dollars)	Workers Involved in Work Stoppages	Wholesale Price Index (1926=100)	GNP	Gross Private Savings	College Degrees Conferred
1940	1,300		1,300	2,508	78.6	100.6	14.59	216,521
1941	1,443		1,374	4,288	87.3	125.8	22.59	
1942	1,709		1,473	2,968	98.9	159.1	41.90	213,491
1943	1,951		1,586	3,752	103.1	192.5	49.30	
1944	2,108		1,686	4,956	104.0	211.4	54.15	141.582
1945	2,189		1,710	4,750	105.8	213.6	44.25	
1946	2,356		1,695	4,985	121.1	210.7	26.52	157,349
1947	2,589		1,628	3,693	152.1	234.3	23.57	
1948	2,795		1,635	3,419	165.1	259.4	37.62	317,607
1949	2,851		1,687	3,606	155.0	258.1	36.10	421,282
1950	3,008		1,759	4,843	161.5	284.6	40.32	496,874

	Families with		Military Personnel on Active Duty	Women in Workforce
	Radio Sets	TV Sets		
1940	28,500	0	458	14,160
1941	29,300	0	1,801	14,640
1942	30,600	0	3,859	16,120
1943	30,800	0	9,045	18,810
1944	32,500	0	11,452	19,370
1945	33,100	0	12,123	19,270
1946	33,998	8	3,030	16,840
1947	35,900	14	1,583	16,915
1948	37,623	172	1,446	17,599
1949	39,300	940	1,615	18,048
1950	40,700	3,875	1,460	18,680

*The statistics for U.S. population, live births, deaths, marriages, divorces, unemployed, workers involved in work stoppages, families with radio and TV sets, military personnel and women in workforce are given in units of one thousand. The two Average Annual Earnings statistics are in dollar units. The first statistic in this category is in "current" dollars rather than in dollars of fixed purchasing power; the second statistic is ascertained by dividing the AAE figure by the appropriate consumer price index for the year, and is a measurement of relative purchasing power. The Gross National Product and the Gross Private Savings are in $1 billion units. The figures in the College Degrees Conferred column represent the total number of degrees earned. No degree statistics are available for the years 1941, 1943, 1945 and 1947.

POSTSCRIPT

Joy and Linda met Skipper at the railroad station in Dallas in mid February 1946, thus ending their period of separation. Skipper never returned to graduate school. Instead, he found employment at Atlantic Richfield in Dallas, Texas. In the 1950s he left Atlantic Richfield to establish his own oil consulting firm. Joy and Skipper eventually had five children: Linda, Skip, Terry, Lyman, and Helen. The third child is one of the coauthors of this volume. Skipper died following brain surgery in 1968. After his death, Joy returned to college to finish her undergraduate degree. She currently resides in Dallas, Texas.

QUESTIONS

Defining Terms

Identify in the context of the chapter each of the following:

V-7 Program   G.I. Bill of Rights
USS *Arenac*   Linda Bilhartz
walkout strikes   VE Day
censorship regulations   demobilization
VJ Day   Wholesale Price Index

Probing the Sources

1. Discuss the emotional pain of war. How do the letters add to your understanding of war, both at home and overseas?

2. How did Americans entertain themselves during the war years? What was the relationship between these modes of amusement and the war effort?

3. Using the anecdotal and statistical evidence in this chapter, describe some of the ways in which World War II altered the lives and/or the attitudes of American women, men, and children. Assess the positive and/or negative aspects of these changes. Were these changes temporary or permanent?

Interpreting the Sources

1. Five decades after the end of World War II, Americans were still debating the appropriateness of Truman's decision to use atomic weapons against Japan. How do you explain the continuing controversy? In your opinion, did Truman make the correct decision? Justify your answer.

2. Compare the exchange of letters during World War II with letter exchanges in more recent American military actions. What is the same and what is different? How do you explain the similarities and the differences?

3. Speculate about the time spent in composing a 500-word letter everyday. From a personal, military, and economic point of view, was this time well spent? What role did the letters play in sustaining family relationships, troop morale, and the national will to fight?

4. After reflecting upon the letters create five questions about World War II that you are curious about. Ask these questions to someone who lived during the war. Write an essay that incorporates the results of your oral or Internet interview.

ADDITIONAL READING

Studs Terkel's *The Good War: An Oral History of World War II* and Michael S. Sherry's *In the Shadow of War* (1995) are excellent general introductions to World War II. For a collection of letters from servicemen to the home front, see Annette Tapert, ed., *Lines of Battle* (1987). John W. Dower's *War Without Mercy* (1986) explores the attitudes of Japanese and American leaders toward their respective enemies. For the impact of the Pacific war on the inhabitants of the various island archipelagos, see Geoffrey White and Lamont Lindstron, ed.

The Pacific Theater (1989). Karen Anderson's *Wartime Women* (1981) discusses the impact of the war on gender roles, family relations, and the status of women. For the impact of the war on Japan, see John Dower, *Embracing Defeat: Japan in the Wake of World War II* (2000).

11

The Cold War

HISTORICAL CONTEXT

What is it exactly that we do as historians? As we have suggested throughout this volume, we search through the documentation of the past—looking for patterns and trends, trying to give order to a chaotic jumble of events and thoughts—and then construct stories. We do not write fiction, but neither do we tell the whole truth, for the absolute truth, the capital "T" truth, is unknowable, and perhaps even an illusion itself. In an attempt to understand and organize the past, we construct and use broad generalities to denote the temper or preoccupation of an era. Look at the organization of the earlier chapters of this book. There are separate sections on the eras of Reconstruction, the Progressive period, World War I, the Twenties, the Great Depression, and World War II. The implication is that, for example, during the Progressive era notions of progress and the improvement of life consumed America. But we know that not all people were involved in progressive crusades—perhaps only the smallest minority were—and that for some people, such as African Americans and many immigrants, the very idea of the Progressive era was a cruel irony. Nevertheless, textbooks and lectures on America in the early twentieth century usually stress Progressivism as the grand organizing principle.

The Cold War forms the organizing principle for the period after World War II. On one level, the rivalry between the United States and the Soviet Union—or between West and East, capitalism and communism—was quite real. The foreign policies of both countries emphasized some form of expansion, whether economic or military or both, and the two world powers generally opposed each other on crucial issues. How and why this rivalry developed is still debated by historians. After all, the two countries had been allies between 1941 and 1945 in the war against Nazi Germany. How had allies become opponents within months of the end of World War II? Without an overtly hostile act by either side, why did they become bitter enemies?

Like most events, the answer is complex. The rivalry began with the November 1917 revolution in Russia. Although United States officials had favored the liberal revolution earlier that year in Russia, a revolution that had overthrown Czar Nicholas and installed a moderate republican government, they did not support the October revolutionaries led by Vladimir Ilyich Lenin, a communist who opposed Russia's participation in World War I. Lenin and his Bolshevik supporters ended Russia's experimentation with democracy and republicanism, pulled their country out of the war, and established the Soviet Union. American leaders reacted by briefly joining a multi-national force to overthrow the Bolsheviks and by supporting a propaganda campaign that placed the Soviet Union in the worst possible light. Catching the temper of the moment, historian David M. Oshinsky observed, "It was claimed that the Soviets had an electric guillotine that chopped off hundreds of heads an hour; Bolshevik leaders drove around in fancy automobiles while businessmen were starving to death; and Russia had nationalized women by requiring them to register at 'bureaus of free love.' The message was the always the same: the Bolsheviks were hated by the people and represented only themselves."

During the 1920s the United States government tried to ignore the Soviet Union as much as possible. Occasionally a popular novelist would criticize the Soviet Union, or a left-leaning idealist would praise Lenin and the Russians, but there was little intellectual or financial commerce between the countries. That changed slightly in November of 1933, sixteen years after the establishment of the communist state, when the Franklin Roosevelt administration officially recognized and established diplomatic relations with the Soviet Union. Mired in the Great Depression, President Roosevelt hoped that the recognition of the Soviet Union would open new markets for American products. The dream of the great Russian market proved largely chimerical. In 1933, American diplomat and Soviet authority George Kennan had argued against recognition of the Soviet Union. Over 30 years later, in his memoirs, he saw no reason to change his position: "Never—neither then nor at any later date—did I consider the Soviet Union a fit ally or associate, actual or potential, for this country."

Some Americans, however, began to regard the Soviet Union in a new light during the 1930s. Faced by economic hardships at home and the growing threat of Nazi Germany in Europe, many Americans, especially those on the political left, believed that the Soviet Union offered the best solution for both the problems. Communism appeared more humane than capitalism during the depression, and collective security seemed more effective than isolationism. Yet other Americans—probably most—continued to view the Soviets as an enemy that would subvert religion, democracy, capitalism, and all that was decent in the world. They pointed to two events as keys to Soviet behavior. The first was a series of purges conducted by Soviet Premier Joseph Stalin. From his first years in office, Stalin had demonstrated a heightened sense of suspicion; he distrusted his own military leaders and government officials; he feared betrayal from those in power, close to power, and far from power. His solution was the ruthless elimination of all suspected enemies. Historians of the purges estimate that about one million people were executed and another twelve million died in labor camps. The purges made Americans question Stalin's methods and the morality of his regime. The questioning turned to outright hatred after the announcement of the German-Soviet Nonaggression Pact in late August 1939. After opposing the Nazis throughout most of the 1930s, Stalin cynically ignored his own expressed beliefs and entered into a pact with Hitler. Making matters worse, in early September the Soviet Union joined Germany in invading and dividing Poland. For most Americans, the purges and the Nonaggression Pact stripped the Soviet Union of its thin veneer of idealism and showed it to be a ruthless, cynical totalitarian state.

But morality is often an inconvenient basis for foreign policy, and in 1941 America's official position with the Soviet Union did an abrupt about-face. First, Hitler violated the 1939 Nonaggression Pact and invaded the Soviet Union. Then—after the Japanese attacked American forces at Pearl Harbor—Germany declared war on the United States. Suddenly the United States and the Soviet Union were allies, partners in an odd marriage of convenience in which neither country really liked or trusted the other. But until Hitler was defeated, it was a marriage in which there could be no divorce.

During World War II, American opinion makers gave Joseph Stalin and the Soviet Union a face lift. Reporters dubbed Stalin "Uncle Joe" and portrayed him as a kindly, if stern, father figure, the sort of patriarch who always had the best interests of the family in mind. In the movie *Mission to Moscow*, Hollywood characterized him as a thoughtful, pipe-smoking, farsighted political leader concerned with collective security, Nazi aggression, and the prosperity and well-being of his country. Other World War II films—*Three Russian Girls, Song of Russia, Boys from Stalingrad, The North Star,* and *Days of Glory*—presented similar views of Stalin and his people. "War has put Hollywood's traditional conception of the Moscovites through the wringer," noted a 1942 *Variety* columnist, "and they have come out, shaved, washed, sober, good to their families, Rotarians, brother Elks, and 33rd Degree Masons." In short, popular culture reinforced official political culture.

After the end of the war relations between the United States and the Soviet Union chilled rapidly. Disputes over the fates of Poland and Eastern Europe, the division of Germany, control over atomic weapons, and other issues divided the two countries, leading to a war of rhetoric and a mood of suspicion. In February 1946, Stalin warned Soviet citizens that there could never be a lasting peace with the capitalistic West, suggesting that economic sacrifices, and even war, lay ahead. Supreme Court Justice William O. Douglas called the speech "the declaration of World War III." And so it went—tough talk on one side resulted in equally strident language on the other, difficult issues assumed insurmountable proportions, and the gulf between the two world superpowers widened.

The result was the Cold War, the central fact of American foreign policy between the end of World War II in 1945 and the end of communist rule in the Soviet Union in 1991. During that 45 year period, thought of one another dominated the foreign policies of the United States and the Soviet Union. Through a series of flashpoints, ranging from Greece, Turkey, and Berlin to Korea, Vietnam, and Cuba, the two sides jockeyed for advantage in a deadly, global game of chess. Without actually ever going to war against each other, they were never fully at peace. To each, the other was an implacable enemy bent on total world domination.

During that period the Cold War also dominated and defined American life. It became the organizing principle of our popular culture, which boiled down to a series of "us" against "them" confrontations. Hollywood parlayed the theme into successful movies, from such "B" films as *I Was a Communist for the FBI, My Son John,* and *Big Jim McLain* to acclaimed works like *Fail Safe, On the Beach,* and *Dr. Strangelove.* From John Wayne's westerns to James Bond's action adventures the Cold War helped to define the plots. Popular writers and television producers also capitalized on the Cold War. John Le Carre, William F. Buckley, Jr., and Tom Clancy wrote best-sellers that revolved around the Cold War, and television shows such as *The Man from U.N.C.L.E.* and *I Spy* used the Cold War to sell consumer products. Even in international sporting events, the Cold War defined the rules of the game, making winning and losing of monumental importance.

The following documents helped define and portray the Soviet Union for the American people. As you read them consider the authorship and the underlying agenda. How did they contribute to the construction of a Cold War mentality? How did they reinforce or call into question the dominant Cold War paradigm? How did they give shape and meaning to the lives of millions of Americans?

THE DOCUMENTS

Introduction to Document 1

During America's honeymoon period with the Soviet Union in the early 1940s, Hollywood made several films that attempted to place Stalin and Russians in the best possible light. *Mission to Moscow,* released by Warner Brothers in 1943, purports to be the story of American ambassador Joseph Davies' mission to the Soviet Union on the eve of war. In reality, it was an attempt to rewrite Soviet history, justify Stalin's purges, and attack American isolationists. The following section of the script portrays Stalin as a far-sighted statesman and hints that he had no choice but to sign the German-Soviet Nonaggression Pact. Try to imagine how the scene was shot and what impact it would have had on Americans in 1943.

DOCUMENT 1   *Mission to Moscow*

Med. Long Shot Stalin from their angle as he walks toward the camera. (NOTE: In his book, Mr. Davies describes Stalin as follows: "His demeanor is kindly, his manner almost deprecatingly simple, his personality and expression of reserved strength and poise very marked." In the writer's opinion these characteristics for the part are even more important than physical verisimilitude.)

Med. Shot the Group as Stalin walks directly to Davies, dispensing with the formality of an introduction. The two men shake hands.

Stalin: Mr. Davies, I am happy to know you.

Davies: Thank you, Mr. Stalin. This is a great pleasure for me . . . (smiles) also considerable of a surprise.

They all smile at this frankness and the ice is broken.

Kalinin: Gentlemen, won't you please have chairs?

Stalin (*as they are seated*):   Besides your work here in Moscow, I understand you have visited many other sections of the Soviet Union.

Davies: And I've been deeply impressed by what I've seen—your industrial plants, the development of your natural resources, and the work being done to improve living conditions everywhere in your country. I believe history will record you as a great builder for the benefit of common men.

Stalin (*with sincere modesty*):   It is not my achievement, Mr. Davies. Our five-year plans were conceived by Lenin and carried out by the people themselves.

Davies: Well, the results have been a revelation to me. I confess I wasn't prepared for all I've found here. (With a smile.) You see, Mr. Stalin, I'm a capitalist, as you probably know.

Stalin (*laughingly*):   Yes, we know you are a capitalist—there can be no doubt about that.

They all join in the laughter.

Kalinin: We also know this about you, Mr. Davies—the worst things you've had to say, you have said to our faces, the best things you have said to our enemies.

Stalin: We want you to realize that we feel more friendly toward the government of the United States than any other nation. If there are any matters that are not settled between us, please take them up with Molotov.

Davies: Thank you . . . Well, gentlemen, I know how busy you are. I mustn't take up more of your time.

He rises, and the others follow suit, but Stalin interposes before the ambassador can move toward the door.

Stalin: Mr. Davies, do you have another appointment?

Davies: No, I don't.

Stalin: Then please do not hurry away.

The CAMERA PANS with the two men as Stalin leads Davies by the arm toward the door of his own office.

Stalin (as they walk):   There are some things on my mind that I would like you to know—and your great president to know.

Full Shot Stalin's Office   An austere room with maps on the wall and a large conference table in the middle of the room. We should give the impression here of two men surrounded by the problems of the world. They should be seen at first as very small in contrast with the table at which they are seated. As Stalin talks, the CAMERA PULLS UP to them.

Stalin: The outlook for European peace is bad—very bad. England and France have allowed Hitler to take Austria without a struggle. They will probably allow him to do the same with Czechoslovakia. They have repudiated their pledges to the League and are throwing the defenseless countries on the mercies of bandits.

Davies: It's clear what they're doing. What I don't understand is *why* they're doing it.

Stalin: I will tell you why, Mr. Davies, and I will tell you frankly because this is a time for plain words—the reactionary elements in England, represented by the Chamberlain government, have determined upon the deliberate policy of making Germany strong. And at the same time they shout lies in their press about the weakness of the Russian army and disorder in the Soviet Union.

Davies: You mean, Mr. Stalin, that these elements are actually encouraging German aggression?

Stalin: There is no doubt that their plan is to push Hitler into a war with this country. Then when the combatants exhaust themselves they will step in to make "peace"—yes, the kind of peace that will serve their own interests.

Davies: But I am sure the English people do not approve of such a policy.

Stalin: In my opinion the present governments of England and France do not represent their people. Finally the Fascist dictators will drive too hard a bargain and the people will call their governments to account—but by then it may be too late.

Davies: Mr. Stalin, may I ask you a very direct question?

Stalin: Of course.

Davies: If Hitler *does* attack Czechoslovakia and if France and England go to her aid—is Russia willing and ready to join them in war against Germany?

Stalin: We have a commitment with France to fight in the event they go to the aid of Czechoslovakia. The Soviet Union has never repudiated a treaty obligation. She would not repudiate this one.

Davies: Your past record speaks well for the future.

Stalin: But we are not going to be put in the position of pulling other people's chestnuts out of the fire. Either we must be able to rely on our mutual guarantees with the other democracies or . . . well, we may be forced to protect ourselves in another way.

Davies: Mr. Stalin, on my way home I'm stopping off in England. May I quote what you have just told me?

Stalin: If you could convince them and your own government that peace or war is in the balance, you would do us all a great service.

    At this point Davies rises and Stalin walks with him slowly toward the door.

Davies: I feel as keenly as you and Mr. Litvinov that collective security is the last bulwark against war.

Stalin: Litvinov has done all he can to make the world realize it. . . .

Davies (earnestly):   Mr. Stalin, a while ago I made the remark that my job was finished. After talking with you, I wonder if it hasn't only begun.

    Stalin looks pleased and gratified.

Introduction to Document 2

On March 12, 1947, President Harry Truman addressed a joint session of Congress in an attempt to win approval for a defense aid package for the governments of Greece and Turkey, which were fighting against internal communist movements. One congressman told Truman that he would have to "scare the hell out of the American people" to get congress to appropriate the money. Consider how Truman tried to successfully achieve that end. How did he characterize the Cold War between East and West, communism and capitalism? How does his language serve to enlarge the nature of the struggle?

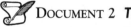 DOCUMENT 2   ***The Truman Doctrine March 12, 1947***

(Congressional Record, March 12, 1947)

The gravity of the situation which confronts the world today necessitates my appearance before a joint session of the Congress. The foreign policy and the national security of this country are involved.

One aspect of the present situation, which I wish to present to you at this time for your consideration and decision, concerns Greece and Turkey.

The United States has received from the Greek Government an urgent appeal for financial and economic assistance. . . .

The very existence of the Greek state is today threatened by the terrorist activities of several thousand armed men, led by Communists, who defy the Government's authority at a number of points, particularly along the northern boundaries. . . .

Greece must have assistance if it is to become a self-supporting and self-respecting democracy. The United States must supply this assistance. We have already extended to Greece certain types of relief and economic aid but these are inadequate. There is no other country to which democratic Greece can turn. No other nation is willing and able to provide the necessary support for a democratic Greek Government.

The British Government, which has been helping Greece, can give no further financial or economic aid after March 31. Great Britain finds itself under the necessity of reducing or liquidating its committments in several parts of the world, including Greece. . . .

Greece's neighbor, Turkey, also deserves our attention. The future of Turkey as an independent and economically sound state is clearly no less important to the freedom-loving peoples of the world than the future of Greece. . . .

As in the case of Greece, if Turkey is to have the assistance it needs, the United States must supply it. We are the only country able to provide that help.

I am fully aware of the broad implications involved if the United States extends assistance to Greece and Turkey, and I shall discuss these implications with you at this time.

One of the primary objectives of the foreign policy of the United States is the creation of conditions in which we and other nations will be able to work out a way of life free from coercion. This was a fundamental issue in the war with Germany and Japan. Our victory was won over countries which sought to impose their will, and their way of life, upon other nations.

To ensure the peaceful development of nations, free from coercion, the United States has taken a leading part in establishing the United Nations. The United Nations is designed to make possible lasting freedom and independence for all its members. We shall not realize our objectives, however, unless we are willing to help free peoples to maintain their free institutions and their national integrity against aggressive movements that seek to impose on them totalitarian regimes. This is no more than a frank recognition that totalitarian regimes imposed on free peoples, by direct or indirect aggression, undermine the foundations of international peace and hence the security of the United States.

The peoples of a number of countries of the world have recently had totalitarian regimes forced upon them against their will. The Government of the United States has made frequent protests against coercion and intimidation, in violation of the Yalta Agreement, in Poland, Rumania and Bulgaria. I must also state that in a number of other countries there have been similar developments.

At the present moment in world history nearly every nation must choose between alternative ways of life. The choice is too often not a free one.

One way of life is based upon the will of the majority, and is distinguished by free institutions, representative government, free elections, guarantees of individual liberty, freedom of speech and religion, and freedom from political oppression.

The second way of life is based upon the will of the minority forcibly imposed upon the majority. It relies upon terror and oppression, a controlled press and radio, fixed elections, and the suppression of personal freedoms.

I believe that it must be the policy of the United States to support free peoples who are resisting attempted subjugation by armed minorities or by outside pressures.

I believe that we must assist free peoples to work out their own destinies in their own way. . . .

The seeds of totalitarian regimes are nurtured by misery and want. They spread and grow in the evil soil of poverty and strife. They reach their full growth when the hope of a people for a better life has died. We must keep that hope alive. The free peoples of the world look to us for support in maintaining their freedoms.

If we falter in our leadership, we may endanger the peace of the world—and we shall surely endanger the welfare of this nation.

Great responsibilities have been placed upon us by the swift movement of events. I am confident that the Congress will face these responsibilities squarely.

Introduction to Document 3

On February 12, 1950, Senator Joseph McCarthy of Wisconsin gave a Lincoln's Birthday speech in Wheeling, West Virginia. After briefly extolling the virtues of the 16th American president, McCarthy quickly turned to his real theme, the subversion of the American government by traitors from within. Note whom he accuses. How did social class play into his charges of treason? The speech, which was inserted into the *Congressional Record*, was a bombshell. For the next few years, McCarthy and his accusations were constantly in the news.

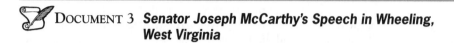DOCUMENT 3 *Senator Joseph McCarthy's Speech in Wheeling, West Virginia*

(Congressional Record)
Joseph McCarthy

. . . Five years after a world war has been won, men's hearts should anticipate a long peace, and men's minds should be free from the heavy weight that comes with war. But this is not such a period—for this is not a period of peace. This is a time of the "cold war." This is a time when all the world is split into two vast, increasingly hostile armed camps—a time of a great armaments race.

Today we can almost physically hear the mutterings and rumblings of an invigorated god of war. You can see it, feel it, and hear it all the way from the hills of Indochina, from the shores of Formosa, right over into the very heart of Europe itself.

The one encouraging thing is that the "mad moment" has not yet arrived for the firing of the gun or the exploding of the bomb which will set civilization about the final task of destroying itself. There is still a hope for peace if we finally decide that no longer can we safely blind our eyes and close our ears to those facts which are shaping up more and more clearly. And that is that we are now engaged in a show-down fight—not the usual war between nations for land areas or other material gains, but a war between two diametrically opposed ideologies.

The great difference between our western Christian world and the atheistic Communist world is not political, ladies and gentlemen, it is moral. There are other differences, of course, but those could be reconciled. For instance, the Marxian idea of confiscating the land and factories and running the entire economy as a single enterprise is momentous. Likewise, Lenin's invention of the one-party police state as a way to make Marx's idea work is hardly less momentous.

Stalin's resolute putting across of these two ideas, of course, did much to divide the world. With only those differences, however, the East and the West could most certainly still live in peace.

The real, basic difference, however, lies in the religion of immoralism—invented by Marx, preached feverishly by Lenin, and carried to unimaginable extremes by Stalin. This religion of immoralism, if the Red half of the world wins—and well it may—this religion of immoralism will more deeply wound and damage mankind than any conceivable economic or political system. . . .

Today we are engaged in a final, all-out battle between communistic atheism and Christianity. The modern champions of communism have selected this as the time. And, ladies and gentlemen, the chips are down—they are truly down. . . .

Lest there be any doubt that the time has been chosen, let us go directly to the leader of communism today—Joseph Stalin. Here is what he said—not back in 1928, not before the war, not during the war—but 2 years after the last war was ended: "To think that the Communist revolution can be carried out peacefully, within the framework of a Christian democracy, means one has either gone out of one's mind and lost all normal understanding, or has grossly and openly repudiated the Communist revolution."

And this is what was said by Lenin in 1919, which was also quoted with approval by Stalin in 1947:

"We are living," said Lenin, "not merely in a state, but in a system of states, and the existence of the Soviet Republic side by side with Christian states for a long time is unthinkable. One or the other must triumph in the end. And before that end supervenes, a series of frightful collisions between the Soviet Republic and the Bourgeois states will be inevitable."

Ladies and gentlemen, can there by anyone here tonight who is so blind as to say that the war is not on? Can there be anyone who fails to realize that the Communist world has said, "The time is now"—that this is the time for the show-down between the democratic Christian world and the Communist atheistic world?

Unless we face this fact, we shall pay the price that must be paid by those who wait too long.

Six years ago, at the time of the first conference to map out peace—Dumbarton Oaks—there was within the Soviet orbit 180,000,000 people. Lined up on the antitotalitarian side there were in the world at that time roughly 1,625,000,000 people. Today, only 6 years later, there are 800,000,000 people under the absolute domination of Soviet Russia—an increase of over 400 percent. On our side, the figure has shrunk to around 500,000,000. In other words, in less than 6 years the odds have changed from 9 to 1 in our favor to 8 to 5 against us. This indicates the swiftness of the tempo of Communist victories and American defeats in the cold war. As one of our outstanding historical figures once said, "When a great democracy is destroyed, it will not be because of enemies from without, but rather because of enemies from within."

The truth of this statement is becoming terrifyingly clear as we see this country each day losing on every front.

At war's end we were physically the strongest nation on earth and, at least potentially, the most powerful intellectually and morally. Ours could have been the honor of being a beacon in the desert of destruction, a shining living proof that civilization was not yet ready to destroy itself. Unfortunately, we have failed miserably and tragically to arise to the opportunity.

The reason why we find ourselves in a position of impotency is not because our only powerful potential enemy has sent men to invade our shores, but rather because of the traitorous actions of those who have been treated so well by this Nation. It has not been the less fortunate or members of minority groups who have been selling this Nation out, but rather those who have had all the benefits that the wealthiest nation on earth has had to offer—the finest homes, the finest college education, and the finest jobs in Government we can give.

This is glaringly true in the State Department. There the bright young men who are born with silver spoons in their mouths are the ones who have been worst. . . . In my opinion the State Department, which is one of the most important government departments, is thoroughly infested with Communists.

I have in my hand 57 cases of individuals who would appear to be either card carrying members or certainly loyal to the Communist Party, but who nevertheless are still helping to shape our foreign policy.

One thing to remember in discussing the Communists in our Government is that we are not dealing with spies who get 30 pieces of silver to steal the blueprints of a new weapon. We are dealing with a far more sinister type of activity because it permits the enemy to guide and shape our policy. . . .

As you hear this story of high treason, I know that you are saying to yourself, "Well, why doesn't the Congress do something about it?" Actually, ladies and gentlemen, one of the important reasons for the graft, the corruption, the dishonesty, the disloyalty, the treason in high Government positions—one of the most important reasons why this continues is a lack of moral uprising on the part of the 140,000,000 American people. In the light of history, however, this is not hard to explain.

It is the result of an emotional hang-over and a temporary moral lapse which follows every war. It is the apathy to evil which people who have been subjected to the tremendous evils of war feel. As the people of the world see mass murder, the destruction of defenseless and innocent people, and all of the crime and lack of morals which go with war, they become numb and apathetic. It has always been thus after war.

However, the morals of our people have not been destroyed. They still exist. This cloak of numbness and apathy has only needed a spark to rekindle them. Happily, this spark has finally been supplied.

As you know, very recently the Secretary of State proclaimed his loyalty to a man guilty of what has always been considered as the most abominable of all crimes—of being a traitor to the people who gave him a position of great trust. The Secretary of State in attempting to justify his continued devotion to the man who sold out the Christian world to the atheistic world, referred to Christ's Sermon on the Mount as a justification and reason therefor, and the reaction of the American people to this would have made the heart of Abraham Lincoln happy.

When this pompous diplomat in striped pants, with a phony British accent, proclaimed to the American people that Christ on the Mount endorsed communism, high treason, and betrayal of a sacred trust, the blasphemy was so great that it awakened the dormant indignation of the American people.

He has lighted the spark which is resulting in a moral uprising and will end only when the whole sorry mess of twisted, warped thinkers are swept from the national scene so that we may have a new birth of national honesty and decency in Government.

Introduction to Document 4

Even poets reacted to the climate created by the cold war. Perhaps most famous was Allan Ginsberg's poem "America," a rebuke in verse to what Ginsberg considered American hypocrisy and paranoia. Note that the poem was written six years after McCarthy first made his charges of internal subversion, when the cold war had become a daily reality. What was Ginsberg's tone? What message was he trying to convey?

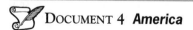 DOCUMENT 4 *America*

Allan Ginsberg

America I've given you all and now I'm nothing.
America two dollars and twentyseven cents January 17, 1956.
I can't stand my own mind.
America when will we end the human war?
Go fuck yourself with your atom bomb.
I don't feel good don't bother me.
I won't write my poem till I'm in my right mind.
America when will you be angelic?
When will you take off your clothes?
When will you look at yourself through the grave?
When will you be worthy of your million Trotskyites?
America why are your libraries full of tears?
America when will you send your eggs to India?
I'm sick of your insane demands.
When can I go into the supermarket and buy what I need with my good looks? . . .

I'm addressing you.
Are you going to let your emotional life be run by Time Magazine?

I'm obsessed by Time Magazine.
I read it every week.
Its cover stares at me every time I slink past the corner candystore.
I read it in the basement of the Berkeley Public Library.
It's always telling me about responsibility. Businessmen are serious. Movie producers
    are serious. Everybody's serious but me.
It occurs to me that I am America.
I am talking to myself again. . . .

America how can I write a holy litany in your silly mood?
I will continue like Henry Ford my strophes are as individual as his automobiles more
    so they're all different sexes.
America I will sell you strophes $2500 apiece $500 down on your old strophe
America free Tom Mooney
America save the Spanish Loyalists
America Sacco & Vanzetti must not die
America I am the Scottsboro boys.
America when I was seven momma took me to Communist Cell meetings they sold
    us garbanzos a handful per ticket a ticket costs a nickel and the speeches were free
    everybody was angelic and sentimental about the workers it was all so sincere you
    have no idea what a good thing the party was in 1935 Scott Nearing was a grand
    old man a real mensch Mother Bloor made me cry I once saw Israel Amter plain.
    Everybody must have been a spy.
America you don't really want to go to war.
America it's them bad Russians.
Them Russians them Russians and them Chinamen. And them Russians.
The Russia wants to eat us alive. The Russia's power mad. She wants to take our cars
    from out our garages.
Her wants to grab Chicago. Her needs a Red Readers' Digest. Her wants our auto
    plants in Siberia. Him big bureaucracy running our fillingstations.
That no good. Ugh. Him make Indians learn read. Him need big black niggers. Hah.
    Her make us all work sixteen hours a day. Help.
America this is quite serious.
America this is the impression I get from looking in the television set.
America is this correct?
I'd better get right down to the job.
It's true I don't want to join the Army or turn lathes in precision parts factories, I'm
    nearsighted and psychopathic anyway.
America I'm putting my queer shoulder to the wheel.

Introduction to Document 5

In 1961, 14 years after Truman addressed Congress about the communist crisis in Greece and Turkey and 11 years after McCarthy emphasized the communist crisis in the State Department, John F. Kennedy was sworn in as president of the United States. The day was bitterly cold in Washington, D.C., but the country enjoyed a springtime of peace. Not only were American troops not engaged in combat, there were no wars looming on the horizon. But like Truman and McCarthy, Kennedy spoke the language of crisis, giving the impression that war might—just might—be close at hand.

DOCUMENT 5   *John F. Kennedy's Inaugural Address January 20, 1961*

(Department of State Bulletin, February 6, 1961)

We observe today not a victory of party but a celebration of freedom—symbolizing an end as well as a beginning—signifying renewal as well as change. For I have sworn before you and Almighty God the same solemn oath our forebearers prescribed nearly a century and three-quarters ago.

The world is very different now. For man holds in his mortal hands the power to abolish all forms of human poverty and all forms of human life. And yet the same revolutionary beliefs for which our forebearers fought are still at issue around the globe—the belief that the rights of man come not from the generosity of the state but from the hand of God.

We dare not forget today that we are the heirs of that first revolution. Let the word go forth from this time and place, to friend and foe alike, that the torch has been passed to a new generation of Americans—born in this century, tempered by war, disciplined by a hard and bitter peace, proud of our ancient heritage—and unwilling to witness or permit the slow undoing of those human rights to which this nation has always been committed, and to which we are committed today at home and around the world.

Let every nation know, whether it wishes us well or ill, that we shall pay any price, bear any burden, meet any hardship, support any friend, oppose any foe to assure the survival and the success of liberty.

This much we pledge—and more.

To those old allies whose cultural and spiritual origins we share, we pledge the loyalty of faithful friends. United, there is little we cannot do in a host of co-operative ventures. Divided, there is little we can do—for we dare not meet a powerful challenge at odds and split asunder.

To those new states whom we welcome to the ranks of the free, we pledge our word that one form of colonial control shall not have passed away merely to be replaced by a far more iron tyranny. We shall not always expect to find them supporting our view. But we shall always hope to find them strongly supporting their own freedom—and to remember that, in the past, those who foolishly sought power by riding the back of the tiger ended up inside.

To those people in the huts and villages of half the globe struggling to break the bonds of mass misery, we pledge our best efforts to help them help themselves, for whatever period is required—not because the Communists may be doing it, not because we seek their votes, but because it is right. If a free society cannot help the many who are poor, it cannot save the few who are rich.

To our sister republics south of our border, we offer a special pledge—to convert our good words into good deeds—in a new alliance for progress—to assist free men and free governments in casting off the chains of poverty. But this peaceful revolution of hope cannot become the prey of hostile powers. Let all our neighbors know that we shall join with them to oppose aggression or subversion anywhere in the Americas. And let every other power know that this hemisphere intends to remain the master of its own house.

To that world assembly of sovereign states, the United Nations, our last best hope in an age where the instruments of war have far outpaced the instruments of peace, we renew our pledge of support—to prevent it from becoming merely a forum for invective—to strengthen its shield of the new and the weak—and to enlarge the area in which its writ may run.

Finally, to those nations who would make themselves our adversary, we offer not a pledge but a request: that both sides begin anew the quest for peace, before the dark powers of destruction unleashed by science engulf all humanity in planned or accidental self-destruction.

We dare not tempt them with weakness. For only when our arms are sufficient beyond doubt can we be certain beyond doubt that they will never be employed.

But neither can two great and powerful groups of nations take comfort from our present course—both sides overburdened by the cost of modern weapons, both rightly alarmed by the steady spread of the deadly atom, yet both racing to alter that uncertain balance of terror that stays the hand of mankind's final war.

So let us begin a new—remembering on both sides that civility is not a sign of weakness, and sincerity is always subject to proof. Let us never negotiate out of fear. But let us never fear to negotiate.

In your hands, my fellow citizens, more than mine, will rest the final success or failure of our course. Since this country was founded, each generation of Americans has been summoned to give testimony to its national loyalty. The graves of young Americans who answered the call to service surround the globe.

Now the trumpet summons us again—not as a call to bear arms, though arms we need—not as a call to battle, though embattled we are—but a call to bear the burden of a long twilight struggle, year in and year out, "rejoicing in hope, patient in tribulation"—a struggle against the common enemies of man: tyranny, poverty, disease, and war itself.

Can we forge against these enemies a grand and global alliance, North and South, East and West, that can assure a more fruitful life for all mankind? Will you join in that historic effort?

In the long history of the world, only a few generations have been granted the role of defending freedom in its hour of maximum danger. I do not shrink from this responsibility—I welcome it. I do not believe that any of us would exchange places with any other people or any other generation. The energy, the faith, the devotion which we bring to this endeavor will light our country and all who serve it—and the glow from that fire can truly light the world.

And so, my fellow Americans: ask not what your country can do for you—ask what you can do for your country.

My fellow citizens of the world: ask not what America will do for you, but what together we can do for the freedom of man.

Finally, whether you are citizens of America or citizens of the world, ask of us here the same high standards of strength and sacrifice which we ask of you. With a good conscience our only sure reward with history the final judge of our deeds let us go forth to lead the land we love, asking His blessing and His help, but knowing that here on earth God's work must truly be our own.

Introduction to Document 6

One of the striking features of the Cold War was the remarkably consistent rhetoric of politicians in both the United States and the Soviet Union. Although there were moments of thawing, and even a few premature predictions of the end of the Cold War, American political leaders often returned to the theme of the basic evil of the Soviet Union. In 1983 President Ronald Reagan, speaking before the National Association of Evangelicals, presented the idea in its clearest form, arguing that the only way to deal with the Soviet Union was from a position of strength. It is interesting to the note the differences and the similarities between Reagan's speech and the earlier ones by Truman and Kennedy.

DOCUMENT 6 *President Ronald Reagan on Russia as an "Evil Empire," 1983*

During my first press conference as President, in answer to a direct question, I pointed out that, as good Marxist-Leninists, the Soviet leaders have openly and publicly declared that the only morality they recognize is that which will further their cause, which is world revolution. I think I should point out I was only quoting Lenin, their guiding spirit, who said in 1920 that they repudiate all morality that proceeds from supernatural ideas—that's their name for religion—or ideas that are outside class conceptions. Morality is entirely subordinate to the interests of class war. And everything is moral that is necessary for the annihilation of the old, exploiting social order and for uniting the proletariat.

Well, I think the refusal of many influential people to accept this elementary fact of Soviet doctrine illustrates an historical reluctance to see totalitarian powers for what they are. We saw this phenomenon in the 1930's. We see it too often today.

This doesn't mean we should isolate ourselves and refuse to seek an understanding with them. I intend to do everything I can to persuade them of our peaceful intent, to remind them that it was the West that refused to use its nuclear monopoly in the forties and fifties for territorial gain and which now proposes 50-percent cut in strategic ballistic missiles and the elimination of an entire class of land-based, intermediate-range nuclear missiles.

At the same time, however, they must be made to understand we will never compromise our principles and standards. We will never give away our freedom. We will never abandon our belief in God. And we will never stop searching for a genuine peace. . . .

A number of years ago, I heard a young father, a very prominent young man in the entertainment world, addressing a tremendous gathering in California. It was during the time of the cold war, and communism and our own way of life were very much on people's minds. And he was speaking to that subject. And suddenly, though, I heard him saying, "I love my little girls more than anything—" And I said to myself, "Oh, no, don't. You can't—don't say that." But I had underestimated him. He went on: "I would rather see my little girls die now, still believing in God, than have them grow up under communism and one day die no longer believing in God."

There were thousands of young people in that audience. They came to their feet with shouts of joy. They had instantly recognized the profound truth in what he had said, with regard to the physical and the soul and what was truly important.

Yes, let us pray for the salvation of all of those who live in that totalitarian darkness—pray they will discover the joy of knowing God. But until they do, let us be aware that while they preach the supremacy of the state, declare its omnipotence over individual man, and predict its eventual domination of all peoples on the Earth, they are the focus of evil in the modern world.

It was C. S. Lewis who, in his unforgettable "Screwtape Letters," wrote: "The greatest evil is not done now in those sordid 'dens of crime' that Dickens loved to paint. It is not even done in concentration camps and labor camps. In those we see its final result. But it is conceived and ordered (moved, seconded, carried and minuted) in clear, carpeted, warmed, and well-lighted offices, by quiet men with white collars and cut fingernails and smooth-shaven cheeks who do not need to raise their voice."

Well, because these "quiet men" do not "raise their voices," because they sometimes speak in soothing tones of brotherhood and peace, because, like other dictators before them, they're always making "their final territorial demand," some would have us accept them at their word and accommodate ourselves to their aggressive impulses. But if history teaches anything, it teaches that simple-minded appeasement or wishful thinking about our adversaries is folly. It means the betrayal of our past, the squandering of our freedom.

So, I urge you to speak out against those who would place the United States in a position of military and moral inferiority. . . . I urge you to beware the temptation of pride—the temptation of blithely declaring yourselves above it all and label both sides equally at fault, to ignore the facts of history and the aggressive impulses of an evil empire, to simply call the arms race a giant misunderstanding and thereby remove yourself from the struggle between right and wrong and good and evil.

I ask you to resist the attempts of those who would have you withhold your support for our efforts, this administration's efforts, to keep America strong and free, while we negotiate real and verifiable reductions in the world's nuclear arsenals and one day, with God's help, their total elimination.

While America's military strength is important, let me add here that I've always maintained that the struggle now going on for the world will never be decided by bombs or rockets, by armies or military might. The real crisis we face today is a spiritual one; at root, it is a test of moral will and faith.

Whittaker Chambers, the man whose own religious conversion made him a witness to one of the terrible traumas of our time, the Hiss-Chambers case, wrote that the crisis of the Western World exists to the degree in which the West is indifferent to God, the degree to which it collaborates in communism's attempt to make man stand alone without God. And then he said, for Marxism-Leninism is actually the second oldest faith, first proclaimed in the Garden of Eden with the words of temptation, "Ye shall be as gods."

The Western World can answer this challenge, he wrote, "but only provided that its faith in God and the freedom He enjoins is as great as communism's faith in Man."

I believe we shall rise to the challenge. I believe that communism is another sad, bizarre chapter in human history whose last pages even now are being written. I believe this because the source of our strength in the quest for human freedom is not material, but spiritual. And because it knows no limitation, it must terrify and ultimately triumph over those who would enslave their fellow man. For in the words of Isaiah: "He giveth power to the faint; and to them that have no might He increased strength. . . . But they that wait upon the Lord shall renew their strength; they shall mount up with wings as eagles; they shall run, and not be weary. . . ."

Yes, change your world. One of our Founding Fathers, Thomas Paine, said, "We have it within our power to begin the world over again." We can do it, doing together what no one church could do by itself.

God bless you, and thank you very much.

Introduction to Document 7

In 1972 the Soviet Union defeated the United States in a controversial basketball game at the Munich Olympics. The game, played in the shadow of Cold War politics, enraged many Americans. In 1973 the Soviet basketball team traveled to the United States on a "goodwill tour." Again, Cold War expectations, stereotypes, and emotions colored how Americans viewed the games. Talking about the 1952 Helsinki Games, United States Olympic decathlon star Bob Mathias commented about competing against the Russians: "They were in a sense the real enemy. You just loved to beat 'em. You just had to beat 'em. . . . The feeling was strong down through the entire team." A generation later the same feeling persisted. The first article was written by Tom Callahan for the Cincinnati *Enquirer*, May 2, 1973; the second, by Jim Murray, appeared in the Los Angeles *Times*, April 26, 1973.

DOCUMENT 7 *The Russian Basketball Tour*

TRENCHES UNDER THOSE BASKETS
Tom Callahan
The Cincinnati Enquirer

THERE IS A microcosmic war on, in case you haven't heard, and our country has chosen Bob Cousy to run it for us.

At first, I thought this was a little like commissioning Jane Fonda, but I was glad, anyway.

Because I know Cousy. I have sat beside him on airplanes at times when discussing basketball would have been too depressing and so we talked instead about his friends from schooldays, the Berrigan brothers, or My Lai and a lot of other things like that.

In a good sense, Cousy is a peacenik along with being a sensitive, understanding man. When I heard Cooz was to be in charge of the United States national basketball team gathering to play Russia, I was glad.

He wouldn't seek reprisals for the loss Russia dealt America's Olympic team in Munich, the first defeat a U.S. basketball team had known in Olympic history.

Nor would he wave the flag excessively to make the competition seem any more important than just six basketball games.

Cooz would be out to win, naturally. But the games, not world supremacy. That's what I thought, anyway.

You can imagine how surprised I was, therefore, to hear the call go out Tuesday for more "muscle." . . . .

"I'm an old alley fighter, but I want equal muscle," said the coach, who means to add a center and "muscular forwards" and forget about finesse because this is war.

"It's organized mayhem under the basket," he said. "Outside fouls are called closely, but the criterion under the basket seems to be blood." . . . .

SWEN NATER IS a dirty player," charged Russian coach Vladimir Kandrashin through an interpreter. The coach motioned with his elbow.

Cousy didn't care what Kandrashin said.

"I wish he could play 40% more aggressive," Cooz said of Nater, a seven-foot center, "and if that means 40% dirtier, that's all right with me." . . . .

"The Russians have guys who really sneak blows," said the Yanks' Bobby Jones.

"I consider them a dirty basketball team," concurred Tom Henderson.

The Soviets aren't as talkative but they have brandished fists a few times during the games that do their talking for them.

"Evidently that's the way the International game is played," shrugged Cousy.

The teams play in Albuquerque tonight and then move on to Indianapolis Saturday, New York May 7 and Baltimore May 9.

IT'S JUST A GAME
Jim Murray
The Los Angeles Times

The way some people carry on, you would think the U.S. vs. Russia basketball game at the last Olympics was a national calamity on the order of the Johnstown Flood, the San Francisco Earthquake or the Chicago Fire.

The opinion persists that this moment will live in perfidy with the sinking of the Maine, the killing of Alexander Hamilton and the British burning of the White House.

We were jobbed by those treacherous foreigners. George Washington was right. We should never have dabbled in entangling alliances like the Olympic Games.

We didn't even show up for the second place medals and lots of people think we should have walked off the floor while we were still ahead—I guess on the theory that self-immolation is the preferable form of extinction.

I don't know who the culprit is supposed to be—the timer, the clock, the public address announcer, or maybe, just the Russian winter. All I know is, with three seconds left the Russians had the ball 91 feet from the basket and they got it there in one prodigious pass which was by far the best offensive play I saw all night.

The real calamity of the evening was that the score should have been close enough for the Russians to win with that one mammoth assist from end-line to offensive boards. By my reckoning the score—based on the personnel I saw on the floor—should have been "U.S. 75, Russia, 40" or thereabouts, by that time.

For one thing, I noticed during the warmups that the U.S. had some kids who just casually hoisted in 10-foot baskets. The Russians looked more like the Green Bay Packers. They had a couple of guys who didn't look as if they could even mail the ball successfully. . . .

Still, Russia won the game now, didn't they, and we did nothing to improve our international image by refusing to show up for our medals. If gold medals are all that important, you have to wonder why a half dozen or so of our finest players have scorned going to the Games to get one over the past few Olympics. We made ourselves look like a nation of sophomores and, in the light of what was happening in Munich that week, I would have to say a basketball bauble was a pretty puny thing to hold your breath and threaten to throw a tantrum over.

I suppose when the Russians beat you to the stars, and then beat you in the sprints, and at basketball, you got to find somebody to blame. I expect even on the day the world comes to an end there will be an American standing in line someplace with a "Beat Stanford" button on, grumbling about the officiating. Some guys never get out of the beanie hat and raccoon coat stage in their whole lives.

Which is why I was delighted to see Bob Cousy, the new coach of the American team, announce that what was going to be played at the Forum this Sunday in The Times-sponsored basketball reencounter between America and Russia, was not World War III or a vendetta or a national crusade but just a game between two squads of, on the whole, pretty nice young men.

I don't think Wall Street will go into a tizzy if the Russians win or that Congress will convene summarily at midnight. I would hope the crowd would leave their flags and noisemakers and "We're No. 1!" badges at home and act more like hosts than hostiles.

I am sure a Bob Cousy team will not sit on the basketball all night as if they thought it would hatch, but I am equally sure that if Russia wins the game in the last two seconds with a length-of-the-court pass, Cousy will be the first to sprint across the court and congratulate the winner.

And, if they should lose and show up cheerfully for the award ceremony later, how is the CIA ever going to live it down that a bunch of Bolsheviks were far better sports than we are?

QUESTIONS

Defining Terms

Identify in the context of the chapter each of the following:

Cold War

List of 57 names

Evil Empire

Truman Doctrine

Them bad Russians

The Goodwill Tour

Kennedy's Inaugural Address

Greece and Turkey

Mission to Moscow

Joseph Stalin

Probing the Sources

1. How and why did Harry Truman try to "scare the hell" out of the American people in order to achieve his foreign policy ends?

2. Did Joseph McCarthy believe that internal or external threats posed the gravest danger for the United States? Did he offer a solution?

3. How did John Kennedy try to give an impression of crisis in his inaugural address?

4. What problems did Allen Ginsberg have with America's Cold War culture?

5. What did Ronald Reagan mean by an "evil empire"?

6. How did Cold War politics spill over into sports?

Interpreting the Sources

1. Were there any points on which Harry Truman, Joe McCarthy, John Kennedy, and Ronald Reagan agreed? Was the Cold War a Democratic or Republican policy?

2. How is the image presented of the Soviets different in the film *Mission to Moscow* and the 1973 Goodwill Tour?

3. How did Allen Ginsberg present the mentality of Americans? What did he believe motivated the actions of Americans?

4. What forces shaped the Cold War and accounts for its long life? Was the Soviet threat real or imaginary?

ADDITIONAL READING

The origin of the Cold War has been one of the most hotly debated topics in American history. An outstanding overview of the Cold War is provided in Walter LaFeber, *America, Russia, and the Cold War* (1985). Daniel Yergin, *Shattered Peace* (1982), recounts the early years of the Cold War. Gar Alperovitz, *Atomic Diplomacy* (1985), suggests that the Cold War began even before the end of World War II, while John L. Gaddis, *The United States and the Origins of the Cold War, 1941–1947* (1972), argues that it evolved and deepened over time. Also see Gaddis's *Strategies of Containment* (1982). The view from the Soviet Union is provided in Vojtech Mastny, *Russia's Road to the Cold War, 1941–1945* (1979). Many of the leading American actors of the period have written memoirs. Among the best are Dean Acheson, *Present at Creation: My Years in the State Department* (1969); and

George F. Kennan, *Memoirs, 1925–1950* (1967). Walter Isaacson and Evan Thomas, *The Wise Men: Six Friends and the World They Made* (1986), presents a group biography of the men who formed America's Cold War policies. For more general works, see James T. Patterson, *Grand Expectations: The United States, 1945–1974* (1996); and Melvin Leffler, *A Preponderance of Power: National Security, The Truman Administration, and the Cold War* (1992). The impact of the Cold War on domestic politics and culture has also been considered in depth. David M. Oshinsky, *A Conspiracy So Immense: The World of Joseph McCarthy* (1983) shows how the Cold War worked its way into politics. Stephen J. Whitfield, *The Culture of the Cold War* (1996) traces the impact of the Cold War on American life. Larry Ceplair and Steven Englund, *The Inquisition in Hollywood: Politics of the Film Industry, 1930–1960* (1983) is a detailed study of the relationship between Washington and Hollywood.

12

The Civil Rights Movement
Freedom Summer, 1964

HISTORICAL CONTEXT

In June 1964, two hundred college students from some of the most prestigious universities in America gathered at the campus of Western College for Women in Oxford, Ohio. They spent several days getting ready for their summer vacations. All were going to Mississippi to participate in one of the most important mass movements in American history. The fact that two hundred *white* students planned to go into the deep South to work in the civil rights movement stirred massive attention in the media. But the fight for equality had already been in high gear for a decade; it was a movement by and for black Americans, with profound consequences for whites.

In 1954, the United States Supreme Court decided unanimously in the landmark case *Brown v. the Board of Education of Topeka, Kansas* that the segregationist doctrine of "separate but equal" public schools for blacks and whites inherently violated constitutional guarantees because segregated black schools were underfunded and inferior. The decision implicitly questioned the entire southern Jim Crow legal system that formally kept blacks and whites apart in schools, hotels, trains, public swimming pools, restrooms, and a variety of other locations. It takes a leap of historical imagination to feel what it must have been like for a black person to confront two drinking fountains—one labeled "White" and the other, probably an inferior facility, labeled "Colored." Most of the time, blacks tried not to notice; but by the mid-1950s, increasing numbers of African Americans stopped looking the other way. It was impossible for them not to be heartened by the *Brown* decision and other court cases in which their rights were upheld; it was equally impossible not to be let down when the federal government hesitated to come through with enforcement of its own laws and judicial decisions. The raising of hopes on the one hand and the failure of fulfillment on the other energized many African Americans to mobilize themselves. Their underlying assumption was that, as Americans, they deserved all of the rights and privileges of other citizens.

Nonviolent direct action became the main technique of the movement for the decade or so beginning with the *Brown* decision and ending with the Mississippi Freedom Summer. Simply put, this technique meant refusing to acquiesce to unjust laws, many of which the courts had overturned. Sit-ins, demonstrations, boycotts, civil disobedience, breaking the law, and filling the jails—all done without committing

227

violence or retaliating against others' aggressions—these were the essence of non-violent direct action.

The most dramatic early example of such techniques came in Montgomery, Alabama, in December 1955. Mrs. Rosa Parks, a black seamstress, rode the bus home after a long day's work. A white man got on, but she refused to give up her seat to him as law and custom required. When she was arrested, blacks began a mass boycott of Montgomery's bus system. Local residents like E. D. Nixon, who had been active in the labor movement as a railroad porter, and 27-year-old Martin Luther King, Jr., of Atlanta, freshly graduated from divinity school at Boston University, helped organize and inspire the year-long boycott. The protesters won their point when the Supreme Court ruled that laws forcing blacks to sit at the back of the bus or to give up their seats to whites were illegal. Once again, however, enforcement was slow.

In 1960, the movement took a new turn as four black students from North Carolina Agricultural and Technical College simply sat down at a segregated lunch counter and waited to be served. Whites berated, abused, then arrested them. For the next few years, sit-ins occurred at public accommodations throughout the South. Protesters requested their rights as citizens and maintained their Gandhian mode of nonviolence; whites responded with increasing levels of bloodshed. Demonstrators were killed and wounded as they registered at previously segregated universities, rode previously segregated buses, and checked into all-white hotels. Boycotts brought local economies to a standstill; massive sit-ins tied up criminal justice systems by filling the jails with protesters; and, above all, evening news images of people protesting peacefully for their rights and being met by police dogs, water cannons, and bludgeons brought considerable sympathy. Even President Kennedy was cautiously supporting new civil rights legislation by the time of his assassination.

Yet, as the summer of 1964 approached, the civil rights movement was coming to a crossroads. The right to be served a cup of coffee, to swim in public pools, or even to go to good schools (and ten years after the *Brown* decision, southern schools remained segregated) were important, but increasingly, the movement was forced to confront issues of politics and power. African Americans in the southern states constituted an enormous potential electorate, yet old legal barriers kept them from voting. This ultimate right of citizenship was next on the movement's agenda, and the Freedom Summer was part of the proposed solution.

Organizational leadership of the movement had been evolving all along. The National Association for the Advancement of Colored People (NAACP) had led the way in bringing civil rights cases to courts, especially in the 1950s, but as the movement turned toward nonviolent direct action, other groups with new leaders such as the Southern Christian Leadership Conference (SCLC) led by Martin Luthur King Jr., and James Farmer's Congress on Racial Equality (CORE) took center stage. Early in the 1960s, however, another organization emerged, the Student Nonviolent Coordinating Committee (SNCC). SNCC was the most militant of these organizations. Its membership drew heavily on young black southerners, many of whom had grown up poor, had seen the rising tide of white resistance, and were skeptical that integration was the answer. SNCC was active in various ways, but concern with issues of power led its members to undertake a massive voter registration drive. The Freedom Summer project was part of this new emphasis.

Sit-in in Jackson, Mississippi, in June 1963. (AP/Wide World)

Under the leadership of Robert Moses, SNCC, CORE, and the NAACP banded together in an umbrella organization known as the Congress of Federated Organizations (COFO). However, the money and manpower for COFO came mainly from SNCC, and the Freedom Summer was effectively a SNCC project. Simply put, the goal was to put hundreds of field-workers in Mississippi to educate poor rural African Americans in their elementary rights and to help them register to vote. Massive participation by idealistic white college students would bring increased press coverage and highlight the oppressive social conditions of the Deep South.

As SNCC planned the Freedom Summer, some leaders objected to involvement by whites. They argued that nonblacks came south, then departed when things got rough; that they stole all of the publicity; and that they monopolized leadership roles. Moses, however, insisted that integration was the ultimate goal and that he would not be a party to any form of segregation. As for whites getting too much media attention, the movement depended on stirring public opinion against segregation, and since the press was more interested in white protesters than black, the whites were useful allies out of proportion to their relatively small numbers.

The following news stories, editorials, photographs, memoranda, and other documents give a sense of the forces at work in Mississippi in the summer of 1964 and of the contending factions and ideologies. The events of that summer shattered the faith of many in nonviolent direct action, and in the coming years, civil rights protests grew increasingly bloody. After 1964, the movement's goals became much more concerned with economic and political power, and its methods more militant.

The results of those early years were mixed. Local governments seemed intransigent, acts of white violence went unpunished, and those sworn to uphold the law, such as the Federal Bureau of Investigation, often took the side of whites who attacked blacks. On the other hand, Congress passed the Civil Rights Act of 1964, which banned discrimination in public accommodations. The pain and indignity of legal apartheid had ended. One year later, President Lyndon Johnson signed the Voting Rights Act of 1965, a law that was gradually enforced, fulfilling (with exceptions) the demonstrators' goal of bringing the vote to southern blacks. Since its passage, thousands of African Americans have been elected to political office. So those who sacrificed so much for equality brought important changes to the South and even to the North, where segregation, by custom if not always by law, was the norm.

Events like the Freedom Summer of 1964—with televised scenes of black martyrdom in the face of white violence—challenged the old power structure and shocked some people into supporting the goals of the movement. Much of the discriminatory legacy of the Jim Crow era remained then and still remains. Especially in the field of economic opportunity, African Americans continue to face obstacles born of racial prejudice. Nonetheless, an ongoing tradition of activism that began in the 1950s continues to this day. Furthermore, that legacy did not remain confined to the field of African Americans' rights, but extended to other racial minorities, to the women's movement, and to the protest against the Vietnam War. The civil rights struggle, then, opened a whole new era of activist politics.

THE DOCUMENTS

The documents in this chapter tell the story of the Freedom Summer as it unfolded. Remember that this was only one episode in a drama that developed over several years. Note the range of opinion expressed by journalists and commentators (for example, the old 1950s technique of red-baiting—making unfounded allegations that individual leaders were communists—was still going strong). Note, too, how the civil rights debate covered a broad area of contested ground: states' rights versus the need for federal intervention; southern folkways versus racial equality; individual security versus group advancement; court cases versus direct action; and nonviolence versus greater militancy.

Introduction to Document 1

Document 1 provides some background for the events of 1964. Anne Moody grew up in Centreville, Mississippi, during the 1940s and 1950s. Her autobiography, *Coming of Age in Mississippi*, published in 1968, described her confusion, agony, and anger as she slowly became conscious of the racism and violence that surrounded her. Moody fought segregation with everything she had, risking her life and pushing herself to the edge of a nervous breakdown. The following passages capture how it felt to work in the civil rights movement in the summer of 1963. Moody was a student at Tougaloo College, but she devoted most of her time to community organizing. Document 1 is excerpted from a chapter in Moody's autobiography; here she describes the situation in Canton, Mississippi.

DOCUMENT 1 *From* Coming of Age in Mississippi

Anne Moody

In July, CORE opened up an office in Canton, Mississippi, to start a voter registration campaign in Madison County. By this time, I was so fed up with the fighting and bickering among the organizations in Jackson, I was ready to go almost anywhere, even Madison County, where Negroes frequently turned up dead. Shortly before Christmas a man's headless corpse had been found on the road between Canton and Tougaloo with the genitals cut off and with K's cut into the flesh all over his body. Around the time the body was found, Tougaloo College had received a lot of threats, so an inventory was made of all the males on campus to see if any were missing.

When Reverend [Ed] King discovered that I had agreed to work with CORE in the area, he was very much concerned. He discussed Canton with me, telling me he thought the place was too rough for girls. Some of my girlfriends also begged me not to go. But I just had to. I don't know why I felt that way, but I did.

Because I had come from Wilkinson County, I just didn't think Madison could be any worse. Things might even be a little better, I thought, since in Madison there were three Negroes to every white. I remembered that in Jackson there had been one point when I could see the white folks actually tremble with fear. At times when we were having mass demonstrations we had them so confused they didn't know that to do. Whenever I could detect the least amount of fear in any white Mississippian, I felt good. I also felt there was a chance of winning the battle regardless of how costly it turned out to be.

Disregarding all acts of violence, Madison County was considered a place with a possible future for Negroes. In addition to the fact that our records showed that there was a population of twenty-nine thousand Negroes as against nine thousand whites, Negroes owned over 40 percent of the land in the county. However, there were only about one hundred and fifty to two hundred registered to vote, and these had registered as a result of a campaign conducted by a few local citizens a couple of years earlier. Of this number, less than half were actually voting.

I arrived in Canton with Dave Dennis one Friday evening, and was taken straight to the CORE office, a small room adjoining a Negro café. The café was owned by C. O. Chinn and his wife, a well-established Negro family. It was located on Franklin Street in the center of one of Canton's Negro sections. Dave and I were just in time to have supper there with George Raymond, the project director, and Bettye Poole, my old Tougaloo buddy.

Dave introduced me to Mrs. Chinn. She was a stout lady with a warm and friendly smile. I liked her right away. I spent the entire evening sitting around the office talking to her and George Raymond about Madison County.

The office had been open only a few weeks, and in that time, Mrs. Chinn had already had her liquor license taken away. The place had been broken into twice, and many Negroes had been physically threatened. George reported that so far mostly teen-agers were involved in the Movement. He said that about fifty dedicated teen-age canvassers showed up each day. They were sent out daily, but had little success. Most of the Negroes just didn't want to be bothered, Mrs. Chinn told me. "That's the way it is all over," I thought. "Most Negroes have been thoroughly brainwashed. If they aren't brainwashed, they are too insecure—either they work for Miss Ann or they live on Mr. Charlie's place."

I just didn't see how the Negroes in Madison County could be so badly off. They should have had everything going for them—out-numbering the whites three to one and owning just about as much land as they did. When I discussed this point with Mrs. Chinn, I discovered that, although they did own the land, they were allowed to farm only so much of it. Cotton is the main crop in Mississippi, and, as Mrs. Chinn explained that night, the federal government controls cotton by giving each state a certain allotment. Each state decides how much each county gets and each county distributes the allotments to the farmers. "It always ends up with the white people getting most of the allotments," Mrs. Chinn said. "The Negroes aren't able to get more, regardless of how much land they have." Most of the farmers in Madison County were barely living off what they made from their land. Besides, they were never clear from debt. The independent farmers were practically like sharecroppers, because they always had their crop pledged in advance. The more I thought about it, the more it seemed that the federal government was directly or indirectly responsible for most of the segregation, discrimination, and poverty in the South. . . .

By the beginning of August . . . Dave Dennis decided to bring in three . . . workers—two girls, who were students from Jackson, and a boy called Flukie, a CORE task force worker. There were now six of us, but there was still more work than we could handle. George and Flukie went out in the country each day to talk with farmers and to scout for churches to conduct workshops in. The rest of us were left to canvass and look after the office.

So far we had only been able to send a handful of Negroes to the courthouse to attempt to register, and those few that went began to get fired from their jobs. This discouraged others who might have registered. Meanwhile, we were constantly being threatened by the whites. Almost every night someone came running by to tell us the whites planned to bump us off.

One evening just before dark, someone took a shot at a pregnant Negro woman who was walking home with her two small sons. This happened in a section where a few poor white families lived. The woman stood in the street with her children, screaming and yelling for help. A Negro truck driver picked them up and drove them to the Boyd Street housing project, which was right across the street from the Freedom House. She was still yelling and screaming when she got out of the truck, and people ran out of all the project houses. The woman stood there telling everyone what had happened. She was so big it looked as though she was ready to have the baby any minute. As I looked at the other women standing around her, I didn't like what I saw in their faces. I could tell what they were thinking—"Why don't you all get out of here before you get us all killed?"

After this incident, Negro participation dropped off to almost nothing, and things got so rough we were afraid to walk the streets. In addition, our money was cut off. We were being paid twenty dollars a week by the Voter Education Project, a Southern agency which supported voter registration for Negroes. They said that since we were not producing registered voters, they could not continue to put money into the area. It seemed things were getting rough from every angle. We sometimes went for days without a meal. I was getting sick and losing lots of weight. . . .

Sunday, September 15, 1963, was my twenty-third birthday. I got up about nine that morning feeling like one hundred and three. Everyone else was sleeping so I just decided to let them sleep. After a shower, I started to fix breakfast even though Mattie had promised to cook that morning. As soon as I finished, I got them up because we were supposed to have a staff meeting later. . . .

We were all eating and listening to the radio when the music stopped abruptly in the middle of a record. "A special news bulletin just in from Birmingham," the DJ was saying. "A church was just bombed in Birmingham, Alabama. It is believed that several Sunday-school students were killed." We all sat glued to our seats, avoiding each other's eyes. No one was eating now. Everyone was waiting for the next report on the bombing. The second report confirmed that four girls had been killed. I looked at George; he sat with his face buried in the palms of his hands. Dave sat motionless with tears in his eyes. Mattie looked at Dave as if she had been grounded by an electric shock. I put my hand up to my face. Tears were pouring out of my eyes, and I hadn't even known I was crying.

"Why! Why! Why! Oh, God, why? Why us? Why us?" I found myself asking. "I gotta find myself some woods, trees, or water—anything. I gotta talk to you, God, and you gotta answer. Please don't play Rip Van Winkle with me today."

I rushed out of the house and started walking aimlessly. I ran up a hill where there were trees. I found myself in a graveyard I didn't even know was there. I sat there looking up through the trees, trying to communicate with God. "Now talk to me, God. Come on down and talk to me.

"You know, I used to go to Sunday school when I was a little girl. I went to Sunday school, church, and B.T.U. every Sunday. We were taught how merciful and forgiving you are. Mama used to tell us that you would forgive us seventy-seven times a day, and I believed in you. I bet you those girls in Sunday school were being taught the same as I was when I was their age. Is that teaching wrong? Are you going to forgive their killers? You not gonna answer me, God, hmm? Well, if you don't want to talk, then listen to me.

"As long as I live, I'll never be beaten by a white man again. Not like in Woolworth's. Not any more. That's out. You know something else, God? Nonviolence is out. I have a good idea Martin Luther King is talking to you, too. If he is, tell him that nonviolence has served its purpose. Tell him that for me, God, and for a lot of other Negroes who must be thinking it today." . . .

A few days later, a Negro high school girl, picking cotton after school out in the country, was raped by a white farmer. The news was whispered throughout Canton. All the Negroes thought it was horrible, but none of them stopped sending their children to pick cotton. They had no choice—the little money the teen-agers made from picking cotton kept them in school. In Madison County, the use of teen-aged labor during the cotton-picking season was an institution. The Negro schools actually closed at noon the first two months of the school year, so that the students would be available to work for the white farmers. Their own parents, who had almost as much land as the whites but received much smaller allotments from the government, practically starved. Most of them couldn't even afford to give their children lunch money and buy them school supplies. . . .

Because the girl came to the CORE office and filled out an affidavit, her father had to resort to packing a gun to protect his family. After that, several open assaults were made on young Negro girls by the white men in the area. The assaults provoked a lot of talk concerning other affairs. . . . It came out in the open that some of the top officials of Madison County had Negro mistresses that they lived with almost full-time. . . .

It was now three weeks since the Birmingham church bombing, and during this time the Klan had been extremely busy. What I feared most was that the threats would stop, and action would begin—that I would see a bunch of Klansmen riding through Canton. If this ever happened, I was sure the streets of Canton would flow with blood for days.

Introduction to Documents 2 through 4

The following internal documents from leaders of the civil rights groups that organized the Freedom Summer set forth the strategy and rationale for the project.

Document 2 is from a pamphlet distributed by SNCC in Spring 1964. It details the conditions of voting rights for blacks in Mississippi. Document 3 is an undated (probably early 1964) summary of SNCC's plans for the Freedom Summer and the reasons for the project. The document is too long to reprint in its entirety; what is left out here goes into great detail about the need to establish "freedom schools," designed to educate black youth in basic literacy skills, and also to identify potential young leaders to strengthen the future of the civil rights movement. Document 4 is a memorandum from Robert Moses to the "Friends of Freedom in Mississippi"—mostly leaders in the movement—asking them to write to President Lyndon Johnson and urge protection for civil rights workers. Documents 3 and 4 were circulated among organizers of the movement; they were not for public consumption.

📜 DOCUMENT 2 *SNCC Pamphlet on Voting Rights*

For the first time in United States history colored citizens are organizing across an entire state to overthrow white supremacy. In Mississippi national and local civil rights, civic and church organizations, through the Council of Federated Organizations, are pulling together for the right to demand changes in the Mississippi Way of Life.

At the same time there are whites throughout the state organizing to crush the movement for change. The dominant white supremacy group is known as the White Citizens' Councils, organized by Mississippi's "leading" citizens in 1954 to combat colored voting rights and resist the Supreme Court school decision that same year.

The Citizens' Councils now maintain a firm stranglehold on the governorship, the state legislature and the federal and state courts. They control local and state education throughout most of the state, and dominate the economic base and activity in the state. . . .

In 1890 there were many more colored citizens than white citizens who were eligible to become qualified electors in Mississippi. Therefore, in that year a Mississippi Constitutional Convention was held to adopt a new State Constitution.

Section 244 of the new Constitution required a new registration of voters starting January 1, 1892. This section also established a new requirement for qualification as a registered voter: a person had to be able to read any section of the Mississippi Constitution, or understand any section when read to him, or give a reasonable interpretation of any section. . . .

Under the new registration the balance of voting power shifted. By 1899 approximately 122,000 (82 percent) of the white males of voting age were registered. But only 18,000 (9 percent) of the colored males qualified. Since 1899 a substantial majority of whites of voting age have become registered voters. But the percentage of colored registered voters declined. . . .

On April 22, 1954, the State Legislature again passed a resolution to amend Section 244. This time however, several new qualifications were included in the proposal.

FIRST, that a person must be able to read and write any section of the Mississippi Constitution; and give a reasonable interpretation of the Constitution to the county registrar.

SECOND, a person must be able to demonstrate to the county registrar a reasonable understanding of the duties and obligations of citizenship under a constitutional form of government.

THIRD, that a person make a sworn written application for registration on a form which would be prescribed by the State Board of Election Commissioners.

FOURTH, that all persons who were registered before January 1, 1954, were expressly exempted from the new requirements. . . .

The burden of the new requirements had to fall on colored citizens because a substantial majority of whites were already registered and therefore exempted from the amendment. Most would still have to apply for registration and therefore have to fulfill the new requirements. In 1954 at least 450,000 (63 percent) of the voting-age whites were registered.

Approximately 22,000 (five percent) of the voting-age colored citizens were registered. With 95 percent of the 472,000 eligible voters white, the proposed amendment to Section 244 was adopted on November 2, 1954. . . .

Without the right to register and vote we cannot take part in any phases of Mississippi's form of republican government.

What recourse do the white supremacists leave Mississippi colored citizens, if they cannot voice their opinions at the polls?

DOCUMENT 3 *Prospectus for the Mississippi Freedom Summer*

It has become evident to the civil rights groups involved in the struggle for freedom in Mississippi that political and social justice cannot be won without the massive aid of the country as a whole, backed by the power and authority of the federal government. Little hope exists that the political leaders of Mississippi will steer even a moderate course in the near future (Governor Johnson's inaugural speech notwithstanding); in fact, the contrary seems true: as the winds of change grow stronger, the threatened political elite of Mississippi becomes more intransigent and fanatical in its support of the status quo. The closed society of Mississippi is, as Professor Silver asserts, without the moral resources to reform itself. And Negro efforts to win the right to vote cannot succeed against the extensive legal weapons and police powers of local and state officials without a nationwide mobilization of support.

A program is planned for this summer which will involve the massive participation of Americans dedicated to the elimination of racial oppression. Scores of college students, law students, medical students, teachers, professors, ministers, technicians, folk artists and lawyers from all over the country have already volunteered to work in Mississippi this summer—and hundreds more are being recruited. . . .

Since 1964 is an election year, the clear-cut issue of voting rights should be brought out in the open. Many SNCC and CORE workers in Mississippi hold the view that Negroes will never vote in large numbers until Federal marshals intervene. At any rate, many Americans must be made to realize that the voting rights they so often take for granted involve considerable risk for Negroes in the South. In the larger context of the national civil rights movement, enough progress has been made during the last year that there can be no turning back. Major victories in Mississippi, recognized as the stronghold of racial intolerance in the South, would speed immeasurably the breaking down of legal and social discrimination in both North and South. . . .

This summer's work in Mississippi is sponsored by COFO, the Council of Federated Organizations, which includes the Student Nonviolent Coordinating Committee (SNCC), the Southern Christian Leadership Conference (SCLC), the Congress of Racial Equality (CORE), and the NAACP, as well as Mississippi community groups. Within the state COFO has made extensive preparations since mid-January to develop structured programs which will put to creative use the talents and energies of the hundreds of expected summer volunteers. . . .

Voter registration workers will be involved in an intensive summer drive to encourage as many Negroes as possible to register. They will participate in COFO's Freedom Registration, launched in early February, to register over 400,000 Negroes on Freedom Registration books. These books will be set up in local Negro establishments and will have simplified standards of registration (the literacy test and the requirement demanding an interpretation of a section of the Mississippi Constitution will be eliminated). Freedom Registration books will serve as the basis of a challenge of the official books of the state and the validity of "official" elections this fall. Finally, registration workers will assist in the campaigns of Freedom candidates who are expected to run for seats in all five of the State's congressional districts and for the seat of Senator John Stennis, who is up for re-election. . . .

DOCUMENT 4 *Robert Moses Memorandum*

Memo to "Friends of Freedom in Mississippi"
Roy Wilkins, James Farmer, Martin Luther King,
James Forman, A. Philip Randolph, Bayard Rustin,
John Lewis, Harry Belafonte, James Baldwin,
Dick Gregory, Ossie Davis, Marlon Brando,
Aaron Henry, Ed King, Robert Spike, Jesse Gray,
Larry Landry, Clyde Ferguson, Noel Day, Ella Baker.

From: Bob Moses

Re: Mississippi Freedom Summer

Dear Sirs:

I am writing on request of the Executive Committee of the Student Nonviolent Co-ordinating Committee and in my function as Program Director of the Council of Federated Organizations (COFO).

You are all aware of the summer program COFO is sponsoring in Mississippi this summer. We expect to field over two thousand workers in Freedom schools, community centers, voter registration drives in every county, and projects in selected white communities. We anticipate up to one thousand volunteers from across the country to join us in this program, including ministers, teachers, lawyers and students.

We have learned through bitter experience in the past three years that the judicial, legislative and executive bodies of Mississippi form a wall of absolute resistance to granting civil rights to Negroes. It is our conviction that only a massive effort by the country backed by the full power of the President can offer some hope for even minimal change in Mississippi.

We have already been accused of launching this project to incite violence and chaos in Mississippi this summer. We have two answers to this charge. For one, violence is prevalent throughout the state; at least six Negroes have been killed by whites in the past three months. And, more important, the responsibility for maintaining law and guaranteeing, at the same time, the right to peaceful protest, must rest, in the final analysis, in the case of Mississippi, with the President of the United States.

The President must be made to understand that this responsibility rests with him, and him alone, and that neither he nor the American people can afford to jeopardize the lives of the people who will be working in Mississippi this summer by failing to take the necessary precautions before the summer begins.

We are writing this letter now to you, to join together as the "Friends of Freedom in Mississippi" to seek a meeting with President Johnson to ask him to do the following things to insure peaceful change in Mississippi this summer.

President Johnson should:

1. Meet in early May with Governor Johnson of Mississippi and extract from Governor Johnson the pledge that he will call together all state and local law enforcement leaders and lay down certain ground rules for the summer. Under these rules the following activities will not only be permitted, but will be protected: peaceful orderly picketing; voter registration; orderly distribution of leaflets; peaceful assembly; freedom of inter-racial groups to live in the Negro communities and to move around the state without molestation.

2. President Johnson will inform the governor that these are clearly established constitutional rights which the federal government has the responsibility to protect, and

that if the governor will not do this, the federal government, will before the summer, establish at key points throughout the state constellations of federal marshalls who will be ready on call to protect these rights by preventive action, including on-the-spot arrests; and that the full power of the federal government stands behind these marshalls. If the governor agrees, but then there is an obvious breaking of the agreement, these marshalls will be immediately moved into Mississippi.

3. President Johnson should pledge to the committee in advance that he will take these actions if the governor refuses. . . .

Introduction to Document 5

Document 5 is a group of news reports on the incidents of Freedom Summer 1964. These reports not only tell us information about events but also give us a sense of how newspapers and magazines both influenced and reflected popular opinion. There are editorials, features, and news stories here, from sources north and south, liberal and conservative, local and national. Note how widely opinions about events ranged, and how even the "facts" were controversial. Try to see how far you can go in reconstructing the known details of the case. Where did ideological positions, value judgments, and clashing perspectives come into play? How did they shape the writers' perceptions of events?

 DOCUMENT 5   *Reporting Freedom Summer*

Mississippi: Allen's Army
NEWSWEEK, FEBRUARY 24, 1964

The second summer of the Negro revolt was still months off. But ever since the first, Allen Thompson, the graying, satin-smooth mayor of unreconstructed Jackson, Miss., has been acting as though Armageddon were just around the corner.

Girding for a new wave of civil-rights demonstrations this summer, Thompson is massing an impressive—and expensive—deterrent force of men and military hardware. To defend the capital city of 144,422, he is building up his young, tough, riot-trained police force from 390 to 450, plus two horses and six dogs. The force is "twice as big as any city our size," Thompson boasted last week—and it will be backed by a reserve pool of deputies, state troopers, civilian city employees, and even neighborhood citizen patrols.

With a hefty $2.2 million budget to spend, the department recently bought 200 new shotguns, stockpiled tear gas, and issued gas masks to every man. Its motor fleet includes three canvas-canopied troop lorries, two half-ton searchlight trucks, and three giant trailer trucks to haul demonstration POW's [prisoners of war] off to two big detention compounds. "I think we can take care of 25,000," the mayor said.

But the pride of Allen's Army is Thompson's Tank—the already popular nickname for a 13,000-pound armored battlewagon built to the mayor's specifications at roughly $1 a pound. The twelve-man tank, abristle with shotguns, tear-gas guns, and a sub-machine gun, flopped on its first mission—putting down a demonstration at all-Negro Jackson State College two weeks ago. As it rolled up, a tear-gas shell went off inside, and all twelve men stumbled out crying. Nevertheless, Thompson says reverently: "It's a wonderful thing."

Would a collision come? Thompson thought so—and so did the young warhawks of the Student Nonviolent Coordinating Committee, already mapping a massive summer campaign in Mississippi. SNCC was dispatching questionnaires last week to prospective recruits for its own nonviolent army of 500 to 1,000—mostly college students—to staff "freedom schools," community centers, and voter-registration drives. "The summer of 1964," SNCC chairman John Lewis said, "could really be *the* year for Mississippi. Before the Negro people get the right to vote, there will have to be a massive confrontation, and it probably will come this summer. . . ."

The mayor insists his army is only a second-strike force designed to preserve law and order. "We have to wait," he told *Newsweek's* Karl Fleming, "until they start trouble." But Thompson is certain trouble will come. "This is it," he said. "They are not bluffing and we are not bluffing. We're going to be ready for them. . . . They won't have a chance."

Western College to Host Civil Rights School
OXFORD PRESS, OXFORD, OHIO, JUNE 4, 1964

The National Council of Churches' Commission on Religion and Race will conduct a two-week instructional program at Western College for Women, June 12–27, President Herrick B. Young announced today.

College students from Yale, Harvard, Oberlin, the University of Illinois, and the University of North Carolina, among other institutions, will be prepared for a civil rights program to be conducted this summer throughout the South.

In making this announcement, President Young stated, "We have made our facilities available for this training program upon the request of the Council. As an institution with a Christian emphasis and an integrated student body, the Western campus is an appropriate setting for such a program."

The students participating in the program will be trained in two groups of three hundred each. The duration of each session will be one week. A staff of approximately fifty lawyers, social workers and educators will conduct the program.

The program will emphasize skills-training, in such matters as voter education, voter registration, remedial reading, how to teach, citizenship education, and the development of community centers. . . .

One-third of those recruited and trained will work in community centers and another third will teach such subjects as reading in summer schools. The rest will work in voter education and registration.

The students also will be trained in nonviolent discipline, because in many cases they may be called on to work under adverse circumstances, a spokesman of the National Council of Churches said.

The week-long course will also screen out those who should not be sent into situations that could become tense, the spokesman said.

Along with the students, the Council plans to send lawyers and ministers. The lawyer will advise on voter rights and other problems and the ministers will act as counselors.

Students Told Dixie Has Perils,
Warned Jailing, Death Possible in Rights Invasion
CHICAGO DAILY NEWS, JUNE 16, 1964

Raymond R. Coffey

OXFORD, Ohio—The barefoot and Bermuda shorts legion of white college students training here for a civil rights invasion of Mississippi will never be able to say they weren't warned.

Still miles and days away from the borders of the Magnolia State, they're ingesting a heavy diet of blood and thunder lectures about what they are likely to encounter before the summer is gone.

They are also being told bluntly that they are being counted on to provide a kind of shield of political protection for the local Negroes they'll be working with.

The students, around 200 of them, from all over the country, are being sent into Mississippi at the end of the week to work in a program of voter registration, "freedom schools" and community centers sponsored jointly by several major civil rights groups.

Their first training sessions—on techniques, security precautions, the politics and economics of Mississippi and so on—were held on the campus of Western College for Women here Monday.

At the first general meeting, James Forman, executive secretary of the Student Non-violent Co-ordinating Committee (SNCC), and a key figure in the program, put it on the line.

At the beginning, he said, the students should be made aware of three things:

They should expect to get beaten up, they should expect to go to jail and they should be aware of the possibility that some one is going to get killed.

"This should be discussed now," he said. "So if anyone wants to turn back, they can turn back now."

Robert Moses, Negro director of the whole project, told the students, many of them from well-to-do families and the nation's top colleges:

"The fact is, you have political influence through your mothers and fathers and congressmen and other people back home. Mississippi Negroes don't."

This influence, he and other speakers indicated, is being counted on to get the federal government to flood Mississippi with agents who will be able to provide some measure of safety for the civil rights workers, white and Negro.

At a section meeting for a small group of students, Stokely Carmichael, 22, a Negro college graduate and veteran of four years in the Mississippi civil rights movement, was more explicit.

The only safe way to "work a plantation," when trying to get Negro field hands to register as voters, he said, "is to have two guys, one of whom stays in the car and keeps the motor running."

Also essential, he said, is a car that can hit at least 85 miles an hour when the time comes to escape.

Matter-of-factly he noted that most plantation roads are privately owned, which gives the white manager the feeling that he can shoot trespassers freely.

"All plantation trucks now carry rifles and some of them have two-way radios," Carmichael explained, because "until about 1962 the boss man's job was just to get the cotton picked, but now he also has to make sure there's no civil rights activity among the field hands."

U.S. Puts Rights Army on Its Own in Dixie
CHICAGO DAILY NEWS, JUNE 20, 1964

Nicholas Von Hoffman

OXFORD, Ohio—They got the word straight from Uncle Sam. It hit with a shock wave of fear and anger.

Some 200 college students, civil rights volunteers bound for Mississippi, have been told to their faces that the Justice Department can't guarantee their physical safety.

The word came from John Doar, a Justice official—and the students responded with catcalls, sarcastic laughter and loud, angry questions. . . .

Doar told the students, the first contingent of 1,000 expected to work on various civil rights and education programs with Mississippi Negroes, that "I admire what you intend to do. The real heroes in this country today are the students."

He said that Mississippi is "a state that has gotten off the track."

"It appears to me," Doar said, "that there are a great many people (in Mississippi) who recognize that Mississippi is part of the United States and want to change, but for the most part they have been silent.

Doar stated that the power of the Ku Klux Klan, the White Citizens' councils and of other extremist groups is being used to "fight at any cost to the country to resist any encroachment on white supremacy."

He said that the extremists are trying to mark the students as people bent on "creating mass disorder in the streets of Mississippi."

He warned the students that, since under the federal system it is the State of Mississippi's job to keep law and order, that it is "impossible for Negroes to be protected" by the federal government.

"I suggest that for now you accept that as a fact," he quietly told the students who listened with tense expressions on their faces until they erupted during the question-answer period. . . .

"The FBI will do its best to keep track of where everybody is in Mississippi," said Doar, "but we cannot protect you in the sense of preventing a crime from occuring against you."

Over 100 Students—Civil Rights Workers Arrive in Mississippi
SHREVEPORT [LOUISIANA] JOURNAL, JUNE 22, 1964

JACKSON, Miss. (AP)—The first wave of Northern and Eastern college students was in Mississippi today to begin work among Negroes.

The Council of Federated Organizations (COFO) said more than 100 students came by bus and car over the weekend, and more were expected.

More than 200 volunteer student workers finished a week of indoctrination for the Mississippi Summer Project conducted by the National Conference of Churches at Oxford, Ohio. They were told how to hold voter registration drives and set up remedial schools.

COFO, which includes major civil rights groups working in the state, has estimated some 1,000 students will come to staff workshops for Negroes this summer.

3 Rights Workers Are Freed After Paying $20 Fines
BATON ROUGE [LOUISIANA] STATE TIMES, JUNE 22, 1964

JACKSON, Miss. (AP)—The Neshoba County sheriff's office said today three civil rights workers were arrested Sunday and released after paying a $20 fine.

The Council of Federated Organizations said the trio has been unaccounted for since Sunday afternoon.

Bill Light, a COFO public information officer, said two white workers and a Meridian Negro left Meridian Sunday for Philadelphia in Neshoba County to check on a report of a Negro church being burned last week.

Light identified the three as Mickey Schwener, 24, New York City, a Congress of Racial Equality field secretary; James Cheney, 22, a Meridian Negro CORE worker; and Allen Goodman, 20, a New York City summer volunteer.

Light said they learned through calling police departments between Jackson and Philadelphia that the three were arrested Sunday for speeding and held briefly. He said they posted a $20 bond and were released.

COFO said they have not been heard from since.

"Freedom" to the Delta
CHARLESTON [SOUTH CAROLINA] POST, JUNE 24, 1964

This week the vanguard of a youthful army left the rolling hill country of southwestern Ohio, where volunteers had spent several weeks being indoctrinated and incensed, for the flat Delta land of Mississippi. The Summer Project, a joint effort of the Student Non-Violent Coordinating Committee (SNICK) and the National Council of Churches, was on the march. . . .

"The real aim of SNICK and the other more extreme Negro organizations is to secure the military occupation of Mississippi by federal troops." This is not the expressed judgment of Mississippi Governor Paul Johnson or even of Senator James Eastland. The words are those of Joseph Alsop, the liberal columnist. Mr. Alsop, however much he may desire civil rights for Negroes, knows that no good can come from this Summer Project, controlled as it is by the most militant of the many civil rights groups and the one whose ranks include, according to Mr. Alsop, more than a few dedicated Communists. . . .

The crusade leaders say publicly that the main thrust of the summer invasion will be directed at voter discrimination in Mississippi, where only 6.6 per cent of Negroes of voting age are registered to vote. Such an effort, conducted with forbearance and directed at helping the Negro improve himself, might produce some good. Judging by the record, however, SNICK is short on forbearance and uncommonly long on making trouble. Nor is the National Council of Churches likely to provide much in the way of restraint.

The Council has invested $260,000 in this project, and it wants more out of that investment than a handful of votes. At a Baltimore meeting last February, during which the Summer Project was under discussion, Council members talked of "social redevelopment" in Mississippi, of applying "corrective treatment" to the Delta region.

"The main problem at this point," the Council's own report of the Baltimore meeting said, "is the concentration of wealth among the few, e.g., on an average, 5 per cent of the farms control 50 percent of all the farmland."

Voting? This has nothing to do with voting. The Council is speaking of agrarian reform of the sort that socialists promote.

From this, the goals of the Summer Project appear to be two-fold: first, indoctrination in socialist economics; second, military occupation of Mississippi if that can be arranged. This is no longer a struggle of black and white. If the reports of even the most liberal observers are to be believed, the Reds predominate and the nation can anticipate a long, hot summer indeed.

Charred Hulk of Car Spurs Intense Search
NEW HAVEN [CONNECTICUT] REGISTER, JUNE 24, 1964

WASHINGTON (AP)—President Johnson conferred today with Allen Dulles, who is flying to Mississippi this afternoon as the President's personal representative to evaluate law observance in the face of an organized civil rights campaign there.

Sitting in on the meeting of Johnson and Dulles, former head of the Central Intelligence Agency, was Atty. Gen. Robert F. Kennedy.

Johnson asked Dulles to undertake the assignment after three civil rights workers disappeared in Mississippi and the car in which they were riding was found burned. . . .

PHILADELPHIA, Miss. (AP)—Three-man teams combed the bayous and red clay hill countryside of east-central Mississippi today for three young civil rights workers who vanished Sunday night.

Federal agents teamed with state and local police in checking every house, shack and barn around the Bogue Chitto swamp, where the youth's fire-gutted station wagon was found by the FBI Tuesday.

Missing are Andy Goodman, 20, and Michael Schwerner, 24, both white from New York City, and James Cheney, a 22-year-old Negro from nearby Meridian.

They vanished mysteriously Sunday night after Cheney paid a $20 fine for speeding. The trio headed southeast toward Meridian but the burned station wagon was found 13.5 miles northeast here.

Mississippi's Lawless Invaders

SHREVEPORT [LOUISIANA] JOURNAL, JUNE 26, 1964

Before summer is over, the country is likely to experience student lawlessness in various places as a result of mixing holiday leisure with too much alcohol. Police in New York, Wisconsin and other states have had to deal firmly with such juvenile riots in the last few years.

This kind of unorganized lawlessness, which violates the rights of peaceful communities, is bad enough. It is symptomatic of rising disrespect for law.

Much worse, however, is the planned lawlessness for which students are training on the campus of the Western College for Women in Oxford, Ohio. We refer to the so-called "student army" that is begining to enter Mississippi to break state laws and foment strife. This "army" of young integrationists was described recently in The Chicago Daily News. Many of the students never have seen Mississippi, the Chicago newspaper reports, but they want to break its laws, nevertheless.

It is shocking that college students should want to devote a summer to lawlessness. It is even more shocking that a college would offer its campus for a course in civil disobedience. Most shocking of all is that a church group, namely the National Council of Churches—as revealed last March 27 in The Journal's editorial, "Mississippi Marked for New Invasion"—should be behind the force of law-breaking demonstrators.

The type of person with whom the National Council of Churches is involved must astonish some of its more innocent supporters. We refer to Myles Horton, head of the Highlander Center in Knoxville, Tenn.

"Horton," says The Chicago Daily News, "is helping the orientation program set up by the National Council of Churches on the campus of Western College for Women for the hundreds of students going into Mississippi to work on civil rights this summer."

As noted by the Charleston, S.C., News and Courier, it would require a book to recount Myles Horton's record of involvement in leftwing causes over the years.

Important documentation of his career was made available last November when Louisiana's Joint Legislative Committee on UnAmerican Activities released a special report. The committee report, based on sworn testimony, included affidavits signed by persons who stated that they had seen Young Communist League cards in the possession of Myles Horton and other Highlander Folk School leaders. Other affidavits told of the Soviet government being praised at Highlander, and of the Russian flag being saluted at that training school.

The appointment of Myles Horton is the strongest indictment we can imagine of the National Council of Churches as a radical action force in politics, masquerading as religious.

As a result of initial forays into the so-called "civil rights" field in Mississippi, three young integrationists—two whites and a Negro—today are the objects of an intensive search. They disappeared mysteriously after paying a traffic fine in Philadelphia, Miss., Sunday. A station wagon in which they were traveling was later found burned, but no trace of the missing trio was detected.

If violence has befallen the invading integrationists, the State of Mississippi can be counted upon to work with federal investigators in bringing the criminals to justice.

But until there is definite proof that harm has befallen the three outsiders, judgment in the case should be withheld. As has been pointed out by Mississippi authorities, it is possible that the missing men are alive and well—and maybe even in another section of the country. President Johnson's unwarranted grandstand action in sending federal forces into Mississippi to "aid" in the search for the missing men is another affront to the South. . . .

Traded: A Birthright for a Mess
CHARLOTTE [NORTH CAROLINA] OBSERVER, JULY 11, 1964
Nine years ago, William Faulkner wrote these words about the South:

> The question is no longer of white against black. It is no longer whether or not white blood shall remain pure, it is whether or not white people remain free.

Faulkner's point has been largely overlooked while the attention of a nation is focused on a more visible struggle of Negro Americans to get their first deep draughts of freedom. Yet today, so soon after Faulkner wrote the question, it no longer can be reasonably asked about his native Mississippi.

For the answer has already been made in Mississippi—the white people have not remained free. Clearly, nowhere in all America has the white citizen been so thoroughly shorn of his native rights as he has in Mississippi.

Of freedom to worship, for example:

"I can't even say God is love without seeing people in the pews getting red and showing signs of anger," said one Jackson minister. "That meant love your brother. And if you love your brother, they think, your daughter will marry a Negro." . . .

White Americans in many locales are in danger of social ostracism or worse if they express praise for the President of the United States, the past President or the preceding President. And if Mississippi goes the route of Alabama, no white American will even be able to vote for the current President.

A petition expressing support for "the governor and city officials in maintaining law and order" was passed around to prominent Jackson businessmen after an outbreak of Ku Klux Klan activities. None dared sign it.

While conversing with a friend, one-time Baptist and native Mississippian Frank Trippett of Newsweek magazine referred to "card-carrying Baptists" in light humor. His friend quickly said, "Shhhh. Man, you're back in the South now."

Thus has a pall of fear stifled any but the most orthodox expression, to a degree that has little parallel in American history.

Of freedom of the press:

Most newspapers dare not cross the invisible line of dissent. Editorials endorsing "law and order" often read like apologies, laced with attacks on everything else it is safe to attack, for insurance against angry reader reaction.

A cross recently was burned at the home of the managing editor of the McComb Daily Enterprise-Journal—not because the paper advocated desegregation, but because it printed stories of Klan terrorism on the front page. . . .

In one respect, the white American in Mississippi has made himself the virtual slave of the Negro. He has so relentlessly pursued the policy of white supremacy that the Negro question has come to dominate almost every aspect of his life—the thinking, the speech, the business, the politics, the education. Everywhere a Mississippian turns, he bumps against the issue he has created.

The cost of keeping the state a "white man's land" was always high, but it has finally taken from the native white American there much of his basic heritage. Until he realizes what he has traded away, his is the central tragedy of American life.

White Moderate Lives in Fear, Very Real Danger in Mississippi
MINNEAPOLIS TRIBUNE, JULY 12, 1964

Dick Cunningham

Jack Hill is not his real name. But he is a real person and he lives in Jackson, Miss., with a very real fear.

He's a white man who has stepped out of line twice.

He stopped paying dues to the White Citizens' Council when the council solicited funds for the defense of Byron De La Beckwith, accused slayer of Negro leader Medgar Evers.

More recently he and his wife went to a play at Negro Tougaloo College near Jackson. They stayed for an integrated dinner and found some of the Negro faculty members "a lot smarter than some of the white people we spend time with."

"But if you print that," Hill said quickly, "I'll call you a liar."

What does Hill fear?

All the things anyone fears who defies convention anywhere plus a specific Mississippi fear.

"There's a man in my area—a funeral director—who keeps his eye on things like this. If he knew what I said, he could ruin my business in a month."

One of the goals of the Council of Federated Organizations (COFO), the alliance of groups that is sponsoring the Negro civil rights drive in Mississippi this summer, is to reach such white moderates as Jack Hill.

A team of white students, mostly Southerners, is seeking to talk to them in churches, business groups, labor unions and college groups.

Talking may be as far as they get this summer, but the ultimate aim, according to COFO director Rober Moses, "is to give the white moderate some relief from his impotence."

Heart of Darkness
NEW YORK TIMES, AUGUST 6, 1964

Only two weeks ago we were blandly assured by Sen. James O. Eastland of Mississippi that the disappearance of three civil rights workers in his state might well turn out to be a hoax. Now three bodies have been found, and the FBI has identified two of them as Mickey Schwerner and Andy Goodman. The third corpse is probably all that is mortal of James Chaney, the Negro companion of the two white youths. Some hoax.

It is true that the North has no right to affect superior airs in lecturing Mississippi on civil rights; bigotry is no respecter of the Mason-Dixon line. But the attitude to murder sets Mississippi apart. A year ago, Medgar Evers [a civil rights leader] was shot in the back. Since then, at least 11 Negroes have been killed in mysterious circumstances in Mississippi, including two whose bodies were believed to have been found in the Mississippi River during the search for three civil rights workers.

Though this bloody business horrifies the rest of the country, the tendency in Mississippi is to shrug it off. In Philadelphia, Miss., a resident who declined to give his name to the Associated Press was quoted as laconically remarking of the three boys, "if they had stayed home where they belonged nothing would have happened to them." Implicit in this attitude is the feeling that Mississippi is not "home" to an American but an alien place to be visited at one's own peril. . . .

These Are the Times . . . That Challenge the South

THE NEW REBEL, NEWSLETTER OF THE SOUTHERN STUDENT ORGANIZING COMMITTEE, OCTOBER 1964

Jim Williams

. . . What are the values we cherish? Most of us grew up in the fifties. In a sense we grew up in a very special and a very fine way. For most of us, the fifties provided an abundance which our parents never shared during their childhood, but which we did receive and take almost for granted. From our middle class and Christian heritage we received these traditions of the South.

We cherish the values of freedom, of liberty and democracy. We strive toward the virtues of charity, compassion and humanity. We thirst after decency, the taste of the Great Society which is a democracy of the whole people with abundance and freedom for all. Many "yankees" poke fun of what seems to them to be an exaggerated sense of manners on the part of southerners. Yet, underlying our obvious mannerism, is a deep sense of values.

Another set of values challenges us today. This new doctrine emphasizes personal aggrandisement versus public comfort, selfishness and callowness in place of altruism. This new doctrine, in the name of "freedom" seeks to destroy freedom by flaunting the constitution and the courts and the laws of the land. Men like George Wallace and Ross Barnett espouse freedom and states' rights on one hand—and deny these by force to their Negro brothers. Along with their friends in the Citizens' Councils, they espouse the freedom to starve, the freedom to be shot by segregationist police, and the freedom to rot in jail for exercising the right to vote.

This view has come to be accepted as that representing the South. And, what else could people think as lynching after lynching continued, after firehoses and police dogs, beatings and burnings and bombings? This, too, has come to be "southern tradition."

We must ask ourselves what part of the southern tradition do we wish to emulate? That of compassion, of the heroism of thousands of southerners in working for a better world through the labor movement and now the civil rights movement—or, the dark tradition of the KKK, the Citizens' Councils and assassination?

Introduction to Document 6

Document 6 contains excerpts from interviews (published in the December 18, 1964, issue of *The Nation*) with civil rights workers who participated in voter registration. Note that the article is not about how Freedom Summer changed the lives of black Mississippians. Rather, the focus is on the feelings of those who went south.

DOCUMENT 6 *Journey to Understanding*

Howard Zinn

Four Witnesses to a Mississippi Summer
THE LAWYER . . . WILLIAM M. KUNSTLER

. . . Recently, I was exchanging views with one of the many young lawyers who had volunteered to serve in Mississippi. "I didn't get a chance to practice much law," he said, "but I never felt more like a lawyer in my life.". . .

In private practice, the lawyer is a detached being who views the conflicts that swirl about him as laboratory problems to be solved by the arts of his ancient profession. He is the ringmaster who, by the toot of his whistle or the snap of his whip, brings order out of chaos. For this performance, he expects and receives recognition in the form of money and prestige.

But the movement lawyer, once he has acclimated himself to the demands and dimensions of his new practice, sees a horizon utterly different from the one that defined his activities back in New York City or Chicago. He is activated, not by the promise of fame and fortune, but by the sharing of a common cause with those he represents.

The transformation does not come overnight. I can still recall with shame my earnest recommendation to a brother attorney during the Freedom Rider trials that he not address our clients at a mass meeting. "A lawyer must remain aloof," I told him. "If we become emotionally involved in our clients' problems we will not be able to be dispassionate courtroom advocates."

Three years later I realized that I was playing a fool's game and that my advice was worse than worthless. No remember of a great social movement can remain untouched by the forces that drive it. When Clarence Darrow left his lucrative job as general counsel to the Chicago & Northwestern Railroad to defend Debs and his American Railway Union, his resignation was testimony that attorneys who would serve humanity rather than individual clients must do so with their hearts as well as their heads. . . .

Mississippi in the summer of 1964 was the catalyst of a growing awareness that the law does not exist in a vacuum but is grounded in life. The young men and women who offered their bodies as a witness to the attainability of a just society shamed the American bar into standing beside them. For generations lawyers had looked aside while Negroes in the Deep South had been systematically dehumanized. All in the name of the law, black men had been driven away from the polls, segregated out of community life, forced back into a slavery every bit as intense as that which had theoretically been lifted from them 100 years earlier. Yet the legal profession uttered not one word of collective protest.

That lawyers should have ignored the plight of the Negro is the bitterest of paradoxes, for lawyers have a special obligation to create and preserve the equality on which our entire system of jurisprudence is expressly founded. On courthouse friezes across the land is engraved some form of the motto: "Equal Justice Under Law."

The law did not change in Mississippi last summer, but the lawyers who journeyed there did. All of us, suddenly and starkly conscious that we had failed in one way or another to live up to the solemn responsibilities of our profession, were grateful for the chance to justify our existences. What had started out as an adventure for many of us had abruptly changed into the lesson of our lives.

THE MINISTER . . . BEVERLY ALLEN ASBURY

. . . Something has happened to my theological thinking as a result of the trip to Mississippi. Nearly twenty years ago at the University of Georgia I started considering the Christian ministry from a real concern for human beings. Later I found a theology to express that concern and to give it definition. Later still, perhaps, theological considerations somewhat replaced the human concern, but Mississippi brought me back to people again and helped me put the theological understanding in a new perspective. The "established" churches I saw in Mississippi, and many of the "established" churches I see in the North, can be described only as religious ghettos. They have to be endured with a great deal of fatigue and boredom, and if I were faced with the attitude which exists in so many of them, I doubt that I could "go to church." I see in them too much of a desire to evangelize the world only when it will yield a direct return to the church in increased membership and financial contributions. The established church I saw in Mississippi holds itself aloof from the world, and the established church I see in Ohio and elsewhere too often refuses to risk itself for the sake of the world.

What I saw caused me to turn, as I turned years before, to an understanding of Jesus. My present theological mood looks increasingly to this Man, the "Man-for-Others." I look to Him as the paradigm of my faith, as the one who gives Himself to suffer at the hands of a godless world precisely out of love for that world. The church must use the persuasion and power of love to bring about reconciliation at every level of human and national life. It must pay whatever the price may be to create a faithful and effective structure for the alleviation of every human need. When it becomes the Church of Jesus Christ, it can do no other than follow its Lord into the suffering of those who cannot cry out for themselves. . . .

THE EDUCATOR . . . RICHARD J. BERNSTEIN

In the early fifties, when I started teaching at Yale, there was a general uneasiness among the politically liberal members of the faculty. The lament at that time centered upon the state of mind of the students. They seemed intimidated by, or indifferent to, the poisoned atmosphere created by [Senator Joseph R.] McCarthy, they were "out for themselves," lacked a developed social conscience, were without a cause. Many of the liberal teachers— the attitude was characteristic of campuses throughout the country—were nostalgic for the thirties. That had been a time of heated political discussion, with students in the thick of radical movements. Why wasn't this generation of students more like what we had been (or like what we conceived ourselves to have been)?

There was an element of bad faith in this pose. Besides romanticizing and exaggerating the effectiveness of the radical past, it betrayed an unwillingness and inability to come to grips with new political realities. It was a time when liberals, of whatever generation, were seized by political impotence. They talked about the ills of modern society and were vociferous in decrying the forms of alienation and estrangement, but when it came down to what to do, they offered few concrete proposals.

In the decade since then, the outlook of American youth has changed dramatically. Out of a generation that never knew the depression, out of a generation nurtured on the myth of American affluence, has emerged a group sensitive to social injustice, committed to do something about it, and with a good practical sense of what must be done. I believe that the influence of this group is far greater than its numbers, and that their activity is re-educating America, reawakening our social conscience, and most important, pointing the way toward effective social action It is from this perspective that we can begin to appreciate the value of the Mississippi Summer Project.

The situation in Mississippi last summer was fully reported, but the press did a good deal to distort what actually took place. The incidents judged noteworthy were those of violence and intimidation. In part, the Council of Federated Organizations was also responsible for playing up this aspect of the situation. Violence is nothing new in Mississippi, but for the first time the national spotlight was focused on it. However, the real heart of the project hardly ever hit the news; that was the day-to-day interaction between COFO workers and the Negro community working together for a common cause. Furthermore, the significance of the experience for the doctors, ministers, lawyers and others who went to participate, or just to see the project in operation, cannot be underestimated. My few days in Mississippi last summer were among the most intense, vital and meaningful in my life. And my experience was certainly not unique. Almost everyone I have met who spent some time in Mississippi, no matter how brief, came away with a similar feeling. This project did as much for the participants as for civil rights. It re-educated us about what civil rights really are. And through those who participated and observed, the spirit of the project is spreading across the country.

THE DOCTOR . . . AARON O. WELLS

. . . Four physicians were selected as an advanced committee to confer in Mississippi with leaders of the Council of Federated Organizations, the National Council of Churches and other leaders in the state. Their task was to determine how our medical presence in Mississippi could be made most effective. They returned with an enthusiastic report, and we assigned medical teams to initiate the program. Before the first team entered Mississippi, this nucleus of dedicated persons found a name—the Medical Committee on Human Rights.

Looking back, I realize that I was slow to decide how I could best serve these obviously dedicated people. A woman colleague whose opinion I have always held invaluable was one of the original members, and her enthusiasm and interest influenced me. Then, too, I had asked my wife, who is a registered nurse, to represent me at an early meeting. Her immediate reaction was to enlist in the project, and soon thereafter she was in Mississippi as the nurse with a medical team.

The response of these two women forced me to consider very seriously my own level of participation. I asked myself whether financial contributions to the various civil rights organizations was sufficient. Would attendance at conferences and occasional health lectures in the context of civil rights fulfill my moral obligation to my people? I decided that these responses were not enough, that I must go to Mississippi.

POSTSCRIPT

After Chaney, Goodman, and Schwerner disappeared, the Johnson administration sent additional federal personnel to aid in the search, protect other civil rights workers, and enforce the law. Not only were these efforts minuscule given the enormity of the problem, but those in positions of power, like FBI chief J. Edgar Hoover, remained openly hostile to the civil rights movement. Nonetheless, several months after the bodies of the three men were found, twenty white men, including the sheriff and a deputy of Nashoba County, were indicted for conspiracy to deprive Chaney, Goodman, and Schwerner of their civil rights. (The state of Mississippi would not charge them with murder, so the federal courts indicted them for the lesser crime.) Evidence procured by a large payoff to an anonymous informant revealed that Deputy Sheriff Cecil Price deliberately released the three, whom he had charged with speeding, into the hands of waiting Klansmen. In 1967, seven of those indicted were convicted and began prison sentences.

Within the movement itself, the Freedom Summer had mixed results. The knowledge that all of the publicity about the three missing men—not to mention the massive federal effort to find them—occurred because two were white, further polarized the movement. Many African Americans resented those who returned at the end of summer to suburban homes or prestigious colleges; most whites could barely begin to comprehend the depths of black fear and rage. Some in the movement turned away from nonviolence to a more militant stance.

But as part of a long-term process, Freedom Summer had lasting results. Roughly fifty freedom schools and fifty community centers opened throughout Mississippi, and those institutions became bases of political power and a training ground for new leaders. Certainly the examples of Chaney, Goodman, and Schwerner, as well as of the hundreds of volunteers who joined the Freedom Summer, inspired many others to labor in the movement. Moreover, the tragedy of that summer focused national attention on the Deep South and helped forge a consensus that the most blatant denial of rights must end.

Perhaps most important, the Freedom Summer began a long chain of events that led to African Americans' gaining not just voting rights, but a share of *political* power, north and south. The most visible sign of this rising tide was the political emergence of a middle-aged black woman, Fanny Lou Hammer, and the Mississippi Freedom Democratic party in late summer 1964.

Ms. Hamer had worked all of her life on plantations. In the early 1960s, despite threats, then beatings, and even attempted murder by the Klan, she put down her hoe to lead local voter registration drives for SNCC. When the Mississippi Democratic party remained unresponsive to African-American citizens, COFO established a rival group, the Freedom Democratic party. The Freedom Democrats enrolled 60,000 members, elected a slate of delegates to the Democratic National Convention, and sent them to Atlantic City in late August 1964 to challenge the right of the regular Democratic delegation to represent the state. The old-line Democrats won at the insistence of party nominee President Lyndon Johnson, but not before the Freedom Democrats made their case before the credentials committee and, more important, before a national television audience. Hamer's account, in her plain-spoken English, of the "woesome time" in Winona, Mississippi, when she and other voter registration workers were taken into the county jail and beaten nearly to death moved Americans as few events of the era. The political process—voting, holding office, participating in the major parties—would never again be so closed to African Americans.

QUESTIONS

Defining Terms

Identify in the context of the chapter each of the following:

Brown v. Board of Education   Rosa Parks
CORE   SNCC
Anne Moody   "freedom schools"
National Council of Churches   voter registration
COFO   Robert Moses

Probing the Sources

1. Describe the social and economic conditions of African Americans in the South of the 1950s.
2. What were the goals of the Freedom Summer of 1964?
3. Discuss the role of violence in the civil rights movement, particularly during the Freedom Summer. What was nonviolent direct action, and how effective was it?
4. How did the Freedom Summer of 1964 fit into the earlier and later history of the civil rights movement?
5. What role did white students have in the Freedom Summer? Why did they participate?
6. How and why were African Americans kept from voting in the South?

Interpreting the Sources

1. Some critics called the leaders of the civil rights movement un-American, yet others responded that the movement was in the mainstream of American democratic traditions. Discuss these points.

2. How successful was the Freedom Summer in particular and the civil rights movement in general?

3. What comparisons do you see between Freedom Summer and the era of Reconstruction? Think about voting rights, federal intervention, and the uses of terrorism.

4. Does reading about the Freedom Summer make you optimistic or pessimistic about the ability of people to reform their world?

5. Were white participants "victimized" by the movement? Why did they join, and what did they receive?

ADDITIONAL READING

One of the best general introductions to the civil rights movement is Harvard Sitkoff, *The Struggle for Black Equality, 1954–1980* (1981). Claybome Carson's *In Struggle: SNCC and the Black Awakening of the 1960s* (1981) provides outstanding background for the Freedom Summer; Doug McAdam's *Freedom Summer* (1988) documents the incidents of 1964 as does Charles Marsh, *God's Long Summer* (1997); and Charles Payne, *I've Got the Light of Freedom* (1995). For good case studies of the movement, see William H. Chafe, *Civilities and Civil Rights: Greensboro, North Carolina, and the Black Struggle for Freedom* (1980); and Robert J. Norrell, *Reaping the Whirlwind: The Civil Rights Movement in Tuskegee* (1985). On the role of federal agents in the movement, try David Garrow, *The FBI and Martin Luther King, Jr.* (1981). For King and his times, see Taylor Branch, *Parting the Waters* (1988) and Branch, *Pillar of Fire* (1998). For a moving oral history by those who participated, see Howell Raines, *My Soul Is Rested* (1977). On the movement after 1964, try William L. Van De Berg, *New Day in Babylon* (1993).

Iron Man in Vietnam

HISTORICAL CONTEXT

For most Americans thousands of miles from the battle sites, the Vietnam War was a montage of images: a naked child, burned by napalm, running down a road; a Vietnamese officer executing a man in civilian clothes in the street on suspicion of being a Vietcong operative; burned-over fields and devastated villages; American soldiers giving gifts to Vietnamese children; Vietnamese peasants working their rice paddies. Every night the evening news provided footage and commentary on the daily events. Pictures of war glared from the covers of *Time*, *Newsweek*, and *Life*. "Hawks" and "doves" invoked these scenes to convince others of their views.

The images of the war that captured the attention of millions of young Americans were on the pages of comic books. Throughout its history, the comic book industry has helped to shape and reflect the popular mood of the nation. Comic book superheroes fought the enemies of America in World War II and the Cold War. They have transformed most—but not all—issues into simple black-and-white morality plays where good battles evil and always wins. They have generally presented the portrait of America that Americans want to see. During the course of the Vietnam War, however, even the comic book industry reflected the ambiguity of the times.

The American comic book emerged during the 1930s and reached its peak in popularity during World War II. Millions of young readers on the home front, as well as members of the armed forces overseas, followed the monthly exploits of superheroes like Superman, Batman, Wonder Woman, Captain America, and Captain Marvel as these superheroes defended American interests and foiled the schemes of villainous Nazis and bestial Japanese. Comic books of the war years frequently incorporated war-related themes and messages that simplified complex international issues. With their unequivocal support for the Allied war effort, even months before the Japanese attack on Pearl Harbor, comic books worked to justify U.S. entry into the conflict and propagate the government's wartime policy.

Most of the superheroes who fought World War II failed to survive the postwar recession in comic book sales. The publishers, hoping to tap into new audiences, diversified their output with crime, romance, western, science-fiction, horror, and humor titles. With the outbreak of the Korean War in 1950, the comic book industry, always quick to cash in on a trend, flooded the newsstands with a plethora of Korean War comic books. The comic book response to the Korean conflict, however, unlike that to World War II, was rather ambivalent. While many of the war comics glorified the heroics of the American armed forces and dehumanized the communist enemy, others presented the conflict as a grim and frustrating struggle against a cunning foe. Some comic books actually qualified as antiwar literature, questioning the wisdom and the value of the seemingly unwinnable stalemate in Korea.

But the most popular and prolific comic books of the early 1950s were not the war titles. American youths, it seemed, were not as interested in blood-and-guts war heroes as they were in the blood and guts splashed shamelessly across the pages of horror comic books. Crime and horror comics had come under attack by a variety of concerned individuals and organizations for their alleged corruption of young minds. Foremost of these critics was the psychologist Dr. Frederic Wertham, who accused the comic book industry of outright subversion in his polemical *Seduction of the Innocent,* published in 1954. That same year saw a U.S. Senate investigation into the comic book industry and the publishers' establishment of a rigid self-regulating Comics Code Authority.

The code effectively forced the discontinuation of all but the most innocuous comic books, and the rise of television as the leading source of visual youth entertainment further crippled the industry. Marvel Comics was one of the relatively few publishing houses to continue production after the code. Having once been among the most prolific of comic book publishers, Marvel at the start of the 1960s was a small operation anchored by writer-editor Stan Lee and a handful of artists. DC Comics captured the largest share of the comic book audience with the renewed popularity of superheroes like Superman, Batman, Green Lantern, and the Flash. Inspired by DC's success, Marvel's Stan Lee introduced a series of innovative superhero titles that led the way in expanding the creative and commercial possibilities of the entire comic book industry.

The Marvel superheroes—the Fantastic Four, the Incredible Hulk, SpiderMan, the Mighty Thor, Dr. Strange, the X-Men, Daredevil, and Iron Man—differed from those of DC and other publishers in some important ways. Departing from the clean-cut "Superman" image of the perfect superhero, Lee endowed his characters with human failings and idiosyncrasies. They could perform superhuman physical feats, but they could also be temperamental, insecure, depressed, or selfish. The stories were set not in mythical locales like Metropolis or Gotham City, but in realistic, identifiable settings: New York City, the New Mexican desert, the Soviet Union, or even Vietnam. Lee's intention was to produce comic book fantasy which would conform as much as possible to readers' expectations of realistic human behavior and social relations. It was part of Lee's conscious effort to go after the adolescent and college-age audience of baby boomers, without losing the younger readership or violating the spirit of the Comics Code, which presumed a juvenile audience. Beyond the colorful costumes and action-packed adventure, then, one can see in the Marvel Comics certain language, ideas, and values that the writers and artists expected would appeal to their young readers.

In the early 1960s, comic book readers were largely adolescent males, those who would soon be thinking about military service; indeed, some already were in the armed forces. For such individuals, the word *Vietnam* barely existed in 1963. John Kennedy was continuing the Cold War strategies of his predecessors, Harry Truman and Dwight Eisenhower. Kennedy was determined not to have more countries "fall" to the communists, so he willingly increased American military involvement in Southeast Asia. In South Vietnam—considered most vulnerable by Cold

War strategists who feared communist North Vietnam—Kennedy inherited an American military presence of under one thousand troops in 1961, but by the time he was assassinated in late 1963, he had increased that number to sixteen thousand. If South Vietnam fell, so the logic went, other Southeast Asian countries—Laos, Cambodia, Thailand—would also fall, just like dominoes.

Lyndon Johnson continued the logic inherited from Kennedy; he would not be the first American president to lose a war, nor would he preside over a communist victory. Despite the South Vietnamese government's corruption, ethnic tensions, and incompetence; despite his own pledges during the 1964 election not to involve America in a land war in Asia; and despite a lack of international support for the war, he increased American troop levels: 25,000 at the end of 1964; nearly 200,000 one year later, which doubled after another year; 500,000 by the beginning of 1968; and 550,000 before the end of the year. Moreover, these soldiers were no longer "advisers" to the South Vietnamese. Americans were initiating combat, dropping unprecedented numbers of bombs, and using new substances like chemical defoliants (to clear away the jungle) and napalm, a flammable jelly that was dropped burning from airplanes and clung to everything it hit. Still, the war was a stalemate. Hundreds of thousands of Vietnamese and tens of thousands of Americans were dying, landscapes were being turned to moonscapes, and many American citizens could not understand why. Protests—on college campuses, in the churches, on the streets—grew in size and strength during the late 1960s.

Richard Nixon was elected in 1968, with a promise that he had a "secret plan" to end the war. But before the end came, he expanded the war into Laos and Cambodia, which brought such powerful protests in spring 1970 that college campuses across the nation were shut down by angry students. Nixon did, finally, agree to a cease-fire in 1973. The brunt of the war fell back on the South Vietnamese soldiers, who were quickly routed by troops from the North and by guerrillas in the South who had opposed the American-backed government. When it was over, hundreds of thousands of Americans had taken to the streets in protest; many young men broke the law to resist the draft; students on college campuses were gassed and occasionally shot; and in Vietnam, 58,000 Americans had died, hundreds of thousands of Vietnamese had been killed, and the United States had spent over $150 billion. The final peace treaty contained pretty much the same terms that the French had agreed to twenty years earlier after their defeat and exit from the region.

The Marvel comic books of the early 1960s initially gave no hint of the political, social, and cultural upheavals that would occur later in the decade. Like America's preeminent hero John F. Kennedy, Marvel's superheroes endorsed a national Cold War consensus against a monolithic communist menace embodied by such stereotypical red villains as the Crimson Dynamo, the Red Barbarian, and General Fang. The most political of Lee's creations was Iron Man, who made his first appearance in 1963. His story testifies to the naive assumptions and expectations that many Americans initially held about Vietnam. The complex political, economic, military, and cultural issues at stake in the conflict were reduced to a simplistic moral struggle of good against evil. Iron Man's victory over the tyrant Wong-Chu is a triumph of Western technology over communist barbarism, and of American valor over red treachery. Commenting on this story in 1975, Stan Lee contended that this interpretation of the Vietnam War was a reflection of a time "when most of us genuinely felt that the conflict in that tortured land really was a simple matter of good versus evil and that the American military action against the Viet Cong was tantamount to St. George's battle against the dragon."

By the end of 1975, however, events in Vietnam had changed Lee's views. The United States had signed a peace treaty with the communist government in North Vietnam and Saigon had been overrun by the communist forces. The end of the conflict led to Iron Man's final reflections on the war, reflections that revealed changes both in the comic book industry and in American perceptions of the Vietnam War.

The commercial success of superheroes like Iron Man allowed Marvel to expand its production staff. By the end of the 1960s, young writers and artists, many of whom had been comic book fans since childhood, had replaced the older comic book producers at both Marvel and DC Comics. The younger generation pushed for greater creative freedom within the medium. The art became more refined, and the story matter more sophisticated. Comic books revealed the cultural changes of the era. The young artists generally abandoned the old hard line on the Cold War themes and began to grapple with such contemporary issues as race relations, poverty, environmentalism, drugs, women's rights, and antiwar sentiment. Forced into an awareness of changing times, the Comics Code was revised in 1971 to allow for a more explicit treatment of such issues. Among the most important provisions dropped was the one that forbade the negative portrayal of "respected" authority figures like police and political leaders.

THE DOCUMENTS

Introduction to Documents 1 and 2

The two editions of "Iron Man" reprinted here framed the war years. The first one appeared in 1963, when few Americans thought very much about Vietnam and, when they did, reacted to it with simple stereotypes. The second "Iron Man" was printed in 1975, as American withdrawal reached its formal conclusion, and the nation was still numb from the divisiveness the war had brought. What were the writers and artists saying (or not saying) in this second "Iron Man"? Your answer will probably be a complex one. Note for example that the cover of this comic book uses the old blood-and-guts formula, but that the story inside does not. Does the work explain how the war happened, or blame anyone—governments, leaders, ideologies—for the carnage? As you read the first "Iron Man," ask yourself what arguments it makes—not just in words but in pictures—that helped prepare young Americans to accept the idea of war in Asia. How does the second "Iron Man" explain the end of that war? Do you believe you can understand people's beliefs and opinions by looking at a popular source like comic books?

DOCUMENT 1 *Iron Man: Iron Man is Born, 1963*

Stan Lee

(Marvel Comics)

IN A SECLUDED AREA SOMEWHERE IN THE U.S. DEFENSE PERIMETER, THERE STANDS A CLOSELY GUARDED BUILDING... THE LABORATORY OF ANTHONY STARK!

BOY! THAT GUY STARK MUST REALLY **RATE**, TO GET A TWENTY-FOUR HOUR GUARD!

HE **RATES**, ALL RIGHT! THE COMMIES WOULD GIVE THEIR **EYETEETH** TO KNOW WHAT HE'S WORKING ON NOW!

AND, INSIDE...

GENERAL, YOU WILL SEE MY TINY TRANSISTOR INCREASE THE POWER OF THIS SMALL MAGNET SO TREMENDOUSLY THAT IT WILL OPEN THAT LOCKED VAULT!

OH, COME NOW, STARK! THAT JUST ISN'T **POSSIBLE!**

THINK SO? **THERE!** I'VE SWITCHED ON THE TRANSISTOR! IT'S ENERGIZING THE MAGNET!

CLICK

THE DOOR --IT'S BEGINNING TO BUDGE!

NATURALLY! MY TINY TRANSISTORS ARE **SO** POWERFUL THAT...

-- THEY CAN INCREASE THE FORCE OF **ANY** DEVICE...

--A THOUSANDFOLD!

CRACK

NOW DO YOU BELIEVE THAT THE TRANSISTORS I'VE INVENTED ARE CAPABLE OF SOLVING YOUR PROBLEM IN VIETNAM?

STARK, AFTER WHAT I'VE JUST SEEN, I'M READY TO BELIEVE **ANYTHING!**

YES, IT **WAS** AN AMAZING DEMONSTRATION! BUT NOW, LET US LEARN **MORE** ABOUT THE MAN WHOSE GENIUS MADE IT POSSIBLE! LET US LEARN MORE ABOUT ANTHONY STARK, THE ONE WHO IS FATED TO BECOME... **IRON MAN!**

ANTHONY STARK... RICH, HANDSOME, KNOWN AS A GLAMOROUS PLAYBOY, CONSTANTLY IN THE COMPANY OF BEAUTIFUL, ADORING WOMEN...

LOOK! THERE'S TONY STARK!

UMMMNN... HE'S THE DREAMIEST THING THIS SIDE OF ROCK HUDSON!

THE RIVIERA WAS A REAL DRAG TILL YOU SHOWED UP, DARLING!

YES, ANTHONY STARK IS BOTH A SOPHISTICATE AND A SCIENTIST! A MILLIONAIRE BACHELOR, AS MUCH AT HOME IN A LABORATORY AS IN HIGH SOCIETY!

BUT, THIS MAN WHO SEEMS SO FORTUNATE, WHO'S ENVIED BY MILLIONS -- IS SOON DESTINED TO BECOME THE MOST TRAGIC FIGURE ON EARTH!

OUR TALE REALLY HAS ITS BEGINNING HALFWAY AROUND THE WORLD, IN A SOUTH VIETNAM JUNGLE, MENACED BY WONG-CHU, THE RED GUERRILLA TYRANT!

HAH! I HAVE BROUGHT ANOTHER VILLAGE TO ITS KNEES!

NOW FOR THE WRESTLING MATCH! IF ANY PRISONER CAN DEFEAT WONG-CHU, I FREE WHOLE VILLAGE!

DESPERATE TO SAVE THEIR VILLAGE, THE STRONGEST OF THE NATIVES ACCEPTS THE WAR LORD'S CHALLENGE...

AH, YOU ARE GOOD! BUT WONG-CHU BETTER!

ANOTHER, AND ANOTHER, TRIES IN VAIN...

I AM STRONGEST OF ALL! NEXT TO WONG-CHU OTHER MEN ARE BUT FLEAS!

IT IS OVER! NOW LET US PLUNDER THE TOWN! FOR NONE CAN STOP THE VICTORIOUS WONG-CHU!

3

IN A FEW DAYS SHRAPNEL WILL REACH HIS HEART-- THEN HE WILL DIE! *NOTHING* CAN SAVE HIM!

BAH! WE CAN *USE* HIS GENIUS! WONG-CHU WILL *TRICK* HIM INTO SPENDING HIS LAST DAYS ON EARTH WORKING FOR *US!* IS HE STRONG ENOUGH NOW?

YES, HE CAN WORK TILL SHRAPNEL REACHES HEART!

WE KNOW YOU ARE AMERICAN WEAPONS INVENTOR! IF YOU DESIGN POWERFUL NEW WEAPON FOR *ME,* AFTER-WARDS I HAVE SURGEON SAVE YOUR LIFE!

HE'S LYING... IF THEY *COULD* DO IT *NOW,* TO BE *SURE* I LIVE LONG ENOUGH TO DESIGN WEAPONS FOR THEM!

I KNOW I'VE ONLY DAYS TO LIVE, BUT MY LAST ACT WILL BE TO DEFEAT THIS GRINNING, SMIRKING, RED TERRORIST!

ALL RIGHT, WONG-CHU, I'LL *DO* IT!

I KNEW YOU WOULD NOT HESITATE TO BETRAY YOUR COUNTRY TO SAVE YOURSELF!

HERE ROOM WHERE YOU WORK! PLENTY OF SCRAP IRON! PLENTY TOOLS!

THIS I PROMISE YOU... I SHALL BUILD THE MOST FANTASTIC WEAPON OF ALL TIME!

I'LL *BUILD* IT, ALL RIGHT, BUT IT WILL BE *MINE...*

--MADE FOR ONLY *ONE* PURPOSE-- TO KEEP ME ALIVE!

CLICK!

EVERY TICK OF THE CLOCK BRINGS THE DEADLY PIECE OF SHRAPNEL CLOSER TO MY HEART! I'VE GOT TO WORK FASTER THAN I'VE EVER WORKED BEFORE! CAN'T AFFORD A SINGLE MISTAKE!

THEN, ON THE SECOND DAY OF TONY STARK'S RACE AGAINST TIME...

THIS OLD ONE, PROFESSOR YINSEN! ONCE GREAT SCIENTIST! NOW LOWLY MAN-SERVANT OF WONG-CHU.. ...WILL *HELP* YOU BUILD WEAPON!

NO! I WILL *NEVER* HELP THE EVIL RED TYRANTS! NEVER!!

PROFESSOR YINSEN, IN COLLEGE I READ YOUR BOOKS! YOU WERE THE GREATEST PHYSICIST OF ALL!! THEN, EVERYONE THOUGHT YOU HAD **DIED!**

I'D HAVE BEEN BETTER OFF IF I **HAD!** I WAS PRESSED INTO SLAVE LABOR BY THE REDS, AND WHEN I RESISTED, WONG-CHU TOOK ME PRISONER!

NO LONGER ABLE TO WORK IN SECRET, ANTHONY STARK MUST REVEAL HIS PLAN TO THE AGED SCHOLAR, THE ONLY HUMAN HE DARES TRUST!

AN **IRON MAN!** FANTASTIC! A MIGHTY, ELECTRONIC BODY, TO KEEP YOUR HEART BEATING AFTER THE SHRAPNEL REACHES IT! WE JUST MIGHT **SUCCEED!**

THINK WHAT A CREATURE WE COULD CREATE! WHAT **WONDERS** HE SHALL PERFORM!

AND THE REDS THEMSELVES GAVE US ALL THE MATERIALS WE WILL NEED!

THUS, A DYING MAN'S DESPERATE RACE AGAINST TIME CONTINUES...

I'VE DONE EXTENSIVE WORK WITH TRANSISTORS! I CAN DESIGN THEM IN ANY SIZE TO PERFORM ANY FUNCTION!

WE SHALL USE THEM TO OPERATE THE MACHINE ELECTRONICALLY TO MOVE COUNTLESS GEARS AND CONTROL LEVERS!

ALL ACTIVITY MUST BE COORDINATED PERFECTLY! THE IRON FRAME MUST DUPLICATE EVERY ACTION OF THE HUMAN BODY!

IT SHALL, MY FRIEND! IT SHALL! THIS SHALL BE THE CROWNING ACHIEVEMENT OF MY LIFE!

HOURS PASS INTO DAYS, AS THE SHRAPNEL MOVES CLOSER AND CLOSER TO ANTHONY STARK'S HEART...

I CAN FEEL THE PRESSURE! MY TIME IS RUNNING OUT! WE MUST WORK **FASTER!**

THERE! THE SELF-LUBRICATION SYSTEM IS COMPLETED! JUST A LITTLE LONGER! YOU MUST HAVE COURAGE!

AND THEN, WHEN THE DOOMED AMERICAN'S CONDITION BECOMES CRITICAL--WHEN HE CAN NO LONGER STAND...

THE LIFE-GIVING HEART OF YOUR IRON BODY IS **READY!** QUICKLY,... CLAMP IT AROUND YOUR CHEST!

6

THEN, EVEN AS PRO-
FESSOR YINSEN BREATHES
HIS LAST, THE
ELECTRONIC MARVEL
BEGINS TO STIR...

THE TRANSISTORS
HAVE SUFFICIENT
ENERGY NOW! MY
HEART IS BEATING
NORMALLY! THE
MACHINE IS
KEEPING ME ALIVE!
ALIVE!!

AND THE TRANSISTOR-
POWERED CIRCUITS
ARE COORDINATED
WITH MY BRAIN
WAVES, JUST AS ANY LIVING
HUMAN'S BRAIN
CONTROLS HIS OWN
BODY!

B-BUT I'M
LOSING MY
BALANCE!

THUD!

I'M LIKE A BABY LEARNING
TO WALK! BUT I HAVEN'T TIME!
I MUST LEARN QUICKLY! I
MUST GET THE KNACK OF
MANIPULATING THIS MASSIVE,
UNBELIEVABLY POWERFUL
IRON SHELL BEFORE THE REDS
FIND ME -- OR ELSE I'LL BE
AT THEIR MERCY!

BUT THE BRAIN WHICH HAS
MASTERED THE SECRETS OF
SCIENCE IS ALSO CAPABLE OF
MASTERING ITS NEW BODY!
AND SO...

I HAVE THE
FEEL OF IT
NOW! I CAN
STAND--
MOVE--EVEN
WALK
WITHOUT
TOPPLING!

MEANWHILE, OUTSIDE THE
LOCKED DOOR...

BREAK IT
DOWN! SMASH IT!
I MUST LEARN
WHAT HAS
HAPPENED IN
THERE!

WHAM
WH

8

THEY'RE COMING! THIS IS MY GREATEST TEST! CAN THE THING I HAVE CREATED SURVIVE? THE THING WHICH IS LESS THAN HUMAN...YET, FAR MORE THAN MERELY HUMAN! THIS THING WHICH IS NOW-- ANTHONY STARK!!

WHAM

MY BRAIN STILL THINKS! MY HEART STILL BEATS! BUT, IN ORDER TO REMAIN ALIVE, I MUST SPEND THE REST OF MY LIFE IN THIS IRON PRISON!!

BUT, THIS BITTER REALIZATION IS SUDDENLY INTERRUPTED, AS THE IRON MAN SNAPS BACK TO REALITY...

THEY'LL SOON BE THRU THE DOOR... I MUST CONCEAL MYSELF UNTIL I CAN PLAN MY NEXT MOVE!

FORTUNATELY, YINSEN AND I EQUIPPED MY IRON BODY WITH MANY ATTACHMENTS, SUCH AS THESE!

I'LL FASTEN THESE SUCTION CUPS TO MY PALMS AND TURN ON MY TRANSISTOR- POWERED AIR- PRESSURE JETS!

THEY WORK! THEY GIVE ME THE POWER TO SOAR INTO THE AIR!

THEY DON'T DREAM OF LOOKING UP HERE IN THE SHADOWS!

THE YANKEE IS GONE! AND HE HAS BUILT US NO WEAPONS!

HE CANNOT BE FAR! FIND HIM AND DISPOSE OF HIM AS YOU DID THE OTHER WHO DARED DEFY ME!

THEY KILLED THE PROFESSOR-- A MAN WHO NEVER HARMED ANYONE IN HIS LIFE! THE MURDERING SWINE! THEY'LL PAY FOR IT! I SWEAR IT! IRON MAN SWEARS IT!

WHILE YOU HUNT DOWN YANKEE, I SHALL AMUSE MYSELF AT MY FAVORITE SPORT

THEN, SECONDS AFTER THE REDS DEPART...

YES, WONG-CHU, AMUSE YOURSELF WHILE YOU STILL CAN! FOR OUR MOMENT OF RECKONING IS ALMOST AT HAND!

9

DON'T MISS MORE OF *IRON MAN* IN THE NEXT GREAT ISSUE OF... *TALES of SUSPENSE!*

DOCUMENT 2 *Iron Man: Vengeance in Viet Nam, 1975*

Stan Lee

(Marvel Comics)

DOESN'T *SEEM* THAT LONG AGO--

--OR *DOES IT*, AVENGER?

A *LOT* HAS HAPPENED SINCE THEN... ONE *HECK* OF A *LOT!*

STARK INDUSTRIES, ONE OF THE WORLD'S FOREMOST *MUNITIONS* MANUFACTURERS, HAS GIVEN WAY TO *STARK INTERNATIONAL*--

--WHOSE BUSINESS IS *PEACE,* PURE AND SIMPLE, AND A *BETTER-MENT* OF MAN THROUGH *TECHNOLOGY!*

AND WHAT ABOUT *YOU,* TONY STARK? ONCE YOU WERE *DO OR DIE* FOR AMERICA AND *MOM'S APPLE PIE!* YOU DIDN'T DO MUCH *SOUL-SEARCHING* BACK THEN, DID YOU?

AS *IRON MAN* YOU BEAT THE *COMMIES* FOR DEMOCRACY WITHOUT EVER *QUESTIONING* JUST *WHOSE* DE-MOCRACY YOU WERE *SERVING*--

--OR JUST *WHAT* THOSE YOU SERVED INTENDED TO *DO* WITH THE WORLD ONCE YOU'D *SAVED* IT FOR THEM! *VIET NAM* RAISED *ALL* THOSE QUESTIONS, DIDN'T IT, TONY?

DIDN'T IT?

"LIKE: 'WHAT *RIGHT* HAD WE TO BE THERE IN THE *FIRST PLACE?'*

HEY YOU *MUD-HUGGERS!* LOOK!!

HOLY SPIT! IT'S *IRON MAN!*

WONDER WHAT *HE'S* DOIN' *HERE?*

"EVEN IF WE COULD'VE ANSWERED *THAT* QUESTION, I WAS STILL LEFT WITH SOME OF MY *OWN...*

PRETTY *IMPRESSIVE,* MAJOR! BUT, LIKE YOU *SAID--*

--IT'S A "TOY" THAT'S NEVER BEEN FIELD-TESTED!

IT WILL BE, *IRON MAN!* AND *SOON--*

"...JUST IGNORANT. GOD HELP US ALL!"

AT *0500 HOURS,* MY MEN CROSSED OVER INTO *ENEMY TERRITORY* AND ENTRENCHED IN *THIS* POSITION!

MY ORDERS WERE *VERBAL,* IRON MAN, SO *NO ONE* WILL EVER KNOW THAT THIS MOVE WAS NOT TAKEN ON MY *OWN INITIATIVE!* IF WE *FAIL, HQ* WILL *DENY* ANY KNOW-LEDGE OF OUR *ACT!*

WHAT EXACTLY *IS* YOUR *MISSION,* MAJOR?

YESTERDAY, STARK'S *SATELLITE* SPOTTED A MASSIVE ENEMY *TROOP MOVEMENT* IN A STRETCH OF JUNGLE ABOUT A *MILE* FROM HERE!

COULD BE A *SUPPLY UNIT, REINFORCEMENTS...* WE DON'T KNOW *WHAT!* BUT I'VE BEEN ORDERED TO *STOP* THAT MOVEMENT AT ANY AND *ALL COSTS!*

EVEN AT THE COST OF VIOLATING *INTERNATIONAL LAW?*

THE *COMMIES* VIOLATE INTERNATIONAL LAW EVERY DAY, IRON MAN! WHY SHOULDN'T *WE* GET THE JUMP ON THEM--

"I DIDN'T SEE THE MOVEMENT IN THE JUNGLE..."

--JUST THIS ONCE--

CRACK!

MAJOR--?

"...AND THE GUNSHOT WAS STILL RINGING IN MY EARS AS I WHIRLED TO SEE..."

MAJOR!!

--UNNGGHH!!

CONTINUED AFTER NEXT PAGE

"...AND MECHANIZED DEATH SILENCED THE GUNS OF THE ENEMY POSITIONS...

"...ONE AFTER ANOTHER AFTER *ANOTHER!*"

THE GUN'S STOPPED *FIRING!*

THAT MEANS IT'S ALL *OVER!* OR--

"--OR THE *HEAT-SEEKING LASERS* HAD LOCKED ONTO ANOTHER TARGET...

"...ONE WHOSE *AFTER-BURNERS* WOULD THROW OFF MORE DETECTABLE *HEAT-EMISSIONS* THAN THOSE OF A HANDFUL OF *GROUND-TROOPS!*"

ENEMY PLANES!

WHOOSH!

WHOOOSH!

AND FROM THE WAY THOSE *MISSILES* ARE *ACTING*--

--THEY'RE EITHER LOCKED ON THE *METAL* OF MY *ARMORED SUIT*--

WHHOOM!

--WHICH MIGHT OR *MIGHT NOT* PROTECT ME FROM THEM! BUT A *REPULSOR-BLAST* WILL SOLVE *THAT* LITTLE PROBLEM--

"--OR THEY WERE LOCKED ONTO THE METAL OF TONY STARK'S --*MY*-- NEWEST PIECE OF WEAPONRY...

KA-WHOM

"...THE *SECOND* GUESS WAS *RIGHT.*"

11

CONTINUED AFTER NEXT PAGE

"A LONG, LONG TIME LATER..."

UNNHHH! MOON'S UP!

I MUST'VE BEEN OUT FOR HOURS!

"I STAGGERED THROUGH THE UNDERGROWTH, NOT SURE WHETHER IT WAS THE SHADOWS OR THE VINES THAT KEPT GRABBING AT MY LEGS."

SOMETHING'S-- WRONG!

CAN'T SEEM TO BREATHE PROPERLY-- ALMOST AS IF--

"MAYBE IT WAS BOTH!"

UNNGGHHH!

"I FELL..."

"...AND THAT'S WHEN IT HIT ME!"

BLAST MUST'VE DAMAGED MY CHEST-PLATE!

I'M LOSING POWER RAPIDLY-- AND ALREADY THE STRAIN IS BEGINNING TO SHOW--

--ON MY HEART!

"I STILL RELIED ON THE MAGNETIC FIELD WITHIN MY METAL CHEST-ARMOR IN THOSE DAYS... AND AS I CRAWLED TOWARDS THE CAMP..."

GOT TO REACH THE CAMP--

YOU'RE *ALIVE,* AVENGER!

ALIVE!!

"*I NEVER REALLY THOUGHT MUCH ABOUT WHAT THAT MEANT BACK THEN--*

"--I GUESS THAT *LIFE* IS ONE OF THOSE THINGS YOU TAKE FOR *GRANTED...*"

SOLDIER? HEY, *SOLDIER ??*

WHY DON'T YOU *ANSWER--*

"...UNTIL *DEATH* STEPS IN TO *REMIND* YOU JUST HOW *EASILY* IT CAN BE *TAKEN AWAY!*"

OH.

OH LORD.

"*I THINK I WENT A LITTLE CRAZY AT THAT POINT...*"

WHY ?? WHY DID THIS *HAPPEN?*

THEY WERE OUT HERE BECAUSE A *WEAPON* I'D *BUILT* GAVE THEM THE *PROMISE* OF A *FASTER KILL,* A WELL-OILED *WAR!!*

KROOM

I *DID* THIS! ME-- TONY STARK, THE PLAYBOY GENIUS--

--THIS IS ALL *MY FAULT!!*

WHAT THE--?

PEEOOW!

PEEOOW!

"...BUT THE TINY PIECES OF *LEAD* THAT STUNG MY ARMORED *BACK* BROUGHT ME *OUT* OF IT... *FAST!*"

CONTINUED AFTER NEXT PAGE

"...AND HE OPENED HIS EYES."

--PLEASE--?

"PINK, FLASH-BURNED PUPILS STARING UNSEEINGLY OUT AT NOTHING!

I--I'M SORRY, SON! YOU MUST'VE BEEN SCARED-- PANICKED AND FIRED AT THE SOUND OF MY VOICE!

YOU'RE... BLIND.

PLEASE--?

THAT THE ONLY ENGLISH WORD YOU KNOW?

IT'S NOT A BAD ONE TO BEGIN WITH! C'MERE, SON--

"HE FELL INTO MY ARMS... DRAWING BACK FROM THE COLD TOUCH OF METAL...

"...BUT HE WAS TOO TIRED AND SICK TO RUN. HE LET HIMSELF BE PICKED UP..."

I HEARD THE MAJOR SAY THAT YOU PEOPLE HAD A LARGE CAMP SOMEWHERE UP AHEAD!

LET'S SEE IF I CAN GET YOU HOME!

"...AND I CARRIED HIM BACK TOWARDS HIS LINES."

"BUT THERE WASN'T MUCH LEFT THERE TO COME BACK TO.

DEAD! ALL DEAD!

LOOKS LIKE MY CANNON WORKED BETTER THAN EVEN I THOUGHT IT WOULD!

HOME?

YOU'RE REALLY GETTING THE HANG OF THE LANGUAGE, SON!

YEAH, WE'RE HOME ALL RIGHT!

I GUESS *BOTH SIDES* BOUGHT IT AT ABOUT THE *SAME TIME!*

NOT MUCH OF A *BATTLE!*

...PLEASE... *HOME?*

NO, SON! NOT ANY *MORE!*

THEY'VE ALL *GONE!* NO MORE *HOME!* GOT THAT?

HOME... NO MORE?

THAT'S IT, SON! HOME *NO MORE!*

AND I *DID IT!* YOU *HEAR* THAT, GOD OR SATAN OR WHOEVER IN *HELL* IS *LISTENING!*

"NO ONE *HEARD* -- OR IF THEY DID, THEY DIDN'T *ANSWER.*"

YOU STAY *HERE,* SON! THERE'S SOMETHING I'VE GOT TO *DO!*

"THE *TRANSISTOR-UNITS* BUILT INTO MY *ARMOR* HAD *ALWAYS* POSSESSED *ENORMOUS POWER...* AND MY *REPULSOR-RAYS* ARE PERHAPS THE *GREATEST* SINGLE CONCENTRATION OF THAT *STRENGTH...*"

REPULSOR'S ARE AT *FULL-FORCE!*

I CAN ONLY KEEP THIS UP A FEW MOMENTS *LONGER* WITHOUT PUTTING TOO GREAT A *STRAIN* ON MY *HEART!*

KHOOMM!

23

CONTINUED AFTER NEXT PAGE

"BUT THE *MOUND ITSELF* WASN'T *ENOUGH.*"

IT NEEDS A *TOMBSTONE!* AN *EPITATH!*

WHY

SOMETHING SO THAT SOMEONE COMING *AFTER* WILL KNOW WHY THE MOUND IS *THERE!*

SO MAYBE THEY'LL ASK *WHAT* THESE PEOPLE *DIED FOR!*

THE ONLY *WORD* THAT COULD ANSWER *THAT*--

--IS ANOTHER *QUESTION!*

WHY?

I THINK THAT *SAYS IT!* I THINK THAT SAYS IT *ALL!*

THE *BOY!* I WASN'T *THINKING!*

ALL THAT *NOISE* MUST'VE SCARED THE *PANTS* OFF OF HIM!

YOU *ALL RIGHT,* SON?

"BUT HE WASN'T *SCARED.* THERE WAS A STRANGE EXPRESSION ON HIS FACE THAT COULD ONLY BE CALLED...

HOME-- O.K.?

"...PEACE."

CONTINUED AFTER NEXT PAGE

QUESTIONS

Defining Terms

Identify in the context of the chapter each of the following:

hawks and doves	Professor Yinsen
Stan Lee	Comics Code Authority
Wong Chu	Marvel Comics
transistors	napalm
Anthony Stark	Reds

Probing the Sources

1. How do the pictures reinforce the message carried by the words in "Iron Man Is Born"? In "Vengeance in Vietnam"?

2. What stereotypes do you find in the two comic books?

3. How are comic books similar to or different from other formula fiction: soap operas, grocery store novels, TV sitcoms?

4. Why do historians use sources like these? What can they teach us?

Interpreting the Sources

1. Do you think that the "Iron Man" comics reflect assumptions about gender? About race? About class?

2. Were these comic books propaganda?

3. What ideas about technology do you find in these comic books?

4. Comic books have to sell themselves and the products advertised in them to make a profit. How do you think this need affects their content? Can you make some guesses about these "Iron Man" comics?

5. How did Anthony Stark's view of the war change between 1963 and 1975? Why ??

ADDITIONAL READING

Bradford Wright, "Comic Books and the Vietnam War," in James S. Olson, ed., *Vietnam: A Handbook of the Literature and Research* (1993), provides an outstanding overview of the comic book industry during the 1960s and 1970s. Wright also helped the authors of this book in the preparation of this section; see his *Comic Book Nation* (2001). William W. Savage, *Comic Books in America, 1945–54* (1990), explores the uses of comic books as a tool for understanding American culture and politics. For general information on the comic book industry, see Mike Benton, *The Comic Book in America* (1989), and Will Jacobs and Gerard Jones, *The Comic Book Heroes* (1985). A useful overview of the Vietnam War is James S. Olson and Randy Roberts, *Where the Domino Fell: America and Vietnam, 1945–1990* (1990). For American foreign policy during the era, see George C. Herring, *America's Longest War: The United States & Vietnam* (1979). An overview of antiwar protest is available in Todd Gitlin, *The Sixties* (1987). For interviews with men and women who served, try Mark Baker, *Nam* (1982), Al Santoli, *Everything We Had* (1981), and Stewart O'Nan, *The Vietnam Reader* (1998). Also see Neil Sheehan, A Bright and Shining Lie (1988); Christian Appy, *Working-Class War* (1993), Michael Herr, *Dispatches* (1977), and Philip Caputo, *A Rumor of War* (1977).

14

HIV-AIDS

HISTORICAL CONTEXT

Our immune systems protect us from disease. The food we eat and the air we breath would be deadly were it not for our bodies' ability to destroy infections that otherwise would multiply within us. Shortly before 1980, a disease appeared on these shores that destroyed the human immune system. No one knew precisely where it came from or how it spread. Because patients exhibited a variety of symptoms, it was unclear at first that a single disease was the root cause of the problem. In the United States during the early 1980s, the illness spread mainly among homosexual men, and doctors initially called it GRIDS, or Gay Related Immune Deficiency Syndrome. This was a mistake, since internationally the disease did not remain confined to any particular social group; in Africa, for example, it spread mainly among heterosexuals. What did become clear with time, however, was the size of the tragedy that was unfolding. Within a few years, GRIDS was renamed AIDS (Acquired Immune Deficiency Syndrome), and soon medical researchers understood that a virus they called HIV (Human Immunodeficiency Virus) was responsible for the onset of AIDS.

Numbers reveal part of the story. While HIV and AIDS were undiagnosed and virtually nonexistent in the United States before 1980, by 1995 half a million Americans (a conservative number, since the disease remains underreported) had come down with it, and sixty percent of them died. The rapid spread of illness was shocking. By mid-1989, the first 100,000 cases were reported; that number doubled in two years. The World Health Organization estimated that by the year 2000 at least fifteen million people worldwide would be infected.

Victims of the disease also changed. HIV-AIDS, doctors learned, is most efficiently passed on through sexual intercourse (especially anal intercourse) or through direct mingling of blood. While gay men remained the largest group of AIDS patients in America during the 1980s, the virus rapidly spread to others. Intravenous drug users who shared needles were a very high risk group; before blood banks screened their supplies, anyone needing a transfusion, especially hemophiliacs, risked infection; and women infected with the virus could pass it through the placenta to their unborn babies. As the incidence of heterosexual transmission increased in America during the 1990s, the danger to women grew dramatically. At the end of the century, heterosexual women were by far the fastest growing group of the afflicted.

By the late 1990s, some good news appeared—the increase in numbers of new cases slowed down a bit, and new drugs helped prolong the lives of those with the disease. Doctors have found ways to slow its course and to treat many of the infections that it engenders. First the drug AZT, then a combination of drug therapies prolonged life and enhanced its quality. But in no sense has the epidemic ended. There is still no cure for AIDS.

In this chapter we focus mainly on the first decade of the crisis, as its magnitude slowly emerged. Americans' reactions to the disease were heavily influenced by the fact that most of its early victims were gay. The earliest cases were at once baffling and terrifying. Young men showed up in doctors' offices with skin cancers (Kaposi's sarcoma) that normally afflicted only the elderly—but in these young men the cancers spread with remarkable rapidity. Other men died of a rare form of pneumonia that usually appeared only in those undergoing chemotherapy and whose immune systems had therefore stopped protecting them. Colloquial terms like gay cancer and gay pneumonia were applied to these maladies, but many scientists, though not the public, quickly learned that such labels were inaccurate. Slowly doctors developed a body of knowledge about the disease: that it was transferred only through blood or semen, that it could be detected by testing for the antibodies that tried to fight it, that it gestated slowly, developed symptoms unpredictably, and killed its victims brutally.

Homosexual men and women have been a sorely stereotyped minority throughout American history. Discrimination against them was rarely questioned by the mainstream society until the 1970s. Gay culture, especially in cities like New York and San Francisco, developed its own leaders, institutions, and intellectual traditions, but a new activism took hold beginning in the 1960s, especially as the black civil rights struggle and the women's liberation movement suggested the possibility of similar activity by gays. A symbolic beginning occurred at a Greenwich Village bar in New York City known as the Stonewall Inn. To put it simply, a riot broke out there in the summer of 1969 when patrons of the bar and others who lived in the area resisted the usual round of mob shakedowns and police harassment. Four officers were injured and thirteen citizens arrested. The Stonewall riot became a founding moment in the gay liberation movement.

The next decade witnessed a remarkable flowering of gay power. No longer willing to accept society's stigma, many gay men and women openly proclaimed their difference from others, their rights to full citizenship, their rejection of shame. Small towns had their gay bars, and large cities developed whole neighborhoods of gay establishments. Gays started successful businesses, voted in blocs for friendly candidates, created a power base much like various ethnic groups. By 1980, 120 American corporations and forty cities had adopted policies forbidding discrimination based on sexual orientation. Of course virulent antigay prejudice remained—everything from crude jokes to violent harassment to systematic job discrimination. Many gays remained "in the closet"—kept their sexual preference a secret—rather than risk having their lives and careers ruined.

But some open space had developed in America for gays where little had existed before. The newly expansive gay culture witnessed an unfolding of gay sexuality. In part this grew out of a nationwide "sexual revolution" in which birth control pills, less restrictive divorce laws, and a growing notion that sex should be joyful rather than repressed unleashed greater openness to all things erotic in the America of the 1960s and 1970s. However, if pride replaced shame for many gays, repression sometimes gave way to promiscuity. Gay bathhouses in large cities became symbols of the new freedom. Local men and those who came to visit from smaller towns—indeed from all over the world—could meet other men and engage in open sexual liaisons. The bathhouses were highly profitable businesses and more, symbols of gays' rejection of homophobia.

Here was a tragic coming together of circumstances. Anal intercourse is a very efficient way to transfer the HIV virus, and the disease entered the country during a tremendous efflorescence of gay sex. Bathhouses facilitated numerous sexual encounters, where some individuals had contact with dozens of partners in a matter of weeks or even days. Before anyone had even developed symptoms, HIV had spread to hundreds of people; once the first cases of full-blown AIDS turned up in doctors' offices, thousands were already infected. And because no one yet understood the nature of this virus, it continued to spread. Perhaps as many as half of the gay men in New York and San Francisco born between the end of World War II and 1960 were HIV positive by the end of the 1980s; many of these were dead within a few years. And the disaster was just beginning.

Diseases come from nature, but the way we label them, think about them, research and treat them comes from human cultures. Randy Shilts, a reporter in San Francisco who later died of AIDS, characterized the first five years of the disease, between 1980 and 1985, in these words:

> People died while Reagan administration officials ignored pleas from government scientists and did not allocate adequate funding for AIDS research. . . .
> People died while scientists did not at first devote appropriate attention to the epidemic because they perceived little prestige to be gained in studying a homosexual affliction. . . .
> People died while public health authorities and the political leaders who guided them refused to take the tough measures necessary to curb the epidemic's spread. . . .
> People died while gay community leaders played politics with the disease, putting political dogma [that closing the bathhouses would be giving in to homophobia] ahead of the preservation of human life.
> People died and nobody paid attention because the mass media did not like covering stories about homosexuals and was especially skittish about stories that involved gay sexuality.

By the mid-1990s, nearly as many died each year as the total number of Americans killed in action for the entire Vietnam War. The massive numbers of deaths—gay and straight—finally broke through the silence of the early eighties. In the following sources, we dwell mostly on the early years of the epidemic. As you read, continue to ask yourself what is natural and what is cultural about HIV-AIDS?

THE DOCUMENTS

Introduction to Document 1

Randy Shilts was a reporter for the *San Francisco Chronicle* who began covering the AIDS crisis full-time in the early 1980s. His news stories became the basis for *And the Band Played On,* the final manuscript of which he delivered to his publisher on the very day he tested positive for HIV (he died in 1994 at age 42). Shilts was born in Davenport, Iowa, grew up in a religious and conservative family in Aurora, Illinois, then discovered himself at the University of Oregon. His was not a dispassionate book, but an outraged indictment. He singled out such largely straight institutions as the medical establishment, government health agencies, and the media, but also wealthy bathhouse owners whose profits were threatened by the crisis, as well as gay politicians and leaders whose fears of social repression by straight culture blinded them to the dangers of the epidemic. The following passage describes events in August, September, and October, 1982.

 DOCUMENT 1 *From* **And the Band Played On**

Randy Shilts

August, 1982
NEW YORK CITY

Dan Rather put on his somber face as he stared into the cameras of the "CBS Evening News."

"Federal health officials consider it an epidemic. Yet you rarely hear a thing about it. At first, it seemed to strike only one segment of the population. Now, Barry Peterson tells us, this is no longer the case."

The story, one of the first network news pieces to appear on AIDS, had all the right elements: Bobbi Campbell talked about how he wanted to survive; Larry Kramer said the lack of government research was because it was perceived as a gay disease; Jim Curran provided the hopeful note that solving AIDS could lead to the elimination of all cancer.

"But there is almost no money being spent so far," concluded reporter Peterson. "For Bobbi Campbell, it is a race against time. How long before he and others who have this disease, finally have answers, finally have the hope of a cure?"

Of all the sentences in this story, probably none was so pointedly directed at the fundamental problem than Rather's own lead-in, "you rarely hear a thing about it." As managing editor of the "CBS Nightly News," Rather passed the news judgment that made AIDS a disease that one rarely heard anything about. Three years later, television commentators would still be talking about AIDS as that disease you rarely heard anything about, as if they were helpless bystanders and not the very people who themselves had decreed the silence in the public media.

Because nobody heard much about this disease, nobody in 1982 really did very much about it, save for a few heroic souls. And they were too few to make much of a difference, ensuring that Bobbi Campbell, like thousands of other Americans, would lose his race against time.

NATIONAL INSTITUTES OF HEALTH, BETHESDA, MARYLAND

Now, more than a year into the epidemic, the National Institutes of Health had no coordinated AIDS plan. Everything was done on the basis of temporary assignments by the handful of doctors who happened to be intrigued by the world's first epidemic of immune disorders. At the sprawling NIH hospitals, a few doctors struggled valiantly with every conceivable medical technology to save the AIDS patients, and they failed. At Bob Gallo's lab at the National Cancer Institute's Division of Tumor Cell Biology, about 10 percent of the staff effort went into poking around the devastated lymphocytes of AIDS patients. In his lab at the NCI, Jim Goedert desperately wanted to bunch full-scale bench investigations into finding the AIDS virus but ran straight into the brick wall of limited resources. The dilemma would be hard to explain to outsiders, he thought. The money was in the budget. Indeed, congress had been generally successful at holding the budget line for health against the Reagan budget cutters. The administration, however, was retaliating by not permitting managers like Goedert to hire anybody. Goedert had enough money to pay for lab tests, to finance computer activities, and to purchase supplies, but he couldn't put any new people on board. So he didn't have the scientists he needed to steer studies, analyze data, and then write it up into papers. . . .

CENTER FOR HUMAN TUMOR VIRUS RESEARCH, UNIVERSITY OF CALIFORNIA, SAN FRANCISCO

The hemophiliac cases convinced Dr. Jay Levy that he needed to shift from studying Kaposi's sarcoma to the blood of AIDS patients to find whatever microbe was knocking out their T-4 cells. While East Coast scientists still squabbled over the syndrome's etiology, West Coast researchers were by now almost unanimously convinced that one infectious agent was at work. The tilt toward single agent raised an entirely new quandary for Levy. Though his tiny eighty-foot-square lab on the twelfth floor of the Medical Sciences building had been fine for studying the skin cancer tumors of KS, the university maintained that the lab did not have the appropriate safety gear for studying an infectious disease. In order to comply with university safety standards, Levy needed to adapt a flow hood with a new $1,500 filter.

Again, Levy was at a loss as to how to comply. Like human tumor virus labs across the country, he had been bled dry by the administration's grant cuts and scientific trends that had put cancer virus research out of vogue. Many of Levy's colleagues were leaving academic medicine to get more secure jobs at private pharmaceutical corporations; some dropped out of science altogether. Levy knew that, within a few years, America would face a severe shortage of retrovirologists because of the funding cutbacks. In 1982, nobody seemed to care; that would be the nightmare of 1985. As it was, Jay Levy went to a wealthy friend in April just to meet the payroll of the only two staffers in his center, a part-time technician and a part-time secretary. He was under orders from the university to come up with grant money or leave. Now, as he was about to start what he felt would be promising research into the cause of AIDS, his efforts were arrested because he did not have $1,500 for a filter. He asked the chancellor's office for a few extra bucks but was turned down; there was no mechanism within the university that would channel him the sum. . . .

NEW YORK

Gays were furious at the city's most prominent gay doctor, Dan William. . . . In a long essay and a subsequent interview in the *New York Native's* [a gay newspaper] voluminous AIDS coverage, William dared suggest that bathhouses should be required to post signs warning about the epidemic and promiscuous sex, the way restaurants post signs explaining the Heimlich maneuver. Bathhouses should work to change sexual behavior and reduce the risk of contracting AIDS, he said, or end up, in effect, being the "Russian roulette" parlors of the gay community.

The very suggestion of turning back a decade of sexual liberation stirred a maelstrom William could hardly have predicted. The *Body Politic*, the leading leftist gay magazine, denounced William as a "monogamist" who was "stirring panic" and an "epidemic of fear." William was surprised at the vehemence of the denunciations but understood, in a personal way, the discomfort that the entire community felt at the prospect of squarely facing a deadly new disease. In early 1981, he had been told he was suffering from a degenerative blood disease and that he could expect to live five, maybe ten years. The ailment was unrelated to the AIDS epidemic, but it let William know the desperation of denial: how, when something is so horrible you don't want to believe it, you want to put it out of your mind and insist it isn't true, and how you hate the person who says it is.

William saw that denial among some patients now, when he told them that something was wrong with their white blood cell counts and they needed to closely monitor their health. He also heard it in the angry voices raised against him. That was denial too, on a social and even political level. It was a phase the gay community would work through, just as he had found a way to work through it. The problem for the community, however, was more burning, because its denial would rob gays of time, the time when they could have begun taking AIDS seriously and time when they could have been protecting themselves. Time would always mean lives in this scourge. . . .

Two salient problems . . . haunted the journalism of AIDS for years. First, reporters were willing to believe any story handed to them in a press release without the slightest inclination to discover whether the reported facts were true. Press-release journalism, out of vogue since the advent of Watergate-style investigative reporting, made a dashing comeback with the AIDS epidemic. The second tendency evident in AIDS journalism was the compulsion to lend a reassuring last note to otherwise bleak stories. Big task forces meant the problem might be solved, and every month or so, tucked away in the second section of most newspapers, a few wire-service paragraphs appeared about this or that breakthrough in AIDS research. There were headlines like, "KS Discovery Brings Glimmer of Hope," but, in truth, there were no glimmers of hope as summer faded to fall in 1982. There were just bureaucrats who thought they could both hold back domestic spending and thwart a virulent new epidemic, as well as newspaper editors who didn't care to run much about a homosexual plague and didn't care whether what they did run was true.

Meanwhile, in the last weeks of August, two more states reported their first AIDS cases. The epidemic now had swept into twenty-six states and a dozen nations.

September 1982
BUREAU OF COMMUNICABLE DISEASE CONTROL, SAN FRANCISCO

In her cramped office, piled high with medical journals and manila folders of disease records, Dr. Selma Dritz was on the phone to Atlanta, wondering whether they understood how serious this all was. Still another disease was starting to appear among gay men, and she was convinced it was related to AIDS. As an epidemiologist, Dritz played a numbers game and she wanted the new disease included in the AIDS numbers. As usual, she was fighting with the Centers for Disease Control about it.

The first patients had gone to their doctors with lymph nodes the size of golf balls. This wasn't your garden variety lymphadenopathy. The diagnosis was Burkitt's lymphoma, a lymph cancer that was among the first human cancers linked to a virus. A number of San Francisco researchers, in fact, had once worked in Africa on studies that connected Burkitt's lymphoma to the Epstein-Barr virus, the microbe that in the United States most commonly caused mononucleosis, or the "kissing disease." Dritz was intrigued because, once again, she was seeing a tumor caused by a virus arising in the immune-deficient gay men, just as Kaposi's sarcoma had been linked to the cytomegalovirus in Africa. The immune deficiency seemed to let these viruses run wild and foster the tumors. The detection of this phenomenon had implications far beyond AIDS; the trend might offer new insight into the relationship between cancer and viruses.

When the first reports came in, casually from doctors she would be chatting with, Dritz did her homework. She checked with the California Tumor Registry in Sacramento, where all California cancer cases are recorded, and found that statisticians expected only two or three cases of the rare cancer for the entire state in two years. Dritz had eight cases, all among San Francisco gay men, in just nine months.

"Burkitt's lymphoma is a form of AIDS," Dritz told the CDC, in her most matter-of-fact Chicago voice. "We should start counting it and let people know."

The CDC demurred that they weren't hearing of it anywhere else. Of course, Dritz thought, no place else is as organized as we are in San Francisco. Health officials in other cities weren't on the phone to doctors every day to tail this horrible marauder of gay men's health. It was one of the things that made Dritz grateful for her complicated network of gay community contacts.

Dritz never nagged, but even as she hung up, the doctors at the CDC were betting that she would keep her own set of statistics now. She'd have one set of statistics that counted AIDS cases by the narrow CDC definition, and she'd have another that counted cases by the definition that gave her the most accurate profile of what was killing people in her city. They were right. The two lists were kept, making it that much easier when the CDC ultimately relented to the no-nonsense health officer and added Burkitt's lymphoma to the ever-lengthening list of AIDS ailments. By now these included fungal infections of birds, sheep, cats, and deer, as well as cancers that appeared all over the body, on the tongue, in the rectum, or most horrifically, in the brain. . . .

FEDERAL BUILDING, SAN FRANCISCO

"How much do you need?" asked the burly congressman flatly. . . .

While Phil Burton waited impatiently for a suggestion, Bill Kraus cast about in his mind for some nice round numbers.

"We should ask for $5 million for the CDC and $5 million for the NIH," suggested Kraus.

"Hell," countered Burton. "Let's ask for $5 million and $10 million."

Kraus realized that such numbers were nothing to Burton, who daily kept tabs on a federal budget that was counted in the hundreds of billions of dollars. But the proposal represented a 3,000 percent markup on AIDS funding, and it was soon introduced into the House.

In Washington, Tim Westmoreland, as chief staffer for the House Health Subcommittee, volunteered to put the legislation into legalese, and it was introduced on September 28. Journalist Larry Bush called it "the first gay pork barrel," and, for a movement that could barely raise the tens of thousands to finance a national organization, the appropriation seemed gargantuan. Phil Burton's bills, Kraus knew, were only symbolic, because the funding ultimately would be written into some larger spending bill, but the bills added Burton's formidable political clout to that of the House health point man, Representative Henry Waxman.

Most of the research that would come from the federal government in the next two years was financed by these bills and prodded through Congress by these two men, who in turn were sparked into action by two of the only openly gay congressional aides on Capitol Hill, Yale Law School graduate Tim Westmoreland and one-time street radical Bill Kraus. No matter what would be said about how the gay community reacted to the epidemic, it is clear that virtually all the money that funded the early scientific advances on AIDS can be credited almost solely to these two gay men. . . .

SAN FRANCISCO BOARD OF SUPERVISORS CHAMBERS, CITY HALL

The supplemental appropriation sailed through the board of supervisors without a dissenting vote. Bill Kraus and Dana Van Gorder had timed the vote perfectly. Half the board was up for reelection in five weeks. Nobody would dare vote against public health money, given the fact that one in four city voters was gay. Mayor Feinstein personally felt the money should come from some other part of the health budget, but Bill Kraus knew her hands were tied as well. She was up for reelection next year and wouldn't dare veto an AIDS funding bill.

It was brute political power moving the San Francisco government to spend $450,000 to finance the world's first AIDS clinic, grief counseling and personal support for AIDS patients through the Shanti Project, and the first locally funded education efforts through the Kaposi's Sarcoma Foundation. Nearly 20 percent of the money committed to fighting the AIDS epidemic for the entire United States, including all the science and epidemiology expenditures by the U.S. government, now was pledged by the city and county of San Francisco. . . .

October 1982
CENTERS FOR DISEASE CONTROL, ATLANTA

The start of the federal government's new fiscal year on October 1 found the AIDS Task Force still scrambling for money. CDC budget managers had to prepare three budgets for its AIDS work before it submitted one that scaled down AIDS spending enough to be acceptable to the administration. When Wilmon Rushing, acting administrative officer for AIDS, sent the final budget to CDC management, he warned, "As you know, the attached budget is insufficient to adequately fund AIDS surveillance and epidemiologic studies. However, we will continue with the highest priority activities until additional funds become available. . . ."

The discovery of cyanide in Tylenol capsules occurred in those same weeks of October 1982. The existence of the poisoned capsules, all found in the Chicago area, was first reported on October 1. *The New York Times* wrote a story on the Tylenol scare every day for the entire month of October and produced twenty-three more pieces in the two months after that. Four of the stories appeared on the front page. The poisoning received comparable coverage in media across the country, inspiring an immense government effort. Within days of the discovery of what proved to be the only cyanide-laced capsules, the Food and Drug Administration issued orders removing the drug from store shelves across the country. Federal, state, and local authorities were immediately on hand to coordinate efforts in states thousands of miles from where the tampered boxes appeared. No action was too extreme and no expense too great, they insisted, to save lives.

Investigators poured into Chicago to crack the mystery. More than 100 state, federal, and local agents worked the Illinois end of the case alone, filling twenty-six volumes with 11,500 pages of probe reports. The Food and Drug Administration had more than 1,100 employees testing 1.5 million similar capsules for evidence of poisoning, and chasing down every faint possibility of a victim of the new terror, according to the breathless news reports of the time. Tylenol's parent company, Johnson & Johnson, estimated spending $100 million in the effort. Within five weeks, the U.S. Department of Health and Human Services issued new regulations on tamper-resistant packaging to avert repetition of such a tragedy.

In the end, the millions of dollars for CDC Tylenol investigations yielded little beyond the probability that some lone crackpot had tampered with a few boxes of the pain reliever. No more cases of poisoning occurred beyond the first handful reported in early October. Yet the crisis showed how the government could spring into action, issue warnings, change regulations, and spend money, lots of money, when they thought the lives of Americans were at stake.

Altogether, seven people died from the cyanide-laced capsules; one other man in Yuba City, California, got sick, but it turned out he was faking it so he could collect damages from Johnson & Johnson.

By comparison, 634 Americans had been stricken with AIDS by October 5, 1982. Of these, 260 were dead. There was no rush to spend money, mobilize public health officials, or issue regulations that might save lives.

The institution that is supposed to be the public's watchdog, the news media, had gasped a collective yawn over the story of dead and dying homosexuals. In New York City, where half the nation's AIDS cases resided, *The New York Times* had written only three stories about the epidemic in 1981 and three more stories in all of 1982. None made the front page. Indeed, one could have lived in New York, or in most of the United States for that matter, and not even have been aware from the daily newspapers that an epidemic was happening, even while government doctors themselves were predicting that the scourge would wipe out the lives of tens of thousands.

Introduction to Document 2

C. Everett Koop became Surgeon General—a member of the President's Cabinet and the chief public health officer in the country—at the beginning of the Reagan administration in 1981. Here he tells the story of how he tried to use his office to inform the public about the growing crisis. Note Koop's assertion that when his report was finally released, he was criticized for his reference to sex education. According to Koop the importance of publicity—of explicit information regarding how the disease was spread and the meaning of safe sex—was lost on those at the highest levels of government, including the President, who found such discussions embarrassing and distasteful.

 DOCUMENT 2   *"The Early Days of AIDS as I Remember Them"*

C. Everett Koop

I was confirmed as Surgeon General in November 1981, but even in those early days of my tenure as Surgeon General, I had to learn about AIDS on my own. I learned about it from the newspapers, and from internal documents of the Public Health Service, to which, of course, I had access. I also read the *Morbidity and Mortality Weekly Report* and I did have discussions with colleagues.

There were two reasons, I think, why it took awhile for public health authorities to get a handle on AIDS in the beginning. First was the relatively small number of trained clinicians and researchers who were familiar with the rare diseases which were turning up as opportunistic infections, and which were occurring in places like San Francisco, Los Angeles, Chicago, and New York. The second reason was that the first patients with those conditions were homosexual men, most of whom had patronized physicians and clinics that were more understanding of their so-called "gay lifestyle." In making that choice for care, which was quite natural, these men effectively placed themselves outside of mainstream clinical medicine and therefore they were very difficult for us to know—to reach—and, of course, to help. As a result, our first public health priority, to stop the further transmission of the AIDS virus, became needlessly mired in the homosexual politics of the early 1980s. We lost a great deal of precious time because of this, and I suspect that we lost some lives as well.

By July of 1985, the CDC had reported just under 12,000 cases of AIDS and just under 6,000 of those people had died. Then only a week later, I recall that the numbers for both the cases and the deaths had jumped by 100. The AIDS epidemic was definitely progressing, and doing so at an accelerated rate.

About that time we were introduced to the death of Rock Hudson, who was the first national figure to die of AIDS. That raised further public concern, of course, about the disease, but for the first time it captured the attention of the Reagan White House because the President, having been a former actor, was still connected with Hollywood people who were now concerned. It touched the White House only rather indirectly. It certainly did not touch it nearly as severely as I wish it might have. . . .

Eventually my personal distance from AIDS information and policy came to an end when President Reagan asked me to write a report for the American people on AIDS. For the next two years, AIDS took over my life. . . .

I assumed that the report was meant to be simple and to be in language that could be understood by the average citizen; that it was meant to allay the panic of those who were afraid they might get AIDS but were never exposed to it; but it was also to warn those who were engaged in rather risky behavior what the inevitable outcome would be if they encountered the AIDS virus. . . .

The official American response to AIDS, as far as the government was concerned, hinged on two Cabinet meetings. Remember this is a report that I wrote, and the only government person that officially screened it was the Secretary of HHS. The next level was the Cabinet. The first meeting was with that part of the Cabinet that deals with domestic affairs. They, plus a lot of other people in the White House, are called the Domestic Policy Council. The second meeting would eventually take place in May of 1987 and would involve the entire Cabinet and the President himself. . . .

I did not receive any comments, but many eyebrows did go up. I reviewed the report for them, page-by-page, but in a rather superficial manner, and there was very little discussion. White House gossip informed me later on that the gentlemen at the meeting did not want to discuss condoms with ladies present. So I knew that what I had said had not been absorbed in any depth by anyone.

But at long last, on October 22, I called a press conference and released the AIDS report. Of all the statements that I made, only two words seemed to be remembered: "Sex education." The next few days were spent fending off the press, and answering questions about my ideas on when sex education should begin. Many of the larger issues in that AIDS report were eclipsed temporarily by this distraction.

In the meantime, having failed to come to grips with the AIDS report when they first read it, the political meddlers in the White House tried to bottle up the whole effort. In a very unusual move, two members of the Domestic Policy Council came across town to the Humphrey Building to interview me. Usually, when the White House calls, it is a command appearance at their place, and you go. What they came to ask me was if I did not think it was time to update the report.

The report was only two weeks old. AIDS was moving along fast, but not that fast. The report did not need any updating. In fact, that report does not need any updating today. Of course, what the members of the Domestic Policy Council wanted me to do was to take out the word "condom," and this I refused to do. Meanwhile the presses were running, the mail trucks were rolling, and the report went out. At last, the people of the country did have something in hand that could tell them what was myth and what was fact about the AIDS epidemic, and they could read it in plain English. . . .

If the general public seemed to be making substantial progress in learning about AIDS, the White House still was not on board. I quickly saw—or it was not quickly; I came to this decision rather slowly—that the Reagan White House, including the President himself, reasoned usually in an anecdotal fashion, instead of examining the evidence and acting upon those conclusions. In one of many examples, at another meeting of the Working Group of the Domestic Policy Council, one member, a nurse no less, said that there were many people in the country who believed that AIDS was transmitted by cats, by mosquitoes, by door knobs, by typewriter keyboards, and toilet seats. She said, "Who was to know? Maybe they are right and the government is wrong?"

These discussions about AIDS with a variety of high level government officials depressed me about the lack of intelligence among some people in high places. The major problem was that the President was reluctant to go out front offering the leadership that only he could provide. At least a dozen times I pleaded with my critics in the White House to let me have a meeting with President Reagan so that he could hear from me my concerns about America and the AIDS epidemic, and what his role in it should be. For months I had been trying to cover the rather embarrassing silence of the Oval Office on the scourge of AIDS. I kept telling myself that the President would soon speak out. Finally he did, in April 1987. The occasion was interesting because it was back in my home town of Philadelphia.

President Reagan went there to celebrate with a speech the 250th anniversary of the oldest coterie of medical people in this country, the College of Physicians of Philadelphia. The day before he went, I received a call from one of his assistants, not from a speechwriter, who asked me, "Do you think the President ought to mention AIDS?" I said I thought that was the purpose of the occasion. Reagan did mention AIDS, for the first time in public in Philadelphia, touching upon the epidemic briefly and superficially in his speech.

That afternoon, when he went to the Philadelphia Airport to get on Air Force One to go home, he was crowded by reporters who kept asking him question after question to which he replied nothing at all until he got to the top step, and was just about to enter Air Force One. Then he turned and said, "Just say no." That night Tom Brokaw reported on the NBC evening news that the President had never read *The Surgeon General's Report on AIDS.* . . .

Introduction to Document 3

Abraham Verghese was born in Ethiopia of Indian parents. He received his medical training in Africa, India, and the United States, and specialized in the study and treatment of infectious diseases. He practiced medicine in Johnson City, Tennessee, where the AIDS epidemic struck in the mid-1980s. His memoir, *My Own Country,* depicts his patients' struggle not only with disease, but with heartland America's attitudes toward both gays and the terminally ill. Verghese also tells his own story of being a doctor and an immigrant, an insider and an outsider. And he describes the strains his life as a doctor for AIDS patients placed on his family. The following passage, which comes near the end of his book, describes a moment of revelation, when a profound cultural pattern emerged from the dozens of cases he treated.

 DOCUMENT 3 *From* **My Own Country: A Doctor's Story**

Abraham Verghese

July 1989.

Rajani and the kids had gone to visit her sister in Washington, D.C., for the weekend. I was alone in the house. . . .

I felt lonely. As if everyone had left me. But at the same time, I felt guilty for some reason, as if I had driven them off. . . . There was something else on my mind, something that hovered near the surface like a familiar name I was struggling to remember. There was a pattern in my HIV practice, a paradigm I could see but wanted to flesh out. I had carried copies of patient files and records from the clinic to my house. I kept feeling if I could concentrate hard enough, step back and look carefully, I could draw a kind of blueprint that explained what was happening here in Johnson City, Tennessee, and perhaps in the process explain what was also happening in every little community like ours across the country. . . .

Here we were in late 1989, and the picture of AIDS in our town had changed radically from the day when I walked into the Connection [Clinic]. In 1985 we were in our age of innocence: I was an AIDS expert with no AIDS in sight, a rookie looking for a challenge. Now, we had over eighty HIV-infected persons in our practice, we were AIDS-seasoned, and all sense of innocence had vanished. Including my own. Our little town in the heart of the country with 50,000 residents had a hundredfold more cases than the CDC would have predicted for us. The belief that AIDS would not touch this town had been absurd. . . .

I compiled a list of every person with HIV that we had seen in the office, the VA, the Miracle Center or the hospitals in our neighboring communities. I made a line-listing with three columns: patient name, address, and a blank column in which I penciled in what I knew about each patient's story, how and where he or she had acquired their illness. I consulted my personal journal, in which for four years now, usually late at night, I had written down the stories behind the medical facts I knew.

I went to Steven's room and took down the map from his wall. Steven loved maps and had a precocious knowledge of the world's geography. He knew India, Ethiopia, Boston, Tennessee, all the places that were significant in his life or that of his parents.

I traced out in pencil a map of the quad-state area—Tennessee, Virginia, North Carolina and Kentucky. I labeled this quad-state map: "Domicile." I penciled in tiny red cannonballs for the *current* residences of my patients.

The dots clustered around Johnson City and included Bristol and Kingsport—the Tri-Cities. But the dots also spilled over the ledge of upper east Tennessee into southwest Virginia and Kentucky and across to North Carolina. Big Stone Gap, Blackwood, Wise, Pennington Gap, Pikeville, Whitesburg, Norton, Pound—our HIV-infected patients were tracking down from the small mining towns of southwest Virginia and Kentucky; they were coming up from the farming towns of east Tennessee like Greeneville, Morristown and Tazewell. They were even coming across the mountains from North Carolina.

Part of the explanation, then, for our high patient numbers was the large catchment area for our medical practice.

Next, I traced out the outline of the entire United States, leaving out all the detail within. I titled this map "Acquisition." I was after something different on this map: I wanted to locate the places where each patient *used* to live between 1979 and 1985. This was the period in time when most of them had *contracted* infection with the AIDS virus. I culled all the stories I had been told to try to arrive at this information. The sentinel patient, for example, the young man who had driven down from New York and come to the Miracle Center and died, he had almost certainly contracted his infection in New York City. I placed a dot there for him. Gordon, the prodigal son, brother of Essie, had come back from a prolonged residence in Florida; I placed his dot in Jacksonville. Otis Jackson had lived in San Francisco in the Castro district before returning. . . .

As I neared the end, I could see a distinct pattern of dots emerging on this larger map of the USA. All evening I had been on the threshold of seeing. Now I fully understood. The paradigm was revealed.

I took the completed maps to the porch. I was proud of my handiwork. I poured myself a scotch and sat on the porch swing, staring at the two maps while moths swarmed around the porch light and threw shadows on the paper.

The dots on the larger map, the "Acquisition" map, were no longer confined to the rectangle of Tennessee and its neighboring states as they had been on the "Domicile" map. Instead they seemed to circle the periphery of the United States, they seemed to wink at me like lights ringing a roadside sign. Here was a tight cluster around New York City. Below that, a few dots around Washington, D.C., and then scattered dots on the eastern seaboard down to Florida, where a clump of dots outlined Miami, and single dots pointed to Fort Pierce, Orlando, Jacksonville and Tallahassee. The middle of the country—the heartland—was bare except for three dots in Chicago. There were isolated dots over Houston and San Antonio and Denver and Salt Lake. But on the western seaboard the dots were clustered again in two spots: San Francisco and Los Angeles.

The numbers were small, but the two maps unequivocally confirmed that individual stories of Otis, Gordon and so many others had suggested: infection with HIV in rural Tennessee was largely an *imported* disease. Imported to the country from the city. Imported by native sons who had left long ago and were now returning because of HIV infection.

But if AIDS was a disease imported to east Tennessee, I needed to explain the dots that were clumped around Johnson City on *both* maps. these were patients who lived in the Tri-Cities *and* acquired their infection in the Tri-Cities—the "local-locals," as we came to refer to them.

The first name I wrote down—Rodney Tester—provided the clue to the "local-locals": he was a hemophiliac. . . . But there were still more "local-locals"—persons whose dots occupied the same position on both maps. There were blood transfusion recipients—persons other than the Johnsons—infected by a batch of tainted blood that had found its way into the blood bank of a regional hospital.

The remaining "local-locals" were partners of infected patients—Jackey McCray was in this group. There were also gay men like Raleigh, Ed Maupin and Bobby Keller who had not resided out of the area that had made frequent trips to big cities (or to highway rest-stops where they had met people from the big cities) and engaged in unprotected and high-risk sexual encounters. Finally, there were a few men like Jackie's husband, Clyde, and Jewell, who did not fit into any category. They may have contracted their HIV infection in Johnson City. Or else they were not entirely forthcoming about their travel and risk factors.

It was after midnight but I was still on the porch. I was too wired to contemplate sleeping. Here in our little corner of rural America, my patients, trickling in over the past several years in ones and twos, had revealed a pattern to me. Their collective story spoke of an elaborate migration. Did this paradigm hold true for rural Iowa or rural Texas just as it did for rural Tennessee?

The first step in this circuitous migration was a disappearance from home, a departure from the country. When I thought of departure, I thought of Hobart Carter. One of Hobart Carter's earliest memories was that of his brother telling him not to "walk like that." By the time I saw him, Hobart was in his late twenties, with a large head and an owl-like face. He carried himself very upright, almost tilting backward, making him appear taller than his six foot two. His protruding lower jaw only exaggerated his peculiar hip-swinging carriage. If that was not enough to make him different, he had started to lose his hair at the age of fifteen.

Was it any surprise that when Hobart Carter realized he was gay, he left home for the city at the first opportunity? Yes, the leaving could be construed as a search for a better job, a better education, a space apart from the family just like any heterosexual male might want. But clearly, his desire to leave had much to do with his awakening sexuality.

At home, his opportunities to meet other gay men would be limited and there would have been his parents to deal with: their knowledge, their attitude. His greatest fear was that he might embarrass them, bring them shame. Perhaps he needed distance from them to really understand if he was gay; to live independently was the only way to define himself. He had to separate, despite the part of him that might have wanted to stay.

The opportunity came when his uncle in California became sick. Hobart, who was eighteen by then and quite close to his uncle, volunteered to move there and take care of him. Hobart's father, a fireman and church deacon, recalls: "While he was in California, Hobart was working in a beer-and-sandwich joint called 'Thirteen Buttons.' I asked him on the phone one time, I said, 'Son, what does thirteen buttons mean? When I was in the Navy, thirteen buttons was a kind of coat navy men wore. Does it have something to do with sailors?' And he said, 'Yes, Father, it has something to do with sailors.' But even then, I didn't make the connection."

After two years, Hobart decided to move to San Francisco. He had a friend there and pretty soon he got a job as a night clerk in a very prestigious hotel in San Francisco. He worked that job for a long time and was happy with it, proud of doing what he did and doing it well. He sent his parents a picture of the hotel and a picture of himself working behind the counter. In it he was wearing a black tuxedo and a bow tie, together with an expression that seemed to say he had found not just a job but a city where he could be himself. He had arrived in Mecca.

San Francisco was perhaps the most comfortable place in America in the 1970s to live an openly gay life. On his days off, Hobart strolled up and down the Castro, shopped at the All American Boy or went for a drink in one of the bars. If he ate in a restaurant, he was surrounded by gay men. The "Castro-cut" which was popular then, exaggerated the natural male-pattern recession on either side of the widow's peak. It was, at least in part, a rebellion against effeminacy. Hobart's baldness, which had embarrassed him in Tennessee, now seemed desirable. It fit into the "clone" look (Levi's 501s, flannel shirts or Izods, lace-up boots) that most gay men seemed to be espousing at that time. Adopting the clone look of that town and that era—and gay men have continued to reinvent the look—seemed a way to signal a union with a community after years of alienation from the rituals and even the dress of the larger community. Hobart was no exception.

There was a point in the paradigm that I was constructing when parents became fully aware that their son was gay. With Hobart it happened years before he got sick. His father recalls:

"Hobart came home one vacation in 1977 and he and I were driving down this bypass just about a mile from the house and Hobart turns to me and says, 'Daddy, I want to tell you something that has been eating me up inside. I'm gay. I've had these feelings in me ever since I can remember, since the age of four or five.' Well, it hit me like a ton of bricks, for him to tell me that. Then Hobart says to me, 'Daddy, if you want to stop the car, I'll be happy to get out now.' I said, 'Why would I want to do that? I don't love homosexuality but I love you and I would never tell you to get out of my house.' We just kept a-driving and a-driving, and I was thinking about it and he was studying me. He asked me whether he should tell his mother and I said no, I better be the one to tell her 'cause you know how Mother is.

"I remember telling Hobart as we were driving around that I had known or suspected this for some time, even if I had never formed the words 'homosexual' or 'gay' in my brain. Hobart says to me, 'Why in God's name did you not say something to me if you knew, Daddy? I've been living with this burden for years and years, from the time I was a small boy. I wish you had said something to me.' I said, 'What would I say to you? And if you were not gay and I had suggested you might be, it would only have hurt you.'

"When we got home, we were at peace with each other. Like I said, it hit me like a ton of bricks, but all the same I felt like I understood my son and that his pain had been eased by telling me. I prayed for guidance on it. When I told Mother, it hit her like a ton of bricks, too. Even though she had suspected the same thing beforehand. Hobart called up his brother and told him as well. Jake and Hobart were never really very close, and after that it seemed as if they were even more distant."

For Hobart, this period of independence and self-definition in California coincided with what was the first period of true gay liberation in the seventies. Hobart was discovering and creating his sexual self and adult identity at a moment when gay men and women across the country were learning for the first time to accept themselves and celebrate this sexuality. For the men, particularly, the search for psychological liberation was combined with a period of sexual revolution, a period of rampant sexuality and exhilaration. The gay community had watched the straights experience the sexual revolution of the sixties. For years before that, they had waited in the closets, often sexually inactive. Now finally it seemed there was freedom, exuberance, fraternity. At this moment, sexual freedom was more than just an expression of lust, it was a celebration of all that had not been previously available.

But no one knew of the existence of the HIV virus, least of all Hobart in San Francisco. By the time he was aware there was a virus, it was already in him, subverting his immune system.

Hobart kept in touch with his parents irregularly. Before Hobart returned, before he fell ill, the Carters had a great desire to go west to San Francisco, a part of the country that they had not seen. Mr. Carter collected travel brochures and used to sit in the evenings studying pictures of the Golden Gate Bridge, Embarcadero, Fisherman's Wharf and imagining how it would be. Every time they made plans, Hobart waved them off. For one reason or another their visit at that time was not convenient. When Mr. Carter related this to me, he did so with sadness and deep disappointment. He and his wife had a hard life with very little variety. The prospect of visiting San Francisco was indescribably exciting.

"I sure would have loved to see that Golden Gate Bridge," Mr. Carter told me. His longing has stayed with me as a symbol of all the pleasures denied by barriers of sexuality and misunderstanding, barriers between parents and their own children. When I think now of the losses caused by AIDS, I am also haunted by the earlier losses, the times that might have been, the communication and sharing that for many will never be possible. I can picture Mr. Carter on his porch, years after his son's death, still fingering brochures and studying pictures of the Golden Gate Bridge.

The first two steps of the paradigm—leaving home and then the period of urban living—were followed by the long voyage back. Four months before I first saw Hobart in clinic, he was admitted to San Francisco General Hospital for an acute attack of shingles, and while there was found to be HIV-positive. When he recovered, the hotel job was gone, his rent was in arrears, and there were no friends willing to take him in.

He called his parents to say he was sick, he had lost his job, and he planned to come home. He told his parents over the phone that he had "the virus that causes AIDS."

To his parents this must have seemed terribly unfair: Mr. Carter had just had diverticulitis and bowel surgery. Mrs. Carter was not herself because of her own medical problems. Now, Hobart, who had never once invited them to San Francisco, was coming home with AIDS.

Hobart's mother was a stern woman. If her husband's face was expressive and warm, hers was an inscrutable mask, and only the wild expression in her eyes revealed her underlying torment. When I met her at her son's bedside, I worried that she was going to explode from all the tension: a husband just weeks out of surgery, a son with AIDS.

If the move back was hard on his parents, it was hell for Hobart. He was once again in the same family environment, the same town that he had once felt imprisoned by. The boyhood room where he had once dreamed of a different life now held him again within its walls. The crucifixes in every room, the framed needlepoint verses in the bathroom and kitchen, the giant, somewhat gaudy rendering of Christ at Gethsemane that dominated the living room harked back to a childhood that had been difficult. His apartment in San Francisco had been like his vision of the world: *his* art objects, *his* framed and signed Mapplethorpe print, *his* color scheme and furnishing. All these affirmations of his own identity sat in a box in a friend's basement in San Francisco, a friend who was also sick and might have to vacate soon.

A few months after returning from San Francisco, Hobart had tried to live in an apartment away from his parents. Rents in Johnson City were so much cheaper than in San Francisco; he was able to use his disability check, food stamps and wages from a part-time accounting job to exist on his own for a while. But his worsening illness made him abandon the apartment and move back with his parents.

The paradigm—the circuitous voyage, the migration and return—ended in death. The last time Hobart came to my office, he looked anxious and apprehensive in addition to being wasted and thin. I knew from his conversation that he feared death greatly. I had no idea how to approach this but I felt reckless, willing to try. I sat him down and asked him a series of questions: Where did he want to die? At home or in the hospital? Who did he want with him at his deathbed? What did he want done with his body? What did he want to do with his remaining possessions? What sort of help could I offer him to alleviate his symptoms near death? What symptom did he fear most? Choking? Gagging? Being wide awake? Thinking of Norman Sanger and his death, I told Hobart how I might prescribe morphine and how it would make him feel. Did he want cremation? Did he want an autopsy performed? What sort of service did he want? What music did he want played? Did he want his father to speak? Anyone else?

He had pondered each question at length, and I was convinced that he had avoided these thoughts before. As he answered I served as his scribe, jotting down his replies on a yellow legal pad. At the end I handed him the sheet of paper. We had addressed all those issues about his death over which he had some control. He left my office helped not so much by the paper, but by the sense of having faced his worst fear and talked about it, walked past it. I resolved after that to discuss death with all my patients when it was appropriate. In many families I noticed it was the last entry on the long list of things not discussed with their sons.

A few weeks after Hobart and I had our talk, Mr. Carter visited me to tell me that his son was fading rapidly. He picked up a prescription for morphine solution to help Hobart rest. Hobart would ask his father to come and lie down with him and hug him just as when he was a little boy. They would stay that way for hours. He said to his father, "Daddy, I love you. I hope you never grow old and die."

Mr. Carter replied: "If I die today, I don't mind. Because of my belief in the Lord I feel I will never die. What about you, Hobart? Is everything all right with you and the Lord?"

"Daddy, it was not for the longest time. But now it is."

It was at this point that he called his brother Jake in Germany and asked him for forgiveness. Jake was puzzled. "Forgiveness for what?" Hobart replied, "Forgiveness for everything I have done to you." He had made a similar phone call to me, to ask me to excuse him for any grief he had caused me. I assured him he had caused me none. I thought guiltily about the yellow piece of paper—had that been too much?

He told his father that he wanted his body cremated. He wanted his ashes thrown over the pond at a farm that his friends owned, a farm where he had house-sat for a few weeks.

On a Saturday morning, I was on the tennis court when the call came that Hobart had died. I went over to the hospital and picked up some "Tru-Cut" biopsy needles and small bottles of formalin. This was his idea. In death he had wanted to give me some clues as to what had gone on from an infectious disease point of view.

I drove to the apartment complex in Bristol where the Carters lived, a thirty-minute drive. For financial reasons, the Carters had sold the family home and moved into an apartment. Outside the building, children were playing. They paused to watch me enter the Carters' flat on the ground floor. Did they know a death had taken place? Did they know a child like them had attempted an escape, tried to create a new life, but after just a few years had it cut short?

The apartment was neatly furnished, with a gleaming white sofa in the living room and pictures of Hobart and Jake on the coffee table. Mr. Carter rose to greet me, gracious as ever. "Praise the Lord, Doctor, he is out of his misery," he said to me. Mrs. Carter sat heavily on the couch; she looked up at me but said nothing. . . .

The weekend was drawing to a close. . . . I hammered out a paper describing the paradigm. The two maps accompanied the manuscript. I submitted it to the *Journal of Infec-*

tious Diseases. The editor for the AIDS section, Dr. Merle Sande of the University of California, San Francisco, an internationally known AIDS expert, called me when he got the manuscript. He loved it! He thought it was important. But would I, instead of including just facts and figures, please add in a few anecdotes, individual case studies? I was delighted to.

The paper was a beginning, a rough start on a larger story, the story of how a generation of young men, raised to self-hatred, had risen above the definitions that their society and upbringings had used to define them. It was the story of the hard and sometimes lonely journeys they took far from home into a world more complicated than they imagined and far more dangerous than anyone could have known. There was something courageous about this voyage, the breakaway, the attempt to create places where they could live with pride.

No matter how long I practice medicine, no matter what happens with this retrovirus, I will not be able to forget these young men, the little towns they came from, and the cruel, cruel irony of what awaited them in the big city.

Introduction to Document 4

Christianity has often had a difficult relationship with sex. On one extreme have been deep suspicions of the body and its pleasures, and the belief that humankind must be on guard against the sins of the flesh. Even lawful joys of the marriage bed, the vigilant suspected, had a way of overflowing their boundaries, of leading people down the path of sin. A less common tradition associated pleasure with holiness, and embraced an expansive ideal that linked physical with spiritual good. The following two pieces, commenting on the epidemic in the 1990s, were taken from the internet. The first is a transcript of a radio commentary linking homosexuality with sin and social decline. The second denies that disease is ever a punishment for sin, and invokes the Christian duty to minister to all of the afflicted.

 DOCUMENT 4 *Religious Responses*

(Radio Show Transcript Follows)
The New World Order is coming
Are you ready?
Stand by for insights so startling
you will never look at the news the same way again.
FOR THE NEXT 30 MINUTES, YOU WILL BE ON
THE CUTTING EDGE

This is David Bay, Director of Old Paths Ministries.

And this is the **Cutting Edge,** a radio program dedicated to warning and informing God's people. We are committed to the study and exposition of the inerrant, inspired and authoritative Word of God. The views expressed belong to us, and are not necessarily shared by this station.

The moral bankruptcy of our society is well-documented.

But, few people understand why we have become morally bankrupt. However, when we look at society through the eyes of God, through the Bible, we can easily see why we are facing the unprecedented troubles today. This study of America through the eyes of God is what we will always try to do here; stay with us for some eye-opening truths.

NEWS BRIEF: Providence Journal Bulletin, July 19, 1992, "Gay, Lesbian Movement Forges Place in Political Mainstream." "For the gay and lesbian movement, the 1992

Democratic Convention will go down as nothing less than a historic watershed, a gathering where homosexuals believe they finally forged their place in the political mainstream. Their agenda was largely incorporated into a party platform. . . . For the first time, a gay man with AIDS and an openly lesbian woman spoke to the convention in prime time. . . . A dramatic reason for the movement's great leap forward . . . is Democratic presidential nominee Bill Clinton. Gay and lesbian leaders say Clinton, a longtime supporter, 'gets it.' They point out that, unlike political leaders of the previous generation, Clinton has openly gay friends and has lost some of them to AIDS. . . . [Clinton] welcomed the gay program early in his campaign. And the goal of gay leaders is to turn out millions of votes for him in November—support that could prove crucial in key states."

The truth of this information is unmistakably clear, and so very troublesome. The Democratic Party has, for many years, been the home to all radical elements of society, including gays and lesbians; but it has always hidden this support from the general population of America, afraid of the inevitable negative backlash. The very idea that they no longer feel under such constraints shows us clearly what conclusion the Democratic leadership has developed about current American society: they believe America has changed so much that no significant backlash need be feared. In other words, the long-term goal of changing the attitudes of the vast majority of Americans away from their traditional Judeo-Christian roots has now been realized. If Americans are deemed to be changed this much in this regard, we can be assured that the leaders of the drive to the New World Order have reached the same conclusions, but to a far wider degree.

Inherent distaste for homosexuality was one of THE most deeply-held positions in the collective American psyche. If this has been changed, then we can know many other, less deeply-held feelings and beliefs have changed as well.

This is one of the clearest signs yet that America is spiritually ready to enter the Satanic New World Order. At this point, let us stop for a Scriptural reality check.

Paul addresses the End of the Age, in 1 Timothy 3, starting with verse 1, ". . . In the last day, will come perilous times of great stress and trouble. . . . For people will be lovers of self and self-centered . . . proud and arrogant and contemptuous boasters, . . . loose in morals and conduct, uncontrolled and fierce, haters of good . . . rash and inflated with self-conceit. They will be lovers of sensual pleasures. . . ."

This passage of Scripture, which Paul sets in the "last days", describes the current gay and lesbian movement very clearly and completely. They are utterly self-centered, proud, arrogant, abusive, unholy, without natural human affection. The leading radical group of gay men is the ACT-UP group, who deliberately and openly carry out acts of violence to shock and destroy the old values of society. The National Organization for Women (NOW) accomplishes the same goals for the women. Members of these groups are certainly "uncontrolled," "fierce," "haters of good."

And now they have been openly accepted by the leadership of the national Democratic Party and by its current leader, Bill Clinton, who conceivably will be the next President of the United States of America. This is a major step toward achieving the New World Order. And we Fundamental Christians know that this is a major step in bringing God's physical judgment down upon America. The total situation, both in America and the world at large, is resembling the judgments of Revelation more clearly every day.

A Christian View of Faith, Hope and Love
FROM METROPOLITAN COMMUNITY CHURCH
IS HIV OR AIDS GOD'S JUDGMENT?

Is HIV, the human immunodeficiency virus, or AIDS, acquired immune deficiency syndrome, a punishment or judgment from God? The short answer, from many people of faith, is *"No! Absolutely not!"*

Yet some people have answered the question, "yes." Indeed, some members of what has come to be known as the radical religious right praise God for the tragic epidemic which is claiming the lives of hundreds of thousands of human beings in every part of the world. Because HIV/AIDS was associated in the first years of the epidemic with the gay male community in the western world, many from the radical religious right have used this pandemic as a weapon to further their own homophobic agendas.

The idea that HIV/AIDS is a punishment from God is based on three faulty assumptions: that homosexual acts are sinful, that God causes suffering, and that God punishes sin with disease. These false assumptions result from a particular way of looking at society, sexuality, and how God works in the world.

Homophobia, (the unrealistic fear, hatred, and rejection of lesbians and gay men) is based on these assumptions and the world view they reflect, and on tragic misunderstanding of the meaning of Christ. It is the responsibility of Christians to overcome this fear and misunderstanding, and to witness to God's love and grace.

ARE HOMOSEXUAL ACTS SINFUL?

There are a few passages in the Bible that have been said to condemn homosexual acts. Currently there is much debate about these passages. Some Christians believe these passages condemn *all* homosexual behavior. But a growing number of Bible experts are convinced *these passages condemn only certain sexual acts that are idolatrous or abusive*.

For example, many Bible scholars believe that the story of Sodom and Gomorrah (Gen. 19), condemns rape, not homosexuality. Rape is a violent act and irrelevant to loving same-sex relationships. Other passages in the Bible, such as Ezekiel 16: 49–50, identify the sin of these cities as injustice and idolatry. Likewise, some religious authorities point out that New Testament passages like I Corinthians 6:9 and Romans 1:24–27 deal with sexual behavior that is unloving and exploitative (such as pedophilia or the temple prostitution common to that era). But even then, the Christian message is one of forgiveness and healing. Jesus said nothing to condemn homosexuality, but he said a great deal about faith, hope and love. . . .

IS SIN PUNISHED WITH DISEASE?

"Is God punishing gay men and lesbians with HIV/AIDS?" These are the kinds of questions that have been asked for centuries before HIV/AIDS became an issue. Each time some mysterious malady or disaster befalls an identified community, there have always been some who claim that God has caused the disaster as a judgment against the affected people. If indeed HIV/AIDS is a plague sent by God into the lesbian and gay community, there are some flaws in the plan. There is the matter of all the other people who are not lesbian or gay who are infected and affected. For example, what is the explanation for the decimation caused by HIV/AIDS in Central Africa, where transmission is primarily heterosexual?

Clearly there is no justification for suggesting that God has unfavorably judged the lesbian and gay community, nor that God has created HIV/AIDS as a punishment. Are all women with breast cancer victims of God's wrath? Are people of African descent being punished with sickle cell anemia? Have Jews done anything to deserve Tay-Sachs disease? It is known that HIV/AIDS is disproportionately affecting communities of color in the United States. Does this mean that God has made a judgment against people of color? Most people would answer these questions with a resounding "No!" . . .

People of faith, like Jesus Christ, must reach out with a healing touch. Rather than being understood as God's retribution, suffering becomes an occasion for God's love to be demonstrated. *When Christians reach out and touch those with HIV or AIDS, they can transform suffering into a living example of God's love.*

Each square of the AIDS quilt is a testament of love to a victim of the disease. (Ron Edmonds/AP/Wide World Photos, Inc.)

Following the example of Jesus, people of faith are called to **eat** with people with HIV/AIDS, and to **share** their home with them (Matthew 25:6); to **touch** people with HIV/AIDS and **give** them intimacy (Matthew 8:2–4); and to **heal** people with HIV/AIDS (Luke 17:11–19). *A faithful, intimate presence in the lives of those with HIV/AIDS, witnessing to them of Jesus' healing touch, is one of the most important responsibilities of all people of faith.*

Is HIV or AIDS a punishment or judgment from God? In the minds and hearts of many people of faith, the answer is clearly, "No! Absolutely not!" This pandemic is a tragedy. It does, however, present people of faith with the opportunity to be faithful witnesses to God's love and healing grace, even in the face of suffering, death, and grief.

Introduction to Document 5

In their book *Women, Poverty and AIDS*, Paul Farmer, Margaret Connors, and Janie Simmons reveal not only that the incidence of HIV-AIDS among women is growing, but that it is growing especially among poor women throughout the world. Poverty exposes women to high-risk behaviors, such as intravenous drug use and prostitution. Equally important, poverty makes it more likely that women will be dependent on men who are also part of high-risk populations. In the following selection, Margaret Connors, a medical anthropologist, discusses the connections between women, poverty, and AIDS.

 Document 5 *Unraveling the Epidemic among Poor Women in the United States*

Margaret Connors

> I was in the bathroom, and I remember I was sitting on the toilet and there was one of those heaters on the wall. I don't know why, but I said, "I'm going to open that." I pulled it out and I found the needle, a cooker and the thing they tie themselves with, the rubber hose. When I saw that my heart went to my feet. . . .

These words come from the story of Mildred, a 29-year-old minister's daughter and mother of three who "was going to die for having loved a heroin addict." Mildred ignored rumors that her husband was injecting drugs until she found evidence that he was in fact using heavily. From that time on her life changed forever. Mildred's story was chronicled by a *Boston Globe* journalist over the course of a year and a half as she battled the virus, placed her children with relatives, and attempted to save a love relationship strained by the demands of the care she required.

It took Mildred almost four years to reveal her HIV infection publicly, using one excuse after another to explain days spent depressed, sick in bed, and struggling to get to her job. But after four years of living with HIV, she developed headaches and extreme exhaustion that proved to be due to meningitis. . . .

While Mildred is no different from most women who become infected, the circumstances of her infection fail to conform to any of the exaggerated stereotypes of "women who get AIDS." She is neither a sex worker [e.g. a prostitute], nor a drug user, nor a woman who "sleeps around." In fact she was infected at about age 23 by the young man she fell in love with at 12 and he 13—"puppy love," she calls it.

This story is about one individual's life. Yet tales like Mildred's—stories about women, about poverty, about drug use, about children deprived of their parents, and much more—are multiplying daily, because women constitute the fastest-growing group of AIDS sufferers. We could tell these stories as hundreds and hundreds of individual accounts of suffering, each with its own unique configuration of personalities and circumstances.

There are, in fact, many versions of the AIDS story. Versions told with statistics often lose the immediacy and concreteness of the tales told about an individual life, but can provide insights about the spread of the disease. We know from demographic data that women are the fastest-growing group of AIDS sufferers. We know that it is not just any woman who is likely to contract AIDS, because it is not merely the individual decisions of women that "cause" them to become infected. Structural factors—social class and economic status—far more than individual decisions and aspirations, explain why HIV increasingly affects women in the United States and elsewhere.

We could go so far as to say that the root cause of the HIV infection is, simply, poverty. Poverty is a condition which puts women at greater and greater risk of contracting the HIV virus. Of course, we might say that there are other factors besides poverty that put women at risk for contracting AIDS—factors such as drug use and prostitution. But . . . drug use and transactional sex often occur as the consequence of poverty.

One way to imagine these "factors" (poverty, gender inequality, racism, drug use) is as vectors that converge in the bodies and lives of individuals; in some lives, more factors converge, placing those people at higher risk of contracting disease. But these vectors do not intersect each other mechanically or add up quantitatively. Ethnographic research suggests a more complex picture, in which each factor tends to implicate the other, forming complex constellations of conditions from which it is difficult for "at-risk" individuals to escape. And poverty, increasing in the United States and world-wide, is at the base of them all.

The overriding risk factor for Mildred was her poverty. As a poor woman in the United States, she is more likely to be sexually involved with an injection drug user. Mildred, like thousands of other women, embodies and lives out statistical risk and structural disadvantage, even as she struggles against them. . . . Women often find themselves in situations where they must weigh the risk of becoming infected against other risks including homelessness, assault, and loss of essential income. The social forces that make HIV infection more likely become embodied as personal risk. Examining these women's lives helps make sense of the circumstances in which many poor women are forced to choose between the risk of HIV and other dangers.

These are the basic facts. But the story of why poor women are at greater risk of contracting the virus does not end there. Systematic disregard by government and state agencies has compounded the devastating effect of poverty in women's lives. Since the beginning of the epidemic, women have been denied federal assistance once gravely ill, denied admission to drug treatment if pregnant or caring for their children, and most recently denied income for basic sustenance through drastic welfare cuts. . . .

Nor does the story end there. Social science studies could illuminate the structural reasons for the spread and perpetuation of this disease in certain populations. But, in fact, social scientists have also tended to sidestep the effect of poverty in their analysis of HIV transmission. Entering the public health arena as cultural experts, they have created a discourse that stresses the idea that cultural sensitivity can have a meaningful impact on HIV risk reduction. Unfortunately, culture has been made the focus at the expense of exploring issues of political economy—that is, how economic instability places women and ethnic minorities at risk for HIV infection. . . .

AIDS became the leading cause of death among Massachusetts residents aged 25–44 in 1993 and among all U.S. citizens in this age category in 1995. Twenty percent of new cases diagnosed in the state are women, up 8 percent from just two years ago. David Mulligan, the Massachusetts Commissioner of Public Health recently said that "AIDS is becoming more heterosexual." What this really means is that AIDS is becoming more gendered; seventy percent of these "heterosexual" cases are now among women.

AIDS is simultaneously becoming less white. Black women die of AIDS nine times more often than white women, Latina women six times more often and nearly two-thirds of all children with AIDS are black. Black and Hispanic men die three times more often than white men, often leaving women alone to provide for children. In fact, the number of African Americans who became newly infected with HIV/AIDS exceeded that of whites last year, although African Americans represent only 12 percent of the nation's population.

New cases also continue to climb among injection drug users (IDUs), as they plateau among gay men. Thirty percent of all people with AIDS are injection drug users and

70 percent of injection drug users with AIDS are minorities. In New York City and the state of Massachusetts, the most common means of infection is now through syringe injection. Nearly fifty percent of women are infected through the use of a dirty needle and 80 percent are IDUs or the sex partner of an IDU. In the Massachusetts prison population, females inmates have about twice the HIV infection rate of men in prison and all those testing HIV-positive have a history of injection drug use.

Not unlike plagues that have come before, the worst of the epidemic will ravage the most disadvantaged in our communities.

POSTSCRIPT

Just as this chapter was sent to the publisher, a small Associated Press Story appeared in the *Chicago Tribune*, under the title "Wider Use of HIV 'Quick Tests' Urged." The Center for Disease Control in Atlanta wanted to use a new procedure for determining who was infected: "Federal health officials said Thursday that expanded use of rapid tests for the AIDS virus could detect thousands more cases of HIV infection every year. . . . Researchers at the center estimated that in one year, almost 8,200 more people would learn they were HIV positive if a 15 minute test is used at publicly funded sites." Beneath this message of hope and progress remains a grim reality—we have here a more efficient way to determine who is infected, which will lead to 8,000 new diagnoses each year, for a disease which has no cure. Those victims with excellent medical care can obtain drugs that slow the disease's progress. But for most, AIDS remains a death sentence. The plague years continue.

QUESTIONS

Defining Terms

Identify in the context of the chapter each of the following:

homophobia   Stonewall Inn
HIV-AIDS   Tylenol
GRIDS   bathhouses
Randy Shilts   C. Everett Koop
CDC   Johnson City

Probing the Sources

1. In what ways do Koop and Shilts agree on the early history of HIV-AIDS? Where do they differ?
2. What was Verghese's revelation?
3. What assumptions do the religious right and left share? How do they differ?

Interpreting the Sources

1. What impact did people's beliefs about homosexuality have on the epidemic during its first decade?
2. Why does Shilts find the role of the media so troubling in the AIDS crisis?
3. When did you first become aware of HIV-AIDS? How has it affected the lives of people you know, or of your community?
4. Does this subject make you uncomfortable? If so, why?

ADDITIONAL READING

On the early history of gay culture, see George Chauncey's excellent *Gay New York: Gender, Urban Culture, and the Making of the Gay Male World, 1890–1940* (1994). Charles Kaiser extends the story in *The Gay Metropolis, 1940–1996* (1997). For a broad synthesis on sexuality, try Estelle B. Freedman and John D'Emilio, *Intimate Matters: A History of Sexuality in America*. The literature on AIDS grows with each passing month, but for some of the most interesting writing from the crisis's first decade, see Susan Sontag, *AIDS and its Metaphors* (1989); Paul Monette, *Borrowed Time* (1988); Larry Kramer, *The Normal Heart* (1985); and Kramer, *Reports from the Holocaust* (1989).

Epilogue: The Election of 2000

HISTORICAL CONTEXT

The study of history is the study of change over time. In 1960, for example, the southern states had laws rigidly segregating blacks from whites; just a few years later, those laws were swept away, though daily life changed much more slowly. All who lived through those times knew that important things were happening, but it was impossible to know for certain just how extraordinary and far reaching the changes would be.

The closer events get to the present, the less comfortable historians become. We rely on the perspective of long periods of time—decades, preferably centuries—to decide what was of fundamental significance and why. As time passes, things that seemed important when they occurred reveal themselves to be transitory, while little noticed events—like the assassination of an Austrian Archduke—loom large.

So it is with some trepidation that we present this epilogue. All who lived through the presidential election of 2000 felt that history was in the making. But what does that mean? Certainly there was the unusualness of events—few political contests have ever been so close, rarely has the loser of the popular vote won the presidency, and the Supreme Court never before intervened so directly. What will be the larger implications of this election? Did the High Court set a precedent for judicial intervention in elections that will be followed in the future? Will the controversial outcome bring a reconciliation of the parties or more bickering? We really will not know for years to come.

Still, the story is irresistible. It was clear by election eve on November 8 that the race was close, very close. When television stations predicted early-on that Vice President Albert Gore would carry the state of Florida with its 25 electoral votes, it looked like a Democratic victory was all but inevitable. Then, just a couple of hours later, those same stations changed their story and reported Florida too close to call. In the wee hours of Wednesday morning, the state was declared for George W. Bush. Then the stations retracted their predictions once again.

When the dust settled in the next day or two, it was apparent that Gore had defeated Bush in the nation's popular vote by the small margin of half a million votes. But in the electoral college, which was what really mattered, Florida was still up in the air. Bush was ahead by about a thousand votes in this state where his brother was governor; if the lead held up, he would win the nation's electoral college by the slimmest of margins. As absentee votes were tabulated and some recounting done, Bush's lead in Florida dwindled to just over 500 votes.

Meanwhile, stories began to circulate of problems. For example, the ballots used in Palm Beach County were allegedly so confusing that hundreds of democrats intending to vote for Gore ended up checking off right-wing third party candidate Pat Buchanan. More important, disputes arose over just what constituted a clearly marked ballot. How should election officials read a voter's intentions from a punch card on which a chad (the tiny paper square beside a candidate's name that was supposed to be poked out completely) had not become detached, but merely "dimpled"? There were racial overtones too—many of the largest controversies concerned African-American voters whose names were left off registration lists, or whose polling places were understaffed and contained the most unreliable equipment. Not just in Florida, but nationwide, votes by African Americans (who were leaning heavily toward the Democrats) were much more likely to be disallowed by officials because the polling equipment in heavily black precincts tended to be unreliable, especially compared to that of wealthier white suburbs.

Democrats claimed that they were disenfranchised because their votes were not being counted; Republicans charged that their opponents now wished to change the rules in the middle of the game. Weeks after the election, Florida's secretary of state, a Republican, certified the results, giving Bush the victory. Gore's people went to court to nullify her decision and, where there were irregularities, allow the ballots to be recounted by hand. After a series of lower court rulings and lawsuits by aggrieved voters, the Florida Supreme Court ruled that recounts must proceed in three counties. Bush's lawyers asked the United States Supreme court for a stay of the Florida Court's order, which was granted. Two days later, the nation's highest court granted a writ of certiorari, took over the case, then ruled for Bush's side that the Florida Supreme Court violated the Equal Protection Clause of the United States Constitution when it failed to specify procedures for recounting votes.

THE DOCUMENTS

We present here excerpts from the Supreme Court's unsigned 5-4 ruling, including the majority opinion (supported by Chief Justice William Rehnquist, and Justices Clarence Thomas, Anthony Scalia, Sandra Day O'Connor, and Anthony M. Kennedy) and dissenting opinions (written by Justices John Paul Stevens, David H. Souter, Ruth Bader Ginsburg, and Stephen G. Breyer.) Do you think future historians will interpret the decision as statesmanship or partisanship? Whose arguments do you find most persuasive, and why? The proper title of this case is George W. Bush et al., *v.* Albert Gore, Jr., et al., on writ of certiorari to the Florida Supreme Court, December 12, 2000.

DOCUMENT 1: *The Majority Opinion*

On December 8, 2000, the Supreme Court of Florida ordered that the Circuit Court of Leon County tabulate by hand 9,000 ballots in Miami-Dade County. It also ordered the inclusion in the certified vote totals of 215 votes identified in Palm Beach County and 168 votes identified in Miami-Dade County for Vice President Albert Gore, Jr., and Senator Joseph Lieberman, Democratic Candidates for President and Vice President. The Supreme Court noted that petitioner, Governor George W. Bush asserted that the net gain for Vice President Gore in Palm Beach County was 176 votes, and directed the Circuit Court to resolve that dispute on remand. The court further held that relief would require manual recounts in all Florida counties where so-called "undervotes" had not been subject to manual tabulation. The court ordered all manual recounts to begin at once. Governor Bush and Richard Cheney, Republican Candidates for the Presidency and Vice

Presidency, filed an emergency application for a stay of this mandate. On December 9, we granted the application, treated the application as a petition for a writ of certiorari, and granted certiorari. . . .

On November 8, 2000, the day following the Presidential election, the Florida Division of Elections reported that petitioner, Governor Bush, had received 2,909,135 votes, and respondent, Vice President Gore, had received 2,907,351 votes, a margin of 1,784 for Governor Bush. Because Governor Bush's margin of victory was less than "one-half of a percent . . . of the votes cast," an automatic machine recount was conducted under §102.141(4) of the election code, the results of which showed Governor Bush still winning the race but by a diminished margin. Vice President Gore then sought manual recounts in Volusia, Palm Beach, Broward, and Miami-Dade Counties, pursuant to Florida's election protest provisions. A dispute arose concerning the deadline for local county canvassing boards to submit their returns to the Secretary of State (Secretary). The Secretary declined to waive the November 14 deadline imposed by statute. The Florida Supreme Court, however, set the deadline at November 26. We granted certiorari and vacated the Florida Supreme Court's decision, finding considerable uncertainty as to the grounds on which it was based. . . .

The Supreme Court held that Vice President Gore had satisfied his burden of proof. Noting the closeness of the election, the Court explained that "[o]n this record, there can be no question that there are legal votes within the 9,000 uncounted votes sufficient to place the results of this election in doubt." A "legal vote," as determined by the Supreme Court, is "one in which there is a 'clear indication of the intent of the voter.' " The court therefore ordered a hand recount of the 9,000 ballots in Miami-Dade County. . . . The Supreme Court further held that the Circuit Court could order "the Supervisor of Elections and the Canvassing Boards, as well as the necessary public officials, in all counties that have not conducted a manual recount or tabulation of the undervotes . . . to do so forthwith, said tabulation to take place in the individual counties where the ballots are located."

The Supreme Court also determined that both Palm Beach County and Miami-Dade County, in their earlier manual recounts, had identified a net gain of 215 and 168 legal votes for Vice President Gore. Rejecting the Circuit Court's conclusion that Palm Beach County lacked the authority to include the 215 net votes submitted past the November 26 deadline, the Supreme Court explained that the deadline was not intended to exclude votes identified after that date through ongoing manual recounts. As to Miami-Dade County, the Court concluded that although the 168 votes identified were the result of a partial recount, they were "legal votes [that] could change the outcome of the election." The Supreme Court therefore directed the Circuit Court to include those totals in the certified results, subject to resolution of the actual vote total from the Miami-Dade partial recount.

The petition presents the following questions: whether the Florida Supreme Court established new standards for resolving Presidential election contests, thereby violating Art. II, §1, cl. 2, of the United States Constitution and failing to comply with 3 U. S C. §5, and whether the use of standardless manual recounts violates the Equal Protection and Due Process Clauses. With respect to the equal protection question we find a violation of the Equal Protection Clause. . . .

Much of the controversy seems to revolve around ballot cards designed to be perforated by a stylus but which, either through error or deliberate omission, have not been perforated with sufficient precision for a machine to count them. In some cases a piece of the card—a chad—is hanging, say by two corners. In other cases there is no separation at all, just an indentation.

The Florida Supreme Court has ordered that the intent of the voter be discerned from such ballots. For purposes of resolving the equal protection challenge, it is not necessary to decide whether the Florida Supreme Court had the authority under the legislative scheme for resolving election disputes to define what a legal vote is and to mandate a manual recount implementing that definition. The recount mechanisms implemented in response to the decisions of the Florida Supreme Court do not satisfy the minimum requirement for non-arbitrary treatment of voters necessary to secure the fundamental right. Florida's basic command for the count of legally cast votes is to consider the "intent of the voter." This is unobjectionable as an abstract proposition and a starting principle. The problem inheres in the absence of specific standards to ensure its equal application. The formulation of uniform rules to determine intent based on these recurring circumstances is practicable and, we conclude, necessary. . . .

The want of those rules here has led to unequal evaluation of ballots in various respects. As seems to have been acknowledged at oral argument, the standards for accepting or rejecting contested ballots might vary not only from county to county but indeed within a single county from one recount team to another.

The record provides some examples. A monitor in Miami-Dade County testified at trial that he observed that three members of the county canvassing board applied different standards in defining a legal vote. And testimony at trial also revealed that at least one county changed its evaluative standards during the counting process. Palm Beach County, for example, began the process with a 1990 guideline which precluded counting completely attached chads, switched to a rule that considered a vote to be legal if any light could be seen through a chad, changed back to the 1990 rule, and then abandoned any pretense of a *per se* rule, only to have a court order that the county consider dimpled chads legal. This is not a process with sufficient guarantees of equal treatment.

The State Supreme Court ratified this uneven treatment. It mandated that the recount totals from two counties, Miami-Dade and Palm Beach, be included in the certified total. The court also appeared to hold *sub silentio* that the recount totals from Broward County, which were not completed until after the original November 14 certification by the Secretary of State, were to be considered part of the new certified vote totals even though the county certification was not contested by Vice President Gore. Yet each of the counties used varying standards to determine what was a legal vote. Broward County used a more forgiving standard than Palm Beach County, and uncovered almost three times as many new votes, a result markedly disproportionate to the difference in population between the counties. . . .

That brings the analysis to yet a further equal protection problem. The votes certified by the court included a partial total from one county, Miami-Dade. The Florida Supreme Court's decision thus gives no assurance that the recounts included in a final certification must be complete. Indeed, it is respondent's submission that it would be consistent with the rules of the recount procedures to include whatever partial counts are done by the time of final certification, and we interpret the Florida Supreme Court's decision to permit this. The press of time does not diminish the constitutional concern. A desire for speed is not a general excuse for ignoring equal protection guarantees.

In addition to these difficulties the actual process by which the votes were to be counted under the Florida Supreme Court's decision raises further concerns. That order did not specify who would recount the ballots. The county canvassing boards were forced to pull together ad hoc teams comprised of judges from various Circuits who had no previous training in handling and interpreting ballots. Furthermore, while others were permitted to observe, they were prohibited from objecting during the recount.

The recount process, in its features here described, is inconsistent with the minimum procedures necessary to protect the fundamental right of each voter in the special instance of a statewide recount under the authority of a single state judicial officer. Our consideration is limited to the present circumstances, for the problem of equal protection in election processes generally presents many complexities.

The question before the Court is not whether local entities, in the exercise of their expertise, may develop different systems for implementing elections. Instead, we are presented with a situation where a state court with the power to assure uniformity has ordered a statewide recount with minimal procedural safeguards. When a court orders a statewide remedy, there must be at least some assurance that the rudimentary requirements of equal treatment and fundamental fairness are satisfied.

Given the Court's assessment that the recount process underway was probably being conducted in an unconstitutional manner, the Court stayed the order directing the recount so it could hear this case and render an expedited decision. The contest provision, as it was mandated by the State Supreme Court, is not well calculated to sustain the confidence that all citizens must have in the outcome of elections. The State has not shown that its procedures include the necessary safeguards.

Upon due consideration of the difficulties identified to this point, it is obvious that the recount cannot be conducted in compliance with the requirements of equal protection and due process without substantial additional work. It would require not only the adoption (after opportunity for argument) of adequate statewide standards for determining what is a legal vote, and practicable procedures to implement them, but also orderly judicial review of any disputed matters that might arise. . . .

The Supreme Court of Florida has said that the legislature intended the State's electors to "participat[e] fully in the federal electoral process," as provided in 3 U. S. C. §5. That statute, in turn, requires that any controversy or contest that is designed to lead to a conclusive selection of electors be completed by December 12. That date is upon us, and there is no recount procedure in place under the State Supreme Court's order that comports with minimal constitutional standards. Because it is evident that any recount seeking to meet the December 12 date will be unconstitutional for the reasons we have discussed, we reverse the judgment of the Supreme Court of Florida ordering a recount to proceed. . . .

None are more conscious of the vital limits on judicial authority than are the members of this Court, and none stand more in admiration of the Constitution's design to leave the selection of the President to the people, through their legislatures, and to the political sphere. When contending parties invoke the process of the courts, however, it becomes our unsought responsibility to resolve the federal and constitutional issues the judicial system has been forced to confront.

The judgment of the Supreme Court of Florida is reversed, and the case is remanded for further proceedings not inconsistent with this opinion. . . .

It is so ordered.

DOCUMENT 2: *Dissenting Opinions*

Justice Stevens, Dissenting

The Constitution assigns to the States the primary responsibility for determining the manner of selecting the Presidential electors. When questions arise about the meaning of state laws, including election laws, it is our settled practice to accept the opinions of the highest courts of the States as providing the final answers. On rare occasions, however, either federal statutes or the Federal Constitution may require federal judicial intervention in state elections. This is not such an occasion. . . .

Even assuming that aspects of the remedial scheme [proposed by the Florida Supreme Court] might ultimately be found to violate the Equal Protection Clause, I could not subscribe to the majority's disposition of the case. As the majority explicitly holds, once a state legislature determines to select electors through a popular vote, the right to have one's vote counted is of constitutional stature. As the majority further acknowledges, Florida law holds that all ballots that reveal the intent of the voter constitute valid votes. Recognizing these principles, the majority nonetheless orders the termination of the contest proceeding before all such votes have been tabulated. Under their own reasoning, the appropriate course of action would be to remand to allow more specific procedures for implementing the legislature's uniform general standard to be established.

In the interest of finality, however, the majority effectively orders the disenfranchisement of an unknown number of voters whose ballots reveal their intent—and are therefore legal votes under state law—but were for some reason rejected by ballot-counting machines. It does so on the basis of the deadlines set forth in Title 3 of the United States Code. But, as I have already noted, those provisions merely provide rules of decision for Congress to follow when selecting among conflicting slates of electors. They do not prohibit a State from counting what the majority concedes to be legal votes until a bona fide winner is determined. Indeed, in 1960, Hawaii appointed two slates of electors and Congress chose to count the one appointed on January 4, 1961, well after the Title 3 deadlines. Thus, nothing prevents the majority, even if it properly found an equal protection violation, from ordering relief appropriate to remedy that violation without depriving Florida voters of their right to have their votes counted. As the majority notes, "[a] desire for speed is not a general excuse for ignoring equal protection guarantees."

Finally, neither in this case, nor in its earlier opinion . . . did the Florida Supreme Court make any substantive change in Florida electoral law. Its decisions were rooted in long-established precedent and were consistent with the relevant statutory provisions, taken as a whole. It did what courts do—it decided the case before it in light of the legislature's intent to leave no legally cast vote uncounted. In so doing, it relied on the sufficiency of the general "intent of the voter" standard articulated by the state legislature, coupled with a procedure for ultimate review by an impartial judge, to resolve the concern about disparate evaluations of contested ballots. If we assume—as I do—that the members of that court and the judges who would have carried out its mandate are impartial, its decision does not even raise a colorable federal question.

What must underlie petitioners' entire federal assault on the Florida election procedures is an unstated lack of confidence in the impartiality and capacity of the state judges who would make the critical decisions if the vote count were to proceed. Otherwise, their position is wholly without merit. The endorsement of that position by the majority of this Court can only lend credence to the most cynical appraisal of the work of judges throughout the land. It is confidence in the men and women who administer the judicial system that is the true backbone of the rule of law. Time will one day heal the wound to that confidence that will be inflicted by today's decision. One thing, however, is certain. Although we may never know with complete certainty the identity of the winner of this year's Presidential election, the identity of the loser is perfectly clear. It is the Nation's confidence in the judge as an impartial guardian of the rule of law.

I respectfully dissent.

Justice Souter, Dissenting

The Court should not have reviewed either *Bush v. Palm Beach County Canvassing Bd.*, or this case, and should not have stopped Florida's attempt to recount all undervote ballots by issuing a stay of the Florida Supreme Court's orders during the period of this review. If this court had allowed the State to follow the course indicated by the opinions of its own Supreme Court, it is entirely possible that there would ultimately have been no issue requiring our review. . . .

I am in substantial agreement with the dissenting opinions of JUSTICE STEVENS, JUSTICE GINSBURG and JUSTICE BREYER. I write separately only to say how straightforward the issues before us really are. . . .

Petitioners have raised an equal protection claim in the charge that unjustifiably disparate standards are applied in different electoral jurisdictions to otherwise identical facts. It is true that the Equal Protection Clause does not forbid the use of a variety of voting mechanisms within a jurisdiction, even though different mechanisms will have different levels of effectiveness in recording voters' intentions; local variety can be justified by concerns about cost, the potential value of innovation, and so on. But evidence in the record here suggests that a different order of disparity obtains under rules for determining a voter's intent that have been applied (and could continue to be applied) to identical types of ballots used in identical brands of machines and exhibiting identical physical characteristics. . . . I can conceive of no legitimate state interest served by these differing treatments of the expressions of voters' fundamental rights. The differences appear wholly arbitrary.

In deciding what to do about this, we should take account of the fact that electoral votes are due to be cast in six days. I would therefore remand the case to the courts of Florida with instructions to establish uniform standards for evaluating the several types of ballots that have prompted differing treatments, to be applied within and among counties when passing on such identical ballots in any further recounting (or successive recounting) that the courts might order.

Unlike the majority, I see no warrant for this Court to assume that Florida could not possibly comply with this requirement before the date set for the meeting of electors, December 18. . . . To recount [votes] manually would be a tall order, but before this Court stayed the effort to do that the courts of Florida were ready to do their best to get that job done. There is no justification for denying the State the opportunity to try to count all disputed ballots now.

I respectfully dissent.

Justice Ginsburg, Dissenting

. . . In deferring to state courts on matters of state law, we appropriately recognize that this Court acts as an "outside[r]'lacking the common exposure to local law which comes from sitting in the jurisdiction." That recognition has sometimes prompted us to resolve doubts about the meaning of state law by certifying issues to a State's highest court, even when federal rights are at stake. Notwithstanding our authority to decide issues of state law underlying federal claims, we have used the certification devise to afford state high courts an opportunity to inform us on matters of their own State's law because such restraint "helps build a cooperative judicial federalism." . . .

Rarely has this Court rejected outright an interpretation of state law by a state high court. . . . The extraordinary setting of this case has obscured the ordinary principle that dictates its proper resolution: Federal courts defer to state high courts' interpretations of their state's own law. This principle reflects the core of federalism, on which all agree. "The Framers split the atom of sovereignty. It was the genius of their idea that our citizens would have two political capacities, one state and one federal, each protected from incursion by the other." Were the other members of this Court as mindful as they generally are of our system of dual sovereignty, they would affirm the judgment of the Florida Supreme Court.

I agree with JUSTICE STEVENS that petitioners have not presented a substantial equal protection claim. Ideally, perfection would be the appropriate standard for judging the recount. But we live in an imperfect world, one in which thousands of votes have not been counted. I cannot agree that the recount adopted by the Florida court, flawed as it may be, would yield a result any less fair or precise than the certification that preceded that recount.

Even if there were an equal protection violation, I would agree with JUSTICE STEVENS, JUSTICE SOUTER, and JUSTICE BREYER that the Court's concern about the

December 12 deadline" is misplaced. Time is short in part because of the Court's entry of a stay on December 9, several hours after an able circuit judge in Leon County had begun to superintend the recount process. More fundamentally, the Court's reluctance to let the recount go forward . . . ultimately turns on its own judgment about the practical realities of implementing a recount, not the judgment of those much closer to the process.

Equally important, as JUSTICE BREYER explains, the December 12 "deadline" lacks the significance the Court assigns it. Were that date to pass, Florida would still be entitled to deliver electoral votes Congress *must* count unless both Houses find that the votes "ha[d] not been . . . regularly given." The statute identifies other significant dates, (specifying December 18 as the date electors "shall meet and give their votes"); (specifying "the fourth Wednesday in December"—this year, December 27—as the date on which Congress, if it has not received a State's electoral votes, shall request the state secretary of state to send a certified return immediately). But none of these dates has ultimate significance in light of Congress' detailed provisions for determining, on "the sixth day of January," the validity of electoral votes.

The Court assumes that time will not permit "orderly judicial review of any disputed matters that might arise." But no one has doubted the good faith and diligence with which Florida election officials, attorneys for all sides of this controversy, and the courts of law have performed their duties. Notably, the Florida Supreme Court has produced two substantial opinions within 29 hours of oral argument. In sum, the Court's conclusion that a constitutionally adequate recount is impractical is a prophecy the Court's own judgment will not allow to be tested. Such an untested prophecy should not decide the Presidency of the United States.

I dissent.

Justice Breyer, Dissenting

The Court was wrong to take this case. It was wrong to grant a stay. It should now vacate that stay and permit the Florida Supreme Court to decide whether the recount should resume.

The political implications of this case for the country are momentous. But the federal legal questions presented, with one exception, are insubstantial. . . .

There is no justification for the majority's remedy, which is simply to reverse the lower court and halt the recount entirely. An appropriate remedy would be, instead, to remand this case with instructions that, even at this late date, would permit the Florida Supreme Court to require recounting *all* undercounted votes in Florida, including those from Broward, Volusia, Palm Beach, and Miami-Dade Counties, whether or not previously recounted prior to the end of the protest period, and to do so in accordance with a single-uniform substandard.

The majority justifies stopping the recount entirely on the ground that there is no more time. In particular, the majority relies on the lack of time for the Secretary to review and approve equipment needed to separate undervotes. But the majority reaches this conclusion in the absence of *any* record evidence that the recount could not have been completed in the time allowed by the Florida Supreme Court. . . . Whether there is time to conduct a recount prior to December 18, when the electors are scheduled to meet, is a matter for the state courts to determine. And whether, under Florida law, Florida could or could not take further action is obviously a matter for Florida courts, not this Court, to decide.

By halting the manual recount, and thus ensuring that the uncounted legal votes will not be counted under any standard, this court crafts a remedy out of proportion to the asserted harm. And that remedy harms the very fairness interests the Court is attempting to protect. The manual recount would itself redress a problem of unequal treatment of ballots. As JUSTICE STEVENS points out, the ballots of voters in counties that use punch-card systems are more likely to be disqualified than those in counties using optical-scanning systems. According to recent news reports, variations in the undervote rate are even more pronounced. Thus, in a system that allows counties to use different types of voting systems, voters already arrive at the polls with an unequal chance that their votes will be counted. I do not see how the fact that this results from counties' selection of different voting machines rather than a court order makes the outcome any more fair. Nor do I understand why the Florida Supreme Court's recount order, which helps to redress this inequity, must be entirely prohibited based on a deficiency that could easily be remedied. . . .

Despite the reminder that this case involves "an election for the President of the United States," no preeminent legal concern, or practical concern relate to legal questions, required this Court to hear this case, let alone to issue a stay that stopped Florida's recount process in its tracks. With one exception, petitioners' claims do not ask us to vindicate a constitutional provision designed to protect a basic human right. Petitioners invoke fundamental fairness, namely, the need for procedural fairness, including finality. But with the one "equal protection" exception, they rely upon law that focuses, not upon that basic need, but upon the constitutional allocation of power. Respondents invoke a competing fundamental consideration—the need to determine the voter's true intent. But they look to state law, not to federal constitutional law, to protect that interest. Neither side claims electoral fraud, dishonesty, or the like. And the more fundamental equal protection claim might have been left to the state court to resolve if and when it was discovered to have mattered. It could still be resolved through a remand conditioned upon issuance of a uniform standard; it does not require reversing the Florida Supreme Court.

Of course, the selection of the President is of fundamental national importance. But that importance is political, not legal. And this Court should resist the temptation unnecessarily to resolve tangential legal disputes, where doing so threatens to determine the outcome of the election.

The Constitution and federal statutes themselves make clear that restraint is appropriate. They set forth a road map of how to resolve disputes about electors, even after an election as close as this one. That road map foresees resolution of electoral disputes by *state* courts. But it nowhere provides for involvement by the United States Supreme Court.

To the contrary, the Twelfth Amendment commits to Congress the authority and responsibility to count electoral votes. A federal statute, the Electoral Count Act, enacted after the close 1876 Hayes-Tilden Presidential election, specifies that, after States have tried to resolve disputes (through "judicial" or other means), Congress is the body primarily authorized to resolve remaining disputes. . . . Nor, for that matter, is there any reason to that think the Constitution's Framers would have reached a different conclusion. Madison, at least, believed that allowing the judiciary to choose the presidential electors "was out of the question."

The decision by both the Constitution's Framers and the 1886 Congress to minimize this Court's role in resolving close federal presidential elections is as wise as it is clear. However awkward or difficult it may be for Congress to resolve difficult electoral disputes, Congress, being a political body, expresses the people's will far more accurately than does an unelected Court. And the people's will is what elections are about. . . .

I fear that in order to bring this agonizingly long election process to a definitive conclusion, we have not adequately attended to that necessary "check upon our own exercise of power," "our own sense of self-restraint." Justice Brandeis once said of the Court, "The most important thing we do is not doing." What it does today, the Court should have left undone. I would repair the damage done as best we now can, by permitting the Florida recount to continue under uniform standards.

I respectfully dissent.

Interpreting the Sources

1. Do you find yourself more in agreement with the majority or the dissenters? Why?

2. It has been quite controversial that the majority used the equal protection clause of the Constitution as the basis for its opinion. Why do you think that might be so?

3. Are you persuaded that the court was right to intervene, and that intervention was absolutely necessary?

4. You lived through this chapter of history; how do your own memories and beliefs influence the way you think about this issue today?

Credits

Page xvii: From Upton Sinclair, *The Jungle* (New Jersey: Sinclair, 1906), Chapters 12–14.

Page xxiii: From *The Independent* 57(2905), August 4, 1904, pp. 245–248.

Page xxvii: From *The Congressional Record*, House, *59th Congress, First Session*, Vol. 40, Part 8, pp. 23–29.

Page xxx: Letter by Louis F. Swift from *The Outlook* magazine, June 23, 1906.

Page 4: Reprinted from Walter L. Fleming, ed., *The Constitution and the Ritual of the Knights of the White Camelia* (Morgantown: West Virginia University, 1904), pp. 21–29.

Page 6: Excerpted from George Rawick, ed., *The American Slave: A Composite Autobiography* (Westport, CT: The Greenwood Press, 1977, 1979), Supp. 1, Vol. 5, p. 426; Supp. 2, Vol. 4, Part 3, p. 957; Supp. 2, Vol. 5, Part 4, pp. 1648–1649. Reprinted with the permission of the publisher.

Page 7: *Testimony Taken by the Joint Select Committee to Inquire into the Condition of Affairs in the Late Insurrectionary States* (Washington, DC: U.S. Government Printing Office, 1872), Vol. 6, pp. 545–546; Vol. 7, pp. 607–611.

Page 11: Excerpted from the *Congressional Record*, May 30, 1872, pp. 1–7.

Page 15: From Benjamin Bryant, *Experience of a Northern Man Among the Ku-Klux, or the Condition of the South* (Hartford, CT, 1872).

Page 16: From W. H. Gannon, *The Grand Army of the Republic Versus the Ku Klux Klan* (Boston: W. F. Brown & Company, 1872).

Page 23: Reprinted from the *North American Review*, 124(258); pp. 332–326.

Page 25: Reprinted from the *North American Review*, 125(258); pp. 351–362.

Page 28: Reprinted from Allan Pinkerton, *Strikers, Communists, Tramps and Detectives* (New York: C. W. Carleton & Co., 1878), pp. 13–21.

Page 29: Excerpted from Samuel Gompers, *Seventy Years of Life and Labor* (New York: E. P. Dutton & Co., 1925), pp. 134–135, 137–141, 155–157. Copyright 1925 by E. P. Dutton, renewed 1953 by Gertrude Gleaves Gompers. Reprinted by permission of the publisher, Dutton, an imprint of New American Library, a division of Penguin Books USA Inc.

Page 32: Excerpted from Mary Harris Jones, *The Autobiography of Mother Jones*, ed., Mary Field Parton (Chicago: Charles H. Kerr Co., 1925), pp. 14–16. © 1925, 1953, 1990 by Charles H. Kerr Publishing Company. Reprinted by permission.

Page 32: Reprinted in the *New York Times*, July 23, 30, 1877.

Page 38: From James Mooney, *The Ghost Dance Religion and the Sioux Outbreak*, Part 2, 14th Annual Report of the Bureau of Ethnology (Washington, DC: Government Printing Office, 1896), pp. 916–917.

Index